## DATE DUE

| OCT 4 00 | | | |
|---|---|---|---|
| DE 16 06 | | | |
| | | | |
| | | | |
| | | | |
| | | | |
| | | | |
| | | | |
| | | | |
| | | | |
| | | | |
| | | | |
| | | | |
| | | | |
| | | | |

DEMCO 38-296

# Americans 55 & Older

# Americans
# 55 & Older

## A Changing Market

edited by Sharon Yntema

New Strategist Publications, Inc.

Ithaca, New York

ISBN 1-885070-10-1

Printed in the United States of America

# Table of Contents

## Chapter 4. Income

## Chapter 5. Labor Force

## Chapter 6. Living Arrangements

## Chapter 7. Population

## Chapter 8.  Spending

## Chapter 9.  Wealth

# Illustrations

### Chapter 7. Population

### Chapter 8. Spending

### Chapter 9. Wealth

# Tables

## Chapter 1.  Attitudes

## Chapter 2.  Education

## Chapter 3.  Health

## Chapter 4.  Income

## Chapter 5. Labor Force

## Chapter 6.  Living Arrangements

## Chapter 7.  Population

## Chapter 8.  Spending

## Chapter 9.  Wealth

# Introduction

A revolution is in the making. The 55-plus population is about to be transformed—radically—by the aging of the baby-boom generation. No segment of the population will change as much as older Americans in the next two decades. For many businesses, the older market offers the greatest opportunities for growth and profit. But for other businesses—the ones not paying attention—this market poses a threat to the bottom line. Those who are unprepared for the new older market are destined to be trampled by their competitors who are.

Unfortunately, many businesses aren't paying attention to the distant drums of the revolution. They're too busy chasing young adults under the mistaken impression that the young are their best customers. But those who examine *Americans 55 & Older: A Changing Market* may discover, to their surprise, that older Americans are their best customers after all.

There are 56 million people aged 55 or older this year. By 2005, the number will have expanded to 66 million as the enormous baby-boom generation (born from 1946

## 55+ Population Projected to Grow More Than 17 Percent

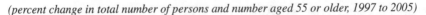

*(percent change in total number of persons and number aged 55 or older, 1997 to 2005)*

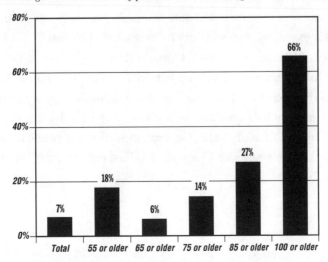

through 1964) enters the age group. The educational level of older Americans, which has been rising steadily for decades, will surge. A larger share of men and women aged 55 or older will be working. The affluent among them will expand by the millions. Already, older Americans are the biggest spenders on many products and services. They spend more than young adults on virtually all products and services. As the sophistication of the older population rises with the aging of the boomers, Americans aged 55-plus will become the prime market for many businesses.

Perhaps the biggest story told by *Americans 55 & Older: A Changing Market* is that the stereotypes of aging—poverty, ill health, and an unwillingness to do or spend—must be put to rest. Older Americans are busy, healthy, and happy. A small minority are poor or sick. We no longer need to wring our hands about the aged, because the aged are doing quite well, thank you.

Whether businesses pay attention to older Americans or not, invariably they will find consumers aged 55 or older making up a larger share of their customers in the years ahead. Those who understand the changing wants and needs of older consumers will prosper. Those who ignore older consumers will be turning their backs on a gold mine.

## How to Use This Book

*Americans 55 & Older: A Changing Market* is designed for easy use. It is divided into nine chapters, organized alphabetically: Attitudes, Education, Health, Income, Labor Force, Living Arrangements, Population, Spending, and Wealth.

Most of the tables in the book are based on data collected by the federal government, in particular the Census Bureau, the Bureau of Labor Statistics, the National Center for Education Statistics, and the National Center for Health Statistics. The federal government continues to be the best source of up-to-date, reliable information on the changing characteristics of Americans. When government data were not available about an important topic, we included data from other surveys and studies. The Attitudes chapter, for example, presents data from the 1994 General Social Survey (GSS) of the University of Chicago's National Opinion Research Center (NORC). NORC is the oldest nonprofit, university-affiliated national survey research facility in the nation. It conducts the GSS every two years using a nationally representative sample of noninstitutionalized English-speaking persons aged 18 or older living in the United States. For more information about the General Social Survey, contact National Opinion Research Center, University of Chicago, 1155 East 60th Street, Chicago, IL, 60637; telephone (312) 753-7500.

As we publish *Americans 55 & Older: A Changing Market*, dramatic technological change is reshaping the demographic reference industry. The government's detailed demographic data, once widely available to all in printed reports, is now accessible only to Internet users or in unpublished tables obtained by calling the appropriate government agency with a specific request. The government's web sites, which house enormous spreadsheets of data, are of great value to researchers with the time and skills to first download and then extract the important nuggets of information. The shift from printed reports to web sites—while convenient for number-crunchers—has made demographic analysis a bigger chore.

The editors of New Strategist have made the job easy for you. While most of the data in *Americans 55 & Older: A Changing Market* were produced by the government, the tables published here are not reprints of the government's tabulations—as is the case in many reference books. Each table was individually compiled and created by New Strategist, with calculations performed by our statisticians to reveal the trends. Each table tells a story about older Americans, a story explained by the accompanying text, which analyzes the data and highlights future trends. If you need more information than the tables and text provide, you can refer to the original data, the source of which is listed at the bottom of each table.

While *Americans 55 & Older: A Changing Market* includes counts of the 55-plus population by region and state, the detailed demographic characteristics of this age group—such as household type and income—are limited to the national level. That's because the only detailed statistics available at the local level are from the 1990 census, which is now woefully out of date for such a rapidly changing population. Researchers looking for up-to-date estimates of the characteristics of older Americans at the local level can get them—for a price—from private data companies.

The book contains a lengthy table list to help you locate the information you need. For a more detailed search, use the index at the back of the book. There you will also find a glossary defining many of the terms commonly used in the tables and text.

*With Americans 55 & Older: A Changing Market* in hand, you will gain an understanding of the revolution now taking place within the 50-plus population.

# 1

# Attitudes

◆ The proportion of Americans who say they are very happy peaks at 34 percent among people aged 60 to 69.

◆ By the time people are in their 60s, most have lost both parents and over half have experienced the death of a sibling.

◆ Only 34 percent of people in their 40s and 50s live in the same place they lived at age 16, versus 39 percent of all Americans.

◆ A substantial 27 percent of people in their 50s stilll have children at home; 5 percent live with both children and grandchildren.

◆ Fifty-eight percent of people in their 50s, 67 percent of those in their 60s, and a full 72 percent of people in their 70s read a newspaper daily.

◆ Most people aged 60 or older did not grow up with a working mother, whereas at least 70 percent of people aged 18 to 39 had working mothers.

◆ Forty-two percent of people aged 60 or older attend religious services at least weekly, compared with only 25 percent of adults under age 40.

◆ Nearly seventy-five percent of people aged 18 to 40 support euthanasia, versus only 53 percent of those aged 70 or older.

◆ Older Americans have more confidence in the leaders of educational institutions and less confidence in the scientific community than do younger Americans.

# Most Fiftysomethings Find Life Exciting

## Most also say their marriages are very happy.

Forty-seven percent of Americans find life exciting, while a nearly equal proportion (48 percent) find it pretty routine. Only 4 percent find it dull. Those most likely to find life exciting are young adults—53 percent of those aged 18 to 29 say life is exciting. Excitement wanes when people are in their 40s, juggling jobs and families. But it rises again to include a majority of those in their 50s. The excitement level drops sharply among people in their 60s and 70s.

Excitement does not necessarily bring happiness. Only 29 percent of all Americans say they are very happy—a much smaller proportion than that of those who find life exciting. And while the amount of excitement in life tends to fall with age, happiness does the opposite: the proportion of those who are very happy peaks at 34 percent among people aged 60 to 69. Overall, at least 80 percent of people aged 50 or older say they are pretty or very happy.

Most married people say their marriages are very happy, regardless of age. Married people aged 30 to 39 and 50 to 59 have a slightly lower level of happiness than those in other age groups. The stresses of parenting for the younger ones and difficulties in adjusting to retirement for the older ones could account for this pattern.

◆ Older Americans may find life less exciting than younger Americans because of their lower level of education. As better-educated generations age, a larger share of older Americans may find life exciting.

### Many Older Americans Are Very Happy

*(percent saying they are "very happy," by age, 1994)*

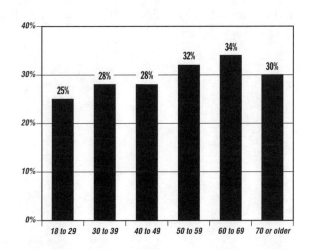

# Is Life Exciting?

"In general, do you find life exciting, pretty routine, or dull?"

*(percent responding by age, 1994)*

|  | exciting | pretty routine | dull |
|---|---|---|---|
| **Total** | **47%** | **48%** | **4%** |
| Aged 18 to 29 | 53 | 43 | 4 |
| Aged 30 to 39 | 50 | 47 | 3 |
| Aged 40 to 49 | 46 | 51 | 3 |
| Aged 50 to 59 | 51 | 44 | 4 |
| Aged 60 to 69 | 39 | 56 | 4 |
| Aged 70 or older | 35 | 52 | 9 |

*Note: Percents may not add to 100 because no opinion and no answer are not included.*
*Source: General Social Survey, National Opinion Research Center, University of Chicago*

# Personal Happiness

"Taken all together, how would you say things are these days—would you say that you are very happy, pretty happy, or not too happy?"

*(percent responding by age, 1994)*

|  | very happy | pretty happy | not too happy |
|---|---|---|---|
| **Total** | **29%** | **59%** | **12%** |
| Aged 18 to 29 | 25 | 63 | 12 |
| Aged 30 to 39 | 28 | 60 | 12 |
| Aged 40 to 49 | 28 | 59 | 13 |
| Aged 50 to 59 | 32 | 57 | 11 |
| Aged 60 to 69 | 34 | 54 | 11 |
| Aged 70 or older | 30 | 56 | 14 |

*Note: Percents may not add to 100 because "don't know" and no answer are not included.*
*Source: General Social Survey, National Opinion Research Center, University of Chicago*

# Marital Happiness

"Taking all things together, how would you describe your marriage? Would you say that your marriage is very happy, pretty happy, or not too happy?"

*(percent responding by age, 1994)*

|  | very happy | pretty happy | not too happy |
|---|---|---|---|
| Total | 60% | 36% | 3% |
| Aged 18 to 29 | 66 | 31 | 3 |
| Aged 30 to 39 | 58 | 37 | 4 |
| Aged 40 to 49 | 61 | 36 | 3 |
| Aged 50 to 59 | 58 | 39 | 3 |
| Aged 60 to 69 | 61 | 34 | 4 |
| Aged 70 or older | 62 | 36 | 1 |

*Note: Asked of people who were married at the time of the survey. Percents may not add to 100 because "don't know" and no answer are not included.*
*Source: General Social Survey, National Opinion Research Center, University of Chicago*

# Death Is No Stranger to Older Americans

**The percentage of Americans having experienced a traumatic event in the past year peaks among those in their 50s.**

The proportion of people experiencing a traumatic event does not vary substantially by age, ranging from a low of 34 percent among those in their 30s to a high of 48 percent among those in their 50s. In some cases the trauma is the death of a friend or relative, in other cases it is a divorce or serious illness.

Overall, 39 percent of people aged 18 or older have been hospitalized in the past five years. Until age 60, the percentage of people who have been hospitalized does not vary much by age. But the figure rises in the older age groups. Among people aged 60 to 69, 47 percent have been hospitalized in the past five years, as have 51 percent of those in their 70s.

The percentage of Americans who have experienced the death of a relative in the past five years rises sharply with age, from only 7 percent of young adults to a majority of people aged 70 or older. Most older Americans no longer have living fathers, but a majority of people in their 50s still have living mothers. By the time people are in their 60s, most have lost both parents and over half have experienced the death of a sibling.

◆ With the baby-boom generation about to enter the age groups in which death and illness become much more common, the opportunity to offer psychological and spiritual counseling abounds for entrepreneurs.

# Traumatic Experiences

Number of traumatic events happening last year.

*(percent responding by age, 1994)*

|  | none | one or more |
|---|---|---|
| **Total** | **60%** | **40%** |
| Aged 18 to 29 | 61 | 39 |
| Aged 30 to 39 | 66 | 34 |
| Aged 40 to 49 | 55 | 45 |
| Aged 50 to 59 | 52 | 48 |
| Aged 60 to 69 | 60 | 40 |
| Aged 70 or older | 58 | 42 |

*Source: General Social Survey, National Opinion Research Center, University of Chicago*

# Hospital Care

**Number of hospitalizations in the past five years.**

*(percent responding by age, 1994)*

|  | none | one or more |
|---|---|---|
| **Total** | **61%** | **39%** |
| Aged 18 to 29 | 67 | 33 |
| Aged 30 to 39 | 62 | 38 |
| Aged 40 to 49 | 64 | 36 |
| Aged 50 to 59 | 67 | 33 |
| Aged 60 to 69 | 53 | 47 |
| Aged 70 or older | 49 | 51 |

*Source: General Social Survey, National Opinion Research Center, University of Chicago*

# Death of Relatives in Past Five Years

Number of relatives who have died in past five years.

*(percent responding by age, 1994)*

|  | none | one or more |
|---|---|---|
| **Total** | **67%** | **33%** |
| Aged 18 to 29 | 94 | 7 |
| Aged 30 to 39 | 73 | 27 |
| Aged 40 to 49 | 62 | 38 |
| Aged 50 to 59 | 51 | 49 |
| Aged 60 to 69 | 55 | 46 |
| Aged 70 or older | 49 | 51 |

*Source: General Social Survey, National Opinion Research Center, University of Chicago*

# Death of Father

**"Is your father still alive?"**

*(percent responding by age, 1994)*

|  | yes | no |
|---|---|---|
| **Total** | **48%** | **52%** |
| Aged 18 to 29 | 85 | 15 |
| Aged 30 to 39 | 74 | 26 |
| Aged 40 to 49 | 46 | 54 |
| Aged 50 to 59 | 25 | 75 |
| Aged 60 to 69 | 4 | 96 |
| Aged 70 or older | 7 | 93 |

*Source: General Social Survey, National Opinion Research Center, University of Chicago*

# Death of Mother

"Is your mother still alive?"

*(percent responding by age, 1994)*

|  | yes | no |
|---|---|---|
| **Total** | **61%** | **39%** |
| Aged 18 to 29 | 87 | 13 |
| Aged 30 to 39 | 86 | 14 |
| Aged 40 to 49 | 69 | 32 |
| Aged 50 to 59 | 54 | 46 |
| Aged 60 to 69 | 20 | 80 |
| Aged 70 or older | 7 | 93 |

*Source: General Social Survey, National Opinion Research Center, University of Chicago*

## Death of Siblings

"Have any siblings or siblings-in-law died?"

*(percent responding by age, 1994)*

|  | yes | no |
|---|---|---|
| **Total** | **21%** | **79%** |
| Aged 18 to 29 | 0 | 100 |
| Aged 30 to 39 | 9 | 91 |
| Aged 40 to 49 | 12 | 88 |
| Aged 50 to 59 | 19 | 81 |
| Aged 60 to 69 | 52 | 48 |
| Aged 70 or older | 64 | 36 |

*Source: General Social Survey, National Opinion Research Center, University of Chicago*

# The Oldest Americans Are Most Likely to Live in Small Towns

**Nearly half the people aged 70 or older live in a small city or town.**

Forty-six percent of people aged 70 or older live in small cities or towns, versus 40 percent of all Americans. Big-city life is most popular among young adults (24 percent of people aged 18 to 29 live in big cities) and, surprisingly, among people aged 60 to 69 (23 percent). The high proportion of sixtysomethings who live in big cities may be accounted for by retirement preferences. Many who longed for city life in middle-age may move to a city after they retire. Living in the suburbs is most popular among people in the peak of their careers—ages 30 to 60. Few Americans of any age live in country villages or on farms.

Although it is widely assumed that mobility has increased over the past few decades, in fact people aged 40 to 59 are more mobile than younger adults. Only 34 percent of those in their 40s and 50s live in the same place they lived at age 16, versus 39 percent of all Americans. The 40-to-59 age group is the one most likely to be living in a different state than when they were 16 (41 percent versus 35 percent of all Americans).

Most Americans live in households that are home to just one generation. The proportion rises with age after age 40, peaking at 92 percent among people aged 70 or older. A substantial 27 percent of people in their 50s still have children at home. In this age group, the proportion of people who live with both children and grandchildren peaks at 5 percent.

◆ While it is often assumed that there are dramatic differences in where people live and how much they have moved around by age, in fact the differences are slight. Living arrangements are much more variable than living locations.

## Community Type

**"How would you describe the place where you live?"**

*(percent responding by age, 1994)*

|  | big city | suburbs or outskirts of a big city | a small city or town | a country village | farm or home in the country |
|---|---|---|---|---|---|
| **Total** | **19%** | **24%** | **40%** | **4%** | **11%** |
| Aged 18 to 29 | 24 | 23 | 44 | 3 | 5 |
| Aged 30 to 39 | 19 | 26 | 39 | 5 | 10 |
| Aged 40 to 49 | 17 | 25 | 39 | 5 | 13 |
| Aged 50 to 59 | 18 | 27 | 36 | 3 | 14 |
| Aged 60 to 69 | 23 | 19 | 36 | 7 | 11 |
| Aged 70 or older | 16 | 18 | 46 | 5 | 12 |

*Note: Percents may not add to 100 because "don't know" and no answer are not included.*
*Source: General Social Survey, National Opinion Research Center, University of Chicago*

# Mobility Since Age 16

"When you were 16 years old, were you living in this same city or state?"

*(percent responding by age, 1994)*

|  | same place | different city | different state |
|---|---|---|---|
| **Total** | **39%** | **26%** | **35%** |
| Aged 18 to 29 | 50 | 24 | 26 |
| Aged 30 to 39 | 42 | 26 | 32 |
| Aged 40 to 49 | 34 | 25 | 41 |
| Aged 50 to 59 | 34 | 25 | 41 |
| Aged 60 to 69 | 35 | 26 | 39 |
| Aged 70 or older | 39 | 26 | 35 |

*Note: Percents may not add to 100 because no answer is not included.*
*Source: General Social Survey, National Opinion Research Center, University of Chicago*

## Extended Families

Number of family generations in household.

*(percent responding by age, 1994)*

| | one | two | | | three | |
| --- | --- | --- | --- | --- | --- | --- |
| | | children | parent(s) | grandchildren | children and grandchildren | children and parents |
| **Total** | **54%** | **41%** | **1%** | **1%** | **2%** | **1%** |
| Aged 18 to 29 | 44 | 53 | 0 | 1 | 2 | 1 |
| Aged 30 to 39 | 36 | 62 | 1 | 0 | 2 | 1 |
| Aged 40 to 49 | 42 | 54 | 1 | 0 | 2 | 1 |
| Aged 50 to 59 | 64 | 27 | 2 | 2 | 5 | 1 |
| Aged 60 to 69 | 84 | 10 | 1 | 1 | 2 | 1 |
| Aged 70 or older | 92 | 6 | 1 | 1 | 1 | 0 |

*Source: General Social Survey, National Opinion Research Center, University of Chicago*

# Older Americans Are Most Fearful of Crime

## Most are afraid to walk alone at night in their neighborhoods.

Among all Americans, 47 percent do not feel safe walking alone at night within a mile of where they live. The youngest and oldest Americans are most afraid. Among those aged 18 to 29, 49 percent are afraid—perhaps reflecting the fact that so many live in big cities, where crime is more prevalent.

Fear of walking alone at night drops to a low of 39 percent among people in their 40s. Again, place of residence may explain this lower level of fear. A large share of people in their 40s live in the (relatively safe) suburbs.

Fear of walking alone at night rises above 50 percent among people aged 60 or older. While many people in their 60s live in big cities, place of residence does not explain why people aged 70 or older are so fearful—since a near majority live in small cities or towns. Behind the fear of older Americans is the fact that most are women—and women are much more fearful of walking alone at night than men. In addition, as people age their sense of vulnerability increases, leading to greater fear.

◆ Because fear of crime rises as people get older, the aging of the population should contribute to a healthy market for home protection systems and other security products and services.

### Fear of Crime Peaks in Older Age Groups

*(percent saying they are afraid to walk alone at night, by age, 1994)*

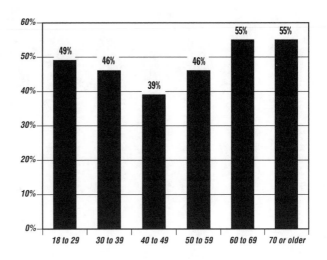

# Fear of Crime

**"Is there an area right around here—that is, within a mile—where you would be afraid to walk alone at night?"**

*(percent responding by age, 1994)*

|  | *yes* | *no* |
|---|---|---|
| **Total** | **47%** | **52%** |
| Aged 18 to 29 | 49 | 51 |
| Aged 30 to 39 | 46 | 54 |
| Aged 40 to 49 | 39 | 60 |
| Aged 50 to 59 | 46 | 54 |
| Aged 60 to 69 | 55 | 44 |
| Aged 70 or older | 55 | 42 |

*Note: Percents may not add to 100 because "don't know" and no answer are not included.*
*Source: General Social Survey, National Opinion Research Center, University of Chicago*

# People Aged 60 or Older Are the Heaviest Consumers of Media

## Older Americans are more likely to read newspapers and watch TV than are younger adults.

At least two-thirds of people aged 60 or older read the newspaper daily, versus only 50 percent of all adults. Over 60 percent watch at least three hours of TV every day, versus 47 percent of the population as a whole. Older Americans are bigger consumers of the media because they have more time to read and watch than do younger adults.

Newspaper readership is lowest among young adults. Only 31 percent of people aged 18 to 29 read a newspaper daily, versus 58 percent of those in their 50s, 67 percent of people in their 60s, and 72 percent of those in their 70s. Television viewership is lowest among middle-aged adults. Over 60 percent of people aged 30 to 49 watch TV for two or fewer hours per day. Only one in five persons in this age group watches TV for four or more hours per day. The proportion who watch TV at least four hours per day is twice as high among people aged 60 or older—44 percent of those aged 60 to 69 and 42 percent of those aged 70 or older.

◆ Older Americans are most likely to be exposed to newspaper and television advertising, which makes these media an excellent way to reach the older market.

◆ Older Americans spend more time watching TV and reading newspapers than younger people because they have more free time. As computers become increasingly prevalent in the homes of older Americans, look for their online use to surpass that of younger and middle-aged adults as well.

## Reading the Newspaper

"How often do you read the newspaper—every day, a few times a week, once a week, less than once a week, or never?"

*(percent responding by age, 1994)*

|  | daily | a few times a week | once a week | less than once a week | never |
|---|---|---|---|---|---|
| Total | 50% | 23% | 13% | 10% | 4% |
| Aged 18 to 29 | 31 | 31 | 19 | 16 | 3 |
| Aged 30 to 39 | 37 | 29 | 18 | 13 | 4 |
| Aged 40 to 49 | 52 | 23 | 14 | 8 | 4 |
| Aged 50 to 59 | 58 | 22 | 8 | 8 | 4 |
| Aged 60 to 69 | 67 | 16 | 9 | 6 | 3 |
| Aged 70 or older | 72 | 10 | 7 | 4 | 7 |

*Note: Percents may not add to 100 because no answer is not included.*
*Source: General Social Survey, National Opinion Research Center, University of Chicago*

# Watching Television

"On the average day, about how many hours do you personally spend watching television?"

*(percent responding by age, 1994)*

|  | none | one | two | three | four or more |
|---|---|---|---|---|---|
| **Total** | **4%** | **22%** | **27%** | **19%** | **28%** |
| Aged 18 to 29 | 4 | 19 | 25 | 20 | 30 |
| Aged 30 to 39 | 4 | 27 | 30 | 18 | 20 |
| Aged 40 to 49 | 5 | 28 | 29 | 19 | 19 |
| Aged 50 to 59 | 3 | 23 | 29 | 18 | 27 |
| Aged 60 to 69 | 2 | 12 | 23 | 18 | 44 |
| Aged 70 or older | 3 | 10 | 21 | 22 | 42 |

*Note: Percents may not add to 100 because no answer is not included.*
*Source: General Social Survey, National Opinion Research Center, University of Chicago*

# Older Americans Are Much Less Likely to Approve of Working Women

## But most people in their 50s say working women, and working mothers, are OK.

Most people aged 60 or older did not grow up with a working mother. Only 29 percent of people aged 70 or older and 41 percent of those aged 60 to 69 say their mother worked for at least one year while they were growing up. Among 50-to-59-year-olds, half had working mothers. In contrast, working mothers were the norm among today's young and middle-aged adults when they were growing up. At least 70 percent of people aged 18 to 39 had working mothers.

Because they did not grow up with working mothers, older Americans are less likely to approve of them. Only 48 percent of people aged 70 or older think a working mother can establish just as warm a relationship with her children as a nonworking mother. Seventy-one percent of the oldest Americans think men should be the achievers outside the home while women take care of home and family. Half the people aged 70 or older say the wife should help her husband's career rather than have a career of her own.

◆ As younger generations age, traditional attitudes toward the roles of men and women are changing. Already, a majority of people in their 50s and 60s approve of working mothers. This approval will continue to grow as boomers enter the older age groups.

# Did Your Mother Work While You Were Growing Up?

"Did your mother ever work for pay for as long as a year when you were growing up?"

*(percent responding by age, 1994)*

|  | *yes* | *no* |
|---|---|---|
| **Total** | **59**% | **40**% |
| Aged 18 to 29 | 79 | 20 |
| Aged 30 to 39 | 71 | 29 |
| Aged 40 to 49 | 61 | 39 |
| Aged 50 to 59 | 50 | 49 |
| Aged 60 to 69 | 41 | 58 |
| Aged 70 or older | 29 | 69 |

*Note: Percents may not add to 100 because "don't know" and no answer are not included.*
*Source: General Social Survey, National Opinion Research Center, University of Chicago*

# Roles of Men and Women

"It is much better for everyone involved if the man is the achiever outside the home and the woman takes care of the home and family—do you agree or disagree?"

*(percent responding by age, 1994)*

|  | agree | disagree |
|---|---|---|
| **Total** | **34%** | **63%** |
| Aged 18 to 29 | 18 | 81 |
| Aged 30 to 39 | 24 | 74 |
| Aged 40 to 49 | 26 | 71 |
| Aged 50 to 59 | 39 | 57 |
| Aged 60 to 69 | 45 | 53 |
| Aged 70 or older | 71 | 24 |

*Note: Percents may not add to 100 because no opinion and no answer are not included.*
*Source: General Social Survey, National Opinion Research Center, University of Chicago*

# Is the Husband's Career More Important?

"It is more important for a wife to help her husband's career than to have one herself—do you agree or disagree?"

*(percent responding by age, 1994)*

|  | *agree* | *disagree* |
|---|---|---|
| **Total** | **21%** | **76%** |
| Aged 18 to 29 | 13 | 95 |
| Aged 30 to 39 | 10 | 87 |
| Aged 40 to 49 | 16 | 80 |
| Aged 50 to 59 | 19 | 76 |
| Aged 60 to 69 | 31 | 66 |
| Aged 70 or older | 51 | 40 |

*Note: Percents may not add to 100 because "don't know" and no answer are not included.*
*Source: General Social Survey, National Opinion Research Center, University of Chicago*

# Who Does the Chores?

**"In your household, who is responsible for doing the following chores?"**

*(percent who say "usually or always" the woman by age, 1994)*

|  | laundry | planning dinner | grocery shopping |
|---|---|---|---|
| **Total** | **65%** | **52%** | **47%** |
| Aged 18 to 29 | 51 | 34 | 37 |
| Aged 30 to 39 | 62 | 49 | 47 |
| Aged 40 to 49 | 64 | 59 | 53 |
| Aged 50 to 59 | 74 | 58 | 49 |
| Aged 60 to 69 | 77 | 57 | 45 |
| Aged 70 or older | 75 | 62 | 48 |

*Note: Percentages are based on respondents who were married or living as married.*
*Source: General Social Survey, National Opinion Research Center, University of Chicago*

# Religion Is Important to Older Americans

**Americans aged 50 or older are more religious than younger adults, and they are more likely to practice their religion every day.**

Regardless of age, most Americans believe in God without any doubts, ranging from 53 percent of Americans aged 18 to 29 to two in three people aged 50 or older. Religious identity varies more by age. At least two in three people aged 50 or older are Protestants, versus a 47 percent minority of 18-to-29-year-olds. Sixteen percent of the youngest adults say they have no religion, versus only 2 percent of the oldest Americans.

Most people aged 50 or older attend religious services at least once per month, with 42 percent of those aged 60 or older attending at least weekly. Only about one in four adults under age 40 attend religious services every week. At least 60 percent of older Americans pray daily, versus fewer than half those under age 40.

Older Amerians are more likely than younger ones to have a great deal of confidence in the leaders of religious institutions. The proportion ranges from 28 percent of those in their 50s to about one-third of those aged 60 or older. A majority of people aged 50 or older agree that we believe too much in science and not enough in faith. Slightly fewer than half the people under age 40 agree.

◆ As younger, less-religious Americans enter the 50-plus age groups, the religious ardor of older Americans will fade. This is already a problem for many churches whose memberships are aging because they cannot attract enough young people.

## A Majority of Americans Pray Daily

*(percent praying at least once per day, by age, 1994)*

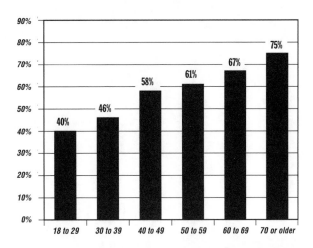

# Belief in God

"Which statement comes closest to expressing what you believe about God?
- I don't believe in God.
- I don't know whether there is a God and I don't believe there is any way to find out.
- I don't believe in a personal God, but I do believe in a Higher Power of some kind.
- I find myself believing in God some of the time, but not at others.
- While I have doubts, I feel that I do believe in God.
- I know God really exists and I have no doubts about it."

*(percent responding by age, 1994)*

| | no doubts | believe, but have doubts | believe sometimes | higher power | don't know, no way to find out | don't believe |
|---|---|---|---|---|---|---|
| **Total** | **62%** | **15%** | **4%** | **10%** | **3%** | **2%** |
| Aged 18 to 29 | 53 | 21 | 4 | 8 | 6 | 4 |
| Aged 30 to 39 | 60 | 19 | 4 | 9 | 3 | 1 |
| Aged 40 to 49 | 62 | 13 | 3 | 12 | 3 | 4 |
| Aged 50 to 59 | 68 | 13 | 3 | 10 | 2 | 1 |
| Aged 60 to 69 | 69 | 9 | 4 | 11 | 0 | 3 |
| Aged 70 or older | 65 | 13 | 4 | 6 | 1 | 3 |

*Note: Percents may not add to 100 because "don't know" and no answer are not included.*
*Source: General Social Survey, National Opinion Research Center, University of Chicago*

# Religious Preference

"What is your religious preference? Is it Protestant, Catholic, Jewish, some other religion, or no religion?"

*(percent responding by age, 1994)*

|  | Protestant | Catholic | Jewish | other | none |
|---|---|---|---|---|---|
| Total | 59% | 25% | 2% | 4% | 9% |
| Aged 18 to 29 | 47 | 29 | 2 | 6 | 16 |
| Aged 30 to 39 | 56 | 25 | 2 | 5 | 11 |
| Aged 40 to 49 | 58 | 26 | 2 | 4 | 11 |
| Aged 50 to 59 | 65 | 25 | 2 | 2 | 5 |
| Aged 60 to 69 | 65 | 25 | 2 | 2 | 5 |
| Aged 70 or older | 73 | 20 | 3 | 1 | 2 |

*Note: Percents may not add to 100 because "don't know" and no answer are not included.*
*Source: General Social Survey, National Opinion Research Center, University of Chicago*

## Attendance at Religious Services

**"How often do you attend religious services?"**

*(percent responding by age, 1994)*

|  | weekly or more | 1 to 3 times per month | up to several times per year | never |
|---|---|---|---|---|
| **Total** | **32%** | **17%** | **34%** | **16%** |
| Aged 18 to 29 | 22 | 18 | 43 | 16 |
| Aged 30 to 39 | 25 | 18 | 39 | 17 |
| Aged 40 to 49 | 33 | 18 | 32 | 16 |
| Aged 50 to 59 | 35 | 18 | 30 | 15 |
| Aged 60 to 69 | 42 | 11 | 30 | 16 |
| Aged 70 or older | 42 | 12 | 27 | 17 |

*Note: Percents may not add to 100 because "don't know" and no answer are not included.*
*Source: General Social Survey, National Opinion Research Center, University of Chicago*

# Frequency of Praying

"About how often do you pray?"

*(percent responding by age, 1994)*

|  | several times per day | once per day | several times per week | once per week | less than once per week | never |
|---|---|---|---|---|---|---|
| **Total** | **23%** | **32%** | **11%** | **8%** | **22%** | **1%** |
| Aged 18 to 29 | 16 | 24 | 13 | 16 | 30 | 2 |
| Aged 30 to 39 | 16 | 30 | 13 | 8 | 30 | 2 |
| Aged 40 to 49 | 23 | 35 | 12 | 7 | 20 | 1 |
| Aged 50 to 59 | 28 | 33 | 11 | 7 | 18 | 1 |
| Aged 60 to 69 | 30 | 37 | 10 | 7 | 15 | 1 |
| Aged 70 or older | 35 | 40 | 6 | 4 | 11 | 1 |

*Note: Percents may not add to 100 because "don't know" and no answer are not included.*
*Source: General Social Survey, National Opinion Research Center, University of Chicago*

# Confidence in the Leaders of Organized Religion

"As far as the people running organized religion are concerned, would you say you have a great deal of confidence, only some confidence, or hardly any confidence at all in them?"

*(percent responding by age, 1994)*

|  | a great deal | only some | hardly any |
|---|---|---|---|
| **Total** | **24%** | **52%** | **22%** |
| Aged 18 to 29 | 22 | 56 | 22 |
| Aged 30 to 39 | 19 | 54 | 24 |
| Aged 40 to 49 | 20 | 53 | 24 |
| Aged 50 to 59 | 28 | 51 | 20 |
| Aged 60 to 69 | 33 | 46 | 20 |
| Aged 70 or older | 32 | 42 | 17 |

*Note: Percents may not add to 100 because "don't know" and no answer are not included.*
*Source: General Social Survey, National Opinion Research Center, University of Chicago*

# Faith or Science?

"We believe too often in science, and not enough in feelings and faith. How much do you agree or disagree?"

*(percent responding by age, 1994)*

|  | agree | neither | disagree |
|---|---|---|---|
| Total | 52% | 23% | 20% |
| Aged 18 to 29 | 47 | 22 | 27 |
| Aged 30 to 39 | 48 | 26 | 22 |
| Aged 40 to 49 | 52 | 25 | 19 |
| Aged 50 to 59 | 55 | 20 | 18 |
| Aged 60 to 69 | 65 | 20 | 10 |
| Aged 70 or older | 55 | 16 | 15 |

*Note: Percents may not add to 100 because "don't know" and no answer are not included.*
*Source: General Social Survey, National Opinion Research Center, University of Chicago*

# Older Americans Are Less Supportive of Euthanasia

**Just over half the people aged 70 or older think euthanasia is OK.**

Younger people are much more willing than older Americans to allow a doctor to end a patient's life painlessly if the patient and his or her family request it. Three in four people aged 18 to 40 would allow doctors to perform euthanasia. This proportion falls with increasing age, to just 53 percent of those aged 70 or older.

The proportion of Americans who think doctors should not be allowed to end a patient's life rises with age, from 24 percent of the youngest adults to 35 percent of the oldest Americans.

◆ As the aged population grows, the issue of euthanasia promises to become more troublesome. If younger adults continue to support this alternative, then euthanasia is likely to become a common practice among the dying. But young adults may change their minds about euthanasia as they get older.

# Attitudes toward Euthanasia

"When a person has a disease that cannot be cured, do you think doctors should be allowed by law to end the patient's life by some painless means if the patient and his family request it?"

*(percent responding by age, 1994)*

|  | *yes* | *no* |
|---|---|---|
| **Total** | **68%** | **27%** |
| Aged 18 to 29 | 74 | 23 |
| Aged 30 to 39 | 74 | 21 |
| Aged 40 to 49 | 70 | 26 |
| Aged 50 to 59 | 61 | 32 |
| Aged 60 to 69 | 63 | 32 |
| Aged 70 or older | 53 | 35 |

*Note: Percents may not add to 100 because "don't know" and no answer are not included.*
*Source: General Social Survey, National Opinion Research Center, University of Chicago*

# Older People Are Cynical Too

**But most think other people try to be helpful most of the time.**

At least half the people aged 50 or older think people try to be helpful most of the time rather than just look out for themselves. In contrast, only 32 percent of people aged 18 to 29 think others are helpful, while 61 percent think people are just looking out for themselves.

Regardless of age, most Americans think the condition of the average person is getting worse. Most also do not think public officials are interested in the problems of the average person. Interestingly, those least cynical about public officials are the youngest Americans. Thirty percent of people aged 18 to 29 think public officials are interested in the problems of the average person, versus only 17 percent of people aged 70 or older.

There is little variation by age in the percentages of Americans who have a "great deal" of confidence in the leaders of a variety of institutions, ranging from the federal government to major companies to the press. Like Americans of all ages, older people have the least confidence in the federal government, Congress, the press, television, and organized labor. They have the most confidence in medicine and the scientific community. Older Americans are much more likely than younger ones to have a great deal of confidence in the leaders of education. They are much less likely than younger adults to have a great deal of confidence in the scientific community.

◆ The growing cynicism of the American public is not limited to the younger age groups. Americans of all ages have been turned off—particularly to the federal government.

# Helpfulness of Others

**"Would you say that most of the time people try to be helpful, or that they are mostly just looking out for themselves?"**

*(percent responding by age, 1994)*

|  | just look out for themselves | try to be helpful |
|---|---|---|
| **Total** | **47%** | **46%** |
| Aged 18 to 29 | 61 | 32 |
| Aged 30 to 39 | 53 | 40 |
| Aged 40 to 49 | 42 | 51 |
| Aged 50 to 59 | 38 | 56 |
| Aged 60 to 69 | 34 | 57 |
| Aged 70 or older | 40 | 52 |

*Note: Numbers may not add to 100 because "other/depends," "don't know" and no answer are not included.*
*Source: General Social Survey, National Opinion Research Center, University of Chicago*

# Are Things Getting Worse?

"In spite of what some people say, the lot (situation/condition) of the average man is getting worse, not better."

*(percent responding by age, 1994)*

|  | agree | disagree |
|---|---|---|
| **Total** | **67%** | **30%** |
| Aged 18 to 29 | 70 | 27 |
| Aged 30 to 39 | 68 | 31 |
| Aged 40 to 49 | 63 | 35 |
| Aged 50 to 59 | 70 | 28 |
| Aged 60 to 69 | 70 | 26 |
| Aged 70 or older | 64 | 29 |

*Note: Percents may not add to 100 because "don't know" and no answer are not included.*
*Source: General Social Survey, National Opinion Research Center, University of Chicago*

# Do Public Officials Really Care?

"Most public officials (people in public office) are not really interested in the problems of the average man."

*(percent of respondents by age, 1994)*

|  | agree | disagree |
|---|---|---|
| **Total** | **74%** | **24%** |
| Aged 18 to 29 | 69 | 30 |
| Aged 30 to 39 | 77 | 22 |
| Aged 40 to 49 | 71 | 26 |
| Aged 50 to 59 | 76 | 23 |
| Aged 60 to 69 | 77 | 21 |
| Aged 70 or older | 74 | 17 |

*Note: Percents may not add to 100 because "don't know" and no answer are not included.*
*Source: General Social Survey, National Opinion Research Center, University of Chicago*

# Confidence in Leaders of Institutions

"How much confidence do you have in the people running this institution? Would you say you had a great deal of confidence, only some confidence, or hardly any confidence at all in them?"

*(percent responding by age, 1994)*

| | federal government | | | Congress | | |
|---|---|---|---|---|---|---|
| | great deal | only some | hardly any | great deal | only some | hardly any |
| Total | 11% | 51% | 35% | 8% | 50% | 39% |
| Aged 18 to 29 | 11 | 56 | 32 | 9 | 54 | 34 |
| Aged 30 to 39 | 10 | 52 | 37 | 6 | 51 | 42 |
| Aged 40 to 49 | 8 | 57 | 34 | 7 | 48 | 43 |
| Aged 50 to 59 | 11 | 50 | 37 | 8 | 49 | 41 |
| Aged 60 to 69 | 16 | 45 | 39 | 10 | 47 | 39 |
| Aged 70 or older | 17 | 43 | 31 | 8 | 50 | 33 |

| | major companies | | | financial institutions | | |
|---|---|---|---|---|---|---|
| | great deal | only some | hardly any | great deal | only some | hardly any |
| Total | 25% | 61% | 10% | 18% | 61% | 20% |
| Aged 18 to 29 | 26 | 65 | 9 | 22 | 61 | 16 |
| Aged 30 to 39 | 25 | 63 | 10 | 15 | 64 | 21 |
| Aged 40 to 49 | 23 | 67 | 9 | 14 | 61 | 24 |
| Aged 50 to 59 | 30 | 58 | 10 | 16 | 60 | 24 |
| Aged 60 to 69 | 26 | 60 | 10 | 18 | 62 | 19 |
| Aged 70 or older | 25 | 49 | 14 | 26 | 53 | 14 |

| | the military | | | Supreme Court | | |
|---|---|---|---|---|---|---|
| | great deal | only some | hardly any | great deal | only some | hardly any |
| Total | 37% | 48% | 12% | 30% | 50% | 16% |
| Aged 18 to 29 | 43 | 41 | 14 | 37 | 50 | 12 |
| Aged 30 to 39 | 33 | 52 | 14 | 30 | 52 | 16 |
| Aged 40 to 49 | 31 | 50 | 16 | 30 | 52 | 16 |
| Aged 50 to 59 | 38 | 52 | 7 | 28 | 51 | 17 |
| Aged 60 to 69 | 36 | 53 | 8 | 29 | 48 | 18 |
| Aged 70 or older | 45 | 40 | 8 | 24 | 42 | 23 |

*(continued)*

*(continued from previous page)*

|  | the press | | | television | | |
|---|---|---|---|---|---|---|
|  | *great deal* | *only some* | *hardly any* | *great deal* | *only some* | *hardly any* |
| **Total** | **10%** | **49%** | **39%** | **9%** | **50%** | **40%** |
| Aged 18 to 29 | 12 | 44 | 42 | 15 | 48 | 36 |
| Aged 30 to 39 | 11 | 53 | 35 | 9 | 52 | 39 |
| Aged 40 to 49 | 7 | 51 | 41 | 6 | 46 | 46 |
| Aged 50 to 59 | 9 | 45 | 45 | 9 | 50 | 40 |
| Aged 60 to 69 | 9 | 54 | 36 | 10 | 48 | 40 |
| Aged 70 or older | 10 | 47 | 36 | 10 | 53 | 33 |

|  | medicine | | | scientific community | | |
|---|---|---|---|---|---|---|
|  | *great deal* | *only some* | *hardly any* | *great deal* | *only some* | *hardly any* |
| **Total** | **41%** | **48%** | **10%** | **38%** | **49%** | **7%** |
| Aged 18 to 29 | 52 | 43 | 6 | 48 | 42 | 7 |
| Aged 30 to 39 | 43 | 47 | 9 | 41 | 49 | 6 |
| Aged 40 to 49 | 36 | 54 | 9 | 39 | 52 | 6 |
| Aged 50 to 59 | 38 | 50 | 11 | 37 | 49 | 10 |
| Aged 60 to 69 | 35 | 48 | 16 | 28 | 56 | 9 |
| Aged 70 or older | 41 | 42 | 12 | 28 | 49 | 6 |

|  | education | | | organized labor | | |
|---|---|---|---|---|---|---|
|  | *great deal* | *only some* | *hardly any* | *great deal* | *only some* | *hardly any* |
| **Total** | **25%** | **56%** | **17%** | **10%** | **52%** | **32%** |
| Aged 18 to 29 | 30 | 54 | 16 | 14 | 60 | 21 |
| Aged 30 to 39 | 19 | 64 | 16 | 8 | 55 | 32 |
| Aged 40 to 49 | 20 | 60 | 19 | 6 | 53 | 39 |
| Aged 50 to 59 | 27 | 54 | 18 | 8 | 50 | 37 |
| Aged 60 to 69 | 28 | 51 | 19 | 14 | 44 | 36 |
| Aged 70 or older | 32 | 44 | 17 | 13 | 41 | 30 |

*Note: Percents may not add to 100 because "don't know" and no answer are not included.*
*Source: General Social Survey, National Opinion Research Center, University of Chicago*

# Education

◆ A substantial 30 percent of Americans aged 55 or older lack a high school diploma, compared with only 18 percent of all Americans aged 25 or older.

◆ Among men aged 55 to 64, 25 percent are college graduates, compared with only 16 percent of men aged 75 or older.

◆ Sixteen percent of women aged 55 to 64 have graduated from college, versus 11 percent of women aged 75 or older.

◆ Twenty-two percent of white men aged 55 or older are college graduates versus only 9 percent of black and 10 percent of Hispanic men in the age group.

◆ Twelve percent of white and 10 percent of black women aged 55 or older are college graduates, compared with only 4 percent of Hispanic women in the same age group.

# Sharp Rise in Educational Attainment of Older Americans

**A high school diploma did not become the norm among people aged 55 or older until the 1980s.**

In 1995, 71 percent of men and 69 percent of women aged 55 or older had a high school education, up from only 16 percent of men and 18 percent of women in 1940. In that year, only 4 percent of men and 2 percent of women aged 55 or older had a college diploma. Now the proportions are 22 and 16 percent, respectively. Despite the dramatic rise in the educational attainment of older Americans, a substantial 30 percent still lack a high school diploma. Among all Americans aged 25 or older, only 18 percent are not high school graduates.

◆ The educational attainment of older Americans is rising because better-educated generations are replacing those with less education. As the baby-boom generation enters the 55-plus age group, the educational level of the older population will continue its rapid rise.

◆ Many marketing strategies that have been successful with older Americans appeal to uneducated and unsophisticated consumers. These strategies will have to be abandoned as the educational level of the market soars.

## Educational Attainment on the Rise

*(percent distribution of men and women aged 55 or older who are high school graduates or more, 1940 and 1996)*

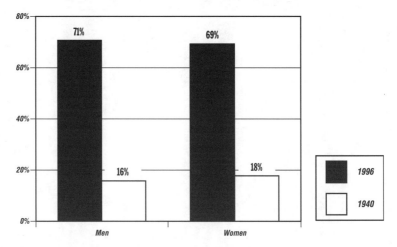

# Educational Attainment of Persons Aged 55 or Older, 1940 to 1996

*(percent distribution of persons aged 55 or older by sex and educational attainment, 1940 to 1996)*

| | total | not a high<br>high school<br>graduate | high school<br>graduate<br>or more | some<br>college | college,<br>four or<br>more years |
|---|---|---|---|---|---|
| **Men** | | | | | |
| 1996 | 100.0% | 29.3% | 70.7% | 18.2% | 21.6% |
| 1995 | 100.0 | 30.5 | 69.5 | 18.6 | 20.4 |
| 1990 | 100.0 | 38.5 | 61.5 | 12.1 | 18.1 |
| 1985 | 100.0 | 44.4 | 55.6 | 10.4 | 15.4 |
| 1980 | 100.0 | 50.4 | 49.6 | 9.9 | 12.6 |
| 1975 | 100.0 | 57.8 | 42.2 | 8.3 | 9.9 |
| 1970 | 100.0 | 65.9 | 34.1 | 6.9 | 8.9 |
| 1960 | 100.0 | 79.2 | 20.8 | 5.7 | 5.3 |
| 1950 | 100.0 | 78.4 | 21.6 | 4.1 | 4.6 |
| 1940 | 100.0 | 84.2 | 15.8 | 3.2 | 3.7 |
| **Women** | | | | | |
| 1996 | 100.0% | 30.7% | 69.3% | 18.3% | 15.6% |
| 1995 | 100.0 | 31.1 | 68.9 | 18.6 | 11.4 |
| 1990 | 100.0 | 38.2 | 61.8 | 12.3 | 10.6 |
| 1985 | 100.0 | 47.1 | 52.9 | 10.8 | 8.8 |
| 1980 | 100.0 | 49.4 | 50.6 | 9.8 | 7.9 |
| 1975 | 100.0 | 56.1 | 43.9 | 8.6 | 6.7 |
| 1970 | 100.0 | 62.8 | 37.2 | 7.7 | 6.3 |
| 1960 | 100.0 | 75.4 | 24.6 | 7.0 | 4.0 |
| 1950 | 100.0 | 76.4 | 23.6 | 5.1 | 3.3 |
| 1940 | 100.0 | 82.2 | 17.8 | 3.8 | 2.2 |

*Source: Bureau of the Census,* Educational Attainment in the United States: March 1996 (Update), *detailed tables for Current Population Reports P20-493, 1997*

# The Oldest Americans Are the Least Educated

**High school and college graduates are much more numerous among 55-to-64-year-olds than among older Americans.**

Men and women aged 55 to 64 are much better educated than their older counterparts. Among men aged 55 to 64, 78 percent are high school graduates. This compares with only 69 percent of men aged 65 to 74 and 59 percent of those aged 75 or older. The proportions among women are almost identical, with 77 percent of women aged 55 to 64 having a high school diploma, versus 69 percent of women aged 65 to 74 and 59 percent of those aged 75 or older.

The gap in the proportions of older Americans with a college diploma is also large. Among men aged 55 to 64, 25 percent are college graduates. This compares with only 16 percent of men aged 75 or older. Among women aged 55 to 64, 16 percent have graduated from college, versus 11 percent of women aged 75 or older.

The proportions of men and women aged 55 to 64 with master's degrees are about double the proportions among their counterparts aged 75 or older. But the share of older Americans with professional or doctoral degrees shows little variation by age.

◆ As well-educated baby boomers begin to dominate the 55-plus population, marketing to older Americans will need to be transformed. Marketing strategies that appealed to the less educated elderly population of the past won't appeal to the sophisticated older population of the future.

# Educational Attainment of Men Aged 55 or Older, 1996

*(number and percent distribution of total men aged 25 or older and men aged 55 or older by educational attainment and age, 1996; numbers in thousands)*

| | | aged 55 or older | | | | |
| | | | | aged 65 or older | | |
| | total | total | 55 to 64 | total | 65 to 74 | 75+ |
|---|---|---|---|---|---|---|
| **Total men, number** | **80,339** | **23,352** | **10,092** | **13,260** | **8,213** | **5,047** |
| Not a high school graduate | 14,534 | 6,851 | 2,260 | 4,591 | 2,525 | 2,066 |
| High school graduate or more | 65,804 | 16,507 | 7,835 | 8,672 | 5,691 | 2,981 |
| High school graduate only | 25,649 | 7,198 | 3,301 | 3,897 | 2,515 | 1,382 |
| Some college, no degree | 13,998 | 3,420 | 1,533 | 1,887 | 1,217 | 670 |
| Associate's degree | 5,303 | 834 | 453 | 381 | 246 | 135 |
| Bachelor's degree or more | 20,854 | 5,055 | 2,548 | 2,507 | 1,714 | 793 |
| Bachelor's degree | 13,219 | 2,845 | 1,415 | 1,430 | 989 | 441 |
| Master's degree | 4,812 | 1,306 | 713 | 593 | 433 | 160 |
| Professional degree | 1,671 | 530 | 215 | 315 | 174 | 141 |
| Doctoral degree | 1,152 | 374 | 205 | 169 | 118 | 51 |
| **Total men, percent** | **100.0%** | **100.0%** | **100.0%** | **100.0%** | **100.0%** | **100.0%** |
| Not a high school graduate | 18.1 | 29.3 | 22.4 | 34.6 | 30.7 | 40.9 |
| High school graduate or more | 81.9 | 70.7 | 77.6 | 65.4 | 69.3 | 59.1 |
| High school graduate only | 31.9 | 30.8 | 32.7 | 29.4 | 30.6 | 27.4 |
| Some college, no degree | 17.4 | 14.6 | 15.2 | 14.2 | 14.8 | 13.3 |
| Associate's degree | 6.6 | 3.6 | 4.5 | 2.9 | 3.0 | 2.7 |
| Bachelor's degree or more | 26.0 | 21.6 | 25.2 | 18.9 | 20.9 | 15.7 |
| Bachelor's degree | 16.5 | 12.2 | 14.0 | 10.8 | 12.0 | 8.7 |
| Master's degree | 6.0 | 5.6 | 7.1 | 4.5 | 5.3 | 3.2 |
| Professional degree | 2.1 | 2.3 | 2.1 | 2.4 | 2.1 | 2.8 |
| Doctoral degree | 1.4 | 1.6 | 2.0 | 1.3 | 1.4 | 1.0 |

*Source: Bureau of the Census,* Educational Attainment in the United States: March 1996 (Update), *detailed tables for Current Population Reports P20-493, 1997*

# Educational Attainment of Women Aged 55 or Older, 1996

*(number and percent distribution of total women aged 25 or older and women aged 55 or older by educational attainment and age, 1996; numbers in thousands)*

| | total | aged 55 or older total | 55 to 64 | aged 65 or older total | 65 to 74 | 75+ |
|---|---|---|---|---|---|---|
| Total women, number | 87,984 | 29,390 | 10,992 | 18,398 | 10,057 | 8,341 |
| Not a high school graduate | 16,190 | 9,030 | 2,494 | 6,536 | 3,079 | 3,457 |
| High school graduate or more | 71,794 | 20,360 | 8,498 | 11,862 | 6,978 | 4,884 |
| High school graduate only | 30,911 | 11,350 | 4,501 | 6,849 | 4,110 | 2,739 |
| Some college, no degree | 15,203 | 4,002 | 1,591 | 2,411 | 1,444 | 967 |
| Associate's degree | 6,868 | 1,385 | 690 | 695 | 419 | 276 |
| Bachelor's degree or more | 18,813 | 3,623 | 1,717 | 1,906 | 1,004 | 902 |
| Bachelor's degree | 13,321 | 2,462 | 1,076 | 1,386 | 710 | 676 |
| Master's degree | 4,288 | 900 | 516 | 384 | 207 | 177 |
| Professional degree | 745 | 138 | 71 | 67 | 42 | 25 |
| Doctoral degree | 459 | 123 | 54 | 69 | 45 | 24 |
| Total women, percent | 100.0% | 100.0% | 100.0% | 100.0% | 100.0% | 100.0% |
| Not a high school graduate | 18.4 | 30.7 | 22.7 | 35.5 | 30.6 | 41.4 |
| High school graduate or more | 81.6 | 69.3 | 77.3 | 64.5 | 69.4 | 58.6 |
| High school graduate only | 35.1 | 38.6 | 40.9 | 37.2 | 40.9 | 32.8 |
| Some college, no degree | 17.3 | 13.6 | 14.5 | 13.1 | 14.4 | 11.6 |
| Associate's degree | 7.8 | 4.7 | 6.3 | 3.8 | 4.2 | 3.3 |
| Bachelor's degree or more | 21.4 | 12.3 | 15.6 | 10.4 | 10.0 | 10.8 |
| Bachelor's degree | 15.1 | 8.4 | 9.8 | 7.5 | 7.1 | 8.1 |
| Master's degree | 4.9 | 3.1 | 4.7 | 2.1 | 2.1 | 2.1 |
| Professional degree | 0.8 | 0.5 | 0.6 | 0.4 | 0.4 | 0.3 |
| Doctoral degree | 0.5 | 0.4 | 0.5 | 0.4 | 0.4 | 0.3 |

*Source: Bureau of the Census,* Educational Attainment in the United States: March 1996 (Update), *detailed tables for Current Population Reports P20-493, 1997*

# Older Whites Are Much Better Educated Than Blacks or Hispanics

## Most black and Hispanic men aged 55 or older do not have a high school diploma.

While 72 percent of white men aged 55 or older are high school graduates, the proportion is much smaller among blacks and Hispanics. Only 50 percent of black men aged 55 or older have a high school diploma. Among Hispanics, the proportion is an even-smaller 37 percent. Similarly, older white women are much better educated than their black or Hispanic counterparts. While 72 percent of white women aged 55 or older are high school graduates, only 51 percent of black and 34 percent of Hispanic women in the age group have a high school diploma.

Among older men, whites are more than twice as likely as blacks or Hispanics to have a college degree. Twenty-two percent of white men aged 55 or older are college graduates versus only 9 percent of black and 10 percent of Hispanic men in the age group. The gap is much smaller between white and black women. Twelve percent of white and 10 percent of black women aged 55 or older are college graduates. Among Hispanic women of the age group, only 4 percent have a college degree.

◆ As the better-educated blacks of the baby-boom generation enter the 55-plus age group, the proportion of blacks with a high school diploma will rise sharply.

◆ Because many younger Hispanics are immigrants with little formal schooling, the educational attainment of the older Hispanic population will not rise much in the future.

# Educational Attainment of Men Aged 55 or Older by Race and Hispanic Origin, 1996

*(number and percent distribution of men aged 55 or older by educational attainment, race, and Hispanic origin, 1996; numbers in thousands)*

|  | white | black | Hispanic |
|---|---|---|---|
| **Men aged 55 or older, number** | **20,867** | **1,834** | **1,296** |
| Not a high school graduate | 5,754 | 926 | 819 |
| High school graduate or more | 15,113 | 908 | 477 |
| High school graduate only | 6,551 | 479 | 224 |
| Some college, no degree | 3,133 | 214 | 95 |
| Associate's degree | 751 | 59 | 28 |
| Bachelor's degree or more | 4,677 | 158 | 132 |
| Bachelor's degree | 2,656 | 70 | 68 |
| Master's degree | 1,194 | 61 | 39 |
| Professional degree | 495 | 8 | 14 |
| Doctoral degree | 332 | 19 | 11 |
| **Men aged 55 or older, percent** | **100.0%** | **100.0%** | **100.0%** |
| Not a high school graduate | 27.6 | 50.5 | 63.2 |
| High school graduate or more | 72.4 | 49.5 | 36.8 |
| High school graduate only | 31.4 | 26.1 | 17.3 |
| Some college, no degree | 15.0 | 11.7 | 7.3 |
| Associate's degree | 3.6 | 3.2 | 2.2 |
| Bachelor's degree or more | 22.4 | 8.6 | 10.2 |
| Bachelor's degree | 12.7 | 3.8 | 5.2 |
| Master's degree | 5.7 | 3.3 | 3.0 |
| Professional degree | 2.4 | 0.4 | 1.1 |
| Doctoral degree | 1.6 | 1.0 | 0.8 |

*Source: Bureau of the Census,* Educational Attainment in the United States: March 1996 (Update), *detailed tables for Current Population Reports P20-493, 1997*

# Educational Attainment of Women Aged 55 or Older by Race and Hispanic Origin, 1996

*(number and percent distribution of women aged 55 or older by educational attainment, race, and Hispanic origin, 1996; numbers in thousands)*

|  | white | black | Hispanic |
|---|---|---|---|
| **Women aged 55 or older, number** | **25,764** | **2,768** | **1,655** |
| Not a high school graduate | 7,317 | 1,365 | 1,088 |
| High school graduate or more | 18,447 | 1,403 | 567 |
| High school graduate only | 10,325 | 780 | 335 |
| Some college, no degree | 3,661 | 265 | 116 |
| Associate's degree | 1,252 | 89 | 47 |
| Bachelor's degree or more | 3,207 | 266 | 66 |
| Bachelor's degree | 2,194 | 163 | 41 |
| Master's degree | 779 | 88 | 19 |
| Professional degree | 120 | 11 | 4 |
| Doctoral degree | 114 | 4 | 2 |
| **Women aged 55 or older, percent** | **100.0%** | **100.0%** | **100.0%** |
| Not a high school graduate | 28.4 | 49.3 | 65.7 |
| High school graduate or more | 71.6 | 50.7 | 34.3 |
| High school graduate only | 40.1 | 28.2 | 20.2 |
| Some college, no degree | 14.2 | 9.6 | 7.0 |
| Associate's degree | 4.9 | 3.2 | 2.8 |
| Bachelor's degree or more | 12.4 | 9.6 | 4.0 |
| Bachelor's degree | 8.5 | 5.9 | 2.5 |
| Master's degree | 3.0 | 3.2 | 1.1 |
| Professional degree | 0.5 | 0.4 | 0.2 |
| Doctoral degree | 0.4 | 0.1 | 0.1 |

*Source: Bureau of the Census,* Educational Attainment in the United States: March 1996 (Update), *detailed tables for Current Population Reports P20-493, 1997*

# 3

# Health

◆ The proportion of people who rate their health as poor peaks at just 12 percent among people aged 65 or older.

◆ Over half of people aged 71 or older would give up their favorite foods to eat healthy foods, compared with only 39 percent of all adults.

◆ Older Americans are much less likely to smoke cigarettes today than they were several decades ago.

◆ Fewer than 1 percent of people aged 65 or older are without health insurance, versus 13 percent of those aged 55 to 64 and 15 percent of all Americans.

◆ People aged 45 or older account for only 20 percent of those suffering from colds, flu, or other acute conditions.

◆ People aged 45 or older account for 83 percent of those suffering from arthritis or high blood pressure.

◆ Only 38 percent of people aged 65 or older are limited by chronic illnesses and just 11 percent are unable to carry out their major activity due to a chronic condition.

◆ The number of older Americans using home health care services is nearly equal to the number in nursing homes.

◆ Eighty-four percent of all deaths in the U.S. occur among people aged 55 or older, with over half occurring among those aged 75 or older.

# Most Older Americans Feel Good

**A majority of older Americans rate their health as excellent or good.**

The proportion of Americans who rate their health as excellent declines with age, from 48 percent of people aged 18 to 24 to 22 percent of people aged 55 or older. The proportion of people who rate their health as good stands at 51 percent among people aged 55 to 64 and at 37 percent among those aged 65 or older. Combining the two categories, a 59 percent majority of people aged 65 or older rate their health as good or excellent. Among those aged 55 to 64, the combination amounts to a substantial 73 percent.

Poor health is more common among older than younger Americans, but even in old age only a small minority are ailing. The proportion of people who rate their health as poor peaks at just 12 percent among people aged 65 or older.

◆ The health of older Americans has been improving as better-educated and more-affluent generations enter the 55-plus age group. As boomers age, the health of older Americans should continue to improve because boomers get more excercise, eat a more nutritious diet, and are less likely to smoke than older Americans did at their age.

# Self-Assessed Health Status, 1994

**"Would you say your own health, in general, is excellent, good, fair, or poor?"**

*(percent responding by age, 1994)*

|  | excellent | good | fair | poor |
|---|---|---|---|---|
| **Total** | **31%** | **47%** | **17%** | **5%** |
| Aged 18 to 24 | 48 | 40 | 11 | 1 |
| Aged 25 to 34 | 37 | 51 | 11 | 1 |
| Aged 35 to 44 | 31 | 50 | 18 | 2 |
| Aged 45 to 54 | 32 | 47 | 16 | 5 |
| Aged 55 to 64 | 22 | 51 | 18 | 9 |
| Aged 65 or older | 22 | 37 | 28 | 12 |

*Note: Percents may not add to 100 because no answer is not included.*
*Source: 1994 General Social Survey, National Opinion Research Center, University of Chicago*

# Older Americans Are Biggest Fitness Fanatics

## Those most likely to exercise frequently are Americans aged 55 or older.

While children and young adults are most likely to be involved in sports, older Americans are most likely to participate in fitness activities. Twenty-eight percent of Americans aged 55 or older frequently participate in fitness activities, a higher share than in any other age group.

People aged 35 to 44 are least likely, among adults, to take part in fitness activities on a regular basis. Most are too busy juggling jobs and family to bother with staying fit. But the percentage of people taking part in regular workouts rises sharply in the 45-to-54 age group, when childrearing responsibilities ease.

◆ As the enormous baby-boom generation enters the 45-plus age groups, the number of older participants in a variety of sport and fitness activities will surge.

## Workouts Increase with Age

*(percent of people frequently participating in fitness activities, by age, 1995)*

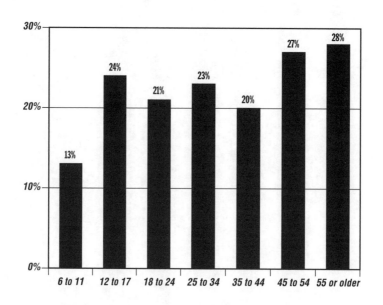

# Sports and Fitness Participation, 1995

*(percent of people frequently participating in sports and fitness activities combined, and percent participating frequently in fitness activities, by age, 1995)*

|  | *sports and fitness* | *fitness only* |
|---|---|---|
| Aged 6 to 11 | 48.1% | 12.8% |
| Aged 12 to 17 | 62.5 | 24.2 |
| Aged 18 to 24 | 38.5 | 21.4 |
| Aged 25 to 34 | 35.9 | 23.0 |
| Aged 35 to 44 | 29.0 | 20.4 |
| Aged 45 to 54 | 35.4 | 26.7 |
| Aged 55 or older | 32.3 | 28.2 |

*Note: Frequent participation in sports activities ranges from 15 to 100 days/year depending on the activity, while frequent participation in fitness activities is 100 or more days/year.*
*Source: Fitness Products Council, North Palm Beach, Florida, 1996*

# The Healthiest Eaters Are Older Americans

**People aged 50 or older are most likely to watch their diets.**

Older Americans are more likely than younger ones to practice healthy eating—probably because they are under doctor's orders to do so. While 79 percent of all Americans say they eat healthy foods, the figure ranges from 83 percent among people aged 50 to 64 to over 90 percent of those aged 71 or older. Older Americans are also more likely than the average person to select foods for healthful reasons, to maintain a low-fat diet, and to maintain a "healthy heart" diet.

When chronic conditions become a factor in people's food choices, they are more likely to forgo their favorite foods in order to eat healthier. People aged 71 or older are much more likely than the average person to avoid favorite foods in order to eat a healthier diet—39 percent of all adults do so versus 52 percent of people aged 71-plus. Older Americans are also more likely than the average person to give up convenience and taste for health benefits.

◆ The rising health consciousness of older Americans is one factor behind their improved physical well-being.

◆ As the population ages, healthy foods are likely to become even more important to food shoppers—particularly as more is discovered about the link between diet and long-term health.

# Healthy Eating Habits, 1996

*(percent of total persons and persons aged 50 or older who always or usually follow selected practices when buying food, by age, 1996)*

| | total | 50 to 64 | 65 to 70 | 71 or older |
|---|---|---|---|---|
| Eat healthy foods | 79% | 83% | 86% | 91% |
| Select foods for healthful reasons | 76 | 78 | 83 | 87 |
| Read labels on food packages | 66 | 68 | 67 | 68 |
| Choose breakfast cereals that are low in fat | 59 | 63 | 62 | 73 |
| Choose low-fat versions of dairy foods | 53 | 59 | 62 | 68 |
| Maintain a "healthy heart" diet | 51 | 57 | 65 | 75 |
| Maintain a low-fat diet | 50 | 53 | 55 | 69 |
| Choose whole grain products over those made with white flour | 49 | 50 | 53 | 60 |
| Take vitamin/mineral supplements at least twice/week | 49 | 49 | 52 | 52 |
| Balance healthy foods with less healthy foods I enjoy more | 43 | 41 | 42 | 41 |
| Avoid some favorite foods in order to eat healthier | 39 | 41 | 43 | 52 |
| Try new foods products | 34 | 31 | 33 | 23 |
| Take vitamin/mineral supplements for certain needs at least twice a week | 32 | 36 | 33 | 38 |
| Give up convenience for health benefits | 28 | 31 | 37 | 43 |
| Maintain a low-calorie diet | 26 | 29 | 31 | 45 |
| Avoid foods that contain red meat | 22 | 20 | 22 | 23 |
| Give up good taste for health benefits | 15 | 17 | 21 | 29 |
| Choose breakfast cereals that are organic | 12 | 11 | 14 | 20 |
| Choose foods that do not contain dairy products | 9 | 10 | 19 | 14 |
| Maintain a vegetarian diet | 9 | 11 | 11 | 11 |

Source: *1996 Healthfocus Trend Report*, HealthFocus, Des Moines, Iowa

# Smoking and Drinking Are Less Common among Older Americans

**People aged 65 or older are less likely to drink or smoke than the average American.**

While 69 percent of Amerians aged 18 or older drink alcoholic beverages at least occasionally, the proportion is slightly lower among people aged 50 to 69 and sharply lower among those aged 70 or older. Over half the people in the 70-plus age group do not drink alcohol at all. In part, this is because alcohol consumption declines with age. It is also because the generations most opposed to alcohol consumption are now in the 70-plus age groups.

Older Americans are much less likely to smoke cigarettes today than they were several decades ago. In 1965, over half the men aged 45 to 64 were smokers. This proportion had fallen to 28 percent by 1994. Among men aged 65 or older, the proportion who smoke fell from 29 to 13 percent during those years. Women aged 45 to 64 are also less likely to smoke than they once were, with the figure falling from 32 to 23 percent. But women aged 65 or older are slightly more likely to smoke because older nonsmokers have been replaced in the age group by women more inclined to smoke.

◆ The decline in cigarette smoking among older Americans has greatly contributed to their improved physical well-being.

◆ Alcohol consumption among people aged 70 or older is likely to rise with the aging of generations more tolerant of drinking.

# Alcohol Consumption by Age, 1994

"Do you ever have occasion to use any alcoholic beverages such as liquor, wine, or beer, or are you a total abstainer?"

*(percent of persons aged 18 or older who currently drink alcohol or abstain, by age, 1994)*

|  | currently use | abstain |
|---|---|---|
| **Total** | **69.1%** | **30.9%** |
| Aged 18 to 29 | 80.6 | 19.4 |
| Aged 30 to 39 | 79.6 | 20.4 |
| Aged 40 to 49 | 67.4 | 35.6 |
| Aged 50 to 59 | 63.5 | 36.5 |
| Aged 60 to 69 | 67.3 | 32.7 |
| Aged 70 to 79 | 43.1 | 56.9 |
| Aged 80 or more | 40.0 | 60.0 |

*Source: 1994 General Social Survey, National Opinion Research Center, University of Chicago*

# Cigarette Smoking by Sex and Age, 1965 and 1994

*(percent of persons aged 18 or older who currently smoke cigarettes by sex and age, 1965 and 1994; percentage point change, 1965-94)*

|  | 1994 | 1965 | percentage point change, 1965-1994 |
|---|---|---|---|
| **Total** | **25.5%** | **42.4%** | **-16.9** |
| **Total men** | **28.2** | **51.9** | **-23.7** |
| Aged 18 to 24 | 29.8 | 54.1 | -24.3 |
| Aged 25 to 34 | 31.4 | 60.7 | -29.3 |
| Aged 35 to 44 | 33.2 | 58.2 | -25.0 |
| Aged 45 to 64 | 28.3 | 51.9 | -23.6 |
| Aged 65 or older | 13.2 | 28.5 | -15.3 |
| **Total women** | **23.1** | **33.9** | **-10.8** |
| Aged 18 to 24 | 25.2 | 38.1 | -12.9 |
| Aged 25 to 34 | 28.8 | 43.7 | -14.9 |
| Aged 35 to 44 | 26.8 | 43.7 | -16.9 |
| Aged 45 to 64 | 22.8 | 32.0 | -9.2 |
| Aged 65 or older | 11.1 | 9.6 | 1.5 |

*Source: National Center for Health Statistics,* Health United States 1996-97 and Injury Chartbook, *1997; calculations by New Strategist*

# People Aged 45 to 64 Had Lots of Children

## The parents of baby boomers had three to four children, on average.

Family size in the United States had been declining for decades until post-World War II young adults married and started having children. Family size rose in the 1950s and 1960s, resulting in the baby-boom generation.

Fifty-one percent of women aged 45 to 64 have had at least three children, according to a 1992 survey. This is greater than the 45 percent of women aged 65 or older who have that many children. Forty-seven percent of men in both age groups have fathered at least three children.

Not only have people aged 45 to 64 had more children than those younger or older, they are also less likely to be childless than those in any other age group. While only 11 percent of women aged 45 to 64 are childless, 16 percent of women aged 65 or older are. Among men aged 45 to 64, 13 percent are childless.

◆ Because today's older Americans had so many children, they are likely to be well cared for in old age since families provide the bulk of care to the frail elderly. The situation will be very different for boomers in old age—many of whom have only one child or no children at all.

### Many Women Aged 45 to 64 Had Three or More Children

*(percent distribution of women aged 45 or older by number of children ever born, 1992)*

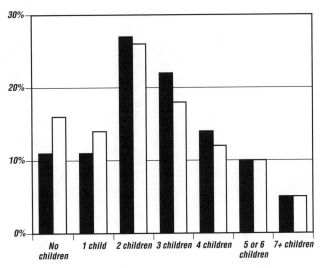

45 to 64
65 or older

# Number of Children Ever Born, 1992

*(percent distribution of total persons aged 18 or older and of persons aged 45 or older by number of children ever born, by sex, 1992)*

| | women | | | men | | |
|---|---|---|---|---|---|---|
| | *total* | *45 to 64* | *65 or older* | *total* | *45 to 64* | *65 or older* |
| **Total** | **100.0%** | **100.0%** | **100.0%** | **100.0%** | **100.0%** | **100.0%** |
| No children | 26.0 | 10.8 | 15.5 | 33.8 | 12.6 | 14.1 |
| One child | 16.3 | 10.9 | 14.3 | 14.9 | 11.1 | 12.5 |
| Two children | 26.5 | 27.4 | 25.5 | 24.1 | 29.3 | 26.7 |
| Three children | 15.5 | 22.2 | 17.5 | 14.0 | 22.7 | 18.8 |
| Four children | 8.2 | 13.9 | 12.4 | 6.9 | 11.9 | 13.0 |
| Five or six children | 5.3 | 10.3 | 9.7 | 4.6 | 9.5 | 9.6 |
| Seven or more children | 2.3 | 4.6 | 5.1 | 1.7 | 2.9 | 5.1 |

*Source: Bureau of the Census,* Fertility of American Men, *Amara Bachu, Population Division Working Paper Series No. 14, 1996*

# Virtually All Americans Aged 65 or Older Have Health Insurance

## But a substantial proportion of those aged 55 to 64 do not.

Overall, 15 percent of Americans do not have health insurance. But among people aged 65 or older, fewer than 1 percent are without insurance coverage. Ninety-six percent of the elderly are covered by Medicare.

A much-larger 13 percent of people aged 55 to 64 do not have health insurance coverage—12 percent of men and 15 percent of women. While men aged 55 to 64 are more likely to have health insurance than the average male, women in that age group are less likely to be covered than the average female. Among the 55-to-64-year-olds who have health insurance, most are covered through their own or their spouse's job.

◆ The years between 55 and 64 are a vulnerable time for many people. They are reaching the age when chronic conditions can become a problem, but millions lack health insurance.

## Health Insurance Coverage by Sex, 1995

*(number and percent distribution of total persons and persons aged 55 or older by source of health insurance coverage and sex, 1995; numbers in thousands)*

| | total persons | covered by private or government health insurance | | | | | | | not covered |
|---|---|---|---|---|---|---|---|---|---|
| | | total | private health insurance | | government health insurance | | | | |
| | | | total | group health | total | Medicaid | Medicare | military | |
| **Total persons** | **264,314** | **223,733** | **185,881** | **161,453** | **69,776** | **31,877** | **34,655** | **9,375** | **40,582** |
| 55 to 64 | 21,084 | 18,270 | 16,124 | 14,098 | 3,790 | 1,415 | 1,660 | 1,231 | 2,814 |
| 65 or older | 31,658 | 31,358 | 21,754 | 11,137 | 30,597 | 2,820 | 30,521 | 1,152 | 300 |
| **Total men** | **129,143** | **107,496** | **91,275** | **80,744** | **30,666** | **13,425** | **14,888** | **5,038** | **21,647** |
| 55 to 64 | 10,092 | 8,873 | 7,947 | 7,144 | 1,772 | 533 | 828 | 629 | 1,219 |
| 65 or older | 13,260 | 13,156 | 9,544 | 5,511 | 12,721 | 898 | 12,676 | 756 | 104 |
| **Total women** | **135,171** | **116,237** | **94,606** | **80,709** | **39,110** | **18,452** | **19,769** | **4,338** | **18,934** |
| 55 to 64 | 10,992 | 9,397 | 8,177 | 6,954 | 2,018 | 882 | 832 | 602 | 1,595 |
| 65 or older | 18,398 | 18,202 | 12,211 | 5,626 | 17,876 | 1,922 | 17,846 | 396 | 196 |
| **Total persons** | **100.0%** | **84.6%** | **70.3%** | **61.1%** | **26.4%** | **12.1%** | **13.1%** | **3.5%** | **15.4%** |
| 55 to 64 | 100.0 | 86.7 | 76.5 | 66.9 | 18.0 | 6.7 | 7.9 | 5.8 | 13.3 |
| 65 or older | 100.0 | 99.1 | 68.7 | 35.2 | 96.6 | 8.9 | 96.4 | 3.6 | 0.9 |
| **Total men** | **100.0** | **83.2** | **70.7** | **62.5** | **23.7** | **10.4** | **11.5** | **3.9** | **16.8** |
| 55 to 64 | 100.0 | 87.9 | 78.7 | 70.8 | 17.6 | 5.3 | 8.2 | 6.2 | 12.1 |
| 65 or older | 100.0 | 99.2 | 72.0 | 41.6 | 95.9 | 6.8 | 95.6 | 5.7 | 0.8 |
| **Total women** | **100.0** | **86.0** | **70.0** | **59.7** | **28.9** | **13.7** | **14.6** | **3.2** | **14.0** |
| 55 to 64 | 100.0 | 85.5 | 74.4 | 63.3 | 18.4 | 8.0 | 7.6 | 5.5 | 14.5 |
| **65 or older** | **100.0** | **98.9** | **66.4** | **30.6** | **97.2** | **10.4** | **97.0** | **2.2** | **1.1** |

*Note: Numbers will not add to total because some people are covered by more than one type of insurance.*
*Source: Bureau of the Census, unpublished tables from the 1996 Current Population Survey*

# Acute Conditions Less Likely in Old Age

## Older Americans account for a tiny share of people suffering from acute health conditions such as colds and flu.

People aged 45 or older accounted for only 20 percent of all acute conditions suffered by Americans in 1994, according to the National Center for Health Statistics. Among the 66 million people suffering from colds severe enough to send them to a doctor or keep them in bed for at least half a day, only 12 million occurred among people aged 45 or older (18 percent). Similarly, of the 90 million flu sufferers who sought medical attention or stayed in bed, only 19 million were older Americans (or 21 percent).

Some acute conditions are common among older Americans, however. People aged 45 or older account for fully 48 percent of acute musculoskeletal conditions, 40 percent of acute eye conditions, 35 percent of acute urinary conditions, and 31 percent of pneumonia and skin conditions.

◆ Older Americans are less likely to experience acute conditions in part because they have developed immunities through years of exposure to many viruses.

# Acute Health Conditions, 1994

*(total number of acute conditions, number and rate per 100 people aged 45 or older, and share of total acute conditions accounted for by age group, 1994; numbers in thousands)*

| | total | aged 45 to 64 | | | aged 65 or older | | |
|---|---|---|---|---|---|---|---|
| | | total | rate | share of total | total | rate | share of total |
| **Total acute conditions** | **445,169** | **56,898** | **112.9** | **12.8**% | **34,100** | **109.9** | **7.7**% |
| **Infective/parasitic diseases** | **54,201** | **3,873** | **7.7** | **7.1** | **1,605** | **5.2** | **3.0** |
| Common childhood diseases | 3,798 | - | - | - | - | - | - |
| Intestinal virus | 11,902 | 951 | 1.9 | 8.0 | 182 | 0.6 | 1.5 |
| Viral infections | 17,257 | 1,562 | 3.1 | 9.1 | 779 | 2.5 | 4.5 |
| Other | 21,244 | 1,360 | 2.7 | 6.4 | 644 | 2.1 | 3.0 |
| **Respiratory conditions** | **208,930** | **27,937** | **55.4** | **13.4** | **13,530** | **43.6** | **6.5** |
| Common cold | 65,968 | 8,372 | 16.6 | 12.7 | 3,822 | 12.3 | 5.8 |
| Other acute upper respiratory infections | 30,866 | 3,351 | 6.6 | 10.9 | 1,476 | 4.8 | 4.8 |
| Influenza | 90,447 | 13,058 | 25.9 | 14.4 | 5,688 | 18.3 | 6.3 |
| Acute bronchitis | 12,149 | 2,101 | 4.2 | 17.3 | 1,137 | 3.7 | 9.4 |
| Pneumonia | 4,220 | 450 | 0.9 | 10.7 | 867 | 2.8 | 20.5 |
| Other respiratory conditions | 5,280 | 605 | 1.2 | 11.5 | 540 | 1.7 | 10.2 |
| **Digestive system conditions** | **15,863** | **2,084** | **4.1** | **13.1** | **1,729** | **5.6** | **10.9** |
| Dental conditions | 2,891 | 437 | 0.9 | 15.1 | 174 | 0.6 | 6.0 |
| Indigestion, nausea, and vomiting | 8,323 | 687 | 1.4 | 8.3 | 565 | 1.8 | 6.8 |
| Other digestive conditions | 4,649 | 961 | 1.9 | 20.7 | 990 | 3.2 | 21.3 |
| **Injuries** | **61,887** | **8,659** | **17.2** | **14.0** | **6,086** | **19.6** | **9.8** |
| Fractures and dislocations | 7,893 | 1,218 | 2.4 | 15.4 | 1,054 | 3.4 | 13.4 |
| Sprains and strains | 14,195 | 2,198 | 4.4 | 15.5 | 1,037 | 3.3 | 7.3 |
| Open wounds and lacerations | 10,874 | 1,105 | 2.2 | 10.2 | 440 | 1.4 | 4.0 |
| Contusions and superficial injuries | 12,117 | 1,796 | 3.6 | 14.8 | 1,856 | 6.0 | 15.3 |
| Other current injuries | 16,807 | 2,341 | 4.6 | 13.9 | 1,700 | 5.5 | 10.1 |
| **Selected other acute conditions** | **71,337** | **8,703** | **17.3** | **12.2** | **5,862** | **18.9** | **8.2** |
| Eye conditions | 3,160 | 316 | 0.6 | 10.0 | 931 | 3.0 | 29.5 |
| Acute ear infections | 24,123 | 1,132 | 2.2 | 4.7 | 447 | 1.4 | 1.9 |
| Other ear conditions | 3,781 | 421 | 0.8 | 11.1 | 434 | 1.4 | 11.5 |
| Acute urinary conditions | 8,140 | 1,406 | 2.8 | 17.3 | 1,425 | 4.6 | 17.5 |
| Disorders of menstruation | 1,146 | 45 | 0.1 | 3.9 | - | - | - |
| Other disorders of female genital tract | 2,652 | 419 | 0.8 | 15.8 | 54 | 0.2 | 2.0 |
| Delivery/other conditions of pregnancy | 3,707 | - | - | - | - | - | - |
| Skin conditions | 6,165 | 1,186 | 2.4 | 19.2 | 728 | 2.3 | 11.8 |
| Acute musculoskeletal conditions | 9,078 | 2,827 | 5.6 | 31.1 | 1,549 | 5.0 | 17.1 |

*(continued)*

*(continued from previous page)*

| | total | aged 45 to 64 | | | aged 65 or older | | |
|---|---|---|---|---|---|---|---|
| | | total | rate | share of total | total | rate | share of total |
| Headache, excluding migraine | 3,975 | 738 | 1.5 | 18.6% | 128 | 0.4 | 3.2% |
| Fever, unspecified | 5,410 | 214 | 0.4 | 4.0 | 166 | 0.5 | 3.1 |
| **All other acute conditions** | **32,952** | **5,642** | **11.2** | **17.1** | **5,289** | **17.0** | **16.1** |

*Note: The acute conditions shown here are those causing people to restrict their activity for at least half a day, or causing people to contact a physician about the illness or injury. (-) means not applicable or sample is too small to make a reliable estimate.*
*Source: National Center for Health Statistics, Current Estimates from the National Health Interview Survey, 1994, Series 10, No. 193, 1995; calculations by New Strategist*

# Chronic Conditions Emerge in Middle Age

**People aged 45 to 64 are much more likely than younger adults to suffer from chronic conditions.**

Although the incidence of acute conditions diminishes as people enter the 45-plus age groups, chronic illnesses begin to emerge. For most chronic conditions, people aged 45 or older account for the majority of sufferers. Some of the exceptions are acne, migraine, asthma, and hay fever.

The most prevalent chonic condition among 45-to-64-year-olds is arthritis (experienced by 24 percent), followed by high blood pressure (22 percent). The most common conditions among those aged 65 or older are arthritis (50 percent), high blood pressure (36 percent), heart disease (33 percent), and hearing impairments (29 percent). People aged 65 or older account for 80 percent of all Americans with cataracts, 73 percent of all those with hardening of the arteries, and 70 percent of all those with emphysema.

◆ As the large baby-boom generation ages into its 50s and 60s, expect to see an enormous increase in the number of people with arthritis, high blood pressure, heart disease, and hearing problems.

# Chronic Health Conditions, 1994

*(total number of persons with chronic condition, number and percent with condition among people aged 45 or older, and share of total chronic conditions accounted for by age group, 1994; numbers in thousands)*

| | total | aged 45 to 64 | | | aged 65 or older | | |
|---|---|---|---|---|---|---|---|
| | | total | rate | share of total | total | rate | share of total |
| **Selected skin and musculoskeletal conditions** | | | | | | | |
| Arthritis | 33,446 | 12,045 | 23.9 | 36.0% | 15,558 | 50.2 | 46.5% |
| Gout | 2,485 | 963 | 1.9 | 38.8 | 1,148 | 3.7 | 46.2 |
| Intervertebral disc disorders | 5,994 | 2,558 | 5.1 | 42.7 | 984 | 3.2 | 16.4 |
| Bone spur or tendinitis | 2,717 | 1,207 | 2.4 | 44.4 | 545 | 1.8 | 20.1 |
| Disorders of bone or cartilage | 1,520 | 430 | 0.9 | 28.3 | 574 | 1.9 | 37.8 |
| Trouble with bunions | 3,296 | 1,078 | 2.1 | 32.7 | 1,109 | 3.6 | 33.6 |
| Bursitis | 5,279 | 2,119 | 4.2 | 40.1 | 1,412 | 4.6 | 26.7 |
| Sebaceous skin cyst | 1,239 | 238 | 0.5 | 19.2 | 255 | 0.8 | 20.6 |
| Trouble with acne | 5,250 | 251 | 0.5 | 4.8 | 84 | 0.3 | 1.6 |
| Psoriasis | 2,571 | 859 | 1.7 | 33.4 | 450 | 1.5 | 17.5 |
| Dermatitis | 9,192 | 1,693 | 3.4 | 18.4 | 1,001 | 3.2 | 10.9 |
| Trouble with dry (itching) skin | 6,166 | 1,660 | 3.3 | 26.9 | 1,156 | 3.7 | 18.7 |
| Trouble with ingrown nails | 5,987 | 1,556 | 3.1 | 26.0 | 1,544 | 5.0 | 25.8 |
| Trouble with corns and calluses | 4,356 | 1,462 | 2.9 | 33.6 | 1,191 | 3.8 | 27.3 |
| **Impairments** | | | | | | | |
| Visual impairment | 8,601 | 2,273 | 4.5 | 26.4 | 2,551 | 8.2 | 29.7 |
| Color blindness | 3,183 | 1,009 | 2.0 | 31.7 | 511 | 1.7 | 16.1 |
| Cataracts | 6,473 | 872 | 1.7 | 13.5 | 5,158 | 16.6 | 79.7 |
| Glaucoma | 2,603 | 593 | 1.2 | 22.8 | 1,673 | 5.4 | 64.3 |
| Hearing impairment | 22,400 | 6,952 | 13.8 | 31.0 | 8,886 | 28.6 | 39.7 |
| Tinnitus | 7,033 | 2,334 | 4.6 | 33.2 | 2,794 | 9.0 | 39.7 |
| Speech impairment | 3,179 | 451 | 0.9 | 14.2 | 278 | 0.9 | 8.7 |
| Absence of extremities | 1,404 | 392 | 0.8 | 27.9 | 553 | 1.8 | 39.4 |
| Paralysis of extremities | 1,416 | 457 | 0.9 | 32.3 | 466 | 1.5 | 32.9 |
| Deformity or orthopedic impairment | 31,068 | 8,570 | 17.0 | 27.6 | 5,138 | 16.6 | 16.5 |
| **Selected digestive conditions** | | | | | | | |
| Ulcer | 4,447 | 1,272 | 2.5 | 28.6 | 979 | 3.2 | 14.7 |
| Hernia of abdominal cavity | 4,778 | 1,574 | 3.1 | 32.9 | 1,997 | 6.4 | 24.2 |
| Gastritis or duodenitis | 3,410 | 888 | 1.8 | 26.0 | 879 | 2.8 | 14.9 |
| Frequent indigestion | 6,957 | 2,060 | 4.1 | 29.6 | 1,385 | 4.5 | 11.2 |
| Enteritis or colitis | 2,014 | 659 | 1.3 | 32.7 | 432 | 1.4 | 11.3 |
| Spastic colon | 2,063 | 633 | 1.3 | 30.7 | 494 | 1.6 | 14.0 |
| Diverticula of intestines | 2,150 | 882 | 1.8 | 41.0 | 1,020 | 3.3 | 26.7 |
| Frequent constipation | 4,040 | 619 | 1.2 | 15.3 | 1,695 | 5.5 | 14.7 |

*(continued)*

*(continued from previous page)*

| | total | aged 45 to 64 | | | aged 65 or older | | |
|---|---|---|---|---|---|---|---|
| | | total | rate | share of total | total | rate | share of total |
| **Selected conditions of the genitourinary, nervous, endocrine, metabolic, or blood systems** | | | | | | | |
| Goiter or other disorders of the thyroid | 4,509 | 1,506 | 3.0 | 33.4% | 1,491 | 4.8 | 33.1% |
| Diabetes | 7,766 | 3,182 | 6.3 | 41.0 | 3,141 | 10.1 | 40.4 |
| Anemias | 4,664 | 889 | 1.8 | 19.1 | 633 | 2.0 | 13.6 |
| Epilepsy | 1,396 | 236 | 0.5 | 16.9 | 177 | 0.6 | 12.7 |
| Migraine | 11,256 | 2,647 | 5.3 | 23.5 | 675 | 2.2 | 6.0 |
| Neuralgia or neuritis | 566 | 189 | 0.4 | 33.4 | 215 | 0.7 | 38.0 |
| Kidney trouble | 3,512 | 867 | 1.7 | 24.7 | 696 | 2.2 | 19.8 |
| Bladder disorders | 3,747 | 852 | 1.7 | 22.7 | 1,231 | 4.0 | 32.9 |
| Diseases of prostate | 2,641 | 689 | 1.4 | 26.1 | 1,636 | 5.3 | 61.9 |
| Diseases of female genital organs | 5,052 | 1,332 | 2.6 | 26.4 | 240 | 0.8 | 4.8 |
| **Selected circulatory conditions** | | | | | | | |
| Rheumatic fever | 2,006 | 623 | 1.2 | 31.1 | 499 | 1.6 | 24.9 |
| Heart disease | 22,279 | 6,838 | 12.6 | 30.7 | 10,080 | 32.5 | 45.2 |
| Ischemic heart disease | 8,004 | 2,842 | 5.6 | 35.5 | 4,711 | 15.2 | 58.9 |
| Heart rhythm disorders | 8,934 | 2,401 | 4.8 | 26.9 | 2,759 | 8.9 | 30.9 |
| Other selected diseases of the heart, excl. hypertension | 5,342 | 1,595 | 3.2 | 29.9 | 2,610 | 8.4 | 48.9 |
| High blood pressure (hypertension) | 28,236 | 11,206 | 22.2 | 39.7 | 11,293 | 36.4 | 40.0 |
| Cerebrovascular disease | 2,978 | 919 | 1.8 | 30.9 | 1,780 | 5.7 | 59.8 |
| Hardening of the arteries | 2,239 | 559 | 1.1 | 25.0 | 1,641 | 5.3 | 73.3 |
| Varicose veins of lower extremities | 7,260 | 2,545 | 5.1 | 35.1 | 2,317 | 7.5 | 31.9 |
| Hemorrhoids | 9,321 | 3,128 | 6.2 | 33.6 | 1,914 | 6.2 | 20.5 |
| **Selected respiratory conditions** | | | | | | | |
| Chronic bronchitis | 14,021 | 3,223 | 6.4 | 23.0 | 1,878 | 6.1 | 13.4 |
| Asthma | 14,562 | 2,561 | 5.1 | 17.6 | 1,566 | 5.1 | 10.8 |
| Hay fever | 26,146 | 6,089 | 12.1 | 23.3 | 2,481 | 8.0 | 9.5 |
| Chronic sinusitis | 34,902 | 9,067 | 18.0 | 26.0 | 4,687 | 15.1 | 13.4 |
| Deviated nasal septum | 2,028 | 674 | 1.3 | 33.2 | 360 | 1.2 | 17.8 |
| Chronic disease of tonsils or adenoids | 2,925 | 150 | 0.3 | 5.1 | 12 | 0.0 | 0.4 |
| Emphysema | 2,028 | 497 | 1.0 | 24.5 | 1,413 | 4.6 | 69.7 |

*Note: Chronic conditions are those that last at least three months or belong to a group of conditions that are considered to be chronic regardless of when they began.*
*Source: National Center for Health Statistics,* Current Estimates from the National Health Interview Survey, 1994, *Series 10, No. 193, 1995; calculations by New Strategist*

# Few Older People Are Limited by Illness

**A tiny minority are unable to carry on their major activity due to a chronic condition.**

Chronic conditions affect the elderly far less than the stereotypes suggest. Although people aged 65 or older are more likely than younger people to have chronic illnesses, only 38 percent are limited by those conditions. Just 11 percent are unable to carry on their major activity due to a chronic condition. Among all Americans, 15 percent are limited in their activities because of a chronic condition, with 5 percent unable to carry on their major activity.

The percentage of older Americans with functional limitations does not become substantial until the 85-plus age group. According to a 1991 study, 35 percent of people aged 85 or older have difficulty walking, 45 percent have trouble getting outside, 31 percent have trouble bathing or showering, and 28 percent have difficulty preparing meals. Among those with difficulties, at least one in four people aged 85 or older receives help getting outside, preparing meals, managing money, or doing light housework.

◆ Most people associate age with disability, but this stereotype should be abandoned. Even among the oldest old—aged 85 or older—a minority of people have difficulty taking care of themselves.

# Limitations Caused by Chronic Conditions by Sex and Age, 1994

*(percent of persons with activity limitations caused by chronic conditions by sex, age, and type of limitation, 1994)*

| | total persons | with no activity limitation | total with activity limitation | limited in major activity | unable to carry on major activity | limited, but not in major activity |
|---|---|---|---|---|---|---|
| **Total persons** | **100.0%** | **85.0%** | **15.0%** | **10.3%** | **4.6%** | **4.7%** |
| Under age 18 | 100.0 | 93.3 | 6.7 | 4.9 | 0.7 | 1.8 |
| Aged 18 to 44 | 100.0 | 89.7 | 10.3 | 7.1 | 3.2 | 3.1 |
| Aged 45 to 64 | 100.0 | 77.4 | 22.6 | 17.1 | 9.2 | 5.5 |
| Aged 65 or older | 100.0 | 61.8 | 38.2 | 22.6 | 10.7 | 15.6 |
| Aged 65 to 69 | 100.0 | 63.3 | 36.7 | 29.3 | 16.7 | 7.3 |
| Aged 70 or older | 100.0 | 61.1 | 38.9 | 19.5 | 8.1 | 19.3 |
| **Total males** | **100.0** | **85.6** | **14.4** | **10.1** | **4.8** | **4.3** |
| Under age 18 | 100.0 | 92.1 | 7.9 | 6.0 | 0.8 | 1.9 |
| Aged 18 to 44 | 100.0 | 89.8 | 10.2 | 7.4 | 3.7 | 2.8 |
| Aged 45 to 64 | 100.0 | 78.7 | 21.3 | 16.8 | 9.9 | 4.6 |
| Aged 65 to 69 | 100.0 | 62.3 | 37.7 | 32.4 | 20.9 | 5.3 |
| Aged 70 or older | 100.0 | 63.5 | 36.5 | 14.5 | 6.5 | 22.0 |
| **Total females** | **100.0** | **84.3** | **15.7** | **10.5** | **4.4** | **5.2** |
| Under age 18 | 100.0 | 94.4 | 5.6 | 3.8 | 0.7 | 1.7 |
| Aged 18 to 44 | 100.0 | 89.7 | 10.3 | 6.9 | 2.8 | 3.5 |
| Aged 45 to 64 | 100.0 | 76.1 | 23.9 | 17.4 | 8.6 | 6.4 |
| Aged 65 to 69 | 100.0 | 64.2 | 35.8 | 26.8 | 13.3 | 9.0 |
| Aged 70 or older | 100.0 | 59.5 | 40.5 | 22.9 | 9.1 | 17.5 |

*Source: National Center for Health Statistics,* Current Estimates from the National Health Interview Survey, 1994, *Vital and Health Statistics, Series 10, No. 193, 1995*

# Functional Limitations of Persons Aged 65 or Older, 1991

*(total number of persons aged 65 or older, percent with difficulty performing selected functions, and percent receiving help performing function, by age and sex, 1991; numbers in thousands)*

| | total persons aged 65 or older | aged 65 to 74 | | | aged 75 to 84 | | | aged 85 or older |
|---|---|---|---|---|---|---|---|---|
| | | total | men | women | total | men | women | |
| **Total number** | **30,748** | **18,397** | **8,264** | **10,133** | **9,920** | **3,906** | **6,014** | **2,430** |
| **Percent with difficulty** | | | | | | | | |
| Walking | 14.3% | 9.2% | 7.4% | 10.5% | 18.8% | 16.2% | 20.4% | 34.9% |
| Getting outside | 15.9 | 8.7 | 5.9 | 10.9 | 22.3 | 15.9 | 26.4 | 44.8 |
| Bathing or showering | 9.4 | 5.6 | 4.0 | 7.0 | 11.3 | 8.6 | 13.0 | 30.6 |
| Getting in or out of bed or chair | 9.0 | 5.9 | 4.8 | 6.9 | 11.6 | 9.3 | 13.1 | 21.9 |
| Dressing | 5.8 | 3.8 | 3.4 | 4.1 | 7.0 | 5.3 | 8.1 | 16.1 |
| Using toilet | 4.2 | 2.0 | 1.5 | 2.5 | 5.7 | 4.2 | 6.8 | 14.2 |
| Eating | 2.1 | 1.3 | 0.8 | 1.7 | 3.1 | 3.1 | 3.1 | 4.1 |
| Preparing meals | 8.6 | 4.5 | 4.0 | 4.9 | 11.7 | 8.7 | 13.6 | 27.6 |
| Managing money | 7.1 | 2.8 | 2.6 | 3.0 | 10.3 | 8.1 | 11.7 | 26.2 |
| Using the telephone | 7.1 | 3.8 | 5.2 | 2.7 | 9.7 | 12.3 | 8.0 | 21.4 |
| Doing light housework | 11.4 | 6.6 | 5.3 | 7.7 | 15.5 | 12.4 | 17.5 | 30.8 |
| **Percent receiving help** | | | | | | | | |
| Walking | 5.9 | 3.3 | 2.9 | 3.5 | 8.2 | 8.4 | 8.0 | 16.8 |
| Getting outside | 13.2 | 6.3 | 3.7 | 8.5 | 18.8 | 13.4 | 22.3 | 42.3 |
| Bathing or showering | 5.9 | 3.3 | 2.6 | 3.8 | 7.0 | 6.2 | 7.5 | 20.9 |
| Getting in or out of bed or chair | 3.9 | 2.5 | 2.2 | 2.7 | 4.8 | 3.9 | 5.4 | 11.0 |
| Dressing | 3.9 | 2.3 | 2.3 | 2.3 | 5.0 | 4.2 | 5.5 | 11.1 |
| Using toilet | 2.6 | 1.3 | 1.0 | 1.5 | 3.9 | 3.4 | 4.1 | 7.8 |
| Eating | 1.1 | 0.5 | 0.4 | 0.6 | 1.9 | 2.2 | 1.7 | 2.5 |
| Preparing meals | 7.5 | 3.6 | 3.7 | 3.5 | 10.5 | 8.5 | 11.7 | 25.4 |
| Managing money | 6.4 | 2.5 | 2.2 | 2.7 | 9.1 | 7.5 | 10.1 | 24.6 |
| Doing light housework | 8.9 | 4.8 | 3.9 | 5.6 | 12.1 | 9.3 | 14.0 | 27.3 |

*Source: Bureau of the Census,* 65+ in the United States, *Current Population Reports, P23-190, 1996*

# Over 22 Million Americans Care for Older People

**Most caregivers are women, with an average age of 46.**

Most care recipients are also women, with an average age of 77, according to a report by the National Alliance for Caregiving and the American Association of Retired Persons. The survey revealed a tripling in the number of American households caring for a relative or friend aged 50 or older, rising from just 7 million in 1988 to more than 22 million in 1996.

The largest share of caregivers (39 percent) are aged 35 to 49. Another 26 percent are aged 50 to 64, while 22 percent are under age 35. Just 12 percent of caregivers are aged 65 or older. Most caregivers are married, most do not have children under age 18 at home, and most are employed full-time.

◆ The number of caregiving households has surged because baby boomers are aging into the prime caregiving age groups.

◆ Because the parents of the baby-boom generation had so many children, boomers with ailing parents can share their caregiving responsibilities with their many siblings, lightening the load.

# Profile of Caregivers, 1996

*(total number of persons providing unpaid care to a relative or friend who is aged 50 or older, and distribution of caregivers by selected characteristics, 1996; numbers in thousands)*

| | |
|---|---|
| **Total number** | **22,411** |
| **Total percent** | **100.0%** |
| **Sex** | |
| Women | 72.5 |
| Men | 27.5 |
| **Age** | |
| Under age 35 | 22.3 |
| Aged 35 to 49 | 39.4 |
| Aged 50 to 64 | 26.0 |
| Aged 65 or older | 12.4 |
| **Marital status** | |
| Married | 65.7 |
| Single, never married | 12.6 |
| Separated or divorced | 13.0 |
| Widowed | 8.0 |
| **Children <18 in household** | |
| No | 57.8 |
| Yes | 41.3 |
| **Educational attainment** | |
| Not a high school graduate | 9.0 |
| High school graduate only | 35.3 |
| Some college | 22.5 |
| College graduate | 20.1 |
| Graduate school | 8.8 |
| Technical school | 3.5 |
| **Employment status** | |
| Employed full-time | 51.8 |
| Employed part-time | 12.3 |
| Retired | 15.9 |
| Not employed | 19.7 |

*(continued)*

*(continued from previous page)*

**Household income**

| | |
|---|---|
| Under $15,000 | 14.0% |
| $15,000 to $24,999 | 18.0 |
| $25,000 to $29,999 | 9.3 |
| $30,000 to $39,999 | 14.0 |
| $40,000 to $49,999 | 10.3 |
| $50,000 to $74,999 | 14.0 |
| $75,000 or more | 10.9 |
| Median income | $35,000 |

*Source: The National Alliance for Caregiving and The American Association of Retired Persons,* Family Caregiving in the U.S.—Findings from a National Survey, *Final Report, 1997*

# Medical Visits Are Most Frequent among Older Americans

**People aged 75 or older go to the doctor twice as often as the average person.**

While the average American goes to the doctor 2.7 times per year, people aged 75 or older see a doctor an average of 5.9 times per year. Men in the 75-plus age group visit doctors more often than women—6.2 versus 5.7 times per year.

Although older Americans go to doctors more frequently than younger people, they account for a minority of all doctor visits. Forty-seven percent of doctor visits are made by people aged 45 or older.

Older Americans are more likely to visit hospital outpatient departments and emergency rooms than are younger Americans. But again, older people account for a minority of all visits to such facilities. People aged 45 or older account for 38 percent of outpatient visits and 29 percent of emergency room visits.

The older age groups dominate hospital discharges, however. People aged 45 or older account for a 57 percent majority of patients discharged from short-stay hospitals. While the hospitalization rate of people aged 45 to 64 is just slightly above average, that of people aged 65 or older is three times the average.

◆ As the large baby-boom generation ages into its 50s and 60s, the 45-plus age group will begin to dominate doctor visits. Doctors who understand the aging process and who cater to the wants and needs of older Americans will be in great demand.

# Physician Visits by Age and Sex, 1995

*(number of office visits to physicians, percent distribution of visits by age, and number of visits per person, by age and sex, 1995)*

| | total | male | female |
|---|---|---|---|
| **Number of visits (000s)** | | | |
| **Total** | **697,082** | **280,762** | **416,320** |
| Under age 15 | 131,548 | 67,094 | 64,454 |
| Aged 15 to 24 | 56,278 | 19,230 | 37,048 |
| Aged 25 to 44 | 181,590 | 63,115 | 118,475 |
| Aged 45 to 64 | 159,531 | 64,193 | 95,337 |
| Aged 65 to 74 | 90,544 | 36,372 | 54,172 |
| Aged 75 or older | 77,591 | 30,758 | 46,833 |
| **Percent distribution** | | | |
| **Total** | **100.0%** | **100.0%** | **100.0%** |
| Under age 15 | 18.9 | 23.9 | 15.5 |
| Aged 15 to 24 | 8.1 | 6.8 | 8.9 |
| Aged 25 to 44 | 26.1 | 22.5 | 28.5 |
| Aged 45 to 64 | 22.9 | 22.9 | 22.9 |
| Aged 65 to 74 | 13.0 | 13.0 | 13.0 |
| Aged 75 or older | 11.1 | 11.0 | 11.2 |
| **Number of visits per person** | | | |
| **Total** | **2.7** | **2.2** | **3.1** |
| Under age 15 | 2.2 | 2.2 | 2.2 |
| Aged 15 to 24 | 1.6 | 1.1 | 2.1 |
| Aged 25 to 44 | 2.2 | 1.5 | 2.8 |
| Aged 45 to 64 | 3.1 | 2.6 | 3.6 |
| Aged 65 to 74 | 4.9 | 4.4 | 5.3 |
| Aged 75 or older | 5.9 | 6.2 | 5.7 |

*Source: National Center for Health Statistics,* National Ambulatory Medical Care Survey: 1995 Summary, *Advance Data, No. 286, 1997*

# Visits to Hospital Outpatient Departments and Emergency Rooms by Age and Sex, 1995

*(number of visits to hospital outpatient departments and emergency rooms, percent distribution of visits by age, and number of visits per 100 persons, by age and sex, 1995)*

| | outpatient departments | | | emergency rooms | | |
|---|---|---|---|---|---|---|
| | *total* | *male* | *female* | *total* | *male* | *female* |
| **Visits (000s)** | | | | | | |
| **Total** | **67,232** | **26,221** | **41,011** | **96,545** | **46,501** | **50,044** |
| Under age 15 | 15,039 | 8,132 | 6,908 | 22,709 | 12,392 | 10,317 |
| Aged 15 to 24 | 8,307 | 2,238 | 6,069 | 15,681 | 7,282 | 8,399 |
| Aged 25 to 44 | 18,588 | 6,247 | 12,341 | 30,086 | 14,519 | 15,568 |
| Aged 45 to 64 | 14,811 | 5,582 | 9,229 | 13,978 | 6,469 | 7,509 |
| Aged 65 to 74 | 6,004 | 2,332 | 3,673 | 6,057 | 2,810 | 3,248 |
| Aged 75 or older | 4,482 | 1,690 | 2,792 | 8,033 | 3,030 | 5,004 |
| **Percent distribution** | | | | | | |
| **Total** | **100.0%** | **100.0%** | **100.0%** | **100.0%** | **100.0%** | **100.0%** |
| Under age 15 | 22.4 | 31.0 | 16.8 | 23.5 | 26.6 | 20.6 |
| Aged 15 to 24 | 12.4 | 8.5 | 14.8 | 16.2 | 15.7 | 16.8 |
| Aged 25 to 44 | 27.6 | 23.8 | 30.1 | 31.2 | 31.2 | 31.1 |
| Aged 45 to 64 | 22.0 | 21.3 | 22.5 | 14.5 | 13.9 | 15.0 |
| Aged 65 to 74 | 8.9 | 8.9 | 9.0 | 6.3 | 6.0 | 6.5 |
| Aged 75 or older | 6.7 | 6.4 | 6.8 | 8.3 | 6.5 | 10.0 |
| **Number of visits per 100 persons** | | | | | | |
| **Total** | **25.7** | **20.6** | **30.5** | **36.9** | **36.5** | **37.3** |
| Under age 15 | 25.3 | 26.7 | 23.8 | 38.2 | 40.7 | 35.5 |
| Aged 15 to 24 | 23.0 | 12.3 | 33.7 | 43.4 | 40.2 | 46.6 |
| Aged 25 to 44 | 22.4 | 15.3 | 29.2 | 36.2 | 35.5 | 36.9 |
| Aged 45 to 64 | 28.6 | 22.4 | 34.5 | 27.0 | 25.9 | 28.1 |
| Aged 65 to 74 | 32.8 | 28.5 | 36.2 | 33.1 | 34.4 | 32.0 |
| Aged 75 or older | 34.0 | 33.9 | 34.1 | 60.9 | 60.7 | 61.0 |

*Source: National Center for Health Statistics,* National Ambulatory Medical Care Survey: 1995 Outpatient Department Summary, *Advance Data, Number 284, 1997; and* National Ambulatory Medical Care Survey: 1995 Emergency Department Summary, *Advance Data, Number 285, 1997*

# Hospital Discharges by Age and Sex, 1994

*(number of inpatients discharged from short-stay, non-federal hospitals, percent distribution of discharges by age, number of discharges per 100 persons, and average length of stay, by age and sex, 1994)*

|  | total | male | female |
|---|---|---|---|
| **Discharges (in 000s)** | | | |
| **Total** | **30,843** | **12,293** | **18,550** |
| Under age 15 | 2,249 | 1,272 | 978 |
| Aged 15 to 44 | 10,956 | 3,146 | 7,810 |
| Aged 45 to 64 | 6,311 | 3,120 | 3,191 |
| Aged 65 or older | 11,327 | 4,756 | 6,571 |
| **Percent distribution** | | | |
| **Total** | **100.0%** | **100.0%** | **100.0%** |
| Under age 15 | 7.3 | 10.3 | 5.3 |
| Aged 15 to 44 | 35.5 | 25.6 | 42.1 |
| Aged 45 to 64 | 20.5 | 25.4 | 17.2 |
| Aged 65 or older | 36.7 | 38.7 | 35.4 |
| **Number of discharges per 100 persons** | | | |
| **Total** | **11.9** | **9.8** | **13.9** |
| Under age 15 | 3.9 | 4.3 | 3.5 |
| Aged 15 to 44 | 9.3 | 5.4 | 13.2 |
| Aged 45 to 64 | 12.4 | 12.7 | 12.1 |
| Aged 65 or older | 34.2 | 35.3 | 33.4 |
| **Length of stay (days)** | | | |
| **Total** | **5.7** | **6.2** | **5.4** |
| Under age 15 | 4.8 | 4.9 | 4.7 |
| Aged 15 to 44 | 4.2 | 5.8 | 3.5 |
| Aged 45 to 64 | 5.9 | 5.8 | 5.9 |
| Aged 65 or older | 7.4 | 7.2 | 7.5 |

*Source: National Center for Health Statistics,* 1994 Summary: National Hospital Discharge Survey, *Advance Data, Number 278, 1996*

# Home Health Care Is Popular among Older Americans

**Home health care services allow the ailing elderly to remain in their own homes rather than move into a nursing home.**

The number of older Americans using home health care services is nearly equal to the number in nursing homes—about 1.4 million each as of the mid-1990s. Home health care has been growing rapidly during the past few years because it has been included in Medicare coverage. It is also growing rapidly because the elderly prefer to remain in their own homes rather than move to an institution if they need care.

Seventy-three percent of the recipients of home health care are aged 65 or older, with half aged 75 or older. More than two in three are women. Among elderly women who receive home health care, most are widows. Forty percent of home health care recipients live alone.

Among all nursing home residents, 90 percent are aged 65 or older, with 74 percent aged 75 or older. Seventy-two percent of nursing home residents are women, and most are widows. The largest share of nursing home residents (41 percent) were in a hospital before their admission to the nursing home.

◆ While home health care benefits are likely to be curtailed in the future, the preferences of older Americans are clear. Look for slowing growth in the nursing home population and continued rapid growth in home health care—even if more of those services must be paid for out-of-pocket.

# Characteristics of Current Elderly Users of Home Health Care, 1994

*(number and percent distribution of current users of home health care aged 65 or older by selected characteristics, 1994)*

| | total | | men | | women | |
|---|---|---|---|---|---|---|
| | *number* | *percent* | *number* | *percent* | *number* | *percent* |
| **Age** | | | | | | |
| **Total users** | **1,889,400** | **100.0%** | **613,400** | **100.0%** | **1,276,000** | **100.0%** |
| Aged 65 or older | 1,379,800 | 73.0 | 399,600 | 65.1 | 980,200 | 76.8 |
| Aged 65 to 74 | 413,700 | 21.9 | 139,700 | 22.8 | 274,000 | 21.5 |
| Aged 75 to 84 | 583,600 | 30.9 | 176,300 | 28.7 | 407,300 | 31.9 |
| Aged 85 or older | 382,500 | 20.2 | 83,600 | 13.6 | 299,000 | 23.4 |
| **Race** | | | | | | |
| White | 943,800 | 68.4 | 274,900 | 68.8 | 668,900 | 68.2 |
| Black | 178,800 | 13.0 | 52,800 | 13.2 | 126,000 | 12.9 |
| **Hispanic origin** | | | | | | |
| Non-Hispanic | 815,200 | 59.1 | 246,100 | 61.6 | 569,100 | 58.1 |
| Hispanic | 50,900 | 3.7 | 13,500 | 3.4 | 37,400 | 3.8 |
| **Marital status** | | | | | | |
| Married | 437,500 | 31.7 | 208,500 | 52.2 | 229,000 | 23.4 |
| Widowed | 641,700 | 46.5 | 112,900 | 28.3 | 528,900 | 54.0 |
| Divorced | 53,100 | 3.8 | 19,500 | 4.9 | 33,600 | 3.4 |
| Never married | 86,900 | 6.3 | 36,500 | 9.1 | 50,400 | 5.1 |
| **Living arrangement** | | | | | | |
| With family members | 702,600 | 50.9 | 261,900 | 65.5 | 440,800 | 45.0 |
| Alone | 553,400 | 40.1 | 110,200 | 27.6 | 443,200 | 45.2 |
| With nonfamily members | 63,200 | 4.6 | 17,000 | 4.3 | 45,500 | 4.6 |

*Note: Numbers may not add to total because unknown is not shown.*
*Source: National Center for Health Statistics,* Characteristics of Elderly Home Health Care Users: Data from the 1994 National Home and Hospice Care Survey, *Number 279, 1996*

# Characteristics of Elderly Nursing Home Residents, 1995

*(number and percent distribution of nursing home residents aged 65 or older by selected characteristics, 1995)*

| | total | | men | | women | |
|---|---|---|---|---|---|---|
| | *number* | *percent* | *number* | *percent* | *number* | *percent* |
| **Total residents** | **1,548,600** | **100.0%** | **428,962** | **100.0%** | **1,119,638** | **100.0%** |
| **Age at admission** | | | | | | |
| Aged 65 or older | 1,385,400 | 89.5 | 342,700 | 79.9 | 1,042,700 | 93.1 |
| Aged 65 to 74 | 242,000 | 15.6 | 93,500 | 21.8 | 148,600 | 13.3 |
| Aged 75 to 84 | 586,300 | 37.9 | 143,400 | 33.4 | 442,900 | 39.6 |
| Aged 85 or older | 557,100 | 36.0 | 105,900 | 24.7 | 451,200 | 40.3 |
| **Race** | | | | | | |
| White | 1,240,000 | 89.5 | 294,500 | 85.9 | 945,500 | 90.7 |
| Black | 117,900 | 17.5 | 37,000 | 10.8 | 80,900 | 7.8 |
| **Hispanic origin** | | | | | | |
| Non-Hispanic | 1,276,000 | 92.1 | 312,600 | 91.2 | 963,400 | 92.4 |
| Hispanic | 32,300 | 2.3 | 13,000 | 3.8 | 19,300 | 1.9 |
| **Marital status** | | | | | | |
| Married | 229,300 | 16.5 | 126,800 | 37.0 | 102,500 | 9.8 |
| Widowed | 914,800 | 66.0 | 127,900 | 37.3 | 786,900 | 75.5 |
| Divorced | 75,800 | 5.5 | 31,600 | 9.2 | 44,200 | 4.2 |
| Never married | 154,300 | 11.1 | 53,000 | 15.5 | 101,300 | 9.7 |
| **Living quarters before nursing home** | | | | | | |
| Private residence | 509,700 | 36.8 | 124,500 | 36.2 | 385,200 | 36.9 |
| Retirement home | 31,100 | 2.2 | 6,600 | 1.9 | 24,400 | 2.3 |
| Residential facility | 68,600 | 4.9 | 15,200 | 4.4 | 53,400 | 5.1 |
| Nursing home | 160,400 | 11.6 | 43,600 | 12.7 | 116,800 | 11.2 |
| Hospital | 562,300 | 40.6 | 138,500 | 40.4 | 423,800 | 40.6 |
| Mental health facility | 14,900 | 1.1 | - | - | 9,700 | 0.9 |

*Note: Numbers may not add to total because unknown is not shown. (-) means sample is too small to make a reliable estimate.*
*Source: National Center for Health Statistics,* Characteristics of Elderly Nursing Home Residents: Data from the 1995 National Nursing Home Survey, *Number 289, 1997*

# Heart Disease Is the Leading Killer of Older Americans

**Over one-third of deaths among Americans aged 55 or older are due to heart disease.**

Among Americans aged 85 or older, 42 percent of deaths are due to heart disease. The second leading cause of death among older Americans—cancer—accounts for just 24 percent of deaths among people aged 55 or older and for only 12 percent of deaths among people aged 85 or older. Eighty-four percent of deaths in the U.S. occur among people aged 55 or older, with over half occurring among people aged 75 or older.

At all ages, males are more likely to die than females. Consequently, life expectancy for females is greater than that for males. At birth, boys have a life expectancy of 72.5 years, while girls can expect to live for 78.9 years. The female advantage in life expectancy persists throughout life, although it diminishes with age. At age 55, women can expect to live 27.0 more years while men have a life expectancy of 22.9 years—a gap of 4.1 years. At age 85, women's life expectancy surpasses men's by just 1.1 year.

Thanks to advances in medical science, death rates due to heart disease have been dropping for the past few decades. Consequently, the life expectancy of older Americans is increasing. In 1995, people aged 65 could expect to live 17.4 more years—18.9 more years for women and 15.6 more years for men. Since 1900, life expectancy at age 65 has increased by 4.5 years overall—a gain of 6.1 years for women and 2.6 years for men.

◆ The life expectancy of older Americans will continue to rise as medical science finds new ways to treat heart disease.

# Causes of Death, 1995: Number

*(number of deaths among total persons and among persons aged 55 or older, for ten leading causes of death among total population and among population aged 65 or older, 1995)*

| Number | total | aged 55 or older | | | | |
|---|---|---|---|---|---|---|
| | | *total* | *55 to 64* | *65 to 74* | *75 to 84* | *85+* |
| **Total deaths** | **2,312,132** | **1,929,838** | **235,512** | **480,890** | **652,177** | **561,259** |
| Diseases of heart* | 737,563 | 683,666 | 68,240 | 150,058 | 230,114 | 235,254 |
| Malignant neoplasms* | 538,455 | 469,040 | 87,898 | 162,864 | 152,108 | 66,170 |
| Cerebrovascular diseases* | 157,991 | 148,497 | 9,735 | 25,734 | 53,654 | 59,374 |
| Chronic obstructive pulmonary diseases* | 102,899 | 98,466 | 9,988 | 30,118 | 39,211 | 19,149 |
| Accidents* | 93,320 | 35,842 | 6,743 | 8,400 | 10,968 | 9,731 |
| Pneumonia and influenza* | 82,923 | 77,755 | 3,458 | 10,737 | 25,985 | 37,575 |
| Diabetes mellitus* | 59,254 | 52,640 | 8,188 | 16,231 | 18,135 | 10,086 |
| Human immunodeficiency virus | 43,115 | 3,090 | 2,320 | 681 | 79 | 10 |
| Suicide | 31,284 | 8,860 | 2,804 | 2,960 | 2,311 | 785 |
| Chronic liver disease and cirrhosis | 25,222 | 15,588 | 5,356 | 5,909 | 3,492 | 831 |
| Nephritis, nephrotic syndrome, nephrosis* | 23,676 | 21,921 | 1,739 | 4,590 | 8,079 | 7,513 |
| Septicemia* | 20,965 | 18,638 | 1,739 | 3,985 | 6,633 | 6,281 |
| Alzheimer's disease* | 20,606 | 20,560 | 330 | 2,083 | 8,182 | 9,965 |
| All other causes | 374,859 | 275,275 | 26,974 | 56,540 | 93,226 | 98,535 |

*\* One of the ten leading causes of death among people aged 65 or older.*
*Source: National Center for Health Statistics,* Report of Final Mortality Statistics, 1995, *Monthly Vital Statistics Report, Vol. 45, No. 11, Supplement 2, 1997; calculations by New Strategist*

# Causes of Death, 1995: Percent Distribution by Cause

*(percent distribution of deaths by selected cause and age, for ten leading causes of death among total population and among population aged 65 or older, 1995)*

| Percent distribution by cause | total | aged 55 or older total | 55 to 64 | 65 to 74 | 75 to 84 | 85+ |
|---|---|---|---|---|---|---|
| **Total deaths** | 100.0% | 100.0% | 100.0% | 100.0% | 100.0% | 100.0% |
| Diseases of heart* | 31.9 | 35.4 | 29.0 | 31.2 | 35.3 | 41.9 |
| Malignant neoplasms* | 23.3 | 24.3 | 37.3 | 33.9 | 23.3 | 11.8 |
| Cerebrovascular diseases* | 6.8 | 7.7 | 4.1 | 5.4 | 8.2 | 10.6 |
| Chronic obstructive pulmonary diseases* | 4.5 | 5.1 | 4.2 | 6.3 | 6.0 | 3.4 |
| Accidents* | 4.0 | 1.9 | 2.9 | 1.7 | 1.7 | 1.7 |
| Pneumonia and influenza* | 3.6 | 4.0 | 1.5 | 2.2 | 4.0 | 6.7 |
| Diabetes mellitus* | 2.6 | 2.7 | 3.5 | 3.4 | 2.8 | 1.8 |
| Human immunodeficiency virus | 1.9 | 0.2 | 1.0 | 0.1 | 0.0 | 0.0 |
| Suicide | 1.4 | 0.5 | 1.2 | 0.6 | 0.4 | 0.1 |
| Chronic liver disease and cirrhosis | 1.1 | 0.8 | 2.3 | 1.2 | 0.5 | 0.1 |
| Nephritis, nephrotic syndrome, nephrosis* | 1.0 | 1.1 | 0.7 | 1.0 | 1.2 | 1.3 |
| Septicemia* | 0.9 | 1.0 | 0.7 | 0.8 | 1.0 | 1.1 |
| Alzheimer's disease* | 0.9 | 1.1 | 0.1 | 0.4 | 1.3 | 1.8 |
| All other causes | 16.2 | 14.3 | 11.5 | 11.8 | 14.3 | 17.6 |

* One of the ten leading causes of death among people aged 65 or older.
Source: National Center for Health Statistics, Report of Final Mortality Statistics, 1995, Monthly Vital Statistics Report, Vol. 45, No. 11, Supplement 2, 1997; calculations by New Strategist

# Causes of Death, 1995: Percent Distribution by Age

*(percent distribution of deaths by age and selected cause, for ten leading causes of death among total population and among population aged 65 or older, 1995)*

| | total | aged 55 or older | | | | |
|---|---|---|---|---|---|---|
| **Percent distribution by age** | | total | 55 to 64 | 65 to 74 | 75 to 84 | 85+ |
| **Total deaths** | 100.0% | 83.5% | 10.2% | 20.8% | 28.2% | 24.3% |
| Diseases of heart* | 100.0 | 92.7 | 9.3 | 20.3 | 31.2 | 31.9 |
| Malignant neoplasms* | 100.0 | 87.1 | 16.3 | 30.2 | 28.2 | 12.3 |
| Cerebrovascular diseases* | 100.0 | 94.0 | 6.2 | 16.3 | 34.0 | 37.6 |
| Chronic obstructive pulmonary diseases* | 100.0 | 95.7 | 9.7 | 29.3 | 38.1 | 18.6 |
| Accidents* | 100.0 | 38.4 | 7.2 | 9.0 | 11.8 | 10.4 |
| Pneumonia and influenza* | 100.0 | 93.8 | 4.2 | 12.9 | 31.3 | 45.3 |
| Diabetes mellitus* | 100.0 | 88.8 | 13.8 | 27.4 | 30.6 | 17.0 |
| Human immunodeficiency virus | 100.0 | 7.2 | 5.4 | 1.6 | 0.2 | 0.0 |
| Suicide | 100.0 | 28.3 | 9.0 | 9.5 | 7.4 | 2.5 |
| Chronic liver disease and cirrhosis | 100.0 | 61.8 | 21.2 | 23.4 | 13.8 | 3.3 |
| Nephritis, nephrotic syndrome, nephrosis* | 100.0 | 92.6 | 7.3 | 19.4 | 34.1 | 31.7 |
| Septicemia* | 100.0 | 88.9 | 8.3 | 19.0 | 31.6 | 30.0 |
| Alzheimer's disease* | 100.0 | 99.8 | 1.6 | 10.1 | 39.7 | 48.4 |
| All other causes | 100.0 | 73.4 | 7.2 | 15.1 | 24.9 | 26.3 |

*\* One of the ten leading causes of death among people aged 65 or older.*
*Source: National Center for Health Statistics,* Report of Final Mortality Statistics, 1995, *Monthly Vital Statistics Report, Vol. 45, No. 11, Supplement 2, 1997; calculations by New Strategist*

# Life Expectancy by Age, Sex and Race, 1995

*(years of life remaining at birth and at exact ages from 55 to 85, by sex and race, 1995)*

|        | total | | | white | | black | |
|--------|-------|-------|-------|-------|-------|-------|-------|
|        | *total* | *men* | *women* | *men* | *women* | *men* | *women* |
| Birth  | 75.8 | 72.5 | 78.9 | 73.4 | 79.6 | 65.2 | 73.9 |
| 55     | 25.1 | 22.9 | 27.0 | 23.2 | 27.3 | 19.6 | 24.4 |
| 60     | 21.1 | 19.1 | 22.9 | 19.3 | 23.0 | 16.4 | 20.6 |
| 65     | 17.4 | 15.6 | 18.9 | 15.7 | 19.1 | 13.6 | 17.1 |
| 70     | 14.1 | 12.4 | 15.3 | 12.5 | 15.4 | 11.0 | 13.9 |
| 75     | 11.0 | 9.7 | 11.9 | 9.7 | 12.0 | 8.8 | 11.1 |
| 80     | 8.3 | 7.2 | 8.9 | 7.2 | 8.9 | 6.8 | 8.4 |
| 85     | 6.0 | 5.2 | 6.3 | 5.2 | 6.3 | 5.1 | 6.2 |

*Source: National Center for Health Statistics,* Report of Final Mortality Statistics, 1995, *Monthly Vital Statistics Report, Vol. 45, No.11, Supplement 2, 1997*

# Life Expectancy at Age 65 by Sex and Race, 1900 to 1995

*(years of life remaining at age 65 by sex and race; change in years of life remaining for selected years, 1900-95)*

| | total | | | white | | black | |
|---|---|---|---|---|---|---|---|
| | *total* | *men* | *women* | *men* | *women* | *men* | *women* |
| 1995 | 17.4 | 15.6 | 18.9 | 15.7 | 19.0 | 13.7 | 17.2 |
| 1990 | 17.2 | 15.1 | 18.9 | 15.2 | 19.1 | 13.2 | 17.2 |
| 1980 | 16.4 | 14.1 | 18.3 | 14.2 | 18.4 | 13.0 | 16.8 |
| 1970 | 15.2 | 13.1 | 17.0 | 13.1 | 17.1 | 12.5 | 15.7 |
| 1960 | 14.3 | 12.8 | 15.8 | 12.9 | 15.9 | 12.7 | 15.1 |
| 1950 | 13.9 | 12.8 | 15.0 | 12.8 | 15.1 | 12.9 | 14.9 |
| 1900 | 11.9 | 11.5 | 12.2 | 11.5 | 12.2 | 10.4 | 11.4 |
| **Change in years** | | | | | | | |
| 1990 to 1995 | 0.2 | 0.5 | 0.0 | 0.5 | -0.1 | 0.5 | 0.0 |
| 1950 to 1995 | 3.3 | 2.3 | 3.9 | 2.4 | 4.0 | 0.3 | 2.3 |
| 1900 to 1995 | 4.5 | 2.6 | 6.1 | 2.7 | 6.2 | 2.6 | 5.4 |

*Source: National Center for Health Statistics,* Births and Deaths: United States, 1995, *Monthly Vital Statistics Report, Vol. 45, No.3, Supplement 2, 1996; calculations by New Strategist*

# 4

# Income

◆ The median income of householders aged 65 or older grew an enormous 17 percent between 1980 and 1995, after adjusting for inflation.

◆ Ten percent of householders aged 55 to 64 have annual incomes of $100,000 or more, as do 4 percent of those aged 65 to 74.

◆ Married couples aged 65 or older have a median household income of $28,862, versus an average of $19,096 for the entire age group.

◆ Personal income of men aged 55 to 64 fell 2 percent between 1980 and 1995, in part because of the growing prevalence of early retirement.

◆ Among full-time workers aged 55 to 64, white men had a median income of $40,095, versus $28,267 for blacks and $22,124 for Hispanics.

◆ The median incomes of women aged 55 to 64 who work full-time range from a high of $25,005 for whites to $19,843 for Hispanics.

◆ Thirteen percent of women and 7 percent of men aged 55 or older are poor.

◆ Social Security is the single most common source of income for Americans aged 65 or older; benefits averaged $7,972 per person in 1995.

# Older Householders Have Seen Incomes Grow

**The median income of older householders has grown faster than that of the average household since 1980.**

The $38,077 median income of householders aged 55 to 64 exceeded that of the average household by several thousand dollars in 1995. While many householders in this age group are retired, those who are still in the labor force are enjoying peak earnings. Householders aged 55 to 64 have seen their median income climb by 5 percent since 1980, after adjusting for inflation. This compares with a gain of 4 percent for households overall.

The median income of householders aged 65 or older has grown an enormous 17 percent since 1980, after adjusting for inflation, from $16,260 to $19,096 in 1995. One reason for this growth is the replacement of a poorer older generation by a more educated and affluent cohort. Older householders are not immune to economic ups and downs. Those aged 65 or older saw their median income drop 3 percent during the first half of the 1990s as interest rates fell during the recession. Their incomes were growing again between 1994 and 1995, however.

◆ The incomes of older householders should continue to rise as the dual earners of the baby-boom generation enter the 55-to-64 age group and as better-educated cohorts fill the 65-plus age groups.

## Elderly Incomes Should Continue to Rise

*(percent change in median income of total households and households headed by persons aged 55 or older, 1980 to 1995; in 1995 dollars)*

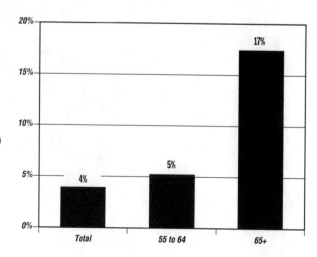

# Median Income of Households Headed by People Aged 55 or Older, 1980 to 1995

*(median income of total households and of households headed by persons aged 55 or older, 1980 to 1995; in 1995 dollars)*

| | total | 55 to 64 | aged 65 or older total | 65 to 74 | 75+ |
|---|---|---|---|---|---|
| 1995 | $34,076 | $38,077 | $19,096 | $23,031 | $15,342 |
| 1994 | 33,178 | 36,230 | 18,608 | 22,029 | 15,148 |
| 1993 | 32,949 | 35,304 | 18,721 | 22,475 | 15,111 |
| 1992 | 33,278 | 36,925 | 18,613 | 22,128 | 14,795 |
| 1991 | 33,709 | 37,265 | 18,994 | 22,449 | 15,590 |
| 1990 | 34,914 | 37,739 | 19,653 | 23,661 | 15,333 |
| 1989 | 35,526 | 37,878 | 19,383 | 23,301 | 14,873 |
| 1988 | 35,073 | 37,234 | 19,225 | 22,510 | 15,209 |
| 1987 | 34,962 | 36,973 | 19,376 | 22,970 | 15,143 |
| 1986 | 34,620 | 37,232 | 19,252 | - | - |
| 1985 | 33,452 | 36,198 | 18,772 | - | - |
| 1984 | 32,878 | 35,341 | 18,774 | - | - |
| 1983 | 31,957 | 34,853 | 17,930 | - | - |
| 1982 | 32,155 | 35,191 | 17,601 | - | - |
| 1981 | 32,263 | 35,590 | 16,750 | - | - |
| 1980 | 32,795 | 36,196 | 16,260 | - | - |
| **Percent change** | | | | | |
| 1994-1995 | 2.7% | 5.1% | 2.6% | 4.5% | 1.3% |
| 1990-1995 | -2.4 | 0.9 | -2.8 | -2.7 | 0.1 |
| 1980-1995 | 3.9 | 5.2 | 17.4 | - | - |

*Note: (-) means data are not available.*
*Source: Bureau of the Census, Internet web site,* http://www.census.gov; *calculations by New Strategist*

# Many Older Householders Are Affluent

**More than 1 million 55-to-64-year-olds have incomes of $100,000 or more.**

Household incomes fall as people age because so many retire from the labor force and live on savings, pensions, and Social Security benefits. The median income of house-holders aged 55 to 64 stood at $38,077 in 1995—greater than the median of $34,076 for all households. But the median income of householders aged 65 to 74 was sharply lower at $23,031. Householders aged 75 or older had a median income of just $15,342.

Many older householders are affluent, however. Ten percent of householders aged 55 to 64 have annual incomes of $100,000 or more, as do 4 percent of those aged 65 to 74. A much larger share of older householders have incomes below $10,000, however, including 28 percent of those aged 75 or older.

◆ If baby boomers stay in the labor force longer than their parents did—as seems likely—the household incomes of the 55-to-64 age group should grow sharply as working boomers enter their late 50s and early 60s after the turn of the century.

# Income Distribution of Households Headed by Persons Aged 55 or Older, 1995

*(number and percent distribution of total households and of households headed by persons aged 55 or older, by income, 1995; households in thousands as of 1996)*

| | | aged 55 or older | | | | |
| | | | | aged 65 or older | | |
| | *total* | *total* | *55 to 64* | *total* | *65 to 74* | *75+* |
|---|---|---|---|---|---|---|
| **Total households** | **99,627** | **33,887** | **12,401** | **21,486** | **11,908** | **9,578** |
| Under $10,000 | 12,190 | 6,097 | 1,463 | 4,634 | 1,983 | 2,651 |
| $10,000 to $19,999 | 17,009 | 8,378 | 1,783 | 6,595 | 3,196 | 3,401 |
| $20,000 to $29,999 | 14,905 | 5,483 | 1,655 | 3,828 | 2,289 | 1,539 |
| $30,000 to $39,999 | 13,129 | 3,879 | 1,593 | 2,286 | 1,471 | 814 |
| $40,000 to $49,999 | 10,565 | 2,626 | 1,283 | 1,343 | 943 | 401 |
| $50,000 to $59,999 | 8,276 | 1,872 | 1,007 | 865 | 609 | 257 |
| $60,000 to $69,999 | 6,332 | 1,381 | 824 | 557 | 405 | 151 |
| $70,000 to $79,999 | 4,571 | 1,011 | 714 | 297 | 210 | 88 |
| $80,000 to $89,999 | 3,256 | 706 | 473 | 233 | 150 | 83 |
| $90,000 to $99,999 | 2,281 | 552 | 371 | 181 | 136 | 44 |
| $100,000 or more | 7,114 | 1,900 | 1,234 | 666 | 518 | 148 |
| Median income | $34,076 | $26,042 | $38,077 | $19,096 | $23,031 | $15,342 |
| **Total households** | **100.0%** | **100.0%** | **100.0%** | **100.0%** | **100.0%** | **100.0%** |
| Under $10,000 | 12.2 | 18.0 | 11.8 | 21.6 | 16.7 | 27.7 |
| $10,000 to $19,999 | 17.1 | 24.7 | 14.4 | 30.7 | 26.8 | 35.5 |
| $20,000 to $29,999 | 15.0 | 16.2 | 13.3 | 17.8 | 19.2 | 16.1 |
| $30,000 to $39,999 | 13.2 | 11.4 | 12.8 | 10.6 | 12.4 | 8.5 |
| $40,000 to $49,999 | 10.6 | 7.7 | 10.3 | 6.3 | 7.9 | 4.2 |
| $50,000 to $59,999 | 8.3 | 5.5 | 8.1 | 4.0 | 5.1 | 2.7 |
| $60,000 to $69,999 | 6.4 | 4.1 | 6.6 | 2.6 | 3.4 | 1.6 |
| $70,000 to $79,999 | 4.6 | 3.0 | 5.8 | 1.4 | 1.8 | 0.9 |
| $80,000 to $89,999 | 3.3 | 2.1 | 3.8 | 1.1 | 1.3 | 0.9 |
| $90,000 to $99,999 | 2.3 | 1.6 | 3.0 | 0.8 | 1.1 | 0.5 |
| $100,000 or more | 7.1 | 5.6 | 10.0 | 3.1 | 4.4 | 1.5 |

*Source: Bureau of the Census, unpublished tables from the 1996 Current Population Survey; calculations by New Strategist*

# Married Couples Have the Highest Incomes

**Older women who live alone have the lowest incomes.**

Married couples have above-average incomes regardless of age. Among householders aged 55 to 64, the median income of married couples stood at $49,898 in 1995—more than $10,000 higher than the median income of the average household in this age group. For couples aged 65 or older, median household income was $28,862 versus $19,096 for the average household in the age group.

The median income of male-headed families surpasses that of married couples in the 75-plus age group, but there are so few of these households (just 145,000 in 1995), that their higher incomes do little to boost the overall median.

Women who live alone have the smallest incomes in all the older age groups. Among householders aged 75 or older, women who live alone had a median income of just $10,619 in 1995, well below the $23,031 median for all households in this age group.

◆ The household incomes of older Americans should rise in the years ahead as generations of working women and dual-earner couples fill the 55-plus age groups.

# Income Distribution of Households by Household Type, 1995: Aged 55 to 64

*(number and percent distribution of households headed by persons aged 55 to 64, by income and household type, 1995; households in thousands as of 1996)*

| | family households | | | | nonfamily households | | | |
| --- | --- | --- | --- | --- | --- | --- | --- | --- |
| | | | | | female householder | | male householder | |
| | total | married couples | female hh no spouse present | male hh no spouse present | total | living alone | total | living alone |
| **Total households** | **12,401** | **7,741** | **1,111** | **283** | **1,967** | **1,852** | **1,299** | **1,089** |
| Under $10,000 | 1,462 | 352 | 174 | 12 | 648 | 637 | 276 | 271 |
| $10,000 to $19,999 | 1,782 | 727 | 245 | 53 | 495 | 474 | 262 | 237 |
| $20,000 to $29,999 | 1,655 | 863 | 222 | 60 | 347 | 322 | 163 | 129 |
| $30,000 to $39,999 | 1,594 | 1,016 | 194 | 40 | 175 | 160 | 169 | 136 |
| $40,000 to $49,999 | 1,284 | 920 | 104 | 18 | 122 | 107 | 120 | 101 |
| $50,000 to $59,999 | 1,006 | 788 | 47 | 16 | 79 | 73 | 76 | 59 |
| $60,000 to $69,999 | 826 | 663 | 40 | 31 | 34 | 26 | 58 | 38 |
| $70,000 to $79,999 | 716 | 601 | 34 | 9 | 33 | 29 | 39 | 30 |
| $80,000 to $89,999 | 472 | 396 | 27 | 9 | 10 | 10 | 30 | 22 |
| $90,000 to $99,999 | 371 | 330 | 5 | 10 | 11 | 3 | 15 | 11 |
| $100,000 or more | 1,233 | 1,084 | 19 | 23 | 15 | 12 | 92 | 56 |
| Median income | $38,077 | $49,898 | $26,919 | $35,836 | $16,879 | $16,164 | $25,917 | $22,062 |
| **Total households** | **100.0%** | **100.0%** | **100.0%** | **100.0%** | **100.0%** | **100.0%** | **100.0%** | **100.0%** |
| Under $10,000 | 11.8 | 4.5 | 15.7 | 4.2 | 32.9 | 34.4 | 21.2 | 24.9 |
| $10,000 to $19,999 | 14.4 | 9.4 | 22.1 | 18.7 | 25.2 | 25.6 | 20.2 | 21.8 |
| $20,000 to $29,999 | 13.3 | 11.1 | 20.0 | 21.2 | 17.6 | 17.4 | 12.5 | 11.8 |
| $30,000 to $39,999 | 12.9 | 13.1 | 17.5 | 14.1 | 8.9 | 8.6 | 13.0 | 12.5 |
| $40,000 to $49,999 | 10.4 | 11.9 | 9.4 | 6.4 | 6.2 | 5.8 | 9.2 | 9.3 |
| $50,000 to $59,999 | 8.1 | 10.2 | 4.2 | 5.7 | 4.0 | 3.9 | 5.9 | 5.4 |
| $60,000 to $69,999 | 6.7 | 8.6 | 3.6 | 11.0 | 1.7 | 1.4 | 4.5 | 3.5 |
| $70,000 to $79,999 | 5.8 | 7.8 | 3.1 | 3.2 | 1.7 | 1.6 | 3.0 | 2.8 |
| $80,000 to $89,999 | 3.8 | 5.1 | 2.4 | 3.2 | 0.5 | 0.5 | 2.3 | 2.0 |
| $90,000 to $99,999 | 3.0 | 4.3 | 0.5 | 3.5 | 0.6 | 0.2 | 1.2 | 1.0 |
| $100,000 or more | 9.9 | 14.0 | 1.7 | 8.1 | 0.8 | 0.6 | 7.1 | 5.1 |

*Source: Bureau of the Census, unpublished tables from the 1996 Current Population Survey; calculations by New Strategist*

# Income Distribution of Households by Household Type, 1995: Aged 65 or Older

*(number and percent distribution of households headed by persons aged 65 or older, by income and household type, 1995; households in thousands as of 1996)*

| | family households | | | | nonfamily households | | | |
| | | | female hh | male hh | female householder | | male householder | |
| | total | married couples | no spouse present | no spouse present | total | living alone | total | living alone |
|---|---|---|---|---|---|---|---|---|
| **Total households** | **21,486** | **9,281** | **1,632** | **394** | **7,731** | **7,534** | **2,448** | **2,307** |
| Under $10,000 | 4,636 | 400 | 210 | 35 | 3,282 | 3,271 | 709 | 693 |
| $10,000 to $19,999 | 6,596 | 2,218 | 436 | 90 | 2,958 | 2,907 | 894 | 867 |
| $20,000 to $29,999 | 3,828 | 2,266 | 360 | 52 | 762 | 694 | 388 | 350 |
| $30,000 to $39,999 | 2,286 | 1,429 | 219 | 72 | 386 | 361 | 180 | 163 |
| $40,000 to $49,999 | 1,343 | 908 | 165 | 45 | 143 | 130 | 82 | 76 |
| $50,000 to $59,999 | 864 | 590 | 102 | 32 | 80 | 71 | 60 | 49 |
| $60,000 to $69,999 | 557 | 389 | 56 | 18 | 54 | 42 | 40 | 36 |
| $70,000 to $79,999 | 296 | 210 | 27 | 19 | 14 | 12 | 26 | 24 |
| $80,000 to $89,999 | 232 | 193 | 16 | 10 | 6 | 6 | 7 | 2 |
| $90,000 to $99,999 | 181 | 134 | 15 | 11 | 12 | 11 | 9 | 8 |
| $100,000 or more | 667 | 544 | 26 | 10 | 34 | 29 | 53 | 39 |
| Median income | $19,096 | $28,862 | $24,585 | $32,056 | $11,428 | $11,217 | $14,993 | $14,486 |
| **Total households** | **100.0%** | **100.0%** | **100.0%** | **100.0%** | **100.0%** | **100.0%** | **100.0%** | **100.0%** |
| Under $10,000 | 21.6 | 4.3 | 12.9 | 8.9 | 42.5 | 43.4 | 29.0 | 30.0 |
| $10,000 to $19,999 | 30.7 | 23.9 | 26.7 | 22.8 | 38.3 | 38.6 | 36.5 | 37.6 |
| $20,000 to $29,999 | 17.8 | 24.4 | 22.1 | 13.2 | 9.9 | 9.2 | 15.8 | 15.2 |
| $30,000 to $39,999 | 10.6 | 15.4 | 13.4 | 18.3 | 5.0 | 4.8 | 7.4 | 7.1 |
| $40,000 to $49,999 | 6.3 | 9.8 | 10.1 | 11.4 | 1.8 | 1.7 | 3.3 | 3.3 |
| $50,000 to $59,999 | 4.0 | 6.4 | 6.3 | 8.1 | 1.0 | 0.9 | 2.5 | 2.1 |
| $60,000 to $69,999 | 2.6 | 4.2 | 3.4 | 4.6 | 0.7 | 0.6 | 1.6 | 1.6 |
| $70,000 to $79,999 | 1.4 | 2.3 | 1.7 | 4.8 | 0.2 | 0.2 | 1.1 | 1.0 |
| $80,000 to $89,999 | 1.1 | 2.1 | 1.0 | 2.5 | 0.1 | 0.1 | 0.3 | 0.1 |
| $90,000 to $99,999 | 0.8 | 1.4 | 0.9 | 2.8 | 0.2 | 0.1 | 0.4 | 0.3 |
| $100,000 or more | 3.1 | 5.9 | 1.6 | 2.5 | 0.4 | 0.4 | 2.2 | 1.7 |

*Source: Bureau of the Census, unpublished tables from the 1996 Current Population Survey; calculations by New Strategist*

# Income Distribution of Households by Household Type, 1995: Aged 65 to 74

*(number and percent distribution of households headed by persons aged 65 to 74, by income and household type, 1995; households in thousands as of 1996)*

| | family households | | | | nonfamily households | | | |
| | | | | | female householder | | male householder | |
| | total | married couples | female hh no spouse present | male hh no spouse present | total | living alone | total | living alone |
|---|---|---|---|---|---|---|---|---|
| **Total households** | **11,907** | **6,175** | **913** | **251** | **3,239** | **3,136** | **1,329** | **1,241** |
| Under $10,000 | 1,985 | 238 | 129 | 25 | 1,228 | 1,226 | 365 | 355 |
| $10,000 to $19,999 | 3,195 | 1,235 | 236 | 61 | 1,226 | 1,201 | 437 | 421 |
| $20,000 to $29,999 | 2,290 | 1,432 | 202 | 29 | 392 | 349 | 235 | 216 |
| $30,000 to $39,999 | 1,471 | 998 | 115 | 49 | 204 | 191 | 105 | 97 |
| $40,000 to $49,999 | 942 | 668 | 94 | 30 | 95 | 90 | 55 | 49 |
| $50,000 to $59,999 | 605 | 457 | 64 | 15 | 26 | 22 | 43 | 35 |
| $60,000 to $69,999 | 406 | 299 | 29 | 10 | 36 | 26 | 32 | 29 |
| $70,000 to $79,999 | 209 | 157 | 20 | 11 | 7 | 7 | 14 | 12 |
| $80,000 to $89,999 | 149 | 132 | 5 | 8 | 2 | 2 | 2 | 0 |
| $90,000 to $99,999 | 136 | 115 | 0 | 7 | 9 | 9 | 5 | 3 |
| $100,000 or more | 519 | 444 | 19 | 6 | 14 | 13 | 36 | 24 |
| Median income | $23,031 | $31,614 | $24,386 | $31,289 | $12,435 | $12,944 | $16,159 | $15,443 |
| **Total households** | **100.0%** | **100.0%** | **100.0%** | **100.0%** | **100.0%** | **100.0%** | **100.0%** | **100.0%** |
| Under $10,000 | 16.7 | 3.9 | 14.1 | 10.0 | 37.9 | 39.1 | 27.5 | 28.6 |
| $10,000 to $19,999 | 26.8 | 20.0 | 25.8 | 24.3 | 37.9 | 38.3 | 32.9 | 33.9 |
| $20,000 to $29,999 | 19.2 | 23.2 | 22.1 | 11.6 | 12.1 | 11.1 | 17.7 | 17.4 |
| $30,000 to $39,999 | 12.4 | 16.2 | 12.6 | 19.5 | 6.3 | 6.1 | 7.9 | 7.8 |
| $40,000 to $49,999 | 7.9 | 10.8 | 10.3 | 12.0 | 2.9 | 2.9 | 4.1 | 3.9 |
| $50,000 to $59,999 | 5.1 | 7.4 | 7.0 | 6.0 | 0.8 | 0.7 | 3.2 | 2.8 |
| $60,000 to $69,999 | 3.4 | 4.8 | 3.2 | 4.0 | 1.1 | 0.8 | 2.4 | 2.3 |
| $70,000 to $79,999 | 1.8 | 2.5 | 2.2 | 4.4 | 0.2 | 0.2 | 1.1 | 1.0 |
| $80,000 to $89,999 | 1.3 | 2.1 | 0.5 | 3.2 | 0.1 | 0.1 | 0.2 | 0.0 |
| $90,000 to $99,999 | 1.1 | 1.9 | 0.0 | 2.8 | 0.3 | 0.3 | 0.4 | 0.2 |
| $100,000 or more | 4.4 | 7.2 | 2.1 | 2.4 | 0.4 | 0.4 | 2.7 | 1.9 |

*Source: Bureau of the Census, unpublished tables from the 1996 Current Population Survey; calculations by New Strategist*

# Income Distribution of Households by Household Type, 1995: Aged 75 or Older

*(number and percent distribution of households headed by persons aged 75 or older, by income and household type, 1995; households in thousands as of 1996)*

| | family households | | | | nonfamily households | | | |
| | | | | | female householder | | male householder | |
| | total | married couples | female hh no spouse present | male hh no spouse present | total | living alone | total | living alone |
|---|---|---|---|---|---|---|---|---|
| Total households | 9,578 | 3,105 | 718 | 145 | 4,494 | 4,398 | 1,119 | 1,066 |
| Under $10,000 | 2,651 | 162 | 82 | 10 | 2,054 | 2,045 | 344 | 338 |
| $10,000 to $19,999 | 3,401 | 983 | 200 | 29 | 1,732 | 1,706 | 457 | 445 |
| $20,000 to $29,999 | 1,539 | 834 | 158 | 23 | 371 | 344 | 152 | 134 |
| $30,000 to $39,999 | 814 | 431 | 105 | 24 | 182 | 170 | 74 | 65 |
| $40,000 to $49,999 | 401 | 240 | 71 | 15 | 48 | 40 | 28 | 27 |
| $50,000 to $59,999 | 255 | 133 | 35 | 17 | 53 | 49 | 17 | 15 |
| $60,000 to $69,999 | 152 | 90 | 27 | 8 | 18 | 16 | 9 | 9 |
| $70,000 to $79,999 | 87 | 52 | 7 | 9 | 7 | 5 | 12 | 12 |
| $80,000 to $89,999 | 84 | 61 | 11 | 2 | 5 | 5 | 5 | 2 |
| $90,000 to $99,999 | 45 | 19 | 15 | 4 | 3 | 2 | 4 | 4 |
| $100,000 or more | 149 | 100 | 7 | 4 | 21 | 16 | 17 | 15 |
| Median income | $23,031 | $24,381 | $24,897 | $33,992 | $10,744 | $10,619 | $14,018 | $13,607 |
| Total households | 100.0% | 100.0% | 100.0% | 100.0% | 100.0% | 100.0% | 100.0% | 100.0% |
| Under $10,000 | 27.7 | 5.2 | 11.4 | 6.9 | 45.7 | 46.5 | 30.7 | 31.7 |
| $10,000 to $19,999 | 35.5 | 31.7 | 27.9 | 20.0 | 38.5 | 38.8 | 40.8 | 41.7 |
| $20,000 to $29,999 | 16.1 | 26.9 | 22.0 | 15.9 | 8.3 | 7.8 | 13.6 | 12.6 |
| $30,000 to $39,999 | 8.5 | 13.9 | 14.6 | 16.6 | 4.0 | 3.9 | 6.6 | 6.1 |
| $40,000 to $49,999 | 4.2 | 7.7 | 9.9 | 10.3 | 1.1 | 0.9 | 2.5 | 2.5 |
| $50,000 to $59,999 | 2.7 | 4.3 | 4.9 | 11.7 | 1.2 | 1.1 | 1.5 | 1.4 |
| $60,000 to $69,999 | 1.6 | 2.9 | 3.8 | 5.5 | 0.4 | 0.4 | 0.8 | 0.8 |
| $70,000 to $79,999 | 0.9 | 1.7 | 1.0 | 6.2 | 0.2 | 0.1 | 1.1 | 1.1 |
| $80,000 to $89,999 | 0.9 | 2.0 | 1.5 | 1.4 | 0.1 | 0.1 | 0.4 | 0.2 |
| $90,000 to $99,999 | 0.5 | 0.6 | 2.1 | 2.8 | 0.1 | 0.0 | 0.4 | 0.4 |
| $100,000 or more | 1.6 | 3.2 | 1.0 | 2.8 | 0.5 | 0.4 | 1.5 | 1.4 |

*Source: Bureau of the Census, unpublished tables from the 1996 Current Population Survey; calculations by New Strategist*

# Older Whites Have Much Higher Incomes than Blacks or Hispanics

## The greatest income disparity is in the 55-to-64 age group.

White householders aged 55 to 64 had a median income of $40,150 in 1995, nearly double the $21,843 median for blacks and $22,859 median for Hispanics. More than 1 million white householders in this age group had incomes of $100,000 or more. White incomes are higher than black because white households in the age group are much more likely to be headed by married couples—many of whom are dual earners. White incomes exceed those of Hispanics because many Hispanics are immigrants with little education, earning power, or pension benefits.

Black householders aged 75 or older have the lowest incomes, just $9,866 in 1995. This is the only age group in which the median household income of Hispanics significantly exceeds that of blacks. Hispanic householders aged 75 or older had a median income of $12,277 in 1995—not far below the $15,807 median for white householders.

◆ The income disparities among older householders by race and ethnicity will persist in the future because their underlying causes—the small proportion of married-couple households among blacks and the immigrant status of Hispanics—also exist in younger generations of Americans.

# Income Distribution of Households by Race and Hispanic Origin of Householder, 1995: Aged 55 to 64

*(number and percent distribution of households headed by persons aged 55 to 64 by income, race, and Hispanic origin, 1995; households in thousands as of 1996)*

| | total | white | black | Hispanic |
|---|---|---|---|---|
| **Number** | | | | |
| **Total households, aged 55 to 64** | **12,806** | **10,613** | **1,385** | **808** |
| Under $10,000 | 1,575 | 1,075 | 337 | 163 |
| $10,000 to $19,999 | 1,908 | 1,437 | 279 | 192 |
| $20,000 to $29,999 | 1,747 | 1,399 | 222 | 126 |
| $30,000 to $39,999 | 1,659 | 1,376 | 173 | 110 |
| $40,000 to $49,999 | 1,304 | 1,120 | 131 | 53 |
| $50,000 to $59,999 | 1,019 | 907 | 56 | 56 |
| $60,000 to $69,999 | 835 | 763 | 40 | 32 |
| $70,000 to $79,999 | 702 | 632 | 50 | 20 |
| $80,000 to $89,999 | 457 | 423 | 25 | 9 |
| $90,000 to $99,999 | 381 | 343 | 16 | 22 |
| $100,000 or more | 1,219 | 1,138 | 56 | 25 |
| Median income | $38,077 | $40,150 | $21,843 | $22,859 |
| **Percent** | | | | |
| **Total households, aged 55 to 64** | **100.0%** | **100.0%** | **100.0%** | **100.0%** |
| Under $10,000 | 12.3 | 10.1 | 24.3 | 20.2 |
| $10,000 to $19,999 | 14.9 | 13.5 | 20.1 | 23.8 |
| $20,000 to $29,999 | 13.6 | 13.2 | 16.0 | 15.6 |
| $30,000 to $39,999 | 13.0 | 13.0 | 12.5 | 13.6 |
| $40,000 to $49,999 | 10.2 | 10.6 | 9.5 | 6.6 |
| $50,000 to $59,999 | 8.0 | 8.5 | 4.0 | 6.9 |
| $60,000 to $69,999 | 6.5 | 7.2 | 2.9 | 4.0 |
| $70,000 to $79,999 | 5.5 | 6.0 | 3.6 | 2.5 |
| $80,000 to $89,999 | 3.6 | 4.0 | 1.8 | 1.1 |
| $90,000 to $99,999 | 3.0 | 3.2 | 1.2 | 2.7 |
| $100,000 or more | 9.5 | 10.7 | 4.0 | 3.1 |

*Note: Numbers will not add to total because Hispanics may be of any race and not all races are shown.*
*Source: Bureau of the Census, unpublished tables from the 1996 Current Population Survey; calculations by New Strategist*

# Income Distribution of Households by Race and Hispanic Origin of Householder, 1995: Aged 65 or Older

*(number and percent distribution of households headed by persons aged 65 or older by income, race, and Hispanic origin, 1995; households in thousands as of 1996)*

| | total | white | black | Hispanic |
|---|---|---|---|---|
| **Number** | | | | |
| **Total households, aged 65 or older** | **21,486** | **19,326** | **1,777** | **898** |
| Under $10,000 | 4,634 | 3,844 | 689 | 345 |
| $10,000 to $19,999 | 6,595 | 6,026 | 487 | 240 |
| $20,000 to $29,999 | 3,828 | 3,516 | 244 | 135 |
| $30,000 to $39,999 | 2,288 | 2,139 | 115 | 65 |
| $40,000 to $49,999 | 1,345 | 1,213 | 104 | 46 |
| $50,000 to $59,999 | 873 | 806 | 41 | 26 |
| $60,000 to $69,999 | 561 | 512 | 35 | 14 |
| $70,000 to $79,999 | 299 | 276 | 17 | 6 |
| $80,000 to $89,999 | 229 | 201 | 20 | 6 |
| $90,000 to $99,999 | 183 | 170 | 6 | 6 |
| $100,000 or more | 651 | 623 | 19 | 9 |
| Median income | $19,096 | $19,590 | $13,246 | $13,513 |
| **Percent** | | | | |
| **Total households, aged 65 or older** | **100.0%** | **100.0%** | **100.0%** | **100.0%** |
| Under $10,000 | 21.6 | 19.9 | 38.8 | 38.4 |
| $10,000 to $19,999 | 30.7 | 31.2 | 27.4 | 26.7 |
| $20,000 to $29,999 | 17.8 | 18.2 | 13.7 | 15.0 |
| $30,000 to $39,999 | 10.6 | 11.1 | 6.5 | 7.2 |
| $40,000 to $49,999 | 6.3 | 6.3 | 5.9 | 5.1 |
| $50,000 to $59,999 | 4.1 | 4.2 | 2.3 | 2.9 |
| $60,000 to $69,999 | 2.6 | 2.6 | 2.0 | 1.6 |
| $70,000 to $79,999 | 1.4 | 1.4 | 1.0 | 0.7 |
| $80,000 to $89,999 | 1.1 | 1.0 | 1.1 | 0.7 |
| $90,000 to $99,999 | 0.9 | 0.9 | 0.3 | 0.7 |
| $100,000 or more | 3.0 | 3.2 | 1.1 | 1.0 |

*Note: Numbers will not add to total because Hispanics may be of any race and not all races are shown.*
*Source: Bureau of the Census, unpublished tables from the 1996 Current Population Survey; calculations by New Strategist*

## Income Distribution of Households by Race and Hispanic Origin of Householder, 1995: Aged 65 to 74

*(number and percent distribution of households headed by persons aged 65 to 74 by income, race, and Hispanic origin, 1995; households in thousands as of 1996)*

|  | total | white | black | Hispanic |
|---|---|---|---|---|
| **Number** | | | | |
| **Total households, aged 65 to 74** | **11,907** | **10,583** | **1,064** | **609** |
| Under $10,000 | 1,983 | 1,593 | 326 | 221 |
| $10,000 to $19,999 | 3,196 | 2,841 | 300 | 149 |
| $20,000 to $29,999 | 2,289 | 2,068 | 177 | 97 |
| $30,000 to $39,999 | 1,471 | 1,370 | 74 | 55 |
| $40,000 to $49,999 | 943 | 848 | 78 | 29 |
| $50,000 to $59,999 | 611 | 568 | 26 | 22 |
| $60,000 to $69,999 | 411 | 373 | 26 | 12 |
| $70,000 to $79,999 | 213 | 190 | 17 | 6 |
| $80,000 to $89,999 | 147 | 125 | 17 | 5 |
| $90,000 to $99,999 | 136 | 128 | 4 | 4 |
| $100,000 or more | 507 | 479 | 19 | 9 |
| Median income | $23,031 | $23,816 | $15,925 | $14,561 |
| **Percent** | | | | |
| **Total households, aged 65 to 74** | **100.0%** | **100.0%** | **100.0%** | **100.0%** |
| Under $10,000 | 16.7 | 15.1 | 30.6 | 36.3 |
| $10,000 to $19,999 | 26.8 | 26.8 | 28.2 | 24.5 |
| $20,000 to $29,999 | 19.2 | 19.5 | 16.6 | 15.9 |
| $30,000 to $39,999 | 12.4 | 12.9 | 7.0 | 9.0 |
| $40,000 to $49,999 | 7.9 | 8.0 | 7.3 | 4.8 |
| $50,000 to $59,999 | 5.1 | 5.4 | 2.4 | 3.6 |
| $60,000 to $69,999 | 3.5 | 3.5 | 2.4 | 2.0 |
| $70,000 to $79,999 | 1.8 | 1.8 | 1.6 | 1.0 |
| $80,000 to $89,999 | 1.2 | 1.2 | 1.6 | 0.8 |
| $90,000 to $99,999 | 1.1 | 1.2 | 0.4 | 0.7 |
| $100,000 or more | 4.3 | 4.5 | 1.8 | 1.5 |

*Note: Numbers will not add to total because Hispanics may be of any race and not all races are shown.*
*Source: Bureau of the Census, unpublished tables from the 1996 Current Population Survey; calculations by New Strategist*

# Income Distribution of Households by Race and Hispanic Origin of Householder, 1995: Aged 75 or Older

*(number and percent distribution of households headed by persons aged 75 or older by income, race, and Hispanic origin, 1995; households in thousands as of 1996)*

| Number | total | white | black | Hispanic |
|---|---|---|---|---|
| Total households, aged 65 to 74 | 9,578 | 8,743 | 713 | 289 |
| Under $10,000 | 2,651 | 2,252 | 362 | 124 |
| $10,000 to $19,999 | 3,402 | 3,184 | 187 | 90 |
| $20,000 to $29,999 | 1,539 | 1,446 | 67 | 37 |
| $30,000 to $39,999 | 814 | 769 | 43 | 11 |
| $40,000 to $49,999 | 401 | 365 | 25 | 19 |
| $50,000 to $59,999 | 257 | 238 | 14 | 4 |
| $60,000 to $69,999 | 151 | 140 | 9 | 1 |
| $70,000 to $79,999 | 88 | 86 | 1 | 0 |
| $80,000 to $89,999 | 83 | 76 | 3 | 1 |
| $90,000 to $99,999 | 48 | 43 | 2 | 2 |
| $100,000 or more | 144 | 144 | 0 | 0 |
| Median income | $15,342 | $15,807 | $9,866 | $12,277 |
| **Percent** | | | | |
| Total households, aged 65 to 74 | 100.0% | 100.0% | 100.0% | 100.0% |
| Under $10,000 | 27.7 | 25.8 | 50.8 | 42.9 |
| $10,000 to $19,999 | 35.5 | 36.4 | 26.2 | 31.1 |
| $20,000 to $29,999 | 16.1 | 16.5 | 9.4 | 12.8 |
| $30,000 to $39,999 | 8.5 | 8.8 | 6.0 | 3.8 |
| $40,000 to $49,999 | 4.2 | 4.2 | 3.5 | 6.6 |
| $50,000 to $59,999 | 2.7 | 2.7 | 2.0 | 1.4 |
| $60,000 to $69,999 | 1.6 | 1.6 | 1.3 | 0.3 |
| $70,000 to $79,999 | 0.9 | 1.0 | 0.1 | 0.0 |
| $80,000 to $89,999 | 0.9 | 0.9 | 0.4 | 0.3 |
| $90,000 to $99,999 | 0.5 | 0.5 | 0.3 | 0.7 |
| $100,000 or more | 1.5 | 1.6 | 0.0 | 0.0 |

*Note: Numbers will not add to total because Hispanics may be of any race and not all races are shown.*
*Source: Bureau of the Census, unpublished tables from the 1996 Current Population Survey; calculations by New Strategist*

# Different Income Trends for Older Men and Women

**Women aged 55 to 64 have seen their incomes grow rapidly, while men in this age group have seen their incomes fall.**

Between 1980 and 1995, men aged 55 to 64 saw their median personal income fall 2 percent, after adjusting for inflation. In contrast, women in this age group experienced a 36 percent increase in median personal income during those years. Nevertheless, men's incomes remain far above women's—$28,980 versus $12,381 in 1995.

Behind the falling incomes of men aged 55 to 64 is the growing prevalence of early retirement. As an ever-larger share of men aged 55 to 64 drop out of the labor force, incomes fall. The opposite trend is occurring among women, whose incomes are rising because a growing share are entering the labor force.

Income trends are relatively similar among men and women aged 65 or older. Both sexes have experienced income gains since 1980, with men's increase slightly greater than women's. As of 1995, men aged 65 or older had a median income of $16,484 versus women's $9,355. Behind the income gains in this age group is a more-prosperous elderly generation replacing less-affluent older people.

◆ The median income of women aged 55 to 64 should continue to surge as the working women of the baby-boom generation enter the age group. Men's incomes could also grow if early retirement loses its popularity.

## Older Women See Income Gains

*(percent change in median income of men and women aged 55 or older, 1980 to 1995; in 1995 dollars)*

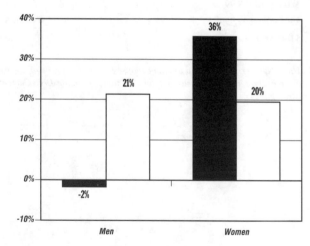

# Median Income of Men Aged 55 or Older, 1980 to 1995

*(median income of total men aged 16 or older and men aged 55 or older, 1980 to 1995; in 1995 dollars)*

| | total men | 55 to 64 | men aged 65 or older | | |
| --- | --- | --- | --- | --- | --- |
| | | | total | 65 to 74 | 75+ |
| 1995 | $22,562 | $28,980 | $16,484 | $18,347 | $14,160 |
| 1994 | 22,336 | 27,842 | 15,682 | 17,069 | 14,046 |
| 1993 | 22,256 | 26,513 | 15,802 | 17,176 | 14,156 |
| 1992 | 22,219 | 27,824 | 15,856 | 17,174 | 13,997 |
| 1991 | 22,904 | 28,488 | 16,065 | 17,159 | 14,588 |
| 1990 | 23,662 | 28,922 | 16,538 | 18,619 | 13,620 |
| 1989 | 24,449 | 20,022 | 16,109 | 17,778 | 13,331 |
| 1988 | 24,358 | 29,175 | 16,066 | 17,959 | 13,176 |
| 1987 | 23,861 | 29,357 | 16,001 | 17,993 | 13,010 |
| 1986 | 23,797 | 29,248 | 16,052 | - | - |
| 1985 | 23,102 | 28,691 | 15,438 | - | - |
| 1984 | 22,882 | 28,642 | 15,328 | - | - |
| 1983 | 22,387 | 28,604 | 14,906 | - | - |
| 1982 | 22,238 | 28,420 | 14,647 | - | - |
| 1981 | 22,789 | 29,372 | 13,765 | - | - |
| 1980 | 23,203 | 29,469 | 13,590 | - | - |
| **Percent change** | | | | | |
| 1994-1995 | 1.0% | 4.1% | 5.1% | 7.5% | 0.8% |
| 1990-1995 | -4.6 | 0.2 | -0.3 | -1.5 | 4.0 |
| 1980-1995 | -2.8 | -1.7 | 21.3 | - | - |

*Note: (-) means data not available.*
*Source: Bureau of the Census, Internet web site, http://www.census.gov; calculations by New Strategist*

# Median Income of Women Aged 55 or Older, 1980 to 1995

*(median income of total women aged 16 or older and women aged 55 or older, 1980 to 1995; in 1995 dollars)*

| | | | women aged 65 or older | | |
|---|---|---|---|---|---|
| | total women | 55 to 64 | total | 65 to 74 | 75+ |
| 1995 | $12,130 | $12,381 | $9,355 | $9,277 | $9,427 |
| 1994 | 11,791 | 11,175 | 9,204 | 9,076 | 9,319 |
| 1993 | 11,650 | 11,421 | 8,964 | 9,120 | 8,822 |
| 1992 | 11,638 | 11,007 | 8,889 | 8,923 | 8,854 |
| 1991 | 11,722 | 11,080 | 9,163 | 9,103 | 9,221 |
| 1990 | 11,742 | 10,961 | 9,380 | 9,550 | 9,201 |
| 1989 | 11,828 | 11,262 | 9,408 | 9,768 | 9,067 |
| 1988 | 11,445 | 10,792 | 9,150 | 9,348 | 8,946 |
| 1987 | 11,128 | 10,117 | 9,251 | 9,372 | 9,120 |
| 1986 | 10,582 | 10,258 | 8,934 | - | - |
| 1985 | 10,222 | 10,160 | 8,941 | - | - |
| 1984 | 10,074 | 10,028 | 8,830 | - | - |
| 1983 | 9,669 | 9,378 | 8,567 | - | - |
| 1982 | 9,385 | 9,417 | 8,553 | - | - |
| 1981 | 9,232 | 9,092 | 7,960 | - | - |
| 1980 | 9,111 | 9,122 | 7,826 | - | - |
| **Percent change** | | | | | |
| 1994-1995 | 2.9% | 10.8% | 1.6% | 2.2% | 1.2% |
| 1990-1995 | 3.3 | 13.0 | -0.3 | -2.9 | 2.5 |
| 1980-1995 | 33.1 | 35.7 | 19.5 | - | - |

*Note: (-) means data not available.*
*Source: Bureau of the Census, Internet web site, http://www.census.gov; calculations by New Strategist*

# High Incomes for Older Workers

## Men aged 65 or older who work full-time had a median income above $41,000 in 1995.

Among full-time workers, those with the highest incomes are the oldest men. Men aged 75 or older who work full-time had a median income of $42,047 in 1995, higher than men in any other age group. But only 3 percent of men in this age group are full-time workers. In the 55-to-64 age group, 54 percent of men work full-time, a figure that falls to just 11 percent among men aged 65 to 74. As men drop out of the labor force, their median income drops sharply with age.

The pattern is the same for women. Among those aged 75 or older who work full-time, median income was $27,411 in 1995—much higher than the $9,427 median income of all women in this age group. Fewer than 1 percent of women aged 75 or older work full-time, however. Among women aged 55 to 64, a substantial 31 percent work full-time, and their median income was $24,121 in 1995.

◆ The proportion of older men and women who work full-time would rise if the federal government eliminated the disincentive to work—Social Security benefits are reduced when beneficiaries earn over a certain income threshhold.

### Older Men Are Highest Paid

*(median income of total men aged 16 or older and men aged 55 or older who are year-round, full-time workers, 1995)*

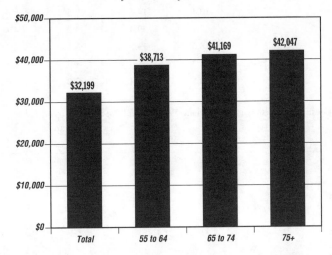

# Income Distribution of Men Aged 55 or Older, 1995

*(number and percent distribution of total men aged 16 or older and men aged 55 or older by income, 1995; men in thousands as of 1996)*

| | total | aged 55 or older total | 55 to 64 | aged 65 or older total | 65 to 74 | 75+ |
|---|---|---|---|---|---|---|
| **Total men, number** | **98,593** | **23,352** | **10,092** | **13,260** | **8,213** | **5,047** |
| **Without income** | **6,527** | **398** | **229** | **169** | **81** | **87** |
| **With income** | **92,066** | **22,955** | **9,863** | **13,092** | **8,131** | **4,960** |
| Under $10,000 | 19,772 | 4,464 | 1,416 | 3,048 | 1,663 | 1,386 |
| $10,000 to $19,999 | 20,674 | 6,910 | 1,954 | 4,956 | 2,822 | 2,134 |
| $20,000 to $29,999 | 16,594 | 4,175 | 1,701 | 2,474 | 1,673 | 800 |
| $30,000 to $39,999 | 12,022 | 2,440 | 1,451 | 989 | 740 | 249 |
| $40,000 to $49,999 | 7,810 | 1,381 | 952 | 429 | 333 | 96 |
| $50,000 to $74,999 | 9,382 | 2,016 | 1,336 | 680 | 498 | 182 |
| $75,000 to $99,999 | 2,874 | 753 | 507 | 246 | 191 | 55 |
| $100,000 or more | 2,937 | 814 | 544 | 270 | 212 | 59 |
| Median income | $22,562 | $21,980 | $28,980 | $16,494 | $18,347 | $14,160 |
| Median income, year-round full-time workers | 32,199 | 39,126 | 38,713 | 41,259 | 41,169 | 42,047 |
| Percent of men who work year-round, full-time | 53.4% | 27.6% | 53.6% | 7.9% | 11.0% | 2.8% |
| **Total men, percent** | **100.0%** | **100.0%** | **100.0%** | **100.0%** | **100.0%** | **100.0%** |
| **Without income** | **6.6** | **1.7** | **2.3** | **1.3** | **1.0** | **1.7** |
| **With income** | **93.4** | **98.3** | **97.7** | **98.7** | **99.0** | **98.3** |
| Under $10,000 | 20.1 | 19.1 | 14.0 | 23.0 | 20.2 | 27.5 |
| $10,000 to $19,999 | 21.0 | 29.6 | 19.4 | 37.4 | 34.4 | 42.3 |
| $20,000 to $29,999 | 16.8 | 17.9 | 16.9 | 18.7 | 20.4 | 15.9 |
| $30,000 to $39,999 | 12.2 | 10.4 | 14.4 | 7.5 | 9.0 | 4.9 |
| $40,000 to $49,999 | 7.9 | 5.9 | 9.4 | 3.2 | 4.1 | 1.9 |
| $50,000 to $74,999 | 9.5 | 8.6 | 13.2 | 5.1 | 6.1 | 3.6 |
| $75,000 to $99,999 | 2.9 | 3.2 | 5.0 | 1.9 | 2.3 | 1.1 |
| $100,000 or more | 3.0 | 3.5 | 5.4 | 2.0 | 2.6 | 1.2 |

*Source: Bureau of the Census, unpublished tables from the 1996 Current Population Survey; calculations by New Strategist*

# Income Distribution of Women Aged 55 or Older, 1995

*(number and percent distribution of total women aged 16 or older and women aged 55 or older by income, 1995; women in thousands as of 1996)*

| | | aged 55 or older | | | | |
| | | | | aged 65 or older | | |
| | *total* | *total* | *55 to 64* | *total* | *65 to 74* | *75+* |
|---|---|---|---|---|---|---|
| **Total women, number** | 106,031 | 29,388 | 10,992 | 18,396 | 10,057 | 8,341 |
| **Without income** | 10,025 | 1,387 | 978 | 409 | 231 | 177 |
| **With income** | 96,007 | 28,004 | 10,014 | 17,990 | 9,826 | 8,163 |
| Under $10,000 | 41,101 | 14,115 | 4,311 | 9,804 | 5,352 | 4,451 |
| $10,000 to $19,999 | 24,619 | 7,969 | 2,522 | 5,447 | 2,817 | 2,629 |
| $20,000 to $29,999 | 14,097 | 2,892 | 1,410 | 1,482 | 886 | 596 |
| $30,000 to $39,999 | 7,831 | 1,414 | 758 | 656 | 396 | 260 |
| $40,000 to $49,999 | 3,971 | 673 | 438 | 235 | 165 | 70 |
| $50,000 to $74,999 | 3,136 | 634 | 378 | 256 | 150 | 106 |
| $75,000 to $99,999 | 708 | 168 | 117 | 51 | 32 | 19 |
| $100,000 or more | 544 | 139 | 81 | 58 | 27 | 31 |
| Median income | $12,130 | $10,487 | $12,381 | $9,355 | $9,277 | $9,427 |
| Median income, year-round full-time workers | 23,777 | 24,432 | 24,121 | 26,606 | 26,215 | 27,411 |
| Percent of women who work year-round, full-time | 33.5% | 13.4% | 31.2% | 2.7% | 4.1% | 0.9% |
| **Total women, percent** | **100.0%** | **100.0%** | **100.0%** | **100.0%** | **100.0%** | **100.0%** |
| **Without income** | **9.5** | **4.7** | **8.9** | **2.2** | **2.3** | **2.1** |
| **With income** | **90.5** | **95.3** | **91.1** | **97.8** | **97.7** | **97.9** |
| Under $10,000 | 38.8 | 48.0 | 39.2 | 53.3 | 53.2 | 53.4 |
| $10,000 to $19,999 | 23.2 | 27.1 | 22.9 | 29.6 | 28.0 | 31.5 |
| $20,000 to $29,999 | 13.3 | 9.8 | 12.8 | 8.1 | 8.8 | 7.1 |
| $30,000 to $39,999 | 7.4 | 4.8 | 6.9 | 3.6 | 3.9 | 3.1 |
| $40,000 to $49,999 | 3.7 | 2.3 | 4.0 | 1.3 | 1.6 | 0.8 |
| $50,000 to $74,999 | 3.0 | 2.2 | 3.4 | 1.4 | 1.5 | 1.3 |
| $75,000 to $99,999 | 0.7 | 0.6 | 1.1 | 0.3 | 0.3 | 0.2 |
| $100,000 or more | 0.5 | 0.5 | 0.7 | 0.3 | 0.3 | 0.4 |

*Source: Bureau of the Census, unpublished tables from the 1996 Current Population Survey; calculations by New Strategist*

# Among Older Men, Whites Have Much Higher Incomes than Blacks or Hispanics

## Gaps between white and black and Hispanic women are much smaller.

Among men aged 55 to 64, 54 percent of whites, 50 percent of Hispanics, and 46 percent of blacks work full-time. Among these full-time workers, white men had a median income of $40,095 versus just $28,267 for blacks and $22,124 for Hispanics. In the 65-plus age group, the income gaps between white and black and Hispanic men shrink considerably because few men work full-time. White men aged 65 or older had a median income of $16,886 versus $11,570 for blacks and $9,794 for Hispanics.

There is less income disparity among older women by race and ethnicity. In the 55-to-64 age group, 31 percent of white women work full-time, as do 30 percent of black and 27 percent of Hispanic women. The median incomes of these full-time workers range from a high of $25,005 for whites to $19,843 for Hispanics. In the 65-plus age group, women's incomes are low regardless of race or Hispanic origin. White women aged 65 or older had an income of just $9,654 in 1995, versus $7,097 for black and $6,652 for Hispanic women.

◆ The incomes of older women should rise in the years ahead as the working women of the baby-boom generation enter the 55-plus age group. But the income disparity by race and ethnicity will persist—and could even increase—because of the higher educational level of whites.

# Income Distribution of Men by Race and Hispanic Origin, 1995: Aged 55 to 64

*(number and percent distribution of men aged 55 to 64 by income, race, and Hispanic origin, 1995; men in thousands as of 1996)*

| | total | white | black | Hispanic |
|---|---|---|---|---|
| **Number** | | | | |
| **Total men, aged 55 to 64** | **10,092** | **8,826** | **934** | **681** |
| **Without income** | **229** | **166** | **41** | **31** |
| **With income** | **9,863** | **8,660** | **893** | **650** |
| Under $10,000 | 1,416 | 1,116 | 229 | 183 |
| $10,000 to $19,999 | 1,954 | 1,647 | 247 | 205 |
| $20,000 to $29,999 | 1,701 | 1,489 | 157 | 108 |
| $30,000 to $39,999 | 1,451 | 1,325 | 87 | 65 |
| $40,000 to $49,999 | 952 | 836 | 83 | 35 |
| $50,000 to $74,999 | 1,336 | 1,254 | 59 | 35 |
| $75,000 to $99,999 | 507 | 467 | 24 | 12 |
| $100,000 or more | 544 | 525 | 8 | 7 |
| Median income | $28,980 | $30,425 | $18,694 | $16,215 |
| Median income, year-round full-time workers | 38,713 | 40,095 | 28,267 | 22,124 |
| Percent of men who work year-round, full-time | 53.6% | 54.1% | 45.5% | 50.2% |
| **Percent** | | | | |
| **Total men, aged 55 to 64** | **100.0%** | **100.0%** | **100.0%** | **100.0%** |
| **Without income** | **2.3** | **1.9** | **4.4** | **4.6** |
| **With income** | **97.7** | **98.1** | **95.6** | **95.4** |
| Under $10,000 | 14.0 | 12.6 | 24.5 | 26.9 |
| $10,000 to $19,999 | 19.4 | 18.7 | 26.4 | 30.1 |
| $20,000 to $29,999 | 16.9 | 16.9 | 16.8 | 15.9 |
| $30,000 to $39,999 | 14.4 | 15.0 | 9.3 | 9.5 |
| $40,000 to $49,999 | 9.4 | 9.5 | 8.9 | 5.1 |
| $50,000 to $74,999 | 13.2 | 14.2 | 6.3 | 5.1 |
| $75,000 to $99,999 | 5.0 | 5.3 | 2.6 | 1.8 |
| $100,000 or more | 5.4 | 5.9 | 0.9 | 1.0 |

*Note: Numbers will not add to total because Hispanics may be of any race and not all races are shown.*
*Source: Bureau of the Census, unpublished tables from the 1996 Current Population Survey; calculations by New Strategist*

# Income Distribution of Men by Race and Hispanic Origin, 1995: Aged 65 or Older

*(number and percent distribution of men aged 65 or older by income, race, and Hispanic origin, 1995; men in thousands as of 1996)*

|  | total | white | black | Hispanic |
|---|---|---|---|---|
| **Number** | | | | |
| Total men, aged 65 or older | **13,260** | **12,041** | **900** | **614** |
| Without income | **169** | **125** | **19** | **36** |
| With income | **13,092** | **11,916** | **881** | **578** |
| Under $10,000 | 3,048 | 2,559 | 389 | 298 |
| $10,000 to $19,999 | 4,956 | 4,571 | 298 | 175 |
| $20,000 to $29,999 | 2,474 | 2,339 | 90 | 54 |
| $30,000 to $39,999 | 989 | 930 | 35 | 23 |
| $40,000 to $49,999 | 429 | 399 | 27 | 11 |
| $50,000 to $74,999 | 680 | 634 | 25 | 11 |
| $75,000 to $99,999 | 246 | 229 | 9 | 1 |
| $100,000 or more | 270 | 256 | 9 | 5 |
| Median income | $16,484 | $16,886 | $11,570 | $9,794 |
| Median income, year-round full-time workers | 41,259 | 41,240 | - | - |
| Percent of men who work year-round, full-time | 7.9% | 7.8% | 8.3% | 7.7% |
| **Percent** | | | | |
| Total men, aged 65 or older | **100.0%** | **100.0%** | **100.0%** | **100.0%** |
| Without income | **1.3** | **1.0** | **2.1** | **5.9** |
| With income | **98.7** | **99.0** | **97.9** | **94.1** |
| Under $10,000 | 23.0 | 21.3 | 43.2 | 48.5 |
| $10,000 to $19,999 | 37.4 | 38.0 | 33.1 | 28.5 |
| $20,000 to $29,999 | 18.7 | 19.4 | 10.0 | 8.8 |
| $30,000 to $39,999 | 7.5 | 7.7 | 3.9 | 3.7 |
| $40,000 to $49,999 | 3.2 | 3.3 | 3.0 | 1.8 |
| $50,000 to $74,999 | 5.1 | 5.3 | 2.8 | 1.8 |
| $75,000 to $99,999 | 1.9 | 1.9 | 1.0 | 0.2 |
| $100,000 or more | 2.0 | 2.1 | 1.0 | 0.8 |

*Note: Numbers will not add to total because Hispanics may be of any race and not all races are shown; (-) means sample is too small to make a reliable estimate.*
*Source: Bureau of the Census, unpublished tables from the 1996 Current Population Survey; calculations by New Strategist*

# Income Distribution of Women by Race and Hispanic Origin, 1995: Aged 55 to 64

*(number and percent distribution of women aged 55 to 64 by income, race, and Hispanic origin, 1995; women in thousands as of 1996)*

| | total | white | black | Hispanic |
|---|---|---|---|---|
| **Number** | | | | |
| **Total women, 55 to 64** | **10,992** | **9,370** | **1,190** | **810** |
| **Without income** | **978** | **751** | **155** | **173** |
| **With income** | **10,014** | **8,619** | **1,035** | **638** |
| Under $10,000 | 4,311 | 3,660 | 496 | 372 |
| $10,000 to $19,999 | 2,522 | 2,144 | 269 | 142 |
| $20,000 to $29,999 | 1,410 | 1,232 | 137 | 72 |
| $30,000 to $39,999 | 758 | 666 | 73 | 27 |
| $40,000 to $49,999 | 438 | 396 | 26 | 12 |
| $50,000 to $74,999 | 378 | 340 | 28 | 10 |
| $75,000 to $99,999 | 117 | 105 | 4 | 0 |
| $100,000 or more | 81 | 76 | 3 | 4 |
| Median income | $12,381 | $12,631 | $10,660 | $7,285 |
| Median income, year-round full-time workers | 24,121 | 25,005 | 20,801 | 19,843 |
| Percent of women who work year-round, full-time | 31.2% | 31.2% | 30.4% | 26.5% |
| **Number** | | | | |
| **Total women, 55 to 64** | **100.0%** | **100.0%** | **100.0%** | **100.0%** |
| **Without income** | **8.9** | **8.0** | **13.0** | **21.4** |
| **With income** | **91.1** | **92.0** | **87.0** | **78.8** |
| Under $10,000 | 39.2 | 39.1 | 41.7 | 45.9 |
| $10,000 to $19,999 | 22.9 | 22.9 | 22.6 | 17.5 |
| $20,000 to $29,999 | 12.8 | 13.1 | 11.5 | 8.9 |
| $30,000 to $39,999 | 6.9 | 7.1 | 6.1 | 3.3 |
| $40,000 to $49,999 | 4.0 | 4.2 | 2.2 | 1.5 |
| $50,000 to $74,999 | 3.4 | 3.6 | 2.4 | 1.2 |
| $75,000 to $99,999 | 1.1 | 1.1 | 0.3 | 0.0 |
| $100,000 or more | 0.7 | 0.8 | 0.3 | 0.5 |

*Note: Numbers will not add to total because Hispanics may be of any race and not all races are shown.*
*Source: Bureau of the Census, unpublished tables from the 1996 Current Population Survey; calculations by New Strategist*

# Income Distribution of Women by Race and Hispanic Origin, 1995: Aged 65 or older

*(number and percent distribution of women aged 65 or older by income, race, and Hispanic origin, 1995; women in thousands as of 1996)*

| | total | white | black | Hispanic |
|---|---|---|---|---|
| **Number** | | | | |
| Total women, 65 or older | 18,396 | 16,395 | 1,577 | 844 |
| Without income | 409 | 260 | 74 | 56 |
| With income | 17,990 | 16,135 | 1,503 | 788 |
| Under $10,000 | 9,804 | 8,455 | 1,110 | 628 |
| $10,000 to $19,999 | 5,447 | 5,110 | 274 | 125 |
| $20,000 to $29,999 | 1,482 | 1,388 | 71 | 24 |
| $30,000 to $39,999 | 656 | 617 | 27 | 5 |
| $40,000 to $49,999 | 235 | 218 | 10 | 0 |
| $50,000 to $74,999 | 256 | 241 | 8 | 3 |
| $75,000 to $99,999 | 51 | 50 | 0 | 3 |
| $100,000 or more | 58 | 56 | 2 | 0 |
| Median income | $9,355 | $9,654 | $7,097 | $6,652 |
| Median income, year-round full-time workers | 26,606 | 26,530 | - | - |
| Percent of women who work year-round, full-time | 2.7% | 2.7% | 2.1% | 2.0% |
| **Percent** | | | | |
| Total women, 65 or older | 100.0% | 100.0% | 100.0% | 100.0% |
| Without income | 2.2 | 1.6 | 4.7 | 6.6 |
| With income | 97.8 | 98.4 | 95.3 | 93.4 |
| Under $10,000 | 53.3 | 51.6 | 70.4 | 74.4 |
| $10,000 to $19,999 | 29.6 | 31.2 | 17.4 | 14.8 |
| $20,000 to $29,999 | 8.1 | 8.5 | 4.5 | 2.8 |
| $30,000 to $39,999 | 3.6 | 3.8 | 1.7 | 0.6 |
| $40,000 to $49,999 | 1.3 | 1.3 | 0.6 | 0.0 |
| $50,000 to $74,999 | 1.4 | 1.5 | 0.5 | 0.4 |
| $75,000 to $99,999 | 0.3 | 0.3 | 0.0 | 0.4 |
| $100,000 or more | 0.3 | 0.3 | 0.1 | 0.0 |

*Note: Numbers will not add to total because Hispanics may be of any race and not all races are shown; (-) means sample is too small to make a reliable estimate.*
*Source: Bureau of the Census, unpublished tables from the 1996 Current Population Survey; calculations by New Strategist*

# College Education Boosts Earnings of Older Men and Women

## Women aged 55 to 64 with a college degree earned nearly twice as much as the average woman in that age group.

College-educated women aged 55 to 64 earned a median of $30,311 in 1995, nearly double the $16,077 median of all women in the age group. Of men aged 55 to 64, those with college degrees earned a median of $47,120, versus $30,639 for the average man of that age.

Getting an education boosts earnings not only because the college-educated command higher salaries at their jobs, but also because they are more likely to have jobs. Among men aged 55 to 64, 81 percent had earnings from a job in 1995. This compares with only 59 percent of men in that age group who did not graduate from high school. The same is true for women aged 55 to 64: 66 percent of those with college educations had earnings from a job, versus a much smaller 36 percent of those who did not graduate from high school.

Even in the 65-plus age group, education still plays a role. The median earnings of men aged 65 or older with a college degree stood at $24,024 in 1995, versus $11,465 for all men in the age group. One-third of men with college degrees had earnings in 1995 versus only 22 percent of all men in the age group.

◆ The rising affluence of older Americans is guaranteed because the highly educated baby-boom generation will soon enter the age group, boosting the proportion of older Americans who work and driving up earnings.

# Earnings Distribution of Men by Education, 1995: Aged 55 to 64

*(number and percent distribution of men aged 55 to 64 by earnings and education, 1995; men in thousands as of 1996)*

| | total | not a high school graduate | high school graduate | some college or assoc. degree | bachelor's degree or more |
|---|---|---|---|---|---|
| **Number** | | | | | |
| Total men, aged 55 to 64 | 10,092 | 2,259 | 3,300 | 1,986 | 2,548 |
| Without earnings | 2,773 | 929 | 862 | 508 | 474 |
| With earnings | 7,319 | 1,330 | 2,438 | 1,478 | 2,074 |
| Under $10,000 | 1,049 | 285 | 373 | 185 | 207 |
| $10,000 to $19,999 | 1,207 | 403 | 419 | 220 | 166 |
| $20,000 to $29,999 | 1,285 | 297 | 530 | 250 | 206 |
| $30,000 to $39,999 | 1,139 | 170 | 469 | 262 | 239 |
| $40,000 to $49,999 | 812 | 84 | 258 | 190 | 278 |
| $50,000 to $74,999 | 1,081 | 64 | 283 | 244 | 491 |
| $75,000 to $99,999 | 361 | 15 | 54 | 69 | 221 |
| $100,000 or more | 386 | 12 | 51 | 57 | 266 |
| Median earnings | $30,639 | $18,926 | $27,186 | $31,644 | $47,120 |
| Median earnings, year-round full-time workers | 26,091 | 22,787 | 31,288 | 38,392 | 52,082 |
| Percent of men who work year-round, full-time | 53.5% | 41.2% | 54.5% | 55.1% | 62.0% |
| **Percent** | | | | | |
| Total men, aged 55 to 64 | 100.0% | 100.0% | 100.0% | 100.0% | 100.0% |
| Without earnings | 27.5 | 41.1 | 26.1 | 25.6 | 18.6 |
| With earnings | 72.5 | 58.9 | 73.9 | 74.4 | 81.4 |
| Under $10,000 | 10.4 | 12.6 | 11.3 | 9.3 | 8.1 |
| $10,000 to $19,999 | 12.0 | 17.8 | 12.7 | 11.1 | 6.5 |
| $20,000 to $29,999 | 12.7 | 13.1 | 16.1 | 12.6 | 8.1 |
| $30,000 to $39,999 | 11.3 | 7.5 | 14.2 | 13.2 | 9.4 |
| $40,000 to $49,999 | 8.0 | 3.7 | 7.8 | 9.6 | 10.9 |
| $50,000 to $74,999 | 10.7 | 2.8 | 8.6 | 12.3 | 19.3 |
| $75,000 to $99,999 | 3.6 | 0.7 | 1.6 | 3.5 | 8.7 |
| $100,000 or more | 3.8 | 0.5 | 1.5 | 2.9 | 10.4 |

*Source: Bureau of the Census, unpublished tables from the 1996 Current Population Survey; calculations by New Strategist*

# Earnings Distribution of Men by Education, 1995: Aged 65 or Older

*(number and percent distribution of men aged 65 or older by earnings and education, 1995; men in thousands as of 1996)*

| | total | not a high school graduate | high school graduate | some college or assoc. degree | bachelor's degree or more |
|---|---|---|---|---|---|
| **Number** | | | | | |
| **Total men, aged 65 or older** | **13,260** | **4,589** | **3,897** | **2,268** | **2,507** |
| **Without earnings** | **10,397** | **3,922** | **3,113** | **1,693** | **1,668** |
| **With earnings** | **2,863** | **667** | **784** | **574** | **838** |
| Under $10,000 | 1,266 | 373 | 402 | 233 | 260 |
| $10,000 to $19,999 | 570 | 140 | 172 | 138 | 119 |
| $20,000 to $29,999 | 250 | 64 | 51 | 52 | 84 |
| $30,000 to $39,999 | 206 | 55 | 50 | 43 | 58 |
| $40,000 to $49,999 | 135 | 5 | 44 | 29 | 56 |
| $50,000 to $74,999 | 235 | 25 | 37 | 58 | 115 |
| $75,000 to $99,999 | 76 | 1 | 10 | 12 | 52 |
| $100,000 or more | 124 | 5 | 17 | 8 | 93 |
| Median earnings | $11,465 | $7,980 | $9,694 | $11,774 | $24,024 |
| Median earnings, year-round full-time workers | 31,756 | 18,616 | 31,211 | 30,659 | 50,077 |
| Percent of men who work year-round, full-time | 7.9% | 5.3% | 6.3% | 8.5% | 14.6% |
| **Percent** | | | | | |
| **Total men, aged 65 or older** | **100.0%** | **100.0%** | **100.0%** | **100.0%** | **100.0%** |
| **Without earnings** | **78.4** | **85.5** | **79.9** | **74.6** | **66.5** |
| **With earnings** | **21.6** | **14.5** | **20.1** | **25.3** | **33.4** |
| Under $10,000 | 9.5 | 8.1 | 10.3 | 10.3 | 10.4 |
| $10,000 to $19,999 | 4.3 | 3.1 | 4.4 | 6.1 | 4.7 |
| $20,000 to $29,999 | 1.9 | 1.4 | 1.3 | 2.3 | 3.4 |
| $30,000 to $39,999 | 1.6 | 1.2 | 1.3 | 1.9 | 2.3 |
| $40,000 to $49,999 | 1.0 | 0.1 | 1.1 | 1.3 | 2.2 |
| $50,000 to $74,999 | 1.8 | 0.5 | 0.9 | 2.6 | 4.6 |
| $75,000 to $99,999 | 0.6 | 0.0 | 0.3 | 0.5 | 2.1 |
| $100,000 or more | 0.9 | 0.1 | 0.4 | 0.4 | 3.7 |

*Source: Bureau of the Census, unpublished tables from the 1996 Current Population Survey; calculations by New Strategist*

# Earnings Distribution of Women by Education, 1995: Aged 55 to 64

*(number and percent distribution of women aged 55 to 64 by earnings and education, 1995; women in thousands as of 1996)*

| | total | not a high school graduate | high school graduate | some college or assoc. degree | bachelor's degree or more |
|---|---|---|---|---|---|
| **Number** | | | | | |
| **Total women, aged 55 to 64** | **10,992** | **2,493** | **4,501** | **2,282** | **1,716** |
| **Without earnings** | **4,973** | **1,606** | **1,963** | **816** | **587** |
| **With earnings** | **6,019** | **887** | **2,538** | **1,466** | **1,129** |
| Under $10,000 | 1,916 | 443 | 827 | 402 | 244 |
| $10,000 to $19,999 | 1,697 | 300 | 866 | 383 | 148 |
| $20,000 to $29,999 | 1,142 | 86 | 553 | 343 | 162 |
| $30,000 to $39,999 | 616 | 44 | 146 | 177 | 251 |
| $40,000 to $49,999 | 329 | 4 | 87 | 87 | 151 |
| $50,000 to $74,999 | 231 | 9 | 44 | 57 | 120 |
| $75,000 to $99,999 | 50 | 2 | 7 | 10 | 32 |
| $100,000 or more | 38 | 0 | 8 | 8 | 22 |
| Median earnings | $16,077 | $10,010 | $14,669 | $18,699 | $30,311 |
| Median earnings, year-round full-time workers | 22,178 | 16,029 | 20,096 | 23,653 | 35,956 |
| Percent of women who work year-round, full-time | 31.2% | 16.7% | 31.9% | 38.9% | 40.2% |
| **Percent** | | | | | |
| **Total women, aged 55 to 64** | **100.0%** | **100.0%** | **100.0%** | **100.0%** | **100.0%** |
| **Without earnings** | **45.2** | **64.4** | **43.6** | **35.8** | **34.2** |
| **With earnings** | **54.8** | **35.6** | **56.4** | **64.2** | **65.8** |
| Under $10,000 | 17.4 | 17.8 | 18.4 | 17.6 | 14.2 |
| $10,000 to $19,999 | 15.4 | 12.0 | 19.2 | 16.8 | 8.6 |
| $20,000 to $29,999 | 10.4 | 3.4 | 12.3 | 15.0 | 9.4 |
| $30,000 to $39,999 | 5.6 | 1.8 | 3.2 | 7.8 | 14.6 |
| $40,000 to $49,999 | 3.0 | 0.2 | 1.9 | 3.8 | 8.8 |
| $50,000 to $74,999 | 2.1 | 0.4 | 1.0 | 2.5 | 7.0 |
| $75,000 to $99,999 | 0.5 | 0.1 | 0.2 | 0.4 | 1.9 |
| $100,000 or more | 0.3 | 0.0 | 0.2 | 0.4 | 1.3 |

*Source: Bureau of the Census, unpublished tables from the 1996 Current Population Survey; calculations by New Strategist*

# Earnings Distribution of Women by Education, 1995: Aged 65 or Older

*(number and percent distribution of women aged 65 or older by earnings and education, 1995; women in thousands as of 1996)*

| | total | not a high school graduate | high school graduate | some college or assoc. degree | bachelor's degree or more |
|---|---|---|---|---|---|
| **Number** | | | | | |
| **Total women, aged 65 or older** | **18,398** | **6,536** | **6,849** | **3,106** | **1,906** |
| **Without earnings** | **16,302** | **6,047** | **6,084** | **2,613** | **1,558** |
| **With earnings** | **2,096** | **490** | **766** | **493** | **348** |
| Under $10,000 | 1,293 | 361 | 476 | 280 | 176 |
| $10,000 to $19,999 | 396 | 90 | 154 | 108 | 46 |
| $20,000 to $29,999 | 240 | 31 | 80 | 68 | 60 |
| $30,000 to $39,999 | 105 | 9 | 40 | 29 | 29 |
| $40,000 to $49,999 | 26 | 0 | 6 | 2 | 20 |
| $50,000 to $74,999 | 33 | 0 | 11 | 6 | 15 |
| $75,000 to $99,999 | 0 | 0 | 0 | 0 | 0 |
| $100,000 or more | 2 | 0 | 0 | 0 | 2 |
| Median earnings | $6,916 | $5,489 | $7,145 | $8,530 | $9,644 |
| Median earnings, year-round full-time workers | 21,504 | - | 20,969 | 21,943 | 28,927 |
| Percent of women who work year-round, full-time | 2.7% | 1.4% | 2.8% | 4.2% | 4.1% |
| **Percent** | | | | | |
| **Total women, aged 65 or older** | **100.0%** | **100.0%** | **100.0%** | **100.0%** | **100.0%** |
| **Without earnings** | **88.6** | **92.5** | **88.8** | **84.1** | **81.7** |
| **With earnings** | **11.4** | **7.5** | **11.2** | **15.9** | **18.3** |
| Under $10,000 | 7.0 | 5.5 | 6.9 | 9.0 | 9.2 |
| $10,000 to $19,999 | 2.2 | 1.4 | 2.2 | 3.5 | 2.4 |
| $20,000 to $29,999 | 1.3 | 0.5 | 1.2 | 2.2 | 3.1 |
| $30,000 to $39,999 | 0.6 | 0.1 | 0.6 | 0.9 | 1.5 |
| $40,000 to $49,999 | 0.1 | 0.0 | 0.1 | 0.1 | 1.0 |
| $50,000 to $74,999 | 0.2 | 0.0 | 0.2 | 0.2 | 0.8 |
| $75,000 to $99,999 | 0.0 | 0.0 | 0.0 | 0.0 | 0.0 |
| $100,000 or more | 0.0 | 0.0 | 0.0 | 0.0 | 0.1 |

*Note: (-) means sample is too small to make a reliable estimate.*
*Source: Bureau of the Census, unpublished tables from the 1996 Current Population Survey; calculations by New Strategist*

# Poverty Rates among Older Americans Are Below Average

**Only 10 percent of people aged 55 or older are poor, versus 14 percent of all Americans.**

Of the nation's 36 million poor in 1995, 5.5 million were aged 55 or older. Older blacks and Hispanics are more than twice as likely to be poor as older whites—23 and 24 percent, respectively, versus just 9 percent of whites. But older blacks and Hispanics are less likely to be poor than the average black (29 percent) or Hispanic (30 percent). Poverty rates rise with age for whites, blacks and Hispanics. Among whites and blacks aged 75 or older, poverty rates are slightly higher than for the entire white and black populations.

Older women are much more likely to be poor than older men—13 percent of women aged 55 or older are poor versus just 7 percent of men. But older women and men are less likely to be poor than the average female (15 percent) or male (12 percent). Black and Hispanic women are much more likely to be poor than their male counterparts. Among blacks aged 75 or older, 38 percent of women and 23 of men are poor. Among Hispanics aged 75 or older, 33 percent of women and 17 percent of men are poor.

◆ American children are much more likely to be poor than the nation's elderly. The disparity between the well-being of older and younger Americans may increase in the future as the more-affluent baby-boom generation ages.

# People in Poverty by Sex, Race, and Hispanic Origin, 1995

*(number and percent of total persons and persons aged 55 or older in poverty, by sex, race, and Hispanic origin, 1995; persons in thousands as of 1996)*

| | total | white | black | Hispanic |
|---|---|---|---|---|
| **Total persons** | | | | |
| **Number in poverty, total** | **36,425** | **24,423** | **9,872** | **8,574** |
| Aged 55 or older | 5,477 | 4,189 | 1,066 | 702 |
| Aged 65 or older | 3,318 | 2,572 | 629 | 342 |
| Aged 75 or older | 1,745 | 1,375 | 328 | 129 |
| Aged 55 to 59 | 1,163 | 840 | 246 | 186 |
| Aged 60 to 64 | 996 | 777 | 191 | 174 |
| Aged 65 to 74 | 1,573 | 1,196 | 301 | 213 |
| **Percent in poverty, total** | **13.8%** | **11.2%** | **29.3%** | **30.3%** |
| Aged 55 or older | 10.4 | 9.0 | 23.2 | 23.8 |
| Aged 65 or older | 10.5 | 9.0 | 25.4 | 23.5 |
| Aged 75 or older | 13.0 | 11.3 | 32.9 | 27.1 |
| Aged 55 to 59 | 10.3 | 8.7 | 21.4 | 23.0 |
| Aged 60 to 64 | 10.2 | 9.2 | 19.5 | 25.4 |
| Aged 65 to 74 | 8.6 | 7.3 | 20.3 | 21.7 |
| **Females** | | | | |
| **Number in poverty, total** | **20,742** | **13,760** | **5,829** | **4,602** |
| Aged 55 or older | 3,808 | 2,856 | 793 | 463 |
| Aged 65 or older | 2,496 | 1,920 | 490 | 244 |
| Aged 75 or older | 1,379 | 1,091 | 256 | 97 |
| Aged 55 to 59 | 718 | 487 | 178 | 111 |
| Aged 60 to 64 | 594 | 449 | 125 | 108 |
| Aged 65 to 74 | 1,117 | 829 | 234 | 147 |
| **Percent in poverty, total** | **15.4%** | **12.4%** | **32.4%** | **32.9%** |
| Aged 55 or older | 13.0 | 11.1 | 28.6 | 28.0 |
| Aged 65 or older | 13.6 | 11.7 | 31.1 | 28.9 |
| Aged 75 or older | 16.5 | 14.6 | 37.6 | 33.2 |
| Aged 55 to 59 | 12.4 | 9.9 | 28.0 | 25.4 |
| Aged 60 to 64 | 11.4 | 10.1 | 22.6 | 29.2 |
| Aged 65 to 74 | 11.1 | 9.3 | 26.1 | 26.6 |

*(continued)*

*(continued from previous page)*

| Males | total | white | black | Hispanic |
|---|---|---|---|---|
| **Number in poverty, total** | **15,863** | **10,664** | **4,043** | **3,972** |
| Aged 55 or older | 1,668 | 1,334 | 272 | 237 |
| Aged 65 or older | 822 | 652 | 138 | 98 |
| Aged 75 or older | 366 | 284 | 72 | 31 |
| Aged 55 to 59 | 444 | 353 | 68 | 74 |
| Aged 60 to 64 | 402 | 329 | 66 | 65 |
| Aged 65 to 74 | 456 | 368 | 66 | 67 |
| **Percent in poverty, total** | **12.2%** | **9.9%** | **25.7%** | **27.7%** |
| Aged 55 or older | 7.1 | 6.4 | 14.8 | 18.3 |
| Aged 65 or older | 6.2 | 5.4 | 15.4 | 16.0 |
| Aged 75 or older | 7.2 | 6.1 | 22.8 | 17.2 |
| Aged 55 to 59 | 8.1 | 7.4 | 13.3 | 20.2 |
| Aged 60 to 64 | 8.8 | 8.2 | 15.6 | 20.8 |
| Aged 65 to 74 | 5.6 | 5.0 | 11.4 | 15.4 |

*Note: Numbers will not add to total because Hispanics may be of any race and not all races are shown.*
*Source: Bureau of the Census,* Poverty in the United States: 1995, *Current Population Reports, P60-194, 1996*

# Most Elderly Americans Receive Social Security

**Ninety-three percent of Americans aged 65 or older get Social Security checks.**

Of the 31 million Americans aged 65 or older, 29 million receive Social Security benefits—averaging $7,972 in 1995. Social Security is the single most common source of income for Americans aged 65 or older. The only other source of income received by a majority of people aged 65 or older is interest. Two in three elderly people get interest income, averaging $3,114 in 1995. Only 32 percent of Americans aged 65 or older have pension income. Those with pensions received an average of $9,595 in 1995 from this source.

Few older Americans work, but those who do receive the largest amount of income from this source rather than from Social Security, interest, or pensions. The 14 percent minority of older Americans with wage or salary income received an average of $19,304 from this source. Similarly, the 3 percent with nonfarm self-employment income received an average of $17,342.

◆ In the years ahead, the proportion of older Americans with wage, salary, or self-employment income will increase, boosting the economic well-being of the elderly.

◆ With baby boomers saving much more for retirement than the current generation of elderly ever did, they are likely to receive more interest income than today's elderly.

# Sources of Income for Persons Aged 65 or Older, 1995

*(number of persons aged 65 or older with income and average income for those with income, by selected sources of income,1995; ranked by number with income; persons in thousands as of 1996)*

| | with income | | average income |
|---|---|---|---|
| | number | percent | |
| **Total** | **31,081** | **100.0%** | **$17,604** |
| Social Security | 28,739 | 92.5 | 7,972 |
| Interest | 20,695 | 66.6 | 3,114 |
| Pensions | 9,977 | 32.1 | 9,595 |
| Dividends | 6,070 | 19.5 | 3,471 |
| Wages and salary | 4,181 | 13.5 | 19,304 |
| Rents, royalties, estates, or trusts | 3,248 | 10.5 | 3,434 |
| Veterans' benefits | 1,155 | 3.7 | 5,369 |
| Nonfarm self-employment | 886 | 2.9 | 17,342 |
| Disability benefits | 233 | 0.7 | 9,768 |
| Public assistance | 81 | 0.3 | 1,706 |
| Education | 21 | 0.1 | 1,382 |
| Child support | 11 | 0.0 | 915 |

*Source: Bureau of the Census,* Money Income in the United States: 1995, *Current Population Reports, P60-193, 1996; calculations by New Strategist*

# 5

# Labor Force

◆ Among older men, the biggest drop in labor force participation rates has been among those aged 65 to 69—down 32 percentage points in the last 40 years.

◆ Among people aged 65 or older, men are nearly twice as likely as women to be in the labor force—17 percent of men versus 9 percent of women.

◆ In the older age groups, Hispanic men and women are more likely to work than their white or black counterparts.

◆ Labor force participation rates for men and women aged 55 to 64 will climb significantly after 2005 as baby boomers fill the age group.

◆ The proportion of couples in which neither husband nor wife works rises from 31 percent among 60-to-64-year-olds to 66 percent among those aged 65 to 74.

◆ Twenty percent of employed men aged 55 or older work part-time, compared with 11 percent of all employed men.

◆ Eighteen percent of men and 12 percent of women aged 55 or older are self-employed, compared with only 8 percent of all workers aged 16 or older.

◆ In 1996, men aged 55 to 64 had been with their current employer a median of 12 years, a 29 percent drop since 1983.

◆ Only 31 percent of workers aged 61 say they will stop working entirely when they retire; 14 percent do not plan to retire at all.

# Early Retirement Has Become Popular among Older Men

**Only 67 percent of men aged 55 to 64 were in the labor force in 1996, down from 87 percent in 1950.**

In contrast to men, older women are more likely to work than they were in 1950. Nearly half the women aged 55 to 64 were in the labor force in 1996, up from just 27 percent in 1950. Several factors account for the divergent labor force trends of men and women. For men, generous pensions and the provision of retiree health insurance has allowed many to retire before age 65. For women, labor force participation rates have increased in all but the oldest ages as younger working women have replaced older housewives.

Among older men, the biggest drop in labor force participation rates has been for those aged 65 to 69—down 32 percentage points in the past four decades. In 1950, 60 percent of men in their late 60s worked; by 1996 the figure was just 28 percent. For women, the biggest increase in labor force participation rates has been among those aged 55 to 59, rising from 26 to 60 percent between 1950 and 1996.

◆ Unlike their parents, baby boomers are not likely to benefit from generous employer-provided pensions or to receive employer-provided retiree health care coverage. Consequently, the labor force participation rate of older men will rise as boomers enter the 55-plus age group after the turn of the century.

## Older Men Are Much Less Likely to Work

*(percentage point change in labor force participation rates for total men and for men aged 55 or older, 1950 to 1996)*

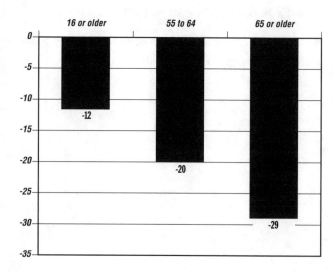

# Labor Force Participation Rates by Sex, 1950 to 1996

*(labor force participation rates for total persons aged 16 or older and for persons aged 55 or older by sex and age, selected years 1950 to 1996; percentage point change, 1950-96)*

| | 1996 | 1990 | 1980 | 1970 | 1960 | 1950 | percentage point change 1950-1996 |
|---|---|---|---|---|---|---|---|
| **Men** | | | | | | | |
| **Aged 16 or older** | **74.9%** | **76.1%** | **77.4%** | **79.7%** | **83.3%** | **86.4%** | **-11.5** |
| Aged 55 to 64 | 67.0 | 67.7 | 72.1 | 83.0 | 86.8 | 86.9 | -19.9 |
| Aged 65 or older | 16.9 | 16.4 | 19.0 | 26.8 | 33.1 | 45.8 | -28.9 |
| Aged 55 to 59 | 77.9 | 78.7 | 80.6 | 86.8 | 87.7 | 86.7 | -8.8 |
| Aged 60 to 64 | 54.3 | 55.1 | 60.4 | 73.0 | 77.6 | 79.4 | -25.1 |
| Aged 65 to 69 | 27.5 | 27.9 | 29.2 | 39.0 | 43.8 | 59.8 | -32.3 |
| Aged 70 to 74 | 17.3 | 16.7 | 18.3 | 22.4 | 28.7 | 38.7 | -21.4 |
| Aged 75 to 79 | - | 10.6 | 16.7 | 14.2 | 19.5 | 24.2 | - |
| Aged 80 to 84 | - | 6.2 | 10.4 | 9.1 | 11.5 | 13.2 | - |
| Aged 85 or older | - | 3.4 | 6.6 | - | 7.0 | 6.9 | - |
| **Women** | | | | | | | |
| **Aged 16 or older** | **59.3** | **57.5** | **51.5** | **43.3** | **37.7** | **33.9** | **25.4** |
| Aged 55 to 64 | 49.6 | 45.3 | 41.3 | 43.0 | 37.2 | 27.0 | 22.6 |
| Aged 65 or older | 8.6 | 8.7 | 8.1 | 9.7 | 10.8 | 9.7 | -1.1 |
| Aged 55 to 59 | 59.8 | 55.4 | 48.4 | 47.4 | 39.7 | 25.9 | 33.9 |
| Aged 60 to 64 | 38.2 | 36.1 | 34.0 | 36.1 | 29.5 | 20.5 | 17.7 |
| Aged 65 to 69 | 17.2 | 16.9 | 15 | 17.2 | 16.6 | 12.8 | 4.4 |
| Aged 70 to 74 | 8.8 | 8.3 | 7.8 | 9.1 | 9.6 | 6.6 | 2.2 |
| Aged 75 to 79 | - | 4.5 | 6.1 | 5.5 | 5.6 | 3.5 | - |
| Aged 80 to 84 | - | 2.2 | 3.7 | 3.5 | 3.0 | 1.7 | - |
| Aged 85 or older | - | 1.0 | 2.5 | - | 2.0 | 1.2 | - |

*Note: (-) means data not available.*
*Sources: Bureau of Labor Statistics,* Employment and Earnings, *January 1997 and January 1991; and* 65+ in the United States, *Current Population Reports, P23-190, 1996; and Bureau of Labor Statistics,* Handbook of Labor Statistics, *Bulletin 2340, 1989; calculations by New Strategist*

# Workers Become a Minority among Men at Age 63

## Transition to retirement with age is slow but steady.

Labor force participation rates fall steadily with age among older men, from a high of 82 percent among men aged 55 to a low of 5 percent among men aged 80 or older. The point at which retirees begin to outnumber workers occurs at age 63 among men.

For women, the dividing line is at age 60. A majority of women aged 55 to 59 are in the labor force. But from age 60 on, women workers are in the minority. Women retire at a younger age than men because most women marry men who are slightly older. When their husbands retire, so do many women.

◆ As boomers enter the older age groups, expect to see labor force participation rates climb for both men and women.

# Labor Force Participation Rates by Single Year of Age and Sex, 1996

*(percent of persons aged 55 or older in the labor force, by sex and age, 1996)*

|  | *men* | *women* |
|---|---|---|
| **Aged 55 or older** | **38.3%** | **23.9%** |
| Aged 55 | 81.9 | 66.0 |
| Aged 56 | 80.8 | 61.2 |
| Aged 57 | 78.2 | 59.2 |
| Aged 58 | 73.9 | 57.6 |
| Aged 59 | 73.6 | 53.7 |
| Aged 60 | 67.5 | 47.9 |
| Aged 61 | 64.8 | 46.4 |
| Aged 62 | 51.5 | 36.1 |
| Aged 63 | 45.2 | 31.1 |
| Aged 64 | 40.6 | 28.3 |
| Aged 65 | 33.4 | 21.6 |
| Aged 66 | 31.7 | 17.7 |
| Aged 67 | 26.5 | 17.1 |
| Aged 68 | 22.7 | 15.7 |
| Aged 69 | 22.2 | 13.6 |
| Aged 70 | 21.3 | 11.6 |
| Aged 71 | 20.1 | 9.5 |
| Aged 72 | 16.3 | 8.3 |
| Aged 73 | 15.1 | 6.8 |
| Aged 74 | 12.9 | 7.2 |
| Aged 75 | 11.9 | 5.7 |
| Aged 76 | 9.6 | 5.5 |
| Aged 77 | 10.4 | 5.3 |
| Aged 78 | 8.3 | 3.7 |
| Aged 79 | 7.2 | 3.1 |
| Aged 80 or older | 4.6 | 1.7 |

*Source: Bureau of Labor Statistics, unpublished data from various Current Population Surveys*

# Unemployment Low for Older Men and Women

## Only 3.4 percent of men and women aged 55 or older were unemployed in 1996.

The unemployment rate of older Americans was a full 2 percentage points below the 5.4 percent rate for the civilian labor force as a whole in 1996. The unemployment rate among older people does not vary much by age.

At all ages, older men are more likely to be in the labor force than older women. Among men aged 55 to 59, for example, 78 percent were in the labor force in 1996. The figure for women in this age group was 60 percent. At ages 60 to 64, most men are still working (54 percent), while a minority of women are still in the labor force (38 percent). At ages 65 or older, few men or women work, but men are nearly twice as likely as women to have jobs. Seventeen percent of men aged 65 or older were in the labor force in 1996, versus 9 percent of women.

◆ The labor force participation rates of older Americans will rise in the coming decades as baby boomers enter the age group. The biggest increase in participation rates is likely to be among women aged 55 to 64 as career-oriented boomer women replace older homemakers.

## Older Workers Have Low Unemployment Rate

*(percent of persons aged 16 or older and aged 55 or older in the civilian labor force who are unemployed, by sex, 1996)*

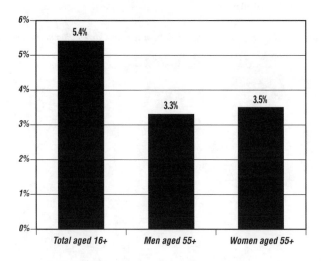

# Employment Status of Persons Aged 55 or Older by Sex, 1996

*(number and percent of persons aged 16 or older and persons aged 55 or older in the civilian labor force by sex, age, and employment status, 1996; numbers in thousands)*

| | | *civilian labor force* | | | *unemployed* | |
|---|---|---|---|---|---|---|
| | *civilian noninstitutional population* | *total* | *percent of population* | *employed* | *number* | *percent of labor force* |
| **Total, aged 16 or older** | **200,591** | **133,943** | **66.8%** | **126,708** | **7,236** | **5.4%** |
| Aged 55 or older | 52,741 | 15,974 | 30.3 | 15,429 | 545 | 3.4 |
| Aged 65 or older | 31,751 | 3,828 | 12.1 | 3,690 | 139 | 3.6 |
| Aged 75 or older | 13,507 | 634 | 4.7 | 614 | 21 | 3.3 |
| Aged 55 to 59 | 11,183 | 7,658 | 68.5 | 7,406 | 252 | 3.3 |
| Aged 60 to 64 | 9,807 | 4,488 | 45.8 | 4,333 | 155 | 3.4 |
| Aged 65 to 69 | 9,683 | 2,124 | 21.9 | 2,039 | 85 | 4.0 |
| Aged 70 to 74 | 8,561 | 1,070 | 12.5 | 1,037 | 33 | 3.1 |
| **Men, aged 16 or older** | **96,206** | **72,087** | **74.9** | **68,207** | **3,880** | **5.4** |
| Aged 55 or older | 23,324 | 8,940 | 38.3 | 8,642 | 299 | 3.3 |
| Aged 65 or older | 13,327 | 2,247 | 16.9 | 2,172 | 76 | 3.4 |
| Aged 75 or older | 5,134 | 375 | 7.3 | 364 | 10 | 2.8 |
| Aged 55 to 59 | 5,373 | 4,184 | 77.9 | 4,048 | 136 | 3.2 |
| Aged 60 to 64 | 4,624 | 2,510 | 54.3 | 2,422 | 88 | 3.5 |
| Aged 65 to 69 | 4,454 | 1,226 | 27.5 | 1,179 | 47 | 3.8 |
| Aged 70 to 74 | 3,739 | 647 | 17.3 | 628 | 18 | 2.9 |
| **Women, aged 16 or older** | **104,385** | **61,857** | **59.3** | **58,501** | **3,356** | **5.4** |
| Aged 55 or older | 29,417 | 7,033 | 23.9 | 6,787 | 246 | 3.5 |
| Aged 65 or older | 18,424 | 1,581 | 8.6 | 1,518 | 63 | 4.0 |
| Aged 75 or older | 8374 | 260 | 3.1 | 249 | 10 | 4.0 |
| Aged 55 to 59 | 5,810 | 3,474 | 59.8 | 3,358 | 116 | 3.3 |
| Aged 60 to 64 | 5,184 | 1,978 | 38.2 | 1,911 | 67 | 3.4 |
| Aged 65 to 69 | 5,229 | 898 | 17.2 | 860 | 38 | 4.3 |
| Aged 70 to 74 | 4,821 | 423 | 8.8 | 409 | 15 | 3.4 |

*Source: Bureau of Labor Statistics,* Employment and Earnings, *January 1997; calculations by New Strategist*

# Labor Force Participation Differs by Race and Hispanic Origin

**Older Hispanics are more likely to work than older whites or blacks.**

Among older men, Hispanics are much more likely to work than whites or blacks. Among men aged 55 or older, only 39 percent of whites and 33 percent of blacks are in the labor force. Among Hispanic men in this age group, a 51 percent majority are working. In the 65-plus age group, 33 percent of Hispanic men are in the labor force versus only 17 percent of white and 13 percent of black men.

This pattern is true for older women as well. Although overall labor force participation rates are higher for white and black women than for Hispanic women, in the older age groups Hispanic women are more likely to work. Among women aged 55 or older, 24 percent of whites, 25 percent of blacks, and 27 percent of Hispanics are in the labor force. The difference increases in the 65-plus age group, with 9 percent of white women, 8 percent of black women, and 14 percent of Hispanic women in the labor force.

◆ Labor force participation rates of older Hispanics are higher because many of them are immigrants. They are less likely than both whites and blacks to have pension or Social Security benefits. They remain in the labor force longer because they cannot afford to retire.

## Older Hispanic Men More Likely to Work

*(percent of men aged 55 or older employed in the civilian labor force, by race and Hispanic origin, 1996)*

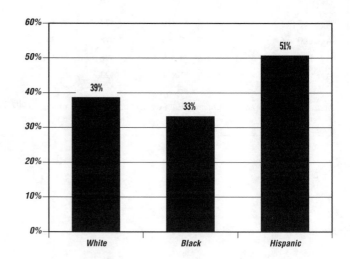

# Employment Status of Men Aged 55 or Older by Race and Hispanic Origin, 1996

*(number and percent of men aged 16 or older and men aged 55 or older in the civilian labor force by race, Hispanic origin, age, and employment status, 1996; numbers in thousands)*

| | civilian noninstitutional population | civilian labor force | | | unemployed | |
| --- | --- | --- | --- | --- | --- | --- |
| | | total | percent of population | employed | number | percent of labor force |
| **Total men, aged 16 or older** | **96,206** | **72,087** | **74.9%** | **68,207** | **3,880** | **5.4%** |
| Aged 55 or older | 23,324 | 8,940 | 38.3 | 8,642 | 299 | 3.3 |
| Aged 65 or older | 13,327 | 2,247 | 16.9 | 2,172 | 76 | 3.4 |
| Aged 75 or older | 5,134 | 375 | 7.3 | 364 | 10 | 2.7 |
| Aged 55 to 59 | 5,373 | 4,184 | 77.9 | 4,048 | 136 | 3.3 |
| Aged 60 to 64 | 4,624 | 2,510 | 54.3 | 2,422 | 88 | 3.5 |
| Aged 65 to 69 | 4,454 | 1,226 | 27.5 | 1,179 | 47 | 3.8 |
| Aged 70 to 74 | 3,739 | 647 | 17.3 | 628 | 18 | 2.8 |
| **White men, aged 16 or older** | **81,489** | **61,783** | **75.8** | **58,888** | **2,896** | **4.7** |
| Aged 55 or older | 20,702 | 7,997 | 38.6 | 7,742 | 255 | 3.2 |
| Aged 65 or older | 11,968 | 2,054 | 17.2 | 1,987 | 67 | 3.3 |
| Aged 75 or older | 4,690 | 349 | 7.4 | 340 | 10 | 2.9 |
| Aged 55 to 59 | 4,669 | 3,698 | 79.2 | 3,589 | 109 | 2.9 |
| Aged 60 to 64 | 4,065 | 2,245 | 55.2 | 2,166 | 79 | 3.5 |
| Aged 65 to 69 | 3,916 | 1,113 | 28.4 | 1,072 | 41 | 3.7 |
| Aged 70 to 74 | 3,362 | 592 | 17.6 | 576 | 16 | 2.7 |
| **Black men, aged 16 or older** | **10,575** | **7,264** | **68.7** | **6,456** | **808** | **11.1** |
| Aged 55 or older | 1,939 | 641 | 33.1 | 608 | 33 | 5.1 |
| Aged 65 or older | 1,025 | 132 | 12.9 | 126 | 7 | 5.3 |
| Aged 75 or older | 337 | 16 | 4.7 | 15 | 1 | 6.3 |
| Aged 55 to 59 | 499 | 331 | 66.3 | 311 | 20 | 6.0 |
| Aged 60 to 64 | 416 | 177 | 42.5 | 171 | 7 | 4.0 |
| Aged 65 to 69 | 411 | 78 | 19.0 | 74 | 4 | 5.1 |
| Aged 70 to 74 | 277 | 39 | 14.1 | 37 | 2 | 5.1 |
| **Hispanic men, aged 16 or older** | **9,604** | **7,646** | **79.6** | **7,039** | **607** | **7.9** |
| Aged 55 or older | 1,342 | 679 | 50.6 | 534 | 40 | 5.9 |
| Aged 55 to 64 | 712 | 469 | 65.9 | 438 | 31 | 6.6 |
| Aged 65 or older | 630 | 210 | 33.3 | 96 | 9 | 4.3 |

*Note: Employment status by detailed age group is not available for Hispanics; (-) means sample is too small to make a reliable estimate.*
*Source: Bureau of Labor Statistics,* Employment and Earnings, *January 1997; calculations by New Strategist*

# Employment Status of Women Aged 55 or Older by Race and Hispanic Origin, 1996

*(number and percent of women aged 16 or older and women aged 55 or older in the civilian labor force by race, Hispanic origin, age, and employment status, 1996; numbers in thousands)*

| | civilian noninstitutional population | civilian labor force | | | unemployed | |
| | | total | percent of population | employed | number | percent of labor force |
|---|---|---|---|---|---|---|
| **Total women, 16 or older** | **104,385** | **61,857** | **59.3%** | **58,501** | **3,356** | **5.4%** |
| Aged 55 or older | 29,417 | 7,033 | 23.9 | 6,787 | 246 | 3.5 |
| Aged 65 or older | 18,424 | 1,581 | 8.6 | 1,518 | 63 | 4.0 |
| Aged 75 or older | 8,374 | 260 | 3.1 | 249 | 10 | 3.8 |
| Aged 55 to 59 | 5,810 | 3,474 | 59.8 | 3,358 | 116 | 3.3 |
| Aged 60 to 64 | 5,184 | 1,978 | 38.2 | 1,911 | 67 | 3.4 |
| Aged 65 to 69 | 5,229 | 898 | 17.2 | 860 | 38 | 4.2 |
| Aged 70 to 74 | 4,821 | 423 | 8.8 | 409 | 15 | 3.5 |
| **White women, 16 or older** | **86,828** | **51,325** | **59.1** | **48,920** | **2,404** | **4.7** |
| Aged 55 or older | 25,821 | 6,137 | 23.8 | 5,934 | 203 | 3.3 |
| Aged 65 or older | 16,419 | 1,431 | 8.7 | 1,376 | 55 | 3.8 |
| Aged 75 or older | 7,552 | 235 | 3.1 | 226 | 9 | 3.8 |
| Aged 55 to 59 | 4,953 | 2,982 | 60.2 | 2,885 | 97 | 3.3 |
| Aged 60 to 64 | 4,449 | 1,724 | 38.8 | 1,672 | 51 | 3.0 |
| Aged 65 to 69 | 4,586 | 813 | 17.7 | 780 | 34 | 4.2 |
| Aged 70 to 74 | 4,281 | 383 | 8.9 | 370 | 12 | 3.1 |
| **Black women, 16 or older** | **13,029** | **7,869** | **60.4** | **7,086** | **784** | **10.0** |
| Aged 55 or older | 2,780 | 687 | 24.7 | 658 | 28 | 4.1 |
| Aged 65 or older | 1,584 | 122 | 7.7 | 115 | 7 | 5.7 |
| Aged 75 or older | 672 | 22 | 3.3 | 20 | 1 | 4.5 |
| Aged 55 to 59 | 641 | 375 | 58.5 | 364 | 11 | 2.9 |
| Aged 60 to 64 | 555 | 190 | 34.2 | 180 | 10 | 5.3 |
| Aged 65 to 69 | 503 | 69 | 13.7 | 66 | 3 | 4.3 |
| Aged 70 to 74 | 409 | 32 | 7.8 | 30 | 2 | 6.3 |
| **Hispanic women, 16 or older** | **9,610** | **5,128** | **53.4** | **4,602** | **525** | **10.2** |
| Aged 55 or older | 1,716 | 460 | 26.8 | 366 | 32 | 7.0 |
| Aged 55 to 64 | 834 | 338 | 40.5 | 310 | 27 | 8.0 |
| Aged 65 or older | 882 | 122 | 13.8 | 56 | 5 | 4.1 |

*Note: Employment status by detailed age group is not available for Hispanics; (-) means sample is too small to make a reliable estimate.*
*Source: Bureau of Labor Statistics,* Employment and Earnings, *January 1997; calculations by New Strategist*

# Older Labor Force Projected to Grow Rapidly

## The number of working women aged 55 to 64 should expand 63 percent between 1994 and 2005.

As the women of the baby-boom generation age into their late 50s and early 60s in the next few years, they will boost the number of working women aged 55 to 64 by over 3 million. The labor force participation rate for women in this age group should climb sharply—from 49 to 57 percent. The labor force participation rate is also expected to rise slightly for women aged 65 or older. Despite these increases, women aged 55 or older will account for only 15 percent of all working women in 2005, up from 11.5 percent in 1994.

The number of men aged 55 to 64 in the labor force is projected to climb 42.5 percent—a gain of 2.7 million. And in a reversal of the early retirement trend of the past several decades, the labor force participation rate for men in this age group will grow—albeit slightly—from 65.5 to 65.6 percent. The participation rate for men aged 65 or older is projected to continue to decline, falling from 16.9 to 16.5 percent.

◆ The labor force participation rate of men aged 55 to 64 will climb significantly after 2005, as baby boomers entirely fill the age group. With employers growing stingy with pension benefits and the age of Social Security eligibility rising, boomers won't retire as early as the current generation of older Americans.

### Older Labor Force Will Grow Rapidly

*(percent change in civilian labor force aged 55 or older, by sex, 1994 to 2005)*

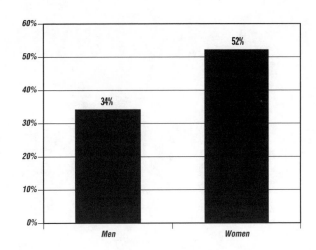

# Labor Force Projections, 1994 to 2005

*(number of persons aged 16 or older and persons aged 55 or older in the civilian labor force, numerical and percent change in number, share of labor force, and labor force participation rate, 1994 and 2005; numbers in thousands)*

| | civilian labor force | | change 1994-2005 | | percent of labor force | | labor force participation rate | |
|---|---|---|---|---|---|---|---|---|
| | 1994 | 2005 | number | percent | 1994 | 2005 | 1994 | 2005 |
| **Men, aged 16 or older** | **70,817** | **76,842** | **6,025** | **8.5%** | **100.0%** | **100.0%** | **75.1%** | **72.9%** |
| Aged 55 or older | 8,600 | 11,536 | 2,936 | 34.1 | 12.1 | 15.0 | 37.8 | 40.6 |
| Aged 55 to 64 | 6,423 | 9,150 | 2,727 | 42.5 | 9.1 | 11.9 | 65.5 | 65.6 |
| Aged 65 or older | 2,177 | 2,386 | 209 | 9.6 | 3.1 | 3.1 | 16.9 | 16.5 |
| | | | | | | | | |
| **Women, aged 16 or older** | **60,239** | **70,263** | **10,024** | **16.6** | **100.0** | **100.0** | **58.8** | **61.7** |
| Aged 55 or older | 6,947 | 10,569 | 3,622 | 52.1 | 11.5 | 15.0 | 24.0 | 30.8 |
| Aged 55 to 64 | 5,289 | 8,613 | 3,324 | 62.8 | 8.8 | 12.3 | 48.9 | 56.6 |
| Aged 65 or older | 1,658 | 1,956 | 298 | 18.0 | 2.8 | 2.8 | 9.2 | 10.2 |

*Source: Bureau of Labor Statistics,* Monthly Labor Review, *November 1995; calculations by New Strategist*

# Few Older Couples Are Dual Earners

**In 48 percent of couples aged 55 or older, neither husband nor wife is in the labor force.**

While 56 percent of all married couples are dual earners—meaning both husband and wife are in the labor force—the proportion is just 25 percent among those aged 55 or older. Dual-earner couples are a minority among older Americans in large part because most older men are retired and most older women spent their lives caring for their families rather than in the labor force.

Among couples headed by 55-to-59-year-olds, however, dual earners are a 54 percent majority. This proportion falls to 33 percent among couples aged 60 to 64. In this age group, the wife is the sole wage earner in 16 percent of couples—a larger share than in any other age group. Behind this is the fact that most women marry men who are slightly older. Many men aged 60 to 64 are retired, while their younger wives are still in the labor force.

The proportion of couples in which neither husband nor wife is in the labor force rises from a 31 percent minority in the 60-to-64 age group to a 66 percent majority in the 65-to-74 age group.

◆ The dual-earner share of older couples will rise in the years ahead as baby boomers enter the age group. Expect to see particularly sharp increases in the dual-earner proportion of couples aged 60 to 64 within 10 years.

# Labor Force Status of Couples Aged 55 or Older, 1996

*(number and percent distribution of total married couples and couples headed by persons aged 55 or older, by labor force status of husband and wife, 1996; numbers in thousands)*

| | total married couples | husband and wife in labor force | husband only in labor force | wife only in labor force | husband and wife not in labor force |
|---|---|---|---|---|---|
| **Total couples, number** | **53,567** | **29,952** | **11,684** | **2,835** | **9,096** |
| Aged 55 or older | 16,671 | 4,224 | 2,812 | 1,655 | 7,979 |
| Aged 65 or older | 8,930 | 793 | 954 | 701 | 6,481 |
| Aged 75 or older | 3,104 | 67 | 168 | 115 | 2,754 |
| Aged 85 or older | 351 | 4 | 6 | 10 | 331 |
| | | | | | |
| Aged 55 to 59 | 4,213 | 2,278 | 1,108 | 408 | 419 |
| Aged 60 to 64 | 3,528 | 1,153 | 750 | 546 | 1,079 |
| Aged 65 to 74 | 6,177 | 730 | 792 | 596 | 4,058 |
| Aged 75 to 84 | 2,753 | 63 | 162 | 105 | 2,423 |
| | | | | | |
| **Total couples, percent** | **100.0%** | **55.9%** | **21.8%** | **5.3%** | **17.0%** |
| Aged 55 or older | 100.0 | 25.3 | 16.9 | 9.9 | 47.9 |
| Aged 65 or older | 100.0 | 8.9 | 10.7 | 7.8 | 72.6 |
| Aged 75 or older | 100.0 | 2.2 | 5.4 | 3.7 | 88.7 |
| Aged 85 or older | 100.0 | 1.1 | 1.7 | 2.8 | 94.3 |
| | | | | | |
| Aged 55 to 59 | 100.0 | 54.1 | 26.3 | 9.7 | 9.9 |
| Aged 60 to 64 | 100.0 | 32.7 | 21.3 | 15.5 | 30.6 |
| Aged 65 to 74 | 100.0 | 11.8 | 12.8 | 9.6 | 65.7 |
| Aged 75 to 84 | 100.0 | 2.3 | 5.9 | 3.8 | 88.0 |

*Source: Bureau of the Census,* Household and Family Characteristics: March 1996, *Current Population Reports, P20-495, 1997; calculations by New Strategist*

# Few Working Americans Are Aged 55 or Older

**Only 12 percent of the 127 million employed Americans are aged 55 or older.**

The share of workers aged 55 or older varies by occupation. Fewer than 10 percent of technicians are aged 55 or older, for example, because so much technological change occurred after older Americans began their careers. Among the nation's 1 million computer scientists, just 5 percent are aged 55 or older. But people aged 55 or older account for 39 percent of farm operators and managers. They are a huge presence in agriculture because changes in the industry over the past few decades have made it more difficult for younger people to take up farming.

The largest share of older workers (16 percent) are executives, administrators, or managers. Forty-six percent of legislators, chief executives, and general administrators in public administration, for example, are aged 55 or older. For workers rising within the government bureaucracy, it takes decades to reach the top.

Workers aged 55 or older are overrepresented among the nation's funeral directors (27 percent), authors (25 percent), real estate salespersons (29 percent), barbers (29 percent), tailors (36 percent), and shoe repairers (29 percent). They are underrepresented among the nation's actors and directors (8 percent), computer programmers (4 percent), and waiters and waitresses (5 percent).

◆ As older Americans are replaced by younger generations, many of the careers in which they are overrepresented may disappear with them. These include barbers (replaced by unisex hairdressers), shoe repairers (replaced by new shoes), and tailors (replaced by off-the-rack clothes).

◆ As boomers age into their late 50s, expect to see a surging share of older workers in technical jobs, including computer programmers and scientists.

# Workers Aged 55 or Older by Occupation, 1996

*(number of total employed persons and employed persons aged 55 or older by occupation, 1996; numbers in thousands)*

| | total | aged 55 or older | | |
| --- | --- | --- | --- | --- |
| | | total | 55 to 64 | 65 or older |
| **Total, employed** | **126,708** | **15,429** | **11,739** | **3,690** |
| **Managerial and professional specialty** | **36,497** | **4,661** | **3,613** | **1,048** |
| Executive, administrative, and managerial | 17,746 | 2,463 | 1,918 | 545 |
| Professional specialty | 18,752 | 2,199 | 1,695 | 504 |
| **Technical, sales, & administrative support** | **37,683** | **4,575** | **3,417** | **1,158** |
| Technicians and related support | 3,926 | 305 | 266 | 39 |
| Sales | 15,404 | 2,061 | 1,441 | 620 |
| Administrative support, including clerical | 18,353 | 2,210 | 1,710 | 500 |
| **Service** | **17,177** | **2,049** | **1,494** | **555** |
| Private household | 804 | 161 | 106 | 55 |
| Protective services | 2,187 | 262 | 174 | 88 |
| Other services | 14,186 | 1,626 | 1,214 | 412 |
| **Precision production, craft, and repair** | **13,587** | **1,421** | **1,191** | **230** |
| Mechanics and repairers | 4,521 | 471 | 390 | 81 |
| Construction trades | 5,108 | 467 | 392 | 75 |
| Extractive occupations | 130 | 9 | 8 | 1 |
| Precision production | 3,828 | 474 | 401 | 73 |
| **Operators, fabricators, and laborers** | **18,197** | **1,936** | **1,582** | **354** |
| Machine operators, assemblers & inspectors | 7,874 | 808 | 695 | 113 |
| Transport and material moving | 5,302 | 749 | 594 | 155 |
| Handlers, equip. cleaners, helpers, & laborers | 5,021 | 378 | 293 | 85 |
| **Farming, forestry, and fishing** | **3,566** | **786** | **442** | **344** |
| Farm operators & managers | 1,314 | 513 | 246 | 267 |
| Other agricultural and related occupations | 2,096 | 245 | 173 | 72 |
| Forestry and logging | 108 | 20 | 16 | 4 |
| Fishing, hunters, and trappers | 49 | 7 | 6 | 1 |

*Source: Bureau of Labor Statistics, unpublished tables from the 1996 Current Population Survey*

# Distribution of Workers Aged 55 or Older by Occupation, 1996

*(percent distribution of total employed persons and employed persons aged 55 or older by occupation, 1996)*

| | total | aged 55 or older | | |
| --- | --- | --- | --- | --- |
| | *total* | *total* | *55 to 64* | *65 or older* |
| **Total employed** | **100.0%** | **100.0%** | **100.0%** | **100.0%** |
| **Managerial and professional specialty** | **28.8** | **30.2** | **30.8** | **28.4** |
| Executive, administrative, and managerial | 14.0 | 16.0 | 16.3 | 14.8 |
| Professional specialty | 14.8 | 14.3 | 14.4 | 13.7 |
| **Technical, sales, & administrative support** | **29.7** | **29.7** | **29.1** | **31.4** |
| Technicians and related support | 3.1 | 2.0 | 2.3 | 1.1 |
| Sales | 12.2 | 13.4 | 12.3 | 16.8 |
| Administrative support, including clerical | 14.5 | 14.3 | 14.6 | 13.6 |
| **Service** | **13.6** | **13.3** | **12.7** | **15.0** |
| Private household | 0.6 | 1.0 | 0.9 | 1.5 |
| Protective services | 1.7 | 1.7 | 1.5 | 2.4 |
| Other service | 11.2 | 10.5 | 10.3 | 11.2 |
| **Precision production, craft, and repair** | **10.7** | **9.2** | **10.1** | **6.2** |
| Mechanics and repairers | 3.6 | 3.1 | 3.3 | 2.2 |
| Construction trades | 4.0 | 3.0 | 3.3 | 2.0 |
| Extractive occupations | 0.1 | 0.1 | 0.1 | 0.0 |
| Precision production | 3.0 | 3.1 | 3.4 | 2.0 |
| **Operators, fabricators, and laborers** | **14.4** | **12.5** | **13.5** | **9.6** |
| Machine operators, assemblers & inspectors | 6.2 | 5.2 | 5.9 | 3.1 |
| Transport and material moving | 4.2 | 4.9 | 5.1 | 4.2 |
| Handlers, equip. cleaners, helpers, & laborers | 4.0 | 2.4 | 2.5 | 2.3 |
| **Farming, forestry, and fishing** | **2.8** | **5.1** | **3.8** | **9.3** |
| Farm operators & managers | 1.0 | 3.3 | 2.1 | 7.2 |
| Other agricultural and related occupations | 1.7 | 1.6 | 1.5 | 2.0 |
| Forestry and logging | 0.1 | 0.1 | 0.1 | 0.1 |
| Fishing, hunters, and trappers | 0.0 | 0.0 | 0.1 | 0.0 |

*Source: Bureau of Labor Statistics, unpublished tables from the 1996 Current Population Survey; calculations by New Strategist*

# Older Worker Share of Occupation, 1996

*(persons aged 55 or older as a share of total employed by occupation, 1996)*

| | total | aged 55 or older | | |
| | | total | 55 to 64 | 65 or older |
|---|---|---|---|---|
| **Total employed** | **100.0%** | **12.2%** | **9.3%** | **2.9%** |
| **Managerial and professional specialty** | **100.0** | **12.8** | **9.9** | **2.9** |
| Executive, administrative, and managerial | 100.0 | 13.9 | 10.8 | 3.1 |
| Professional specialty | 100.0 | 11.7 | 9.0 | 2.7 |
| **Technical, sales, & administrative support** | **100.0** | **12.1** | **9.1** | **3.1** |
| Technicians and related support | 100.0 | 7.8 | 6.8 | 1.0 |
| Sales | 100.0 | 13.4 | 9.4 | 4.0 |
| Administrative support, including clerical | 100.0 | 12.0 | 9.3 | 2.7 |
| **Service** | **100.0** | **11.9** | **8.7** | **3.2** |
| Private household | 100.0 | 20.0 | 13.2 | 6.8 |
| Protective services | 100.0 | 12.0 | 8.0 | 4.0 |
| Other service | 100.0 | 11.5 | 8.6 | 2.9 |
| **Precision production, craft, and repair** | **100.0** | **10.5** | **8.8** | **1.7** |
| Mechanics and repairers | 100.0 | 10.4 | 8.6 | 1.8 |
| Construction trades | 100.0 | 9.1 | 7.7 | 1.5 |
| Extractive occupations | 100.0 | 6.9 | 6.2 | 0.8 |
| Precision production | 100.0 | 12.4 | 10.5 | 1.9 |
| **Operators, fabricators, and laborers** | **100.0** | **10.6** | **8.7** | **1.9** |
| Machine operators, assemblers & inspectors | 100.0 | 10.3 | 8.8 | 1.4 |
| Transport and material moving | 100.0 | 14.1 | 11.2 | 2.9 |
| Handlers, equip. cleaners, helpers, & laborers | 100.0 | 7.5 | 5.8 | 1.7 |
| **Farming, forestry, and fishing** | **100.0** | **22.0** | **12.4** | **9.6** |
| Farm operators & managers | 100.0 | 39.0 | 18.7 | 20.3 |
| Other agricultural and related occupations | 100.0 | 11.7 | 8.3 | 3.4 |
| Forestry and logging | 100.0 | 18.5 | 14.8 | 3.7 |
| Fishing, hunters, and trappers | 100.0 | 14.3 | 12.2 | 2.0 |

*Source: Bureau of Labor Statistics, unpublished tables from the 1996 Current Population Survey; calculations by New Strategist*

# Employed Persons Aged 55 or Older by Detailed Occupation, 1996

*(number of total workers and workers aged 55 or older by selected detailed occupation; persons aged 55 or older as a percent of total workers by occupation, 1996; numbers in thousands)*

| | total employed | aged 55 or older employed | aged 55 or older percent of total |
|---|---|---|---|
| **Total** | **126,708** | **15,429** | **12.2%** |
| Legislators, chief exec., & gen admin., public admin. | 26 | 12 | 46.2 |
| Officials and administrators, public administrators | 636 | 110 | 17.3 |
| Funeral directors | 55 | 15 | 27.3 |
| Managers and administrators, other | 7,107 | 1,065 | 15.0 |
| Engineers | 1,960 | 266 | 13.6 |
| Aerospace engineers | 80 | 16 | 20.0 |
| Computer systems analysts and scientists | 1,093 | 51 | 4.7 |
| Physicians | 667 | 110 | 16.5 |
| Teachers, postsecondary | 889 | 161 | 18.1 |
| Teachers, except postsecondary | 4,724 | 500 | 10.6 |
| Lawyers | 880 | 109 | 12.4 |
| Authors | 114 | 28 | 24.6 |
| Actors and directors | 136 | 11 | 8.1 |
| Editors and reporters | 280 | 35 | 12.5 |
| Public relations specialists | 150 | 16 | 10.7 |
| Airplane pilots & navigators | 114 | 16 | 14.0 |
| Computer programmers | 561 | 24 | 4.3 |
| Insurance sales | 625 | 93 | 14.9 |
| Real estate sales | 737 | 210 | 28.5 |
| Securities & financial services | 406 | 44 | 10.8 |
| Advertising sales | 158 | 16 | 10.1 |
| Sales workers, motor vehicles & boats | 304 | 50 | 16.4 |
| Sales workers, apparel | 451 | 57 | 12.6 |
| Street & door-to-door sales | 360 | 52 | 14.4 |
| Secretaries | 3,164 | 479 | 15.1 |
| Receptionists | 960 | 118 | 12.3 |
| File clerks | 309 | 34 | 11.0 |
| Bookkeepers | 1,774 | 299 | 16.9 |
| Telephone operators | 164 | 27 | 16.5 |
| Bank tellers | 431 | 28 | 6.5 |
| Teachers' aides | 623 | 68 | 10.9 |
| Firefighters | 231 | 7 | 3.0 |
| Police & detectives | 960 | 42 | 4.4 |
| Waiters & waitresses | 1,375 | 63 | 4.6 |

*(continued)*

*(continued from previous page)*

| | total employed | aged 55 or older | |
|---|---|---|---|
| | | employed | percent of total |
| Cooks | 2,061 | 210 | 10.2% |
| Nursing aides | 1,850 | 243 | 13.1 |
| Janitors & cleaners | 2,205 | 418 | 19.0 |
| Barbers | 85 | 25 | 29.4 |
| Hairdressers and cosmetologists | 737 | 65 | 8.8 |
| Automobile mechanics | 889 | 76 | 8.5 |
| Carpenters | 1,220 | 100 | 8.2 |
| Electricians | 763 | 74 | 9.7 |
| Plumbers | 555 | 76 | 13.7 |
| Machinists | 491 | 49 | 10.0 |
| Tailors | 44 | 16 | 36.4 |
| Shoe repairers | 17 | 5 | 29.4 |
| Machine operators, assemblers, & inspectors | 7,874 | 808 | 10.3 |
| Truck drivers | 3,019 | 405 | 13.4 |
| Bus drivers | 512 | 123 | 24.0 |
| Taxi cab drivers | 203 | 47 | 23.2 |
| Farm operators & managers | 1,314 | 513 | 39.0 |
| Farm workers | 840 | 100 | 11.9 |

*Source: Bureau of Labor Statistics, unpublished tables from the 1996 Current Population Survey; calculations by New Strategist*

# Many Older Workers Work Part-Time

## Nearly half the men aged 65 or older are part-time workers.

While only 11 percent of all employed men work part-time, the proportion is 20 percent among those aged 55 or older. The figure rises to 48 percent among working men aged 65 or older, and to a 56 percent majority of working men aged 75 or older.

The proportions are even higher among older women. Overall, 27 percent of employed women work part-time, but among those aged 55 or older the figure is 35 percent. A 64 percent majority of working women aged 65 or older work part-time.

◆ Many older Americans work part-time because Social Security benefits are reduced if earnings rise above a certain income threshold. If the federal government eliminated this disincentive to work, a larger proportion of older Americans would work full-time.

◆ As boomers enter the older age groups, the part-time labor force is likely to surge since many will want to live a retirement lifestyle while still earning a living.

### Part-Time Workers Increase with Age

*(percent of employed men and women aged 55 or older who work part-time, 1996)*

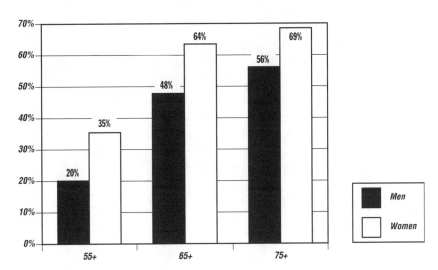

# Full-Time and Part-Time Workers by Sex, 1996

*(number and percent distribution of total employed persons aged 16 or older and employed persons aged 55 or older by full- and part-time status, by age and sex, 1996; numbers in thousands)*

| | men | | | women | | |
|---|---|---|---|---|---|---|
| | *total* | *full-time* | *part-time* | *total* | *full-time* | *part-time* |
| **Number** | | | | | | |
| **Total employed** | **72,086** | **64,037** | **8,049** | **61,857** | **45,303** | **16,554** |
| Aged 55 or older | 8,941 | 7,143 | 1,798 | 7,034 | 4,541 | 2,493 |
| Aged 65 or older | 2,247 | 1,173 | 1,074 | 1,581 | 577 | 1,004 |
| Aged 75 or older | 374 | 164 | 210 | 260 | 82 | 178 |
| Aged 55 to 64 | 6,693 | 5,970 | 723 | 5,452 | 3,964 | 1,488 |
| Aged 65 to 69 | 1,226 | 699 | 527 | 898 | 363 | 535 |
| Aged 70 to 74 | 647 | 309 | 338 | 423 | 132 | 291 |
| **Percent** | | | | | | |
| **Total employed** | **100.0%** | **88.8%** | **11.2%** | **100.0%** | **73.2%** | **26.8%** |
| Aged 55 or older | 100.0 | 79.9 | 20.1 | 100.0 | 64.6 | 35.4 |
| Aged 65 or older | 100.0 | 52.2 | 47.8 | 100.0 | 36.5 | 63.5 |
| Aged 75 or older | 100.0 | 43.9 | 56.1 | 100.0 | 31.5 | 68.5 |
| Aged 55 to 64 | 100.0 | 89.2 | 10.8 | 100.0 | 72.7 | 27.3 |
| Aged 65 to 69 | 100.0 | 57.0 | 43.0 | 100.0 | 40.4 | 59.6 |
| Aged 70 to 74 | 100.0 | 47.8 | 52.2 | 100.0 | 31.2 | 68.8 |

*Source: Bureau of Labor Statistics, unpublished data from the 1996 Current Population Survey; calculations by New Strategist*

# Self-Employment Is Popular among Older Americans

**Men and women aged 65 or older are more likely than those younger to work for themselves.**

While only 8 percent of all nonagricultural workers aged 16 or older are self-employed, 24 percent of workers aged 65 or older are self-employed. To become self-employed usually requires specialized skills, and those most likely to have a specialty are older Americans who have had decades to develop expertise. Men and women aged 55 or older account for 21 percent of all self-employed workers, much greater than the self-employed's 12 percent share of all workers.

Older men are more likely to be self-employed than older women. While 18 percent of men aged 55 or older work for themselves, the proportion is just 12 percent among women in this age group. Fully 29 percent of men aged 65 or older are self-employed, versus 17 percent of their female counterparts.

◆ As boomers enter the 55-or-older age group, the number of self-employed Americans will rise sharply. The share of the self-employed who are aged 55 or older will also increase.

◆ Older Americans will be an increasingly important segment of the market for home-based business products and services.

## Self-Employed Workers Aged 55 or Older by Sex, 1996

*(number of nonagricultural workers aged 16 or older and aged 55 or older whose longest job in 1996 was self-employment, percent who are self-employed, and percent of total self-employed, by sex and age, 1995; numbers in thousands)*

|  | number of self-employed | percent who are self-employed | percent of total self-employed |
|---|---|---|---|
| **Total, self-employed** | **8,971** | **7.9%** | **100.0%** |
| Aged 55 or older | 1,906 | 15.0 | 21.2 |
| Aged 55 to 64 | 1,262 | 12.6 | 14.1 |
| Aged 65 or older | 644 | 23.9 | 7.2 |
| **Total, self-employed men** | **5,465** | **9.1** | **100.0** |
| Aged 55 or older | 1,228 | 17.9 | 22.5 |
| Aged 55 to 64 | 796 | 14.8 | 14.6 |
| Aged 65 or older | 432 | 29.4 | 7.9 |
| **Total, self-employed women** | **3,506** | **6.5** | **100.0** |
| Aged 55 or older | 678 | 11.5 | 19.3 |
| Aged 55 to 64 | 466 | 10.0 | 13.3 |
| Aged 65 or older | 212 | 17.2 | 6.0 |

*Source: Bureau of Labor Statistics,* Employment and Earnings, *January 1997; calculations by New Strategist*

# Many Older Americans Are "Alternative" Workers

## Men and women aged 55 or older account for a disproportionate share of independent contractors.

Alternative workers are defined by the Bureau of Labor Statistics as independent contractors, on-call workers, temporary-help agency workers, or workers provided by contract firms. Older Americans are much more likely to be independent contractors than younger Americans. Men aged 55 or older account for just 13 percent of all employed men, but for 22 percent of men who are independent contractors. Similarly, women in that age group account for 12 percent of all employed women, but for 18 percent of women who are independent contractors. Independent contractors include most of the nation's self-employed.

One in five employed men aged 65 or older is an independent contractor, as is one in 10 employed women in that age group.

Older workers are more likely than their younger counterparts to be on-call workers—a category that includes substitute teachers. They are less likely to be temps and about equally likely to work for contract firms.

◆ Older men and women are much more likely to be independent contractors than younger people because this work is often part-time—a preferred schedule for many older people.

◆ As entrepreneurial baby boomers enter the 55-plus age group, the number of independent contractors should surge.

# Workers in Alternative Work Arrangements, 1995

*(number and percent distribution of total employed workers and workers in alternative work arrangements, for workers aged 16 or older and aged 55 or older, by sex, 1995; numbers in thousands)*

| | total employed workers | independent contractors | on-call workers | temporary-help agency workers | workers provided by contract firms |
|---|---|---|---|---|---|
| **MEN, number** | | | | | |
| **Total workers** | **66,290** | **5,595** | **1,042** | **557** | **466** |
| Aged 55 or older | 8,259 | 1,204 | 146 | 46 | 61 |
| Aged 55 to 64 | 6,187 | 795 | 76 | 33 | 34 |
| Aged 65 or older | 2,072 | 409 | 70 | 13 | 27 |
| **Percent distribution by age** | | | | | |
| **Total workers** | **100.0%** | **8.4%** | **1.6%** | **0.8%** | **0.7%** |
| Aged 55 or older | 100.0 | 14.6 | 1.8 | 0.6 | 0.7 |
| Aged 55 to 64 | 100.0 | 12.8 | 1.2 | 0.5 | 0.5 |
| Aged 65 or older | 100.0 | 19.7 | 3.4 | 0.6 | 1.3 |
| **Percent distribution by work arrangement** | | | | | |
| **Total workers** | **100.0%** | **100.0%** | **100.0%** | **100.0%** | **100.0%** |
| Aged 55 or older | 12.5 | 21.5 | 14.0 | 8.3 | 13.1 |
| Aged 55 to 64 | 9.3 | 14.2 | 7.3 | 5.9 | 7.3 |
| Aged 65 or older | 3.1 | 7.3 | 6.7 | 2.3 | 5.8 |
| **WOMEN, number** | | | | | |
| **Total workers** | **56,918** | **2,714** | **1,036** | **624** | **186** |
| Aged 55 or older | 6,662 | 486 | 178 | 43 | 10 |
| Aged 55 to 64 | 5,183 | 336 | 115 | 34 | 10 |
| Aged 65 or older | 1,479 | 150 | 63 | 9 | - |
| **Percent distribution by age** | | | | | |
| **Total workers** | **100.0%** | **4.8%** | **1.8%** | **1.1%** | **0.3%** |
| Aged 55 or older | 100.0 | 7.3 | 2.7 | 0.6 | 0.2 |
| Aged 55 to 64 | 100.0 | 6.5 | 2.2 | 0.7 | 0.2 |
| Aged 65 or older | 100.0 | 10.1 | 4.3 | 0.6 | - |
| **Percent distribution by work arrangement** | | | | | |
| **Total workers** | **100.0%** | **100.0%** | **100.0%** | **100.0%** | **100.0%** |
| Aged 55 or older | 11.7 | 17.9 | 17.2 | 6.9 | 5.4 |
| Aged 55 to 64 | 9.1 | 12.4 | 11.1 | 5.4 | 5.4 |
| Aged 65 or older | 2.6 | 5.5 | 6.1 | 1.4 | - |

*Note: Independent contractors are wage and salary workers who obtain customers on their own to provide a product or service. The self-employed are included, except those who are incorporated. On-call workers are in a pool of workers who are called to work only as needed, such as substitute teachers and construction workers supplied by a union hiring hall. Temporary-help agency workers are those who said they are paid by a temporary-help agency. Workers provided by contract firms are those employed by a company that provides employees or their services to others under contract, such as in security, landscaping, and computer programming.*
*Source: Bureau of Labor Statistics,* Monthly Labor Review, *June 1997; calculations by New Strategist*

# Job Tenure Falls for Older Men

## But women's job tenure remains high.

The number of years workers have been with their current employer is on the decline—particularly among older men, according to the Employee Benefit Research Institute.

Since 1983, when job tenure peaked for all but the youngest men, the sharpest declines in job tenure have been among the oldest male workers. Men aged 55 to 64 had been with their current employer a median of 17 years in 1983. By 1996, job tenure for this age group had fallen to 12 years—a 29 percent drop.

In contrast to men, job tenure has changed little among older women since 1983. This stability is due to women's increasing attachment to the labor force as career-oriented younger women replace older just-a-job women.

◆ Job tenure declines when workers voluntarily switch jobs and when they are laid off and forced to find new jobs. The decline in job tenure among men is due to a combination of these factors, but its concentration among older men points toward involuntary lay-offs as the biggest factor.

# Job Tenure by Sex and Age, 1983 to 1996

*(median number of years workers aged 25 to 64 have been with their current employer by sex and age, 1983 to 1996; and change in years 1983-96)*

|  | 1996 | 1991 | 1987 | 1983 | change 1983-96 |
|---|---|---|---|---|---|
| **Men** | | | | | |
| Aged 25 to 34 | 3.0 | 3.7 | 3.7 | 3.4 | -0.4 |
| Aged 35 to 44 | 6.0 | 7.2 | 7.6 | 7.7 | -1.7 |
| Aged 45 to 54 | 10.0 | 12.2 | 12.3 | 13.4 | -3.4 |
| Aged 55 to 64 | 12.0 | 15.5 | 15.7 | 17.0 | -5.0 |
| **Women** | | | | | |
| Aged 25 to 34 | 2.7 | 3.2 | 3.1 | 3.1 | -0.4 |
| Aged 35 to 44 | 5.0 | 5.0 | 4.9 | 4.6 | 0.4 |
| Aged 45 to 54 | 7.0 | 7.3 | 7.3 | 6.9 | 0.1 |
| Aged 55 to 64 | 10.0 | 10.4 | 10.3 | 10.5 | -0.5 |

*Source: Employee Benefit Research Institute,* 1996 Data on the Mobility of American Workers, *1997; calculations by New Strategist*

# Many Older Americans Have Not Thought Much about Retirement

## A minority of older workers plan to stop working entirely when they retire.

A large proportion of older workers do not have plans for retirement, according to a 1992 survey. The figure ranges from 44 percent of workers aged 51 to a still-substantial 28 percent of workers aged 61. Only 31 percent of workers aged 61 say they will stop working entirely when they retire, while 20 percent plan to reduce their hours of work. Fourteen percent do not plan to retire at all.

One reason why so few older Americans have thought about retirement is that many have trouble envisioning it. While 30 percent of retirees say retirement means freedom, only 19 percent of workers think of retirement as freedom. Twenty-one percent of retirees say retirement means time for family and hobbies, versus just 15 percent of workers. The largest share of workers (45 percent) think of retirement simply as not working or working less. Only 20 percent of retirees think this narrowly about retirement.

Workers may not want to envision retirement because they are worried about it. Workers are less likely than retirees to be "very" confident in their ability to afford to live where they want, to be healthy enough to enjoy retirement, and to have enough money for leisure and medical expenses

◆ The scare stories in the media about the financial problems facing future retirees have had their impact. Workers' fear of retirement may boost savings, but it could also have the opposite effect—causing workers to give up trying to save for retirement.

# Expected Retirement Patterns by Age, 1992

*(percent distribution of workers aged 51 to 61 by expected pattern of retirement, 1992)*

| | no thought given | stop working | continue as is | work fewer hours | change kind of work, work for self, other |
|---|---|---|---|---|---|
| **Total, aged 51 to 61** | **37%** | **24%** | **13%** | **16%** | **10%** |
| Age 51 | 44 | 18 | 12 | 13 | 12 |
| Age 52 | 41 | 19 | 11 | 17 | 11 |
| Age 53 | 43 | 21 | 9 | 15 | 10 |
| Age 54 | 39 | 22 | 13 | 17 | 10 |
| Age 55 | 40 | 24 | 13 | 14 | 8 |
| Age 56 | 35 | 27 | 12 | 15 | 9 |
| Age 57 | 37 | 24 | 14 | 16 | 10 |
| Age 58 | 32 | 26 | 15 | 19 | 7 |
| Age 59 | 33 | 25 | 18 | 15 | 10 |
| Age 60 | 32 | 29 | 8 | 18 | 12 |
| Age 61 | 28 | 31 | 15 | 20 | 7 |

*Source: Employee Benefit Research Institute estimates from the* 1992 Health and Retirement Study, Wave 1, *in* Employee Benefits, Retirement Patterns, and Implications for Increased Work Life, *EBRI Issue Brief Number 184, 1997*

# What Retirement Means, 1996

*(percent of workers and retirees citing characteristic as what retirement means to them, 1996; ranked by percent citing characteristic)*

|  | percent |
|---|---|
| **Retirees** | |
| Freedom | 30% |
| Relaxing, enjoying life | 24 |
| Time for family, hobbies, or volunteering | 21 |
| Not working, working less | 20 |
| Financial struggles, bad health, depression | 18 |
| Financial security | 3 |
| **Workers** | |
| Not working, working less | 45 |
| Relaxing, enjoying life | 23 |
| Freedom | 19 |
| Time for family, hobbies, or volunteering | 15 |
| Financial security | 12 |
| Financial struggles, bad health, depression | 4 |

*Source: Employee Benefit Research Institute, American Savings Education Council, and Mathew Greenwald & Associates, Inc.,* Retirement Confidence Survey Wave VI, *1996*

# Confidence in Retirement, 1996

*(percent distribution of workers and retirees by level of confidence in specific attributes of retirement, 1996)*

| | retirees | workers |
|---|---|---|
| **Able to afford to live where you want** | | |
| Very | 49% | 35% |
| Somewhat | 28 | 40 |
| Not too/not at all | 21 | 24 |
| **Have enough money for basic expenses** | | |
| Very | 45 | 41 |
| Somewhat | 39 | 42 |
| Not too/not at all | 14 | 15 |
| **Healthy enough to enjoy retirement** | | |
| Very | 40 | 34 |
| Somewhat | 32 | 51 |
| Not too/not at all | 22 | 12 |
| **Have enough money for leisure** | | |
| Very | 36 | 20 |
| Somewhat | 29 | 46 |
| Not too/not at all | 30 | 34 |
| **Good preparation for retirement** | | |
| Very | 35 | 27 |
| Somewhat | 37 | 48 |
| Not too/not at all | 24 | 24 |
| **Have enough money for medical expenses** | | |
| Very | 34 | 18 |
| Somewhat | 36 | 39 |
| Not too/not at all | 25 | 40 |

*Source: Employee Benefit Research Institute, American Savings Education Council, and Mathew Greenwald & Associates, Inc.,* Retirement Confidence Survey, *1996*

# 6

# Living Arrangements

◆ Only 60 percent of the 34 million households headed by people aged 55 or older are families.

◆ The number of households headed by 55-to-64-year-olds will grow 41 percent between 1995 and 2005.

◆ Fully 71 percent of households headed by Americans aged 85 or older are home to just one person.

◆ Eighteen percent of householders aged 55 or older live with children, most of whom are adults.

◆ Among householders aged 85 or older, Hispanics are much more likely to be heading families than whites or blacks.

◆ Most women spend the end of their lives alone, while most men die while still married.

# Family Households Lose Ground with Age

**Only 60 percent of households headed by older Americans are families.**

Of the nation's 100 million households in 1996, 70 percent were families. But among the 34 million households headed by people aged 55 or older, only 60 percent were families. Older people are less likely than the average American to live with family members because of an important transition in living arrangements that occurs in the 65-plus age groups. While married couples account for an above-average share of households headed by 55-to-64-year-olds (62 percent), this proportion falls to a 37 percent minority of households in the 75-to-84 age group. Only 17 percent of households headed by people aged 85 or older are married couples.

The married-couple share of older households falls sharply with age as women become widowed and begin to live alone. Female-headed nonfamily households account for 29 percent of all households headed by people aged 55 or older, ranging from just 16 percent of those headed by 55-to-64-year-olds to 44 percent of households headed by 65-to-74-year-olds. Among households headed by people aged 85 or older, 59 percent are nonfamily households headed by women. Older Americans head a 58 percent majority of the nation's female-headed nonfamily households.

◆ Marketers targeting older householders must consider the unique consumer profile of each age group. While couples dominate households headed by 55-to-64-year-olds, female householders are the decision makers among people aged 75 or older.

# Households Headed by Persons Aged 55 or Older by Type, 1996

*(number of total households and households headed by persons aged 55 or older, percent distribution by age and by household type; numbers in thousands, 1996)*

| | | aged 55 or older | | | | | |
| | | | | aged 65 or older | | | |
| | total | total | 55 to 64 | total | 65 to 74 | 75 to 84 | 85 or older |
|---|---|---|---|---|---|---|---|
| **Number** | | | | | | | |
| **Total households** | **99,627** | **33,887** | **12,401** | **21,486** | **11,908** | **7,552** | **2,026** |
| Family households | 69,594 | 20,440 | 9,134 | 11,306 | 7,340 | 3,424 | 542 |
| Married couples | 53,567 | 17,022 | 7,741 | 9,281 | 6,177 | 2,753 | 351 |
| Female hh, no spouse present | 12,514 | 2,741 | 1,111 | 1,630 | 914 | 552 | 164 |
| Male hh, no spouse present | 3,513 | 678 | 283 | 395 | 249 | 119 | 27 |
| Nonfamily households | 30,033 | 13,447 | 3,267 | 10,180 | 4,568 | 4,128 | 1,484 |
| Female householder | 16,685 | 9,700 | 1,967 | 7,733 | 3,240 | 3,310 | 1,183 |
| Male householder | 13,348 | 3,746 | 1,299 | 2,447 | 1,328 | 818 | 301 |
| **Percent distribution by age** | | | | | | | |
| **Total households** | **100.0%** | **100.0%** | **100.0%** | **100.0%** | **100.0%** | **100.0%** | **100.0%** |
| Family households | 69.9 | 60.3 | 73.7 | 52.6 | 61.6 | 45.3 | 26.8 |
| Married couple | 53.8 | 50.2 | 62.4 | 43.2 | 51.9 | 36.5 | 17.3 |
| Female hh, no spouse present | 12.6 | 8.1 | 9.0 | 7.6 | 7.7 | 7.3 | 8.1 |
| Male hh, no spouse present | 3.5 | 2.0 | 2.3 | 1.8 | 2.1 | 1.6 | 1.3 |
| Nonfamily households | 30.1 | 39.7 | 26.3 | 47.4 | 38.4 | 54.7 | 73.2 |
| Female householder | 16.7 | 28.6 | 15.9 | 36.0 | 27.2 | 43.8 | 58.4 |
| Male householder | 13.4 | 11.1 | 10.5 | 11.4 | 11.2 | 10.8 | 14.9 |
| **Percent distribution by type** | | | | | | | |
| **Total households** | **100.0** | **34.0** | **12.4** | **21.6** | **12.0** | **7.6** | **2.0** |
| Family households | 100.0 | 29.4 | 13.1 | 16.2 | 10.5 | 4.9 | 0.8 |
| Married couple | 100.0 | 31.8 | 14.5 | 17.3 | 11.5 | 5.1 | 0.7 |
| Female hh, no spouse present | 100.0 | 21.9 | 8.9 | 13.0 | 7.3 | 4.4 | 1.3 |
| Male hh, no spouse present | 100.0 | 19.3 | 8.1 | 11.2 | 7.1 | 3.4 | 0.8 |
| Nonfamily households | 100.0 | 44.8 | 10.9 | 33.9 | 15.2 | 13.7 | 4.9 |
| Female householder | 100.0 | 58.1 | 11.8 | 46.3 | 19.4 | 19.8 | 7.1 |
| Male householder | 100.0 | 28.1 | 9.7 | 18.3 | 9.9 | 6.1 | 2.3 |

*Source: Bureau of Census,* Household and Family Characteristics: March 1996, *Current Population Reports, PPL-66, 1997; calculations by New Strategist*

# Households Headed by 55-to-64-Year-Olds Will Grow Rapidly

## But the number of householders aged 65 to 74 will decline between 1995 and 2005.

As the baby-boom generation begins to fill the 55-to-64 age group at the turn of the century, the number of householders in this age group will grow 41 percent, according to projections by the Bureau of the Census. In contrast, the number headed by people aged 65 to 74 will decline 2 percent as the small generation born during the Depression moves into this age bracket. The number of households headed by people aged 75 or older is projected to increase 21 percent.

The biggest gains among householders aged 55 to 64 will be in male-headed families, projected to more than double between 1995 and 2005. But there are so few of these households that a doubling will still leave them well below 1 million. Married couples aged 55 to 64 will increase more slowly than other household types because the divorce-prone baby-boom generation will be entering the age group. Nonfamily households in this age group will grow by a much higher rate of 52 percent as divorcing men and women opt to live alone.

◆ In the coming decade, the older market will be a changing market. Not only is growth uneven by age, but the attitudes and lifestyles of the younger end of the market will be transformed by aging baby boomers.

### Growth in Households Will Vary by Age

*(percent change in number of households headed by persons aged 55 or older, 1995 to 2005)*

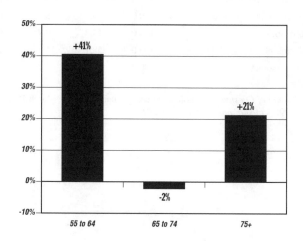

# Projections of Households Headed by Persons Aged 55 or Older by Type, 1995 to 2005

*(number and percent distribution of total households and households headed persons aged 55 or older, 1995 and 2005; numerical and percent change, 1995 and 2005; numbers in thousands)*

| | number | | percent change | percent distribution | |
|---|---|---|---|---|---|
| | 1995 | 2005 | 1995-2005 | 1995 | 2005 |
| **Total, aged 55 to 64** | **12,331** | **17,331** | **40.5%** | **100.0%** | **100.0%** |
| Family households | 9,134 | 12,374 | 35.5 | 74.1 | 71.4 |
| Married couples | 7,521 | 10,097 | 34.2 | 61.0 | 58.3 |
| Female hh, no spouse present | 1,168 | 1,666 | 42.6 | 9.5 | 9.6 |
| Male hh, no spouse present | 283 | 611 | 116.1 | 2.3 | 3.5 |
| Nonfamily households | 3,267 | 4,957 | 51.7 | 26.5 | 28.6 |
| Female householder | 1,967 | 2,794 | 42.1 | 16.0 | 16.1 |
| Living alone | 1,830 | 2,611 | 42.7 | 14.8 | 15.1 |
| Male householder | 1,299 | 2,162 | 66.4 | 10.5 | 12.5 |
| Living alone | 1,134 | 1,868 | 64.7 | 9.2 | 10.8 |
| **Total, aged 65 to 74** | **11,849** | **11,597** | **-2.1** | **100.0** | **100.0** |
| Family households | 7,437 | 7,357 | -1.1 | 62.8 | 63.4 |
| Married couples | 6,255 | 6,229 | -0.4 | 52.8 | 53.7 |
| Female hh, no spouse present | 922 | 852 | -7.6 | 7.8 | 7.3 |
| Male hh, no spouse present | 260 | 276 | 6.2 | 2.2 | 2.4 |
| Nonfamily households | 4,413 | 4,240 | -3.9 | 37.2 | 36.6 |
| Female householder | 3,230 | 2,985 | -7.6 | 27.3 | 25.7 |
| Living alone | 3,124 | 2,888 | -7.6 | 26.4 | 24.9 |
| Male householder | 1,183 | 1,255 | 6.1 | 10.0 | 10.8 |
| Living alone | 1,077 | 1,143 | 6.1 | 9.1 | 9.9 |
| **Total, aged 75 or older** | **9,454** | **11,462** | **21.2** | **100.0** | **100.0** |
| Family households | 4,202 | 5,346 | 27.2 | 44.4 | 46.6 |
| Married couples | 3,297 | 4,291 | 30.1 | 34.9 | 37.4 |
| Female hh, no spouse present | 722 | 833 | 15.4 | 7.6 | 7.3 |
| Male hh, no spouse present | 183 | 222 | 21.3 | 1.9 | 1.9 |
| Nonfamily households | 5,251 | 6,116 | 16.5 | 55.5 | 53.4 |
| Female householder | 4,219 | 4,864 | 15.3 | 44.6 | 42.4 |
| Living alone | 4,124 | 4,754 | 15.3 | 43.6 | 41.5 |
| Male householder | 1,032 | 1,252 | 21.3 | 10.9 | 10.9 |
| Living alone | 974 | 1,182 | 21.4 | 10.3 | 10.3 |

*Source: Bureau of the Census, Projections of the Number of Households and Families in the United States: 1995 to 2010, Current Population Reports, P25-1129, 1996; calculations by New Strategist*

# Older Households Are Small

**Households headed by people aged 55 or older average only 1.97 people.**

The average U.S. household is home to 2.65 people. Household size peaks in middle age, when couples are raising children. It falls steadily in the 55-plus age groups, from an average of 2.36 people for householders aged 55 to 64 to just 1.37 persons for house-holders aged 85 or older.

The most-common household size among householders aged 55 to 74 is two persons. After age 74, single-person households are most common. Fully 71 percent of households headed by the oldest Americans (aged 85 or older) are home to just one person—most of them widows. Overall, householders aged 55 or older account for over half the nation's single-person households.

◆ The wants and needs of married couples are different from those of people who live alone. Businesses targeting older Americans must carefully dissect the market by age in order to find receptive consumers.

# Households Headed by People Aged 55 or Older by Size, 1996

*(number of total households and households headed by persons aged 55 or older by size of household, percent distribution by age of householder and by size of household, 1996; numbers in thousands)*

| | | aged 55 or older | | | | | |
| | | | | aged 65 or older | | | |
| | total | total | 55 to 64 | total | 65 to 74 | 75 to 84 | 85 or older |
|---|---|---|---|---|---|---|---|
| **Number** | | | | | | | |
| **Total households** | **99,627** | **33,887** | **12,401** | **21,486** | **11,908** | **7,552** | **2,026** |
| One person | 24,900 | 12,782 | 2,941 | 9,841 | 4,377 | 4,021 | 1,443 |
| Two persons | 32,526 | 15,641 | 6,067 | 9,574 | 6,032 | 3,051 | 491 |
| Three persons | 16,724 | 3,270 | 1,870 | 1,400 | 980 | 362 | 58 |
| Four persons | 15,118 | 1,267 | 896 | 371 | 296 | 55 | 20 |
| Five persons | 6,631 | 511 | 342 | 169 | 121 | 37 | 11 |
| Six persons | 2,357 | 245 | 168 | 77 | 67 | 10 | - |
| Seven or more persons | 1,372 | 169 | 117 | 52 | 34 | 15 | 3 |
| Average household size | 2.65 | 1.97 | 2.36 | 1.75 | 1.90 | 1.61 | 1.40 |
| **Percent distribution by age** | | | | | | | |
| **Total households** | **100.0%** | **100.0%** | **100.0%** | **100.0%** | **100.0%** | **100.0%** | **100.0%** |
| One person | 25.0 | 37.7 | 23.7 | 45.8 | 36.8 | 53.2 | 71.2 |
| Two persons | 32.6 | 46.2 | 48.9 | 44.6 | 50.7 | 40.4 | 24.2 |
| Three persons | 16.8 | 9.6 | 15.1 | 6.5 | 8.2 | 4.8 | 2.9 |
| Four persons | 15.2 | 3.7 | 7.2 | 1.7 | 2.5 | 0.7 | 1.0 |
| Five persons | 6.7 | 1.5 | 2.8 | 0.8 | 1.0 | 0.5 | 0.5 |
| Six persons | 2.4 | 0.7 | 1.4 | 0.4 | 0.6 | 0.1 | - |
| Seven or more persons | 1.4 | 0.5 | 0.9 | 0.2 | 0.3 | 0.2 | 0.1 |
| **Percent distribution by size** | | | | | | | |
| **Total households** | **100.0** | **34.0** | **12.4** | **21.6** | **12.0** | **7.6** | **2.0** |
| One person | 100.0 | 51.3 | 11.8 | 39.5 | 17.6 | 16.1 | 5.8 |
| Two persons | 100.0 | 48.1 | 18.7 | 29.4 | 18.5 | 9.4 | 1.5 |
| Three persons | 100.0 | 19.6 | 11.2 | 8.4 | 5.9 | 2.2 | 0.3 |
| Four persons | 100.0 | 8.4 | 5.9 | 2.5 | 2.0 | 0.4 | 0.1 |
| Five persons | 100.0 | 7.7 | 5.2 | 2.5 | 1.8 | 0.6 | 0.2 |
| Six persons | 100.0 | 10.4 | 7.1 | 3.3 | 2.8 | 0.4 | - |
| Seven or more persons | 100.0 | 12.3 | 8.5 | 3.8 | 2.5 | 1.1 | 0.2 |

*Source: Bureau of the Census,* Household and Family Characteristics: March 1996, *Current Population Reports, PPL-66, 1997; calculations by New Strategist*

# Many Older Householders Still Have Children at Home

**Six million of the 34 million householders aged 55 or older share their homes with children.**

Eighteen percent of householders aged 55 or older live with children of any age, and the figure for householders aged 55 to 64 is an even more substantial 28 percent. Most of those children are adults, probably living with Mom and Dad while they attend college, hunt for a job, or recover from divorce. Despite the rise of older parents in the past few decades, only 6 percent of householders aged 55 to 64 have children under age 18 at home.

The proportion of older householders with children of any age in their home stands at 15 percent among householders aged 65 to 74 and falls to 8 percent among householders aged 85 or older. Some of the oldest householders who live with children are probably being cared for by them.

◆ Not only do many older Americans still live with their children, but those who don't are almost certain to have children and grandchildren living elsewhere. Appealing to family values can be a powerful marketing tool throughout life.

## Children Live with Many Older Householders

*(percent of households headed by persons aged 55 or older with children of any age at home, 1996)*

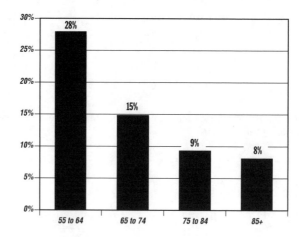

# Households Headed by Persons Aged 55 or Older with Children at Home, 1996

*(number and percent distribution of total households and households headed by persons aged 55 or older, by age of own children at home, 1996; numbers in thousands)*

| | | aged 55 or older | | | | | |
| | | | | aged 65 or older | | | |
| | *total* | *total* | *55 to 64* | *total* | *65 to 74* | *75 to 84* | *85 or older* |
|---|---|---|---|---|---|---|---|
| **Number** | | | | | | | |
| **Total households** | **99,627** | **33,887** | **12,401** | **21,486** | **11,908** | **7,552** | **2,026** |
| With children of any age | 44,144 | 6,083 | 3,454 | 2,629 | 1,759 | 705 | 165 |
| With children <age 25 | 39,307 | 2,158 | 1,843 | 315 | 305 | 10 | - |
| With children <age 18 | 34,203 | 884 | 744 | 140 | 130 | 10 | - |
| With children <age 12 | 25,576 | 317 | 268 | 49 | 41 | 8 | - |
| With children <age 6 | 15,450 | 82 | 62 | 20 | 16 | 4 | - |
| **Percent** | | | | | | | |
| **Total households** | **100.0%** | **100.0%** | **100.0%** | **100.0%** | **100.0%** | **100.0%** | **100.0%** |
| With children of any age | 44.3 | 18.0 | 27.9 | 12.2 | 14.8 | 9.3 | 8.1 |
| With children <age 25 | 39.5 | 6.4 | 14.9 | 1.5 | 2.6 | 0.1 | - |
| With children <age 18 | 34.3 | 2.6 | 6.0 | 0.7 | 1.1 | 0.1 | - |
| With children <age 12 | 25.7 | 0.9 | 2.2 | 0.2 | 0.3 | 0.1 | - |
| With children <age 6 | 15.5 | 0.2 | 0.5 | 0.1 | 0.1 | 0.1 | - |

*Note: Own children includes stepchildren and adopted children of the householder; (-) means sample is too small to make a reliable estimate.*
*Source: Bureau of the Census,* Household and Family Characteristics: March 1996, *Current Population Reports, PPL-66, 1997; calculations by New Strategist*

# Composition of Older Households
# Differs Sharply by Race and Hispanic Origin

**The married-couple share ranges from 52 percent among white householders aged 55 or older to 32 percent among households headed by blacks.**

Married couples dominate both white and Hispanic households headed by people aged 55 or older. While a majority of white households in this age group are headed by couples, among Hispanics the figure is a slightly smaller 48 percent. Among blacks, only one-third of older households are headed by couples, while 30 percent are women living alone or with nonrelatives and 21 percent are families headed by women.

Lifestyle differences persist into the older age groups. The oldest Hispanic householders are much more likely to be heading families, for example, than are whites or blacks. Forty-seven percent of Hispanic households headed by people aged 85 or older are families, versus 31 percent of black and 26 percent of white households in this age group.

◆ Many Hispanics are immigrants from Mexico and other Spanish-speaking countries who bring with them their traditional family structure.

## Married Couples Are Most Common among Whites

*(married couples as a percent of households headed by persons aged 55 or older, by race and Hispanic origin, 1996)*

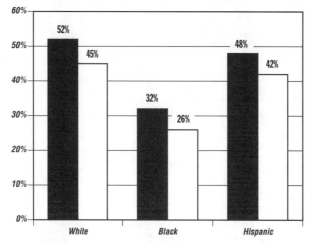

# White Households Headed by Persons Aged 55 or Older by Type, 1996

*(number and percent distribution of total white households and white households headed by persons aged 55 or older, by type, 1996; numbers in thousands)*

| | total white households | aged 55 or older | | aged 65 or older | | | |
| --- | --- | --- | --- | --- | --- | --- | --- |
| | | total | 55 to 64 | total | 65 to 74 | 75 to 84 | 85 or older |
| **Number** | | | | | | | |
| **Total households** | **84,511** | **29,940** | **10,614** | **19,326** | **10,583** | **6,892** | **1,851** |
| Family households | 58,869 | 18,078 | 7,903 | 10,175 | 6,574 | 3,120 | 481 |
| Married couples | 47,873 | 15,578 | 6,943 | 8,635 | 5,720 | 2,590 | 325 |
| Female hh, no spouse present | 8,284 | 1,966 | 730 | 1,236 | 666 | 440 | 130 |
| Male hh, no spouse present | 2,712 | 545 | 240 | 305 | 188 | 90 | 27 |
| Nonfamily households | 25,642 | 11,852 | 2,701 | 9,151 | 4,009 | 3,772 | 1,370 |
| Female householder | 14,275 | 8,586 | 1,617 | 6,969 | 2,860 | 3,035 | 1,074 |
| Male householder | 11,367 | 3,266 | 1,085 | 2,181 | 1,149 | 737 | 295 |
| **Percent** | | | | | | | |
| **Total households** | **100.0%** | **100.0%** | **100.0%** | **100.0%** | **100.0%** | **100.0%** | **100.0%** |
| Family households | 69.7 | 60.4 | 74.5 | 52.6 | 62.1 | 45.3 | 26.0 |
| Married couples | 56.6 | 52.0 | 65.4 | 44.7 | 54.0 | 37.6 | 17.6 |
| Female hh, no spouse present | 9.8 | 6.6 | 6.9 | 6.4 | 6.3 | 6.4 | 7.0 |
| Male hh, no spouse present | 3.2 | 1.8 | 2.3 | 1.6 | 1.8 | 1.3 | 1.5 |
| Nonfamily households | 30.3 | 39.6 | 25.4 | 47.4 | 37.9 | 54.7 | 74.0 |
| Female householder | 16.9 | 28.7 | 15.2 | 36.1 | 27.0 | 44.0 | 58.0 |
| Male householder | 13.5 | 10.9 | 10.2 | 11.3 | 10.9 | 10.7 | 15.9 |

*Source: Bureau of the Census,* Household and Family Characteristics: March 1996, *Current Population Reports, PPL-66, 1997; calculations by New Strategist*

# Black Households Headed by Persons Aged 55 or Older by Type, 1996

*(number and percent distribution of total black households and black households headed by persons aged 55 or older, by type, 1996; numbers in thousands)*

| | total black households | aged 55 or older | | aged 65 or older | | | |
| --- | --- | --- | --- | --- | --- | --- | --- |
| | | total | 55 to 64 | total | 65 to 74 | 75 to 84 | 85 or older |
| **Number** | | | | | | | |
| **Total households** | **11,577** | **3,161** | **1,384** | **1,777** | **1,064** | **563** | **150** |
| Family households | 8,055 | 1,794 | 904 | 890 | 599 | 245 | 46 |
| Married couples | 3,713 | 1,004 | 539 | 465 | 319 | 125 | 21 |
| Female hh, no spouse present | 3,769 | 678 | 327 | 351 | 226 | 100 | 25 |
| Male hh, no spouse present | 573 | 113 | 38 | 75 | 54 | 21 | - |
| Nonfamily households | 3,521 | 1,368 | 480 | 888 | 465 | 318 | 105 |
| Female householder | 1,989 | 952 | 291 | 661 | 318 | 244 | 99 |
| Male householder | 1,532 | 416 | 190 | 226 | 147 | 73 | 6 |
| **Percent** | | | | | | | |
| **Total households** | **100.0%** | **100.0%** | **100.0%** | **100.0%** | **100.0%** | **100.0%** | **100.0%** |
| Family households | 69.6 | 56.8 | 65.3 | 50.1 | 56.3 | 43.5 | 30.7 |
| Married couples | 32.1 | 31.8 | 38.9 | 26.2 | 30.0 | 22.2 | 14.0 |
| Female hh, no spouse present | 32.6 | 21.4 | 23.6 | 19.8 | 21.2 | 17.8 | 16.7 |
| Male hh, no spouse present | 4.9 | 3.6 | 2.7 | 4.2 | 5.1 | 3.7 | - |
| Nonfamily households | 30.4 | 43.3 | 34.7 | 50.0 | 43.7 | 56.5 | 70.0 |
| Female householder | 17.2 | 30.1 | 21.0 | 37.2 | 29.9 | 43.3 | 66.0 |
| Male householder | 13.2 | 13.2 | 13.7 | 12.7 | 13.8 | 13.0 | 4.0 |

*Source: Bureau of the Census,* Household and Family Characteristics: March 1996, *Current Population Reports, PPL-66, 1997; calculations by New Strategist*

# Hispanic Households Headed by Persons Aged 55 or Older by Type, 1996

*(number and percent distribution of total Hispanic households and Hispanic households headed by persons aged 55 or older, by type, 1996; numbers in thousands)*

| | total Hispanic households | aged 55 or older | | aged 65 or older | | | |
|---|---|---|---|---|---|---|---|
| | | total | 55 to 64 | total | 65 to 74 | 75 to 84 | 85 or older |
| **Number** | | | | | | | |
| **Total households** | **7,939** | **1,705** | **808** | **897** | **609** | **220** | **68** |
| Family households | 6,287 | 1,115 | 596 | 519 | 382 | 105 | 32 |
| Married couples | 4,247 | 817 | 441 | 376 | 283 | 73 | 20 |
| Female hh, no spouse present | 1,604 | 235 | 113 | 122 | 86 | 27 | 9 |
| Male hh, no spouse present | 436 | 63 | 42 | 21 | 13 | 5 | 3 |
| Nonfamily households | 1,652 | 590 | 212 | 378 | 227 | 115 | 36 |
| Female householder | 787 | 406 | 123 | 283 | 171 | 83 | 29 |
| Male householder | 865 | 184 | 89 | 95 | 56 | 32 | 7 |
| **Percent** | | | | | | | |
| **Total households** | **100.0%** | **100.0%** | **100.0%** | **100.0%** | **100.0%** | **100.0%** | **100.0%** |
| Family households | 79.2 | 65.4 | 73.8 | 57.9 | 62.7 | 47.7 | 47.1 |
| Married couples | 53.5 | 47.9 | 54.6 | 41.9 | 46.5 | 33.2 | 29.4 |
| Female hh, no spouse present | 20.2 | 13.8 | 14.0 | 13.6 | 14.1 | 12.3 | 13.2 |
| Male hh, no spouse present | 5.5 | 3.7 | 5.2 | 2.3 | 2.1 | 2.3 | 4.4 |
| Nonfamily households | 20.8 | 34.6 | 26.2 | 42.1 | 37.3 | 52.3 | 52.9 |
| Female householder | 9.9 | 23.8 | 15.2 | 31.5 | 28.1 | 37.7 | 42.6 |
| Male householder | 10.9 | 10.8 | 11.0 | 10.6 | 9.2 | 14.5 | 10.3 |

*Source: Bureau of the Census,* Household and Family Characteristics: March 1996, *Current Population Reports, PPL-66, 1997; calculations by New Strategist*

# Lives of Men and Women Diverge in Old Age

## Most older men live with their wives, while most older women are on their own.

The lifestyles of men and women become increasingly different with age. Because men die at a younger age than women, and because women tend to marry men who are slightly older, most women spend the end of their lives alone while most men die while still married.

In the 55-to-64 age group, 66 percent of women and 79 percent of men live with a spouse. This 13 percentage point gap in living arrangements grows to a 42 percentage point chasm in the 75-to-84 age group—when a substantial 73 percent of men, but only 30 percent of women, still live with a spouse.

Women aged 85 or older are more likely to live with relatives other than a spouse (25 percent) than with a husband (10 percent). Among men in this age group, only 10 percent live with relatives other than a spouse, while 47 percent still live with their wives.

Older women who live alone become the majority in the 75-to-84 age group. Sixty-one percent of women aged 85 or older live alone, versus just 36 percent of their male counterparts.

◆ Married couples dominate consumers aged 55 to 64, but in older age groups single women are the dominant consumers. Businesses targeting older Americans must design their products and services and craft their messages accordingly.

### Most Older Men Are Married

*(percent of men and women aged 55 or older who live with a spouse or live alone, 1995)*

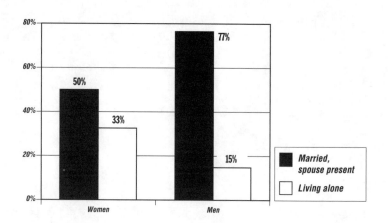

# Living Arrangements of People Aged 55 or Older by Sex, 1995

*(number and percent distribution of total persons aged 15 or older and persons aged 55 or older by sex, age, and living arrangement, 1995; numbers in thousands)*

| | total | married, spouse present | married, spouse absent | living with other relatives | living alone | living with nonrelatives only |
|---|---|---|---|---|---|---|
| **Total women, number** | **105,028** | **54,944** | **4,040** | **25,213** | **14,592** | **6,239** |
| Aged 55 or older | 29,142 | 14,572 | 737 | 3,746 | 9,504 | 583 |
| Aged 65 or older | 18,264 | 7,420 | 346 | 2,585 | 7,591 | 322 |
| Aged 75 or older | 8,147 | 2,057 | 139 | 1,434 | 4,351 | 166 |
| Aged 85 or older | 2,025 | 196 | 39 | 506 | 1,236 | 48 |
| Aged 55 to 64 | 10,878 | 7,152 | 391 | 1,161 | 1,913 | 261 |
| Aged 65 to 74 | 10,117 | 5,363 | 207 | 1,151 | 3,240 | 156 |
| Aged 75 to 84 | 6,122 | 1,861 | 100 | 928 | 3,115 | 118 |
| **Total women, percent** | **100.0%** | **52.3%** | **3.8%** | **24.0%** | **13.9%** | **5.9%** |
| Aged 55 or older | 100.0 | 50.0 | 2.5 | 12.9 | 32.6 | 2.0 |
| Aged 65 or older | 100.0 | 40.6 | 1.9 | 14.2 | 41.6 | 1.8 |
| Aged 75 or older | 100.0 | 25.2 | 1.7 | 17.6 | 53.4 | 2.0 |
| Aged 85 or older | 100.0 | 9.7 | 1.9 | 25.0 | 61.0 | 2.4 |
| Aged 55 to 64 | 100.0 | 65.7 | 3.6 | 10.7 | 17.6 | 2.4 |
| Aged 65 to 74 | 100.0 | 53.0 | 2.0 | 11.4 | 32.0 | 1.5 |
| Aged 75 to 84 | 100.0 | 30.4 | 1.6 | 15.2 | 50.9 | 1.9 |

*(continued)*

*(continued from previous page)*

| | total | married, spouse present | married, spouse absent | living with other relatives | living alone | living with nonrelatives only |
|---|---|---|---|---|---|---|
| **Total men, number** | **97,704** | **54,944** | **2,806** | **21,377** | **10,140** | **8,437** |
| Aged 55 or older | 22,881 | 17,514 | 606 | 820 | 3,391 | 550 |
| Aged 65 or older | 13,003 | 9,693 | 330 | 531 | 2,254 | 195 |
| Aged 75 or older | 4,906 | 3,353 | 121 | 239 | 1,120 | 73 |
| Aged 85 or older | 840 | 393 | 39 | 85 | 300 | 23 |
| Aged 55 to 64 | 9,878 | 7,821 | 276 | 289 | 1,137 | 355 |
| Aged 65 to 74 | 8,097 | 6,340 | 209 | 214 | 1,134 | 200 |
| Aged 75 to 84 | 4,066 | 2,960 | 82 | 154 | 820 | 50 |
| **Total men, percent** | **100.0%** | **56.2%** | **2.9%** | **21.9%** | **10.4%** | **8.6%** |
| Aged 55 or older | 100.0 | 76.5 | 2.6 | 3.6 | 14.8 | 2.4 |
| Aged 65 or older | 100.0 | 74.5 | 2.5 | 4.1 | 17.3 | 1.5 |
| Aged 75 or older | 100.0 | 68.3 | 2.5 | 4.9 | 22.8 | 1.5 |
| Aged 85 or older | 100.0 | 46.8 | 4.6 | 10.1 | 35.7 | 2.7 |
| Aged 55 to 64 | 100.0 | 79.2 | 2.8 | 2.9 | 11.5 | 3.6 |
| Aged 65 to 74 | 100.0 | 78.3 | 2.6 | 2.6 | 14.0 | 2.5 |
| Aged 75 to 84 | 100.0 | 72.8 | 2.0 | 3.8 | 20.2 | 1.2 |

*Source: Bureau of the Census,* Marital Status and Living Arrangements: March 1995, *Current Population Reports, P20-491, 1996; calculations by New Strategist*

# People Aged 55 or Older Who Live Alone by Sex, 1995

*(number and percent of total persons aged 15 or older and persons aged 55 or older who live alone by sex and age, 1995; numbers in thousands)*

| | | living alone | |
|---|---|---|---|
| | *total* | *number* | *percent* |
| **Total persons** | **202,732** | **24,732** | **12.2%** |
| Aged 55 or older | 52,022 | 13,458 | 25.9 |
| Aged 65 or older | 31,267 | 10,128 | 32.4 |
| Aged 75 or older | 13,053 | 5,593 | 42.8 |
| Aged 85 or older | 2,865 | 1,561 | 54.5 |
| Aged 55 to 64 | 20,755 | 3,330 | 16.0 |
| Aged 65 to 74 | 18,214 | 4,535 | 24.9 |
| Aged 75 to 84 | 10,188 | 4,032 | 39.6 |
| **Total women** | **105,028** | **14,592** | **13.9** |
| Aged 55 or older | 29,142 | 9,504 | 32.6 |
| Aged 65 or older | 18,264 | 7,591 | 41.6 |
| Aged 75 or older | 8,147 | 4,351 | 53.4 |
| Aged 85 or older | 2,025 | 1,236 | 61.0 |
| Aged 55 to 64 | 10,878 | 1,913 | 17.6 |
| Aged 65 to 74 | 10,117 | 3,240 | 32.0 |
| Aged 75 to 84 | 6,122 | 3,115 | 50.9 |
| **Total men** | **97,704** | **10,140** | **10.4** |
| Aged 55 or older | 22,881 | 3,391 | 14.8 |
| Aged 65 or older | 13,003 | 2,254 | 17.3 |
| Aged 75 or older | 4,906 | 1,120 | 22.8 |
| Aged 85 or older | 840 | 300 | 35.7 |
| Aged 55 to 64 | 9,878 | 1,137 | 11.5 |
| Aged 65 to 74 | 8,097 | 1,134 | 14.0 |
| Aged 75 to 84 | 4,066 | 820 | 20.2 |

*Source: Bureau of the Census,* Marital Status and Living Arrangements: March 1995, *Current Population Reports, P20-491, 1996; calculations by New Strategist*

# Most Older Americans Are Married

**Men are more likely to be married than women, however.**

While 53 percent of women aged 55 or older are currently married, the proportion among men is a much-higher 79 percent. Reasons for this difference include the fact that women tend to marry men who are a few years older and that men die at a younger age than women. Consequently, women are much more likely than men to be widowed in old age.

The percentage of women who are widows stands at 35 percent among all women aged 55 or older, ranging from a low of 13 percent among those aged 55 to 64 to a high of 81 percent among those aged 85 or older. Only 9 percent of men aged 55 or older are widowed, but 41 percent of those aged 85 or older are.

Marital-status patterns are the same regardless of race and ethnicity. Widowhood is uncommon among white, black, and Hispanic women aged 55 to 64. But in the 85-plus age group, eight in ten women are widows. Among men, the married proportion never falls below 50 percent, even in the oldest age group and regardless of race or Hispanic origin. The widowed proportion peaks at just 37 to 41 percent in the 85-plus age group.

◆ Marriage is much more popular among older Americans than among the baby-boom generation. As boomers age, the proportion of older Americans who are married will decline.

# Marital Status of Persons Aged 55 or Older by Sex, 1995

*(number and percent distribution of total persons aged 15 or older and persons aged 55 or older by sex and marital status, 1995; numbers in thousands)*

| | | aged 55 or older | | | | | |
| | | | | aged 65 or older | | | |
| | *total* | *total* | *55 to 64* | *total* | *65 to 74* | *75 to 84* | *85 or older* |
|---|---|---|---|---|---|---|---|
| **Total women, number** | **105,028** | **29,142** | **10,878** | **18,264** | **10,117** | **6,122** | **2,025** |
| Never married | 24,693 | 1,235 | 467 | 768 | 408 | 255 | 105 |
| Married | 58,984 | 15,310 | 7,543 | 7,767 | 5,571 | 1,961 | 235 |
| Divorced | 10,270 | 2,554 | 1,463 | 1,091 | 786 | 264 | 41 |
| Widowed | 11,082 | 10,041 | 1,405 | 8,636 | 3,352 | 3,641 | 1,643 |
| **Total women, percent** | **100.0%** | **100.0%** | **100.0%** | **100.0%** | **100.0%** | **100.0%** | **100.0%** |
| Never married | 23.5 | 4.2 | 4.3 | 4.2 | 4.0 | 4.2 | 5.2 |
| Married | 56.2 | 52.5 | 69.3 | 42.5 | 55.1 | 32.0 | 11.6 |
| Divorced | 9.8 | 8.8 | 13.4 | 6.0 | 7.8 | 4.3 | 2.0 |
| Widowed | 10.6 | 34.5 | 12.9 | 47.3 | 33.1 | 59.5 | 81.1 |
| **Total men, number** | **97704** | **22,881** | **9878** | **13,003** | **8097** | **4066** | **840** |
| Never married | 30286 | 1,037 | 494 | 543 | 342 | 160 | 41 |
| Married | 57750 | 18,120 | 8097 | 10,023 | 6549 | 3042 | 432 |
| Divorced | 7383 | 1,692 | 1011 | 681 | 513 | 144 | 24 |
| Widowed | 2284 | 2,030 | 275 | 1,755 | 693 | 720 | 342 |
| **Total men, percent** | **100.0%** | **100.0%** | **100.0%** | **100.0%** | **100.0%** | **100.0%** | **100.0%** |
| Never married | 31.0 | 4.5 | 5.0 | 4.2 | 4.2 | 3.9 | 4.9 |
| Married | 59.1 | 79.2 | 82.0 | 77.1 | 80.9 | 74.8 | 51.4 |
| Divorced | 7.6 | 7.4 | 10.2 | 5.2 | 6.3 | 3.5 | 2.9 |
| Widowed | 2.3 | 8.9 | 2.8 | 13.5 | 8.6 | 17.7 | 40.7 |

*Source: Bureau of the Census,* Marital Status and Living Arrangements: March 1995, *Current Population Reports, P20-491, 1996*

# Marital Status of Women Aged 55 or Older by Race and Hispanic Origin 1995

*(number and percent distribution of women aged 55 or older by marital status, race, and Hispanic origin, 1995; numbers in thousands)*

|  | total | white | black | Hispanic |
|---|---|---|---|---|
| **Women, aged 55 to 64** | **10,878** | **9,323** | **1,174** | **791** |
| **Percent** | **100.0%** | **100.0%** | **100.0%** | **100.0%** |
| Never married | 4.3 | 3.8 | 9.3 | 6.6 |
| Married | 69.3 | 71.5 | 52.7 | 66.3 |
| Divorced | 13.4 | 13.3 | 14.0 | 12.6 |
| Widowed | 12.9 | 11.4 | 24.0 | 14.5 |
| **Women, aged 65 to 74** | **10,117** | **8,953** | **895** | **513** |
| **Percent** | **100.0%** | **100.0%** | **100.0%** | **100.0%** |
| Never married | 3.8 | 3.7 | 7.5 | 8.8 |
| Married | 71.5 | 56.8 | 38.3 | 47.6 |
| Divorced | 13.3 | 7.4 | 12.5 | 11.8 |
| Widowed | 11.4 | 32.2 | 41.7 | 31.8 |
| **Women, aged 75 to 84** | **6,122** | **5,538** | **473** | **215** |
| **Percent** | **100.0%** | **100.0%** | **100.0%** | **100.0%** |
| Never married | 4.2 | 4.0 | 4.6 | 6.2 |
| Married | 32.0 | 33.0 | 20.4 | 26.2 |
| Divorced | 4.3 | 4.3 | 5.1 | 5.0 |
| Widowed | 59.5 | 58.7 | 69.9 | 62.6 |
| **Women, aged 85 or older** | **2,125** | **1,811** | **185** | **66** |
| **Percent** | **100.0%** | **100.0%** | **100.0%** | **100.0%** |
| Never married | 5.2 | 5.3 | 5.2 | 3.0 |
| Married | 11.7 | 12.1 | 6.8 | 16.7 |
| Divorced | 2.0 | 1.9 | 3.2 | 1.5 |
| Widowed | 81.0 | 80.7 | 84.7 | 78.8 |

*Note: Numbers will not add to total because Hispanics may be of any race and not all races are shown.*
*Sources: Bureau of the Census,* Marital Status and Living Arrangements: March 1995, *Current Population Reports, P20-491, 1996*

# Marital Status of Men Aged 55 or Older by Race and Hispanic Origin 1995

*(number and percent distribution of men aged 55 or older by marital status, race, and Hispanic origin, 1995; numbers in thousands)*

|  | total | white | black | Hispanic |
|---|---|---|---|---|
| **Men, aged 55 to 64** | **9,878** | **8,712** | **896** | **603** |
| **Percent** | **100.0%** | **100.0%** | **100.0%** | **100.0%** |
| Never married | 5.0 | 4.3 | 12.7 | 5.2 |
| Married | 82.0 | 83.2 | 68.3 | 82.9 |
| Divorced | 10.2 | 10.0 | 12.6 | 8.9 |
| Widowed | 2.8 | 2.5 | 6.4 | 3.0 |
| **Men, aged 65 to 74** | **8,097** | **7,248** | **646** | **446** |
| **Percent** | **100.0%** | **100.0%** | **100.0%** | **100.0%** |
| Never married | 4.2 | 4.1 | 4.9 | 2.3 |
| Married | 80.9 | 82.0 | 68.5 | 74.6 |
| Divorced | 6.3 | 6.1 | 9.9 | 8.7 |
| Widowed | 8.6 | 7.8 | 16.7 | 14.4 |
| **Men, aged 75 to 84** | **4,066** | **3,673** | **296** | **144** |
| **Percent** | **100.0%** | **100.0%** | **100.0%** | **100.0%** |
| Never married | 3.9 | 3.5 | 10.0 | 4.7 |
| Married | 74.9 | 76.2 | 56.2 | 62.6 |
| Divorced | 3.5 | 3.5 | 5.2 | 10.5 |
| Widowed | 17.7 | 16.8 | 28.6 | 22.2 |
| **Men, aged 85 or older** | **840** | **762** | **57** | **44** |
| **Percent** | **100.0%** | **100.0%** | **100.0%** | **100.0%** |
| Never married | 4.9 | 4.1 | 10.9 | 4.5 |
| Married | 51.5 | 51.5 | 51.3 | 50.0 |
| Divorced | 2.9 | 3.2 | 1.0 | 4.5 |
| Widowed | 40.7 | 41.2 | 36.8 | 40.9 |

*Note: Numbers will not add to total because Hispanics may be of any race and not all races are shown.*
*Sources: Bureau of the Census,* Marital Status and Living Arrangements: March 1995, *Current Population Reports, P20-491, 1996*

# Population

◆ Only 46 percent of 65-to-69-year-olds are men, a figure that drops to 31 percent of 85-to-89-year-olds and to just 16 percent of people aged 100 or older.

◆ While the number of 55-to-64-year-olds will grow 43 percent between 1997 and 2005, the number of people aged 70 to 74 will decline nearly 5 percent.

◆ Although 11 percent of the total population are Hispanic, only 6 percent of people aged 55 or older are Hispanic.

◆ People aged 55 or older are far less likely to move than younger people. When they do move, however, they are more likely than average to move to a different state.

◆ The number of 65-to-74-year-olds is projected to decline 10 percent between 1995 and 2000 in New England and to grow 10 percent in the Mountain states.

◆ In every state but Alaska, women are at least 52 percent of the population aged 55 or older and 70 percent of the 85-or-older population.

◆ The elderly populations of Alaska, Colorado, Nevada, and Utah will surge more than 135 percent between 1995 and 2025.

# Older Women Outnumber Older Men

**There are only 77 men aged 55 or older for every 100 women in that age group.**

At birth males outnumber females, but by the early 30s the ratio tips in favor of women. This trend gains strength with age because men are more likely to die than women at any age. The average life expectancy of newborn boys is 72.5 years, but for females it is 78.9 years. By age 55, women can expect to live 27 more years, compared to men's 23. Thus, women increasingly outnumber men in the older age groups.

In the 65-to-69 age group, there are only 84 men per 100 women—or 46 percent of the population. This figure falls to 31 percent in the 85-to-89 age group. Only 16 percent of the nation's centenarians are men.

◆ The older market is increasingly a women's market—especially among the very old, aged 85 or older.

◆ Because men die younger than women, the share of older women who are widows rises dramatically—from 13 percent among women aged 55 to 64 to 81 percent among women aged 85 or older. With age, then, women become increasingly independent consumers.

## Women Increasingly Outnumber Men with Age

*(males per 100 females, by age, 1997)*

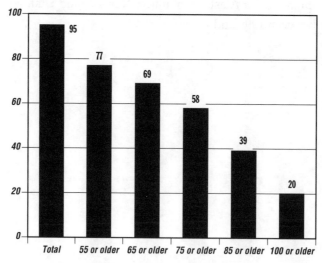

# Population Aged 55 or Older, 1997

*(total number of persons and number aged 55 or older by age and sex, and sex ratio by age, 1997; numbers in thousands)*

|  | total | men | women | males per 100 females |
|---|---|---|---|---|
| **Total persons** | **267,645** | **130,712** | **136,933** | **95** |
| Aged 55 or older | 55,912 | 24,364 | 31,546 | 77 |
| Aged 65 or older | 34,097 | 13,975 | 20,120 | 69 |
| Aged 75 or older | 15,586 | 5,709 | 9,874 | 58 |
| Aged 55 to 64 | 21,815 | 10,389 | 11,426 | 91 |
| Aged 65 to 74 | 18,511 | 8,266 | 10,246 | 81 |
| Aged 75 to 84 | 11,724 | 4,621 | 7,102 | 65 |
| Aged 85 or older | 3,862 | 1,088 | 2,772 | 39 |
| Aged 55 to 59 | 11,754 | 5,642 | 6,111 | 92 |
| Aged 60 to 64 | 10,062 | 4,747 | 5,315 | 89 |
| Aged 65 to 69 | 9,758 | 4,454 | 5,305 | 84 |
| Aged 70 to 74 | 8,753 | 3,812 | 4,941 | 77 |
| Aged 75 to 79 | 7,072 | 2,914 | 4,157 | 70 |
| Aged 80 to 84 | 4,652 | 1,707 | 2,945 | 58 |
| Aged 85 to 89 | 2,451 | 755 | 1,695 | 45 |
| Aged 90 to 94 | 1,051 | 262 | 789 | 33 |
| Aged 95 to 99 | 299 | 61 | 238 | 26 |
| Aged 100 or older | 61 | 10 | 50 | 20 |

*Source: Bureau of the Census,* Population Projections of the United States by Age, Sex, Race, and Hispanic Origin: 1995 to 2050, *Current Population Reports, P25-1130, 1996; calculations by New Strategist*

# Greatest Growth Forecast for People Aged 55 to 59

**The number of people aged 55 to 59 is projected to increase by over 5 million between 1997 and 2005 as boomers enter the age group.**

While the number of people in their late 50s is projected to grow the most, in percentage terms the oldest old should grow the fastest between 1997 and 2005. The number of people aged 100 or older is projected to grow 66 percent during those years. This figure represents a gain of just 40,000 people, however.

Because of baby booms and busts over most of this century, the growth of the population aged 55 or older during the next decade will vary sharply by age group. The number of people aged 55 to 64 will grow 36 percent, for example, but the number of those aged 70 to 74 will decline nearly 5 percent as the small generation born during the Depression enters the age group.

◆ Businesses looking for growth in the older market should target the extremes. The younger (55 to 64) and older (85+) ends of the market will experience rapid growth, while the number of people in the middle will expand little, if at all.

◆ This split in the older market suggests a two-tiered marketing strategy. On the one hand, businesses targeting the very old can continue with their traditional marketing strategies. But businesses wanting to appeal to the expanding number of Americans in their 50s should craft a new approach to appeal to the vastly different baby-boom generation.

## Increase in Older Americans Will Vary by Age

*(percent change in population by age, 1997 to 2005)*

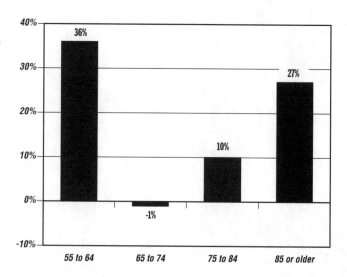

# Population Aged 55 or Older, 1997 to 2005

*(total number of persons and number aged 55 or older, 1997, 2000, and 2005; numerical and percent change, 1997-2005; numbers in thousands)*

| | 1997 | 2000 | 2005 | change, 1997-2005 | |
|---|---|---|---|---|---|
| | | | | number | percent |
| **Total persons** | **267,645** | **274,634** | **285,981** | **18,336** | **6.9%** |
| Aged 55 or older | 55,912 | 58,673 | 65,771 | 9,859 | 17.6 |
| Aged 65 or older | 34,097 | 34,711 | 36,165 | 2,068 | 6.1 |
| Aged 75 or older | 15,586 | 16,575 | 17,796 | 2,210 | 14.2 |
| Aged 55 to 64 | 21,815 | 23,962 | 29,606 | 7,791 | 35.7 |
| Aged 65 to 74 | 18,511 | 18,136 | 18,369 | -142 | -0.8 |
| Aged 75 to 84 | 11,724 | 12,315 | 12,898 | 1,174 | 10.0 |
| Aged 85 or older | 3,862 | 4,260 | 4,898 | 1,036 | 26.8 |
| Aged 55 to 59 | 11,754 | 13,307 | 16,798 | 5,044 | 42.9 |
| Aged 60 to 64 | 10,062 | 10,654 | 12,807 | 2,746 | 27.3 |
| Aged 65 to 69 | 9,758 | 9,410 | 10,037 | 279 | 2.9 |
| Aged 70 to 74 | 8,753 | 8,726 | 8,332 | -421 | -4.8 |
| Aged 75 to 79 | 7,072 | 7,415 | 7,393 | 321 | 4.5 |
| Aged 80 to 84 | 4,652 | 4,900 | 5,505 | 853 | 18.3 |
| Aged 85 to 89 | 2,451 | 2,679 | 2,993 | 542 | 22.1 |
| Aged 90 to 94 | 1,051 | 1,153 | 1,373 | 322 | 30.6 |
| Aged 95 to 99 | 299 | 356 | 431 | 132 | 44.1 |
| Aged 100 or older | 61 | 72 | 101 | 40 | 65.6 |

*Source: Bureau of the Census,* Population Projections of the United States by Age, Sex, Race, and Hispanic Origin: 1995 to 2050, *Current Population Recport, P25-1130, 1996; calculations by New Strategist*

# Little Diversity among Older Americans

**Fully 83 percent of people aged 55 or older are non-Hispanic white.**

Although the population of younger Americans is becoming increasingly diverse, older Americans still look like the U.S. population as a whole did decades ago—with few blacks, Asians, and Hispanics among them.

While only 73 percent of all Americans are non-Hispanic white, the proportion is 85 percent among people aged 65 or older and 87 percent among those aged 85 or older. Just 9 percent of older Americans are non-Hispanic black, while only 2 percent are non-Hispanic Asian.

Among the population as a whole, 11 percent are Hispanic. But among people aged 55 or older, only 6 percent are Hispanic. This figure falls to less than 4 percent among people aged 85 or older.

◆ The older market is the last gasp of the way things used to be, with consumers a homogeneous mass of non-Hispanic whites. As boomers enter the market in the next few years, its diversity will begin to increase. But it won't be until Generation X hits its 50s that diversity will be the rule.

# Non-Hispanics Aged 55 or Older by Race, 1997

*(number and percent distribution of total persons and persons aged 55 or older who are non-Hispanics by race, 1997; numbers in thousands)*

| | total | non-Hispanic total | white | black | Asian | Native American |
|---|---|---|---|---|---|---|
| **Number** | | | | | | |
| **Total persons** | **267,645** | **238,964** | **195,091** | **32,396** | **9,497** | **1,980** |
| Aged 55 or older | 55,913 | 52,768 | 46,352 | 4,829 | 1,325 | 262 |
| Aged 65 or older | 34,097 | 32,453 | 28,939 | 2,705 | 671 | 138 |
| Aged 75 or older | 15,586 | 14,960 | 13,548 | 1,124 | 229 | 59 |
| Aged 55 to 64 | 21,816 | 20,315 | 17,413 | 2,124 | 654 | 124 |
| Aged 65 to 74 | 18,511 | 17,493 | 15,391 | 1,581 | 442 | 79 |
| Aged 75 to 84 | 11,724 | 11,246 | 10,178 | 838 | 188 | 42 |
| Aged 85 or older | 3,862 | 3,714 | 3,370 | 286 | 41 | 17 |
| Aged 55 to 59 | 11,754 | 10,927 | 9,341 | 1,157 | 360 | 69 |
| Aged 60 to 64 | 10,062 | 9,388 | 8,072 | 967 | 294 | 55 |
| Aged 65 to 69 | 9,758 | 9,181 | 7,995 | 893 | 249 | 44 |
| Aged 70 to 74 | 8,753 | 8,312 | 7,396 | 688 | 193 | 35 |
| Aged 75 to 79 | 7,072 | 6,775 | 6,105 | 522 | 122 | 26 |
| Aged 80 to 84 | 4,652 | 4,471 | 4,073 | 316 | 66 | 16 |
| Aged 85 to 89 | 2,451 | 2,356 | 2,153 | 167 | 27 | 9 |
| Aged 90 to 94 | 1,051 | 1,012 | 915 | 83 | 9 | 5 |
| Aged 95 to 99 | 299 | 288 | 254 | 28 | 4 | 2 |
| Aged 100 or older | 61 | 58 | 48 | 8 | 1 | 1 |

*(continued)*

*(continued from previous page)*

| Percent | total | non-Hispanic total | white | black | Asian | Native American |
|---|---|---|---|---|---|---|
| **Total persons** | **100.0%** | **89.3%** | **72.9%** | **12.1%** | **3.5%** | **0.7%** |
| Aged 55 or older | 100.0 | 94.4 | 82.9 | 8.6 | 2.4 | 0.5 |
| Aged 65 or older | 100.0 | 95.2 | 84.9 | 7.9 | 2.0 | 0.4 |
| Aged 75 or older | 100.0 | 96.0 | 86.9 | 7.2 | 1.5 | 0.4 |
| Aged 55 to 64 | 100.0 | 93.1 | 79.8 | 9.7 | 3.0 | 0.6 |
| Aged 65 to 74 | 100.0 | 94.5 | 83.1 | 8.5 | 2.4 | 0.4 |
| Aged 75 to 84 | 100.0 | 95.9 | 86.8 | 7.1 | 1.6 | 0.4 |
| Aged 85 or older | 100.0 | 96.2 | 87.3 | 7.4 | 1.1 | 0.4 |
| Aged 55 to 59 | 100.0 | 93.0 | 79.5 | 9.8 | 3.1 | 0.6 |
| Aged 60 to 64 | 100.0 | 93.3 | 80.2 | 9.6 | 2.9 | 0.5 |
| Aged 65 to 69 | 100.0 | 94.1 | 81.9 | 9.2 | 2.6 | 0.5 |
| Aged 70 to 74 | 100.0 | 95.0 | 84.5 | 7.9 | 2.2 | 0.4 |
| Aged 75 to 79 | 100.0 | 95.8 | 86.3 | 7.4 | 1.7 | 0.4 |
| Aged 80 to 84 | 100.0 | 96.1 | 87.6 | 6.8 | 1.4 | 0.3 |
| Aged 85 to 89 | 100.0 | 96.1 | 87.8 | 6.8 | 1.1 | 0.4 |
| Aged 90 to 94 | 100.0 | 96.3 | 87.1 | 7.9 | 0.9 | 0.5 |
| Aged 95 to 99 | 100.0 | 96.3 | 84.9 | 9.4 | 1.3 | 0.7 |
| Aged 100 or older | 100.0 | 95.1 | 78.7 | 13.1 | 1.6 | 1.6 |

*Source: Bureau of the Census,* Population Projections of the United States by Age, Sex, Race, and Hispanic Origin: 1995 to 2050, *Current Population Report, P25-1130, 1996; calculations by New Strategist*

# Hispanics Aged 55 or Older by Race, 1997

*(number and percent distribution of Hispanics aged 55 or older by race, 1997; numbers in thousands)*

| | total | Hispanic total | white | black | Asian | Native American |
|---|---|---|---|---|---|---|
| **Number** | | | | | | |
| **Total persons** | **267,645** | **28,680** | **26,072** | **1,679** | **605** | **325** |
| Aged 55 or older | 55,913 | 3,149 | 2,888 | 172 | 58 | 28 |
| Aged 65 or older | 34,097 | 1,648 | 1,519 | 83 | 29 | 14 |
| Aged 75 or older | 15,586 | 628 | 584 | 27 | 10 | 5 |
| Aged 55 to 64 | 21,816 | 1,501 | 1,369 | 89 | 29 | 14 |
| Aged 65 to 74 | 18,511 | 1,020 | 935 | 56 | 19 | 9 |
| Aged 75 to 84 | 11,724 | 478 | 442 | 23 | 9 | 4 |
| Aged 85 or older | 3,862 | 150 | 142 | 4 | 1 | 1 |
| Aged 55 to 59 | 11,754 | 827 | 753 | 50 | 16 | 8 |
| Aged 60 to 64 | 10,062 | 674 | 616 | 39 | 13 | 6 |
| Aged 65 to 69 | 9,758 | 578 | 529 | 34 | 10 | 5 |
| Aged 70 to 74 | 8,753 | 442 | 406 | 22 | 9 | 4 |
| Aged 75 to 79 | 7,072 | 297 | 274 | 15 | 6 | 2 |
| Aged 80 to 84 | 4,652 | 181 | 168 | 8 | 3 | 2 |
| Aged 85 to 89 | 2,451 | 95 | 89 | 3 | 1 | 1 |
| Aged 90 to 94 | 1,051 | 40 | 38 | 1 | 0 | 0 |
| Aged 95 to 99 | 299 | 12 | 12 | 0 | 0 | 0 |
| Aged 100 or older | 61 | 3 | 3 | 0 | 0 | 0 |

*(continued)*

*(continued from previous page)*

| | total | Hispanic total | white | black | Asian | Native American |
|---|---|---|---|---|---|---|
| **Percent** | | | | | | |
| **Total persons** | 100.0% | 10.7% | 9.7% | 0.6% | 0.2% | 0.1% |
| Aged 55 or older | 100.0 | 5.6 | 5.2 | 0.3 | 0.1 | 0.1 |
| Aged 65 or older | 100.0 | 4.8 | 4.5 | 0.2 | 0.1 | 0.0 |
| Aged 75 or older | 100.0 | 4.0 | 3.7 | 0.2 | 0.1 | 0.0 |
| Aged 55 to 64 | 100.0 | 6.9 | 6.3 | 0.4 | 0.1 | 0.1 |
| Aged 65 to 74 | 100.0 | 5.5 | 5.1 | 0.3 | 0.1 | 0.0 |
| Aged 75 to 84 | 100.0 | 4.1 | 3.8 | 0.2 | 0.1 | 0.0 |
| Aged 85 or older | 100.0 | 3.9 | 3.7 | 0.1 | 0.0 | 0.0 |
| Aged 55 to 59 | 100.0 | 7.0 | 6.4 | 0.4 | 0.1 | 0.1 |
| Aged 60 to 64 | 100.0 | 6.7 | 6.1 | 0.4 | 0.1 | 0.1 |
| Aged 65 to 69 | 100.0 | 5.9 | 5.4 | 0.3 | 0.1 | 0.1 |
| Aged 70 to 74 | 100.0 | 5.0 | 4.6 | 0.3 | 0.1 | 0.0 |
| Aged 75 to 79 | 100.0 | 4.2 | 3.9 | 0.2 | 0.1 | 0.0 |
| Aged 80 to 84 | 100.0 | 3.9 | 3.6 | 0.2 | 0.1 | 0.0 |
| Aged 85 to 89 | 100.0 | 3.9 | 3.6 | 0.1 | 0.0 | 0.0 |
| Aged 90 to 94 | 100.0 | 3.8 | 3.6 | 0.1 | 0.0 | 0.0 |
| Aged 95 to 99 | 100.0 | 4.0 | 4.0 | 0.0 | 0.0 | 0.0 |
| Aged 100 or older | 100.0 | 4.9 | 4.9 | 0.0 | 0.0 | 0.0 |

*Source: Bureau of the Census,* Population Projections of the United States by Age, Sex, Race, and Hispanic Origin: 1995 to 2050, *Current Population Report, P25-1130, 1996; calculations by New Strategist*

# Older Americans Not Likely to Move

## Each year, only 6 percent of people aged 55 or older move.

Despite images of older Americans moving en masse to Florida and other warm states upon retirement, people aged 55 or older are far less likely to move than younger people. Overall, 16 percent of Americans moved between March 1993 and March 1994, nearly three times the proportion of those aged 55 or older who moved.

Some older people do move when they retire, but not enough to boost their mobility rates very much. While 6.2 percent of people aged 60 to 64 move in a year's time, among those aged 65 to 69 the figure is a slightly higher 6.4 percent. Mobility bottoms out in the 75-to-79 age group at 4.4 percent, then rises above 5 percent at age 80 or older. The higher mobility among the very old occurs as women become widowed and move from retirement locales to be closer to their families.

Older Americans who do move are more likely to move out-of-state than movers in general. Only 16 percent of all movers aged 1 or older moved to a different state between 1993 and 1994. But among those aged 55 or older, 21 percent moved to a different state. And among movers aged 65 to 69, 25 percent moved to a different state.

◆ Between 1993 and 1994, 623,000 Americans aged 55 or older moved to a different state. As the large baby-boom generation ages into its late 50s, the number of older interstate movers should surge, surpassing 1 million.

# Geographical Mobility, 1993 to 1994

*(total number and percent of persons aged 1 or older and aged 55 or older who moved between March 1993 and March 1994, by type of move; numbers in thousands)*

| | | same house (non- movers) | different house in the U.S | | different county | | different state | | | movers from abroad |
| | total | | total | same county | total | same state | total | same region | different region | |
|---|---|---|---|---|---|---|---|---|---|---|
| **Total, 1 or older** | **255,774** | **212,939** | **41,590** | **26,638** | **14,952** | **8,226** | **6,726** | **3,591** | **3,135** | **1,245** |
| Aged 55 or older | 51,513 | 48,373 | 3,057 | 1,782 | 1,274 | 623 | 652 | 380 | 269 | 81 |
| Aged 65 or older | 30,778 | 29,050 | 1,690 | 973 | 716 | 341 | 376 | 238 | 135 | 36 |
| Aged 55 to 59 | 10,730 | 9,957 | 742 | 424 | 319 | 149 | 169 | 78 | 91 | 31 |
| Aged 60 to 64 | 10,005 | 9,366 | 625 | 385 | 239 | 133 | 107 | 64 | 43 | 14 |
| Aged 65 to 69 | 9,595 | 8,965 | 616 | 320 | 296 | 145 | 151 | 104 | 46 | 14 |
| Aged 70 to 74 | 8,490 | 8,043 | 442 | 273 | 169 | 79 | 90 | 55 | 35 | 4 |
| Aged 75 to 79 | 5,979 | 5,705 | 266 | 164 | 102 | 45 | 57 | 45 | 11 | 8 |
| Aged 80 to 84 | 3,879 | 3,666 | 207 | 119 | 87 | 44 | 43 | 22 | 21 | 6 |
| Aged 85 or older | 2,835 | 2,671 | 159 | 97 | 62 | 28 | 35 | 12 | 22 | 4 |
| Median age | 33.8 | 36.0 | 26.8 | 26.4 | 27.5 | 27.3 | 27.9 | 28.0 | 27.8 | 26.5 |
| **Total, 1 or older** | **100.0%** | **83.3%** | **16.3%** | **10.4%** | **5.8%** | **3.2%** | **2.6%** | **1.4%** | **1.2%** | **0.5%** |
| Aged 55 or older | 100.0 | 93.9 | 5.9 | 3.5 | 2.5 | 1.2 | 1.3 | 0.7 | 0.5 | 0.2 |
| Aged 65 or older | 100.0 | 94.4 | 5.5 | 3.2 | 2.3 | 1.1 | 1.2 | 0.8 | 0.4 | 0.1 |
| Aged 55 to 59 | 100.0 | 92.8 | 6.9 | 4.0 | 3.0 | 1.4 | 1.6 | 0.7 | 0.8 | 0.3 |
| Aged 60 to 64 | 100.0 | 93.6 | 6.2 | 3.8 | 2.4 | 1.3 | 1.1 | 0.6 | 0.4 | 0.1 |
| Aged 65 to 69 | 100.0 | 93.4 | 6.4 | 3.3 | 3.1 | 1.5 | 1.6 | 1.1 | 0.5 | 0.1 |
| Aged 70 to 74 | 100.0 | 94.7 | 5.2 | 3.2 | 2.0 | 0.9 | 1.1 | 0.6 | 0.4 | 0.0 |
| Aged 75 to 79 | 100.0 | 95.4 | 4.4 | 2.7 | 1.7 | 0.8 | 1.0 | 0.8 | 0.2 | 0.1 |
| Aged 80 to 84 | 100.0 | 94.5 | 5.3 | 3.1 | 2.2 | 1.1 | 1.1 | 0.6 | 0.5 | 0.2 |
| Aged 85 or older | 100.0 | 94.2 | 5.6 | 3.4 | 2.2 | 1.0 | 1.2 | 0.4 | 0.8 | 0.1 |

*Source: Bureau of the Census,* Geographical Mobility: March 1993 to March 1994, *Current Population Reports, P20-485, 1995*

# In Every Region, Older Women Outnumber Older Men

## Women's share of the older population does not vary much by region.

In the Northeast, 58 percent of people aged 55 or older are women—the highest share among the regions. In the West, women account for 55 percent of the population aged 55 or older—the smallest share among the regions.

With increasing age, women outnumber men by a growing margin. In the Northeast, 73 percent of people aged 85 or older are women. In the West, 69 percent are women.

◆ Whether businesses are national or regional in scope, the fundamentals of marketing to the older population are the same. The majority of your customers are women.

# Population Aged 55 or Older by Region and Sex, 1995

*(total number of persons and number aged 55 or older by region, division, and sex; and percent female, 1995; numbers in thousands)*

| | total | women | men | percent women |
|---|---|---|---|---|
| **TOTAL, UNITED STATES** | **262,755** | **134,441** | **128,314** | **51.2%** |
| Total aged 55 or older | 54,663 | 30,930 | 23,733 | 56.6 |
| Aged 55 to 64 | 21,131 | 11,087 | 10,044 | 52.5 |
| Aged 65 to 74 | 18,759 | 10,417 | 8,342 | 55.5 |
| Aged 75 to 84 | 11,145 | 6,815 | 4,330 | 61.1 |
| Aged 85 or older | 3,628 | 2,611 | 1,017 | 72.0 |
| **TOTAL, NORTHEAST** | **51,466** | **26,652** | **24,814** | **51.8** |
| Total aged 55 or older | 11,595 | 6,666 | 4,929 | 57.5 |
| Aged 55 to 64 | 4,302 | 2,273 | 2,029 | 52.8 |
| Aged 65 to 74 | 4,030 | 2,267 | 1,763 | 56.3 |
| Aged 75 to 84 | 2,450 | 1,529 | 921 | 62.4 |
| Aged 85 or older | 813 | 597 | 216 | 73.4 |
| **Total, New England** | **13,312** | **6,867** | **6,445** | **51.6** |
| Total aged 55 or older | 2,908 | 1,669 | 1,239 | 57.4 |
| Aged 55 to 64 | 1,045 | 546 | 499 | 52.2 |
| Aged 65 to 74 | 1,004 | 562 | 442 | 56.0 |
| Aged 75 to 84 | 637 | 396 | 241 | 62.2 |
| Aged 85 or older | 222 | 165 | 57 | 74.3 |
| **Total, Middle Atlantic** | **38,153** | **19,785** | **18,368** | **51.9** |
| Total aged 55 or older | 8,688 | 4,997 | 3,691 | 57.5 |
| Aged 55 to 64 | 3,257 | 1,727 | 1,530 | 53.0 |
| Aged 65 to 74 | 3,026 | 1,706 | 1,320 | 56.4 |
| Aged 75 to 84 | 1,813 | 1,132 | 681 | 62.4 |
| Aged 85 or older | 592 | 432 | 160 | 73.0 |
| **TOTAL, MIDWEST** | **61,804** | **31,708** | **30,096** | **51.3** |
| Total aged 55 or older | 13,156 | 7,457 | 5,699 | 56.7 |
| Aged 55 to 64 | 5,062 | 2,636 | 2,426 | 52.1 |
| Aged 65 to 74 | 4,418 | 2,443 | 1,975 | 55.3 |
| Aged 75 to 84 | 2,732 | 1,690 | 1,042 | 61.9 |
| Aged 85 or older | 944 | 688 | 256 | 72.9 |

*(continued)*

*(continued from previous page)*

| | total | women | men | percent women |
|---|---|---|---|---|
| **Total, East North Central** | **43,456** | **22,325** | **21,131** | **51.4%** |
| Total aged 55 or older | 9,132 | 5,182 | 3,950 | 56.7 |
| Aged 55 to 64 | 3,560 | 1,858 | 1,702 | 52.2 |
| Aged 65 to 74 | 3,099 | 1,722 | 1,377 | 55.6 |
| Aged 75 to 84 | 1,863 | 1,156 | 707 | 62.1 |
| Aged 85 or older | 610 | 446 | 164 | 73.1 |
| **Total, West North Central** | **18,348** | **9,383** | **8,965** | **51.1** |
| Total aged 55 or older | 4,023 | 2,276 | 1,747 | 56.6 |
| Aged 55 to 64 | 1,502 | 778 | 724 | 51.8 |
| Aged 65 to 74 | 1,319 | 722 | 597 | 54.7 |
| Aged 75 to 84 | 869 | 534 | 335 | 61.4 |
| Aged 85 or older | 333 | 242 | 91 | 72.7 |
| **TOTAL, SOUTH** | **91,890** | **47,219** | **44,671** | **51.4** |
| Total aged 55 or older | 19,248 | 10,927 | 8,321 | 56.8 |
| Aged 55 to 64 | 7,565 | 4,006 | 3,559 | 53.0z |
| Aged 65 to 74 | 6,642 | 3,705 | 2,937 | 55.8 |
| Aged 75 to 84 | 3,832 | 2,347 | 1,485 | 61.2 |
| Aged 85 or older | 1,209 | 869 | 340 | 71.9 |
| **Total, South Atlantic** | **46,995** | **24,190** | **22,805** | **51.5** |
| Total aged 55 or older | 10,351 | 5,871 | 4,480 | 56.7 |
| Aged 55 to 64 | 3,907 | 2,074 | 1,833 | 53.1 |
| Aged 65 to 74 | 3,671 | 2,048 | 1,623 | 55.8 |
| Aged 75 to 84 | 2,128 | 1,289 | 839 | 60.6 |
| Aged 85 or older | 645 | 460 | 185 | 71.3 |
| **Total, East South Central** | **16,067** | **8,324** | **7,743** | **51.8** |
| Total aged 55 or older | 3,424 | 1,969 | 1,455 | 57.5 |
| Aged 55 to 64 | 1,396 | 744 | 652 | 53.3 |
| Aged 65 to 74 | 1,144 | 646 | 498 | 56.5 |
| Aged 75 to 84 | 666 | 420 | 246 | 63.1 |
| Aged 85 or older | 218 | 159 | 59 | 72.9 |
| **Total, West South Central** | **28,828** | **14,704** | **14,124** | **51.0** |
| Total aged 55 or older | 5,472 | 3,088 | 2,384 | 56.4 |
| Aged 55 to 64 | 2,262 | 1,189 | 1,073 | 52.6 |
| Aged 65 to 74 | 1,827 | 1,012 | 815 | 55.4 |
| Aged 75 to 84 | 1,037 | 637 | 400 | 61.4 |
| Aged 85 or older | 346 | 250 | 96 | 72.3 |

*(continued)*

*(continued from previous page)*

| | total | women | men | percent women |
|---|---|---|---|---|
| **TOTAL, WEST** | **57,596** | **28,862** | **28,734** | **50.1%** |
| Total aged 55 or older | 10,665 | 5,881 | 4,784 | 55.1 |
| Aged 55 to 64 | 4,202 | 2,172 | 2,030 | 51.7 |
| Aged 65 to 74 | 3,670 | 2,001 | 1,669 | 54.5 |
| Aged 75 to 84 | 2,131 | 1,250 | 881 | 58.7 |
| Aged 85 or older | 662 | 458 | 204 | 69.2 |
| **Total, Mountain** | **15,645** | **7,868** | **7,777** | **50.3** |
| Total aged 55 or older | 2,988 | 1,626 | 1,362 | 54.4 |
| Aged 55 to 64 | 1,222 | 629 | 593 | 51.5 |
| Aged 65 to 74 | 1,018 | 545 | 473 | 53.5 |
| Aged 75 to 84 | 576 | 334 | 242 | 58.0 |
| Aged 85 or older | 172 | 118 | 54 | 68.6 |
| **Total, Pacific** | **41,951** | **20,995** | **20,956** | **50.0** |
| Total aged 55 or older | 7,675 | 4,255 | 3,420 | 55.4 |
| Aged 55 to 64 | 2,980 | 1,543 | 1,437 | 51.8 |
| Aged 65 to 74 | 2,652 | 1,456 | 1,196 | 54.9 |
| Aged 75 to 84 | 1,554 | 916 | 638 | 58.9 |
| Aged 85 or older | 489 | 340 | 149 | 69.5 |

*Source: Bureau of the Census,* Population Projections for States by Age, Sex, Race, and Hispanic Origin: 1995 to 2025, *PPL-47, 1996; calculations by New Strategist*

# Mountain States Will See Fastest Growth in Number of Older Americans

**The number of people aged 55 or older should climb 21 percent in the Mountain states between 1995 and 2000.**

The slowest growth in the 55-plus population by region and division is projected for the Middle Atlantic states, up less than 2 percent between 1995 and 2000.

In most regions and divisions, the population aged 65 to 74 is projected to shrink as the small generation born during the Depression enters the age group. The greatest decline will occur in New England, where a 10 percent drop in the number of people aged 65 to 74 is forecast. In contrast, the number of people in this age group in the Mountain states should grow 10 percent.

The population aged 85 or older should grow the fastest in every region and division, ranging from an increase of 35 percent in the Mountain states to a gain of 11 percent in the Middle Atlantic states.

◆ In most regions of the country, businesses marketing to older Americans will have to adapt to the booms and busts of the age groups.

◆ The oldest boomers will not reach age 55 until 2001. After that time, businesses in every region can expect rapid growth in the 55-to-64 age group.

## Growth Varies by Division

*(percent change in number of persons aged 55 or older, by division, 1995 to 2000)*

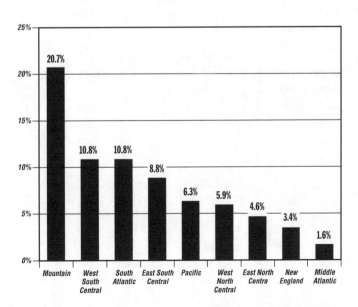

# Population Aged 55 or Older by Region, 1995 and 2000

*(total number of persons and number aged 55 or older by region and division, 1995 and 2000; percent change 1995-2000; numbers in thousands)*

| | 1995 | 2000 | percent change |
|---|---|---|---|
| **TOTAL, UNITED STATES** | **262,755** | **274,634** | **4.5%** |
| Total aged 55 or older | 54,661 | 58,671 | 7.3 |
| Aged 55 to 64 | 21,131 | 23,961 | 13.4 |
| Aged 65 to 74 | 18,760 | 18,136 | -3.3 |
| Aged 75 to 84 | 11,143 | 12,315 | 10.5 |
| Aged 85 or older | 3,627 | 4,259 | 17.5 |
| **TOTAL, NORTHEAST** | **51,465** | **52,107** | **1.2** |
| Total aged 55 or older | 11,596 | 11,837 | 2.1 |
| Aged 55 to 64 | 4,302 | 4,648 | 8.0 |
| Aged 65 to 74 | 4,030 | 3,668 | -9.0 |
| Aged 75 to 84 | 2,450 | 2,609 | 6.5 |
| Aged 85 or older | 814 | 912 | 12.0 |
| **Total, New England** | **13,312** | **13,581** | **2.0** |
| Total aged 55 or older | 2,908 | 3,007 | 3.4 |
| Aged 55 to 64 | 1,045 | 1,167 | 11.7 |
| Aged 65 to 74 | 1,004 | 907 | -9.7 |
| Aged 75 to 84 | 637 | 678 | 6.4 |
| Aged 85 or older | 222 | 255 | 14.9 |
| **Total, Middle Atlantic** | **38,153** | **38,526** | **1.0** |
| Total aged 55 or older | 8,688 | 8,829 | 1.6 |
| Aged 55 to 64 | 3,257 | 3,481 | 6.9 |
| Aged 65 to 74 | 3,026 | 2,760 | -8.8 |
| Aged 75 to 84 | 1,813 | 1,931 | 6.5 |
| Aged 85 or older | 592 | 657 | 11.0 |
| **TOTAL, MIDWEST** | **61,804** | **63,502** | **2.7** |
| Total aged 55 or older | 13,155 | 13,812 | 5.0 |
| Aged 55 to 64 | 5,062 | 5,539 | 9.4 |
| Aged 65 to 74 | 4,418 | 4,251 | -3.8 |
| Aged 75 to 84 | 2,732 | 2,939 | 7.5 |
| Aged 85 or older | 943 | 1,083 | 14.8 |

*(continued)*

*(continued from previous page)*

| | 1995 | 2000 | percent change |
|---|---|---|---|
| **Total, East North Central** | **43,456** | **44,419** | **2.2%** |
| Total aged 55 or older | 9,132 | 9,551 | 4.6 |
| Aged 55 to 64 | 3,560 | 3,877 | 8.9 |
| Aged 65 to 74 | 3,099 | 2,948 | -4.9 |
| Aged 75 to 84 | 1,863 | 2,021 | 8.5 |
| Aged 85 or older | 610 | 705 | 15.6 |
| **Total, West North Central** | **18,348** | **19,082** | **4.0** |
| Total aged 55 or older | 4,023 | 4,261 | 5.9 |
| Aged 55 to 64 | 1,502 | 1,662 | 10.7 |
| Aged 65 to 74 | 1,319 | 1,304 | -1.1 |
| Aged 75 to 84 | 869 | 917 | 5.5 |
| Aged 85 or older | 333 | 378 | 13.5 |
| **TOTAL, SOUTH** | **91,890** | **97,613** | **6.2** |
| Total aged 55 or older | 19,247 | 21,257 | 10.4 |
| Aged 55 to 64 | 7,565 | 8,809 | 16.4 |
| Aged 65 to 74 | 6,642 | 6,648 | 0.1 |
| Aged 75 to 84 | 3,831 | 4,342 | 13.3 |
| Aged 85 or older | 1,209 | 1,458 | 20.7 |
| **Total, South Atlantic** | **46,995** | **50,147** | **6.7** |
| Total aged 55 or older | 10,351 | 11,467 | 10.8 |
| Aged 55 to 64 | 3,907 | 4,634 | 18.6 |
| Aged 65 to 74 | 3,671 | 3,591 | -2.2 |
| Aged 75 to 84 | 2,128 | 2,443 | 14.8 |
| Aged 85 or older | 645 | 799 | 23.9 |
| **Total, East South Central** | **16,067** | **16,918** | **5.3** |
| Total aged 55 or older | 3,424 | 3,727 | 8.8 |
| Aged 55 to 64 | 1,396 | 1,586 | 13.6 |
| Aged 65 to 74 | 1,144 | 1,164 | 1.7 |
| Aged 75 to 84 | 666 | 728 | 9.3 |
| Aged 85 or older | 218 | 249 | 14.2 |
| **Total, West South Central** | **28,828** | **30,548** | **6.0** |
| Total aged 55 or older | 5,472 | 6,062 | 10.8 |
| Aged 55 to 64 | 2,262 | 2,589 | 14.5 |
| Aged 65 to 74 | 1,827 | 1,892 | 3.6 |
| Aged 75 to 84 | 1,037 | 1,170 | 12.8 |
| Aged 85 or older | 346 | 411 | 18.8 |

*(continued)*

*(continued from previous page)*

| | 1995 | 2000 | percent change |
|---|---|---|---|
| **TOTAL, WEST** | **57,596** | **61,413** | **6.6%** |
| Total aged 55 or older | 10,663 | 11,765 | 10.3 |
| Aged 55 to 64 | 4,202 | 4,965 | 18.2 |
| Aged 65 to 74 | 3,670 | 3,569 | -2.8 |
| Aged 75 to 84 | 2,130 | 2,425 | 13.8 |
| Aged 85 or older | 661 | 806 | 21.9 |
| **Total, Mountain** | **15,645** | **17,725** | **13.3** |
| Total aged 55 or older | 2,988 | 3,606 | 20.7 |
| Aged 55 to 64 | 1,222 | 1,545 | 26.4 |
| Aged 65 to 74 | 1,018 | 1,118 | 9.8 |
| Aged 75 to 84 | 576 | 711 | 23.4 |
| Aged 85 or older | 172 | 232 | 34.9 |
| **Total, Pacific** | **41,951** | **43,687** | **4.1** |
| Total aged 55 or older | 7,675 | 8,159 | 6.3 |
| Aged 55 to 64 | 2,980 | 3,420 | 14.8 |
| Aged 65 to 74 | 2,652 | 2,451 | -7.6 |
| Aged 75 to 84 | 1,554 | 1,714 | 10.3 |
| Aged 85 or older | 489 | 574 | 17.4 |

*Source: Bureau of the Census,* Population Projections for States by Age, Sex, Race, and Hispanic Origin: 1995 to 2025, *PPL-47, 1996; calculations by New Strategist*

# Older Women Outnumber Older Men in Every State but Alaska

## In Alaska, only 49 percent of people aged 55 or older are women.

Women are a minority of Alaska's 55-plus population because the state's mining industries attract so many men. In every other state, women are at least a 52 percent majority of the population aged 55 or older. States where men and women are most evenly represented among the older population are Hawaii, Idaho, Nevada, and Montana.

States with the highest proportions of women in their 55-plus populations include Massachusetts, Mississippi, New York, Pennsylvania, Rhode Island, Tennessee, and West Virginia. In these states, 58 percent of people aged 55 or older are women.

In most states, women account for at least 70 percent of the population aged 85 or older. But in Alaska, women are just 50 percent of the oldest old.

◆ Although women's share of the older population is not uniform across the country, businesses in every state but one (Alaska) can count on women being the dominant consumers among the older population.

# Population Aged 55 or Older by State and Sex, 1995

*(total number of persons and number aged 55 or older by state and sex; percent women; 1995; numbers in thousands)*

| | total | women | men | percent women |
|---|---|---|---|---|
| **Total, United States** | **262,755** | **134,440** | **128,315** | **51.2%** |
| Total aged 55 or older | 54,663 | 30,935 | 23,728 | 56.6 |
| Aged 55 to 64 | 21,131 | 11,086 | 10,045 | 52.5 |
| Aged 65 to 74 | 18,759 | 10,418 | 8,341 | 55.5 |
| Aged 75 to 84 | 11,145 | 6,818 | 4,327 | 61.2 |
| Aged 85 or older | 3,628 | 2,613 | 1,015 | 72.0 |
| **Total, Alabama** | **4,253** | **2,212** | **2,041** | **52.0** |
| Total aged 55 or older | 927 | 536 | 391 | 57.8 |
| Aged 55 to 64 | 375 | 201 | 174 | 53.6 |
| Aged 65 to 74 | 312 | 177 | 135 | 56.7 |
| Aged 75 to 84 | 182 | 115 | 67 | 63.2 |
| Aged 85 or older | 58 | 43 | 15 | 74.1 |
| **Total, Alaska** | **604** | **286** | **318** | **47.4** |
| Total aged 55 or older | 68 | 33 | 35 | 48.5 |
| Aged 55 to 64 | 38 | 18 | 20 | 47.4 |
| Aged 65 to 74 | 20 | 10 | 10 | 50.0 |
| Aged 75 to 84 | 8 | 4 | 4 | 50.0 |
| Aged 85 or older | 2 | 1 | 1 | 50.0 |
| **Total, Arizona** | **4,218** | **2,132** | **2,086** | **50.5** |
| Total aged 55 or older | 886 | 486 | 400 | 54.9 |
| Aged 55 to 64 | 326 | 171 | 155 | 52.5 |
| Aged 65 to 74 | 323 | 175 | 148 | 54.2 |
| Aged 75 to 84 | 186 | 106 | 80 | 57.0 |
| Aged 85 or older | 51 | 34 | 17 | 66.7 |
| **Total, Arkansas** | **2,484** | **1,285** | **1,199** | **51.7** |
| Total aged 55 or older | 583 | 330 | 253 | 56.6 |
| Aged 55 to 64 | 223 | 118 | 105 | 52.9 |
| Aged 65 to 74 | 196 | 108 | 88 | 55.1 |
| Aged 75 to 84 | 123 | 75 | 48 | 61.0 |
| Aged 85 or older | 41 | 29 | 12 | 70.7 |

*(continued)*

*(continued from previous page)*

| | total | women | men | percent women |
|---|---|---|---|---|
| **Total, California** | **31,589** | **15,797** | **15,792** | **50.0%** |
| Total aged 55 or older | 5,647 | 3,145 | 2,502 | 55.7 |
| Aged 55 to 64 | 2,184 | 1,135 | 1,049 | 52.0 |
| Aged 65 to 74 | 1,967 | 1,086 | 881 | 55.2 |
| Aged 75 to 84 | 1,137 | 674 | 463 | 59.3 |
| Aged 85 or older | 359 | 250 | 109 | 69.6 |
| **Total, Colorado** | **3,747** | **1,889** | **1,858** | **50.4** |
| Total aged 55 or older | 673 | 372 | 301 | 55.3 |
| Aged 55 to 64 | 298 | 153 | 145 | 51.3 |
| Aged 65 to 74 | 216 | 118 | 98 | 54.6 |
| Aged 75 to 84 | 119 | 72 | 47 | 60.5 |
| Aged 85 or older | 40 | 29 | 11 | 72.5 |
| **Total, Connecticut** | **3,275** | **1,687** | **1,588** | **51.5** |
| Total aged 55 or older | 734 | 418 | 316 | 56.9 |
| Aged 55 to 64 | 267 | 139 | 128 | 52.1 |
| Aged 65 to 74 | 250 | 139 | 111 | 55.6 |
| Aged 75 to 84 | 163 | 100 | 63 | 61.3 |
| Aged 85 or older | 54 | 40 | 14 | 74.1 |
| **Total, Delaware** | **717** | **368** | **349** | **51.3** |
| Total aged 55 or older | 149 | 83 | 66 | 55.7 |
| Aged 55 to 64 | 58 | 30 | 28 | 51.7 |
| Aged 65 to 74 | 54 | 30 | 24 | 55.6 |
| Aged 75 to 84 | 28 | 17 | 11 | 60.7 |
| Aged 85 or older | 9 | 6 | 3 | 66.7 |
| **Total, District of Columbia** | **554** | **295** | **259** | **53.2** |
| Total aged 55 or older | 122 | 74 | 48 | 60.7 |
| Aged 55 to 64 | 45 | 25 | 20 | 55.6 |
| Aged 65 to 74 | 43 | 26 | 17 | 60.5 |
| Aged 75 to 84 | 25 | 16 | 9 | 64.0 |
| Aged 85 or older | 9 | 7 | 2 | 77.8 |
| **Total, Florida** | **14,166** | **7,301** | **6,865** | **51.5** |
| Total aged 55 or older | 3,886 | 2,173 | 1,713 | 55.9 |
| Aged 55 to 64 | 1,255 | 673 | 582 | 53.6 |
| Aged 65 to 74 | 1,459 | 800 | 659 | 54.8 |
| Aged 75 to 84 | 901 | 519 | 382 | 57.6 |
| Aged 85 or older | 271 | 181 | 90 | 66.8 |

*(continued)*

*(continued from previous page)*

| | *total* | *women* | *men* | *percent women* |
|---|---|---|---|---|
| **Total, Georgia** | **7,201** | **3,700** | **3,501** | **51.4%** |
| Total aged 55 or older | 1,259 | 725 | 534 | 57.6 |
| Aged 55 to 64 | 541 | 286 | 255 | 52.9 |
| Aged 65 to 74 | 412 | 235 | 177 | 57.0 |
| Aged 75 to 84 | 234 | 150 | 84 | 64.1 |
| Aged 85 or older | 72 | 54 | 18 | 75.0 |
| **Total, Hawaii** | **1,187** | **587** | **600** | **49.5** |
| Total aged 55 or older | 243 | 130 | 113 | 53.5 |
| Aged 55 to 64 | 93 | 49 | 44 | 52.7 |
| Aged 65 to 74 | 90 | 48 | 42 | 53.3 |
| Aged 75 to 84 | 47 | 25 | 22 | 53.2 |
| Aged 85 or older | 13 | 8 | 5 | 61.5 |
| **Total, Idaho** | **1,163** | **583** | **580** | **50.1** |
| Total aged 55 or older | 225 | 122 | 103 | 54.2 |
| Aged 55 to 64 | 93 | 47 | 46 | 50.5 |
| Aged 65 to 74 | 72 | 38 | 34 | 52.8 |
| Aged 75 to 84 | 46 | 27 | 19 | 58.7 |
| Aged 85 or older | 14 | 10 | 4 | 71.4 |
| **Total, Illinois** | **11,830** | **6,067** | **5,763** | **51.3** |
| Total aged 55 or older | 2,436 | 1,390 | 1,046 | 57.1 |
| Aged 55 to 64 | 952 | 498 | 454 | 52.3 |
| Aged 65 to 74 | 813 | 454 | 359 | 55.8 |
| Aged 75 to 84 | 504 | 315 | 189 | 62.5 |
| Aged 85 or older | 167 | 123 | 44 | 73.7 |
| **Total, Indiana** | **5,803** | **2,982** | **2,821** | **51.4** |
| Total aged 55 or older | 1,220 | 694 | 526 | 56.9 |
| Aged 55 to 64 | 486 | 254 | 232 | 52.3 |
| Aged 65 to 74 | 411 | 229 | 182 | 55.7 |
| Aged 75 to 84 | 242 | 151 | 91 | 62.4 |
| Aged 85 or older | 81 | 60 | 21 | 74.1 |
| **Total, Iowa** | **2,842** | **1,459** | **1,383** | **51.3** |
| Total aged 55 or older | 680 | 386 | 294 | 56.8 |
| Aged 55 to 64 | 248 | 129 | 119 | 52.0 |
| Aged 65 to 74 | 221 | 121 | 100 | 54.8 |
| Aged 75 to 84 | 152 | 93 | 59 | 61.2 |
| Aged 85 or older | 59 | 43 | 16 | 72.9 |

*(continued)*

*(continued from previous page)*

| | total | women | men | percent women |
|---|---|---|---|---|
| **Total, Kansas** | **2,565** | **1,304** | **1,261** | **50.8%** |
| Total aged 55 or older | 553 | 314 | 239 | 56.8 |
| Aged 55 to 64 | 203 | 105 | 98 | 51.7 |
| Aged 65 to 74 | 183 | 101 | 82 | 55.2 |
| Aged 75 to 84 | 120 | 74 | 46 | 61.7 |
| Aged 85 or older | 47 | 34 | 13 | 72.3 |
| **Total, Kentucky** | **3,860** | **1,988** | **1,872** | **51.5** |
| Total aged 55 or older | 825 | 470 | 355 | 57.0 |
| Aged 55 to 64 | 338 | 178 | 160 | 52.7 |
| Aged 65 to 74 | 275 | 154 | 121 | 56.0 |
| Aged 75 to 84 | 160 | 100 | 60 | 62.5 |
| Aged 85 or older | 52 | 38 | 14 | 73.1 |
| **Total, Louisiana** | **4,342** | **2,252** | **2,090** | **51.9** |
| Total aged 55 or older | 845 | 485 | 360 | 57.4 |
| Aged 55 to 64 | 351 | 188 | 163 | 53.6 |
| Aged 65 to 74 | 285 | 161 | 124 | 56.5 |
| Aged 75 to 84 | 159 | 99 | 60 | 62.3 |
| Aged 85 or older | 50 | 37 | 13 | 74.0 |
| **Total, Maine** | **1,241** | **637** | **604** | **51.3** |
| Total aged 55 or older | 276 | 156 | 120 | 56.5 |
| Aged 55 to 64 | 103 | 54 | 49 | 52.4 |
| Aged 65 to 74 | 95 | 52 | 43 | 54.7 |
| Aged 75 to 84 | 57 | 35 | 22 | 61.4 |
| Aged 85 or older | 21 | 15 | 6 | 71.4 |
| **Total, Maryland** | **5,042** | **2,593** | **2,449** | **51.4** |
| Total aged 55 or older | 963 | 544 | 419 | 56.5 |
| Aged 55 to 64 | 391 | 203 | 188 | 51.9 |
| Aged 65 to 74 | 332 | 186 | 146 | 56.0 |
| Aged 75 to 84 | 183 | 113 | 70 | 61.7 |
| Aged 85 or older | 57 | 42 | 15 | 73.7 |
| **Total, Massachusetts** | **6,074** | **3,148** | **2,926** | **51.8** |
| Total aged 55 or older | 1,332 | 772 | 560 | 58.0 |
| Aged 55 to 64 | 471 | 248 | 223 | 52.7 |
| Aged 65 to 74 | 461 | 260 | 201 | 56.4 |
| Aged 75 to 84 | 296 | 186 | 110 | 62.8 |
| Aged 85 or older | 104 | 78 | 26 | 75.0 |

*(continued)*

*(continued from previous page)*

| | total | women | men | percent women |
|---|---|---|---|---|
| **Total, Michigan** | **9,549** | **4,904** | **4,645** | **51.4%** |
| Total aged 55 or older | 1,945 | 1,097 | 848 | 56.4 |
| Aged 55 to 64 | 763 | 398 | 365 | 52.2 |
| Aged 65 to 74 | 670 | 370 | 300 | 55.2 |
| Aged 75 to 84 | 390 | 240 | 150 | 61.5 |
| Aged 85 or older | 122 | 89 | 33 | 73.0 |
| **Total, Minnesota** | **4,610** | **2,341** | **2,269** | **50.8** |
| Total aged 55 or older | 926 | 520 | 406 | 56.2 |
| Aged 55 to 64 | 353 | 181 | 172 | 51.3 |
| Aged 65 to 74 | 298 | 162 | 136 | 54.4 |
| Aged 75 to 84 | 199 | 122 | 77 | 61.3 |
| Aged 85 or older | 76 | 55 | 21 | 72.4 |
| **Total, Mississippi** | **2,697** | **1,404** | **1,293** | **52.1** |
| Total aged 55 or older | 553 | 321 | 232 | 58.0 |
| Aged 55 to 64 | 222 | 120 | 102 | 54.1 |
| Aged 65 to 74 | 184 | 105 | 79 | 57.1 |
| Aged 75 to 84 | 110 | 69 | 41 | 62.7 |
| Aged 85 or older | 37 | 27 | 10 | 73.0 |
| **Total, Missouri** | **5,324** | **2,750** | **2,574** | **51.7** |
| Total aged 55 or older | 1,192 | 680 | 512 | 57.0 |
| Aged 55 to 64 | 452 | 237 | 215 | 52.4 |
| Aged 65 to 74 | 399 | 221 | 178 | 55.4 |
| Aged 75 to 84 | 249 | 155 | 94 | 62.2 |
| Aged 85 or older | 92 | 67 | 25 | 72.8 |
| **Total, Montana** | **870** | **438** | **432** | **50.3** |
| Total aged 55 or older | 191 | 103 | 88 | 53.9 |
| Aged 55 to 64 | 77 | 39 | 38 | 50.6 |
| Aged 65 to 74 | 61 | 32 | 29 | 52.5 |
| Aged 75 to 84 | 40 | 23 | 17 | 57.5 |
| Aged 85 or older | 13 | 9 | 4 | 69.2 |
| **Total, Nebraska** | **1,637** | **837** | **800** | **51.1** |
| Total aged 55 or older | 362 | 204 | 158 | 56.4 |
| Aged 55 to 64 | 134 | 69 | 65 | 51.5 |
| Aged 65 to 74 | 118 | 64 | 54 | 54.2 |
| Aged 75 to 84 | 78 | 48 | 30 | 61.5 |
| Aged 85 or older | 32 | 23 | 9 | 71.9 |

*(continued)*

*(continued from previous page)*

| | total | women | men | percent women |
|---|---|---|---|---|
| **Total, Nevada** | **1,530** | **751** | **779** | **49.1%** |
| Total aged 55 or older | 309 | 159 | 150 | 51.5 |
| Aged 55 to 64 | 133 | 65 | 68 | 48.9 |
| Aged 65 to 74 | 112 | 57 | 55 | 50.9 |
| Aged 75 to 84 | 52 | 29 | 23 | 55.8 |
| Aged 85 or older | 12 | 8 | 4 | 66.7 |
| **Total, New Hampshire** | **1,148** | **584** | **564** | **50.9** |
| Total aged 55 or older | 219 | 122 | 97 | 55.7 |
| Aged 55 to 64 | 83 | 42 | 41 | 50.6 |
| Aged 65 to 74 | 76 | 41 | 35 | 53.9 |
| Aged 75 to 84 | 45 | 28 | 17 | 62.2 |
| Aged 85 or older | 15 | 11 | 4 | 73.3 |
| **Total, New Jersey** | **7,945** | **4,098** | **3,847** | **51.6** |
| Total aged 55 or older | 1,761 | 1,004 | 757 | 57.0 |
| Aged 55 to 64 | 670 | 352 | 318 | 52.5 |
| Aged 65 to 74 | 613 | 344 | 269 | 56.1 |
| Aged 75 to 84 | 364 | 225 | 139 | 61.8 |
| Aged 85 or older | 114 | 83 | 31 | 72.8 |
| **Total, New Mexico** | **1,685** | **855** | **830** | **50.7** |
| Total aged 55 or older | 318 | 174 | 144 | 54.7 |
| Aged 55 to 64 | 135 | 70 | 65 | 51.9 |
| Aged 65 to 74 | 107 | 58 | 49 | 54.2 |
| Aged 75 to 84 | 58 | 34 | 24 | 58.6 |
| Aged 85 or older | 18 | 12 | 6 | 66.7 |
| **Total, New York** | **18,136** | **9,417** | **8,719** | **51.9** |
| Total aged 55 or older | 3,958 | 2,282 | 1,676 | 57.7 |
| Aged 55 to 64 | 1,534 | 816 | 718 | 53.2 |
| Aged 65 to 74 | 1,349 | 764 | 585 | 56.6 |
| Aged 75 to 84 | 798 | 500 | 298 | 62.7 |
| Aged 85 or older | 277 | 202 | 75 | 72.9 |
| **Total, North Carolina** | **7,195** | **3,704** | **3,491** | **51.5** |
| Total aged 55 or older | 1,508 | 868 | 640 | 57.6 |
| Aged 55 to 64 | 609 | 325 | 284 | 53.4 |
| Aged 65 to 74 | 523 | 295 | 228 | 56.4 |
| Aged 75 to 84 | 289 | 183 | 106 | 63.3 |
| Aged 85 or older | 87 | 65 | 22 | 74.7 |

*(continued)*

*(continued from previous page)*

| | total | women | men | percent women |
|---|---|---|---|---|
| **Total, North Dakota** | **641** | **322** | **319** | **50.2** |
| Total aged 55 or older | 146 | 81 | 65 | 55.5 |
| Aged 55 to 64 | 53 | 27 | 26 | 50.9 |
| Aged 65 to 74 | 46 | 25 | 21 | 54.3 |
| Aged 75 to 84 | 34 | 20 | 14 | 58.8 |
| Aged 85 or older | 13 | 9 | 4 | 69.2 |
| **Total, Ohio** | **11,151** | **5,764** | **5,387** | **51.7** |
| Total aged 55 or older | 2,435 | 1,388 | 1,047 | 57.0 |
| Aged 55 to 64 | 944 | 496 | 448 | 52.5 |
| Aged 65 to 74 | 842 | 471 | 371 | 55.9 |
| Aged 75 to 84 | 492 | 306 | 186 | 62.2 |
| Aged 85 or older | 157 | 115 | 42 | 73.2 |
| **Total, Oklahoma** | **3,278** | **1,678** | **1,600** | **51.2** |
| Total aged 55 or older | 732 | 414 | 318 | 56.6 |
| Aged 55 to 64 | 289 | 152 | 137 | 52.6 |
| Aged 65 to 74 | 242 | 133 | 109 | 55.0 |
| Aged 75 to 84 | 148 | 91 | 57 | 61.5 |
| Aged 85 or older | 53 | 38 | 15 | 71.7 |
| **Total, Oregon** | **3,141** | **1,591** | **1,550** | **50.7** |
| Total aged 55 or older | 681 | 377 | 304 | 55.4 |
| Aged 55 to 64 | 255 | 132 | 123 | 51.8 |
| Aged 65 to 74 | 230 | 125 | 105 | 54.3 |
| Aged 75 to 84 | 149 | 87 | 62 | 58.4 |
| Aged 85 or older | 47 | 33 | 14 | 70.2 |
| **Total, Pennsylvania** | **12,072** | **6,270** | **5,802** | **51.9** |
| Total aged 55 or older | 2,969 | 1,712 | 1,257 | 57.7 |
| Aged 55 to 64 | 1,053 | 559 | 494 | 53.1 |
| Aged 65 to 74 | 1,064 | 598 | 466 | 56.2 |
| Aged 75 to 84 | 651 | 407 | 244 | 62.5 |
| Aged 85 or older | 201 | 148 | 53 | 73.6 |
| **Total, Rhode Island** | **990** | **514** | **476** | **51.9** |
| Total aged 55 or older | 231 | 136 | 95 | 58.9 |
| Aged 55 to 64 | 75 | 40 | 35 | 53.3 |
| Aged 65 to 74 | 84 | 48 | 36 | 57.1 |
| Aged 75 to 84 | 54 | 34 | 20 | 63.0 |
| Aged 85 or older | 18 | 14 | 4 | 77.8 |

*(continued)*

*(continued from previous page)*

| | total | women | men | percent women |
|---|---|---|---|---|
| **Total, South Carolina** | **3,673** | **1,902** | **1,771** | **51.8%** |
| Total aged 55 or older | 745 | 428 | 317 | 57.4 |
| Aged 55 to 64 | 305 | 163 | 142 | 53.4 |
| Aged 65 to 74 | 261 | 148 | 113 | 56.7 |
| Aged 75 to 84 | 139 | 87 | 52 | 62.6 |
| Aged 85 or older | 40 | 30 | 10 | 75.0 |
| **Total, South Dakota** | **729** | **370** | **359** | **50.8** |
| Total aged 55 or older | 164 | 90 | 74 | 54.9 |
| Aged 55 to 64 | 59 | 30 | 29 | 50.8 |
| Aged 65 to 74 | 54 | 28 | 26 | 51.9 |
| Aged 75 to 84 | 37 | 22 | 15 | 59.5 |
| Aged 85 or older | 14 | 10 | 4 | 71.4 |
| **Total, Tennessee** | **5,256** | **2,720** | **2,536** | **51.8** |
| Total aged 55 or older | 1,120 | 644 | 476 | 57.5 |
| Aged 55 to 64 | 462 | 246 | 216 | 53.2 |
| Aged 65 to 74 | 373 | 210 | 163 | 56.3 |
| Aged 75 to 84 | 215 | 136 | 79 | 63.3 |
| Aged 85 or older | 70 | 52 | 18 | 74.3 |
| **Total, Texas** | **18,724** | **9,489** | **9,235** | **50.7** |
| Total aged 55 or older | 3,313 | 1,859 | 1,454 | 56.1 |
| Aged 55 to 64 | 1,398 | 731 | 667 | 52.3 |
| Aged 65 to 74 | 1,104 | 609 | 495 | 55.2 |
| Aged 75 to 84 | 608 | 373 | 235 | 61.3 |
| Aged 85 or older | 203 | 146 | 57 | 71.9 |
| **Total, Utah** | **1,951** | **981** | **970** | **50.3** |
| Total aged 55 or older | 293 | 159 | 134 | 54.3 |
| Aged 55 to 64 | 121 | 62 | 59 | 51.2 |
| Aged 65 to 74 | 96 | 51 | 45 | 53.1 |
| Aged 75 to 84 | 58 | 34 | 24 | 58.6 |
| Aged 85 or older | 18 | 12 | 6 | 66.7 |
| **Total, Vermont** | **585** | **297** | **288** | **50.8** |
| Total aged 55 or older | 116 | 64 | 52 | 55.2 |
| Aged 55 to 64 | 45 | 23 | 22 | 51.1 |
| Aged 65 to 74 | 39 | 21 | 18 | 53.8 |
| Aged 75 to 84 | 23 | 14 | 9 | 60.9 |
| Aged 85 or older | 9 | 6 | 3 | 66.7 |

*(continued)*

*(continued from previous page)*

| | total | women | men | percent women |
|---|---|---|---|---|
| **Total, Virginia** | **6,618** | **3,380** | **3,238** | **51.1%** |
| Total aged 55 or older | 1,261 | 714 | 547 | 56.6 |
| Aged 55 to 64 | 524 | 273 | 251 | 52.1 |
| Aged 65 to 74 | 428 | 240 | 188 | 56.1 |
| Aged 75 to 84 | 237 | 147 | 90 | 62.0 |
| Aged 85 or older | 72 | 54 | 18 | 75.0 |
| **Total, Washington** | **5,431** | **2,732** | **2,699** | **50.3** |
| Total aged 55 or older | 1,038 | 571 | 467 | 55.0 |
| Aged 55 to 64 | 410 | 209 | 201 | 51.0 |
| Aged 65 to 74 | 345 | 188 | 157 | 54.5 |
| Aged 75 to 84 | 215 | 126 | 89 | 58.6 |
| Aged 85 or older | 68 | 48 | 20 | 70.6 |
| **Total, West Virginia** | **1,828** | **948** | **880** | **51.9** |
| Total aged 55 or older | 457 | 263 | 194 | 57.5 |
| Aged 55 to 64 | 178 | 95 | 83 | 53.4 |
| Aged 65 to 74 | 158 | 89 | 69 | 56.3 |
| Aged 75 to 84 | 92 | 58 | 34 | 63.0 |
| Aged 85 or older | 29 | 21 | 8 | 72.4 |
| **Total, Wisconsin** | **5,123** | **2,608** | **2,515** | **50.9** |
| Total aged 55 or older | 1,097 | 613 | 484 | 55.9 |
| Aged 55 to 64 | 414 | 212 | 202 | 51.2 |
| Aged 65 to 74 | 363 | 197 | 166 | 54.3 |
| Aged 75 to 84 | 236 | 144 | 92 | 61.0 |
| Aged 85 or older | 84 | 60 | 24 | 71.4 |
| **Total, Wyoming** | **480** | **239** | **241** | **49.8** |
| Total aged 55 or older | 94 | 50 | 44 | 53.2 |
| Aged 55 to 64 | 40 | 20 | 20 | 50.0 |
| Aged 65 to 74 | 31 | 16 | 15 | 51.6 |
| Aged 75 to 84 | 17 | 10 | 7 | 58.8 |
| Aged 85 or older | 6 | 4 | 2 | 66.7 |

*Source: Bureau of the Census,* Population Projections for States by Age, Sex, Race, and Hispanic Origin: 1995 to 2025, *PPL-47, 1996; calculations by New Strategist*

# Wide Variation in Growth of 55-Plus Population Projected for States

**While the number of people aged 55 or older will grow 7 percent nationally between 1995 and 2000, the figure is much higher in some states.**

Between 1995 and 2000, the greatest growth in the number of people aged 55 or older is projected for Nevada, up 32 percent. In contrast, the number of people in this age group is projected to drop 0.4 percent in Rhode Island.

This age group will increase less than 2 percent in Pennsylvania and less than 1 percent in New York. But in Alaska, Colorado, Idaho, Nevada, and Utah the number of people aged 55 or older will grow more than 20 percent in just five years.

The population aged 65 to 74 is projected to decline in most states as the small generation born during the Depression enters this age group. But in some rapidly growing states, even this age group will grow. While Pennsylvania shows a loss of 10 percent in the number of 65-to-74-year-olds, for example, Oregon's population in this age group will grow 3 percent and Nevada's 15 percent.

The oldest old, aged 85 or older, are projected to increase in every state except Alaska and the District of Columbia between 1995 and 2005. In Nevada, this age group should expand 50 percent.

◆ The oldest boomers will reach age 55 in 2001, assuring the growth of the 55-to-64 age group in virtually every state after the turn of the century. Businesses poised to market to aging boomers—who are vastly different from today's older Americans—will benefit from this expansion.

## States with Fastest Growth in 55+ Population

*(percent change in number of persons aged 55 or older, top five states)*

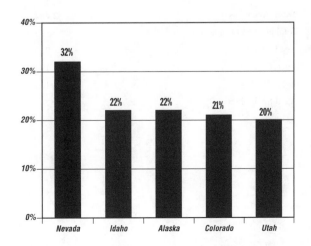

# Population Aged 55 or Older by State, 1995 and 2000

*(total number of persons and number aged 55 or older by state, 1995 and 2000; percent change 1995-2000; numbers in thousands)*

|  | 1995 | 2000 | percent change |
|---|---|---|---|
| **Total, United States** | **262,755** | **274,634** | **4.5%** |
| Total aged 55 or older | 54,663 | 58,671 | 7.3 |
| Aged 55 to 64 | 21,131 | 23,961 | 13.4 |
| Aged 65 to 74 | 18,759 | 18,136 | -3.3 |
| Aged 75 to 84 | 11,145 | 12,315 | 10.5 |
| Aged 85 or older | 3,628 | 4,259 | 17.4 |
| **Total, Alabama** | **4,253** | **4,451** | **4.7** |
| Total aged 55 or older | 927 | 1,003 | 8.2 |
| Aged 55 to 64 | 375 | 421 | 12.3 |
| Aged 65 to 74 | 312 | 317 | 1.6 |
| Aged 75 to 84 | 182 | 198 | 8.8 |
| Aged 85 or older | 58 | 67 | 15.5 |
| **Total, Alaska** | **604** | **653** | **8.1** |
| Total aged 55 or older | 68 | 83 | 22.1 |
| Aged 55 to 64 | 38 | 45 | 18.4 |
| Aged 65 to 74 | 20 | 25 | 25.0 |
| Aged 75 to 84 | 8 | 11 | 37.5 |
| Aged 85 or older | 2 | 2 | 0.0 |
| **Total, Arizona** | **4,218** | **4,798** | **13.8** |
| Total aged 55 or older | 886 | 1,062 | 19.9 |
| Aged 55 to 64 | 326 | 427 | 31.0 |
| Aged 65 to 74 | 323 | 339 | 5.0 |
| Aged 75 to 84 | 186 | 226 | 21.5 |
| Aged 85 or older | 51 | 70 | 37.3 |
| **Total, Arkansas** | **2,484** | **2,631** | **5.9** |
| Total aged 55 or older | 583 | 644 | 10.5 |
| Aged 55 to 64 | 223 | 267 | 19.7 |
| Aged 65 to 74 | 196 | 200 | 2.0 |
| Aged 75 to 84 | 123 | 130 | 5.7 |
| Aged 85 or older | 41 | 47 | 14.6 |

*(continued)*

*(continued from previous page)*

| | 1995 | 2000 | percent change |
|---|---|---|---|
| **Total, California** | **31,589** | **32,521** | **3.0%** |
| Total aged 55 or older | 5,657 | 5,817 | 2.8 |
| Aged 55 to 64 | 2,184 | 2,430 | 11.3 |
| Aged 65 to 74 | 1,967 | 1,757 | -10.7 |
| Aged 75 to 84 | 1,137 | 1,226 | 7.8 |
| Aged 85 or older | 369 | 404 | 9.5 |
| **Total, Colorado** | **3,747** | **4,168** | **11.2** |
| Total aged 55 or older | 673 | 815 | 21.1 |
| Aged 55 to 64 | 298 | 363 | 21.8 |
| Aged 65 to 74 | 216 | 246 | 13.9 |
| Aged 75 to 84 | 119 | 152 | 27.7 |
| Aged 85 or older | 40 | 54 | 35.0 |
| **Total, Connecticut** | **3,275** | **3,284** | **0.3** |
| Total aged 55 or older | 734 | 753 | 2.6 |
| Aged 55 to 64 | 267 | 292 | 9.4 |
| Aged 65 to 74 | 250 | 224 | -10.4 |
| Aged 75 to 84 | 163 | 173 | 6.1 |
| Aged 85 or older | 54 | 64 | 18.5 |
| **Total, Delaware** | **717** | **768** | **7.1** |
| Total aged 55 or older | 149 | 164 | 10.1 |
| Aged 55 to 64 | 58 | 67 | 15.5 |
| Aged 65 to 74 | 54 | 51 | -5.6 |
| Aged 75 to 84 | 28 | 35 | 25.0 |
| Aged 85 or older | 9 | 11 | 22.2 |
| **Total, District of Columbia** | **554** | **523** | **-5.6** |
| Total aged 55 or older | 122 | 115 | -5.7 |
| Aged 55 to 64 | 45 | 46 | 2.2 |
| Aged 65 to 74 | 43 | 36 | -16.3 |
| Aged 75 to 84 | 25 | 24 | -4.0 |
| Aged 85 or older | 9 | 9 | 0.0 |
| **Total, Florida** | **14,166** | **15,233** | **7.5** |
| Total aged 55 or older | 3,886 | 4,281 | 10.2 |
| Aged 55 to 64 | 1,255 | 1,526 | 21.6 |
| Aged 65 to 74 | 1,459 | 1,384 | -5.1 |
| Aged 75 to 84 | 901 | 1,028 | 14.1 |
| Aged 85 or older | 271 | 343 | 26.6 |

*(continued)*

*(continued from previous page)*

| | *1995* | *2000* | *percent change* |
|---|---|---|---|
| **Total, Georgia** | **7,201** | **7,875** | **9.4%** |
| Total aged 55 or older | 1,259 | 1,433 | 13.8 |
| Aged 55 to 64 | 541 | 654 | 20.9 |
| Aged 65 to 74 | 412 | 429 | 4.1 |
| Aged 75 to 84 | 234 | 263 | 12.4 |
| Aged 85 or older | 72 | 87 | 20.8 |
| **Total, Hawaii** | **1,187** | **1,257** | **5.9** |
| Total aged 55 or older | 243 | 264 | 8.6 |
| Aged 55 to 64 | 93 | 107 | 15.1 |
| Aged 65 to 74 | 90 | 83 | -7.8 |
| Aged 75 to 84 | 47 | 56 | 19.1 |
| Aged 85 or older | 13 | 18 | 38.5 |
| **Total, Idaho** | **1,163** | **1,347** | **15.8** |
| Total aged 55 or older | 225 | 275 | 22.2 |
| Aged 55 to 64 | 93 | 118 | 26.9 |
| Aged 65 to 74 | 72 | 82 | 13.9 |
| Aged 75 to 84 | 46 | 55 | 19.6 |
| Aged 85 or older | 14 | 20 | 42.9 |
| **Total, Illinois** | **11,830** | **12,051** | **1.9** |
| Total aged 55 or older | 2,436 | 2,509 | 3.0 |
| Aged 55 to 64 | 952 | 1,025 | 7.7 |
| Aged 65 to 74 | 813 | 767 | -5.7 |
| Aged 75 to 84 | 504 | 529 | 5.0 |
| Aged 85 or older | 167 | 188 | 12.6 |
| **Total, Indiana** | **5,803** | **6,045** | **4.2** |
| Total aged 55 or older | 1,220 | 1,304 | 6.9 |
| Aged 55 to 64 | 486 | 541 | 11.3 |
| Aged 65 to 74 | 411 | 402 | -2.2 |
| Aged 75 to 84 | 242 | 268 | 10.7 |
| Aged 85 or older | 81 | 93 | 14.8 |
| **Total, Iowa** | **2,842** | **2,900** | **2.0** |
| Total aged 55 or older | 680 | 708 | 4.1 |
| Aged 55 to 64 | 248 | 266 | 7.3 |
| Aged 65 to 74 | 221 | 217 | -1.8 |
| Aged 75 to 84 | 152 | 158 | 3.9 |
| Aged 85 or older | 59 | 67 | 13.6 |

*(continued)*

*(continued from previous page)*

| | 1995 | 2000 | percent change |
|---|---|---|---|
| **Total, Kansas** | **2,565** | **2,668** | **4.0%** |
| Total aged 55 or older | 553 | 581 | 5.1 |
| Aged 55 to 64 | 203 | 222 | 9.4 |
| Aged 65 to 74 | 183 | 179 | -2.2 |
| Aged 75 to 84 | 120 | 128 | 6.7 |
| Aged 85 or older | 47 | 52 | 10.6 |
| **Total, Kentucky** | **3,860** | **3,995** | **3.5** |
| Total aged 55 or older | 825 | 891 | 8.0 |
| Aged 55 to 64 | 338 | 382 | 13.0 |
| Aged 65 to 74 | 275 | 279 | 1.5 |
| Aged 75 to 84 | 160 | 173 | 8.1 |
| Aged 85 or older | 52 | 57 | 9.6 |
| **Total, Louisiana** | **4,342** | **4,425** | **1.9** |
| Total aged 55 or older | 845 | 910 | 7.7 |
| Aged 55 to 64 | 351 | 387 | 10.3 |
| Aged 65 to 74 | 285 | 289 | 1.4 |
| Aged 75 to 84 | 159 | 176 | 10.7 |
| Aged 85 or older | 50 | 58 | 16.0 |
| **Total, Maine** | **1,241** | **1,259** | **1.5** |
| Total aged 55 or older | 276 | 289 | 4.7 |
| Aged 55 to 64 | 103 | 117 | 13.6 |
| Aged 65 to 74 | 95 | 89 | -6.3 |
| Aged 75 to 84 | 57 | 61 | 7.0 |
| Aged 85 or older | 21 | 22 | 4.8 |
| **Total, Maryland** | **5,042** | **5,275** | **4.6** |
| Total aged 55 or older | 963 | 1,039 | 7.9 |
| Aged 55 to 64 | 391 | 450 | 15.1 |
| Aged 65 to 74 | 332 | 312 | -6.0 |
| Aged 75 to 84 | 183 | 211 | 15.3 |
| Aged 85 or older | 57 | 66 | 15.8 |
| **Total, Massachusetts** | **6,074** | **6,199** | **2.1** |
| Total aged 55 or older | 1,332 | 1,365 | 2.5 |
| Aged 55 to 64 | 471 | 522 | 10.8 |
| Aged 65 to 74 | 461 | 413 | -10.4 |
| Aged 75 to 84 | 296 | 311 | 5.1 |
| Aged 85 or older | 104 | 119 | 14.4 |

*(continued)*

*(continued from previous page)*

| | 1995 | 2000 | percent change |
|---|---|---|---|
| **Total, Michigan** | **9,549** | **9,679** | **1.4%** |
| Total aged 55 or older | 1,945 | 2,036 | 4.7 |
| Aged 55 to 64 | 763 | 839 | 10.0 |
| Aged 65 to 74 | 670 | 627 | -6.4 |
| Aged 75 to 84 | 390 | 427 | 9.5 |
| Aged 85 or older | 122 | 143 | 17.2 |
| **Total, Minnesota** | **4,610** | **4,830** | **4.8** |
| Total aged 55 or older | 926 | 1,001 | 8.1 |
| Aged 55 to 64 | 353 | 405 | 14.7 |
| Aged 65 to 74 | 298 | 296 | -0.7 |
| Aged 75 to 84 | 199 | 211 | 6.0 |
| Aged 85 or older | 76 | 89 | 17.1 |
| **Total, Mississippi** | **2,697** | **2,816** | **4.4** |
| Total aged 55 or older | 553 | 593 | 7.2 |
| Aged 55 to 64 | 222 | 249 | 12.2 |
| Aged 65 to 74 | 184 | 187 | 1.6 |
| Aged 75 to 84 | 110 | 116 | 5.5 |
| Aged 85 or older | 37 | 41 | 10.8 |
| **Total, Missouri** | **5,324** | **5,540** | **4.1** |
| Total aged 55 or older | 1,192 | 1,260 | 5.7 |
| Aged 55 to 64 | 452 | 505 | 11.7 |
| Aged 65 to 74 | 399 | 391 | -2.0 |
| Aged 75 to 84 | 249 | 263 | 5.6 |
| Aged 85 or older | 92 | 101 | 9.8 |
| **Total, Montana** | **870** | **950** | **9.2** |
| Total aged 55 or older | 191 | 221 | 15.7 |
| Aged 55 to 64 | 77 | 93 | 20.8 |
| Aged 65 to 74 | 61 | 66 | 8.2 |
| Aged 75 to 84 | 40 | 45 | 12.5 |
| Aged 85 or older | 13 | 17 | 30.8 |
| **Total, Nebraska** | **1,637** | **1,705** | **4.2** |
| Total aged 55 or older | 362 | 383 | 5.8 |
| Aged 55 to 64 | 134 | 144 | 7.5 |
| Aged 65 to 74 | 118 | 120 | 1.7 |
| Aged 75 to 84 | 78 | 83 | 6.4 |
| Aged 85 or older | 32 | 36 | 12.5 |

*(continued)*

*(continued from previous page)*

| | 1995 | 2000 | percent change |
|---|---|---|---|
| **Total, Nevada** | **1,530** | **1,871** | **22.3%** |
| Total aged 55 or older | 309 | 407 | 31.7 |
| Aged 55 to 64 | 133 | 188 | 41.4 |
| Aged 65 to 74 | 112 | 129 | 15.2 |
| Aged 75 to 84 | 52 | 72 | 38.5 |
| Aged 85 or older | 12 | 18 | 50.0 |
| **Total, New Hampshire** | **1,148** | **1,224** | **6.6** |
| Total aged 55 or older | 219 | 242 | 10.5 |
| Aged 55 to 64 | 83 | 100 | 20.5 |
| Aged 65 to 74 | 76 | 72 | -5.3 |
| Aged 75 to 84 | 45 | 51 | 13.3 |
| Aged 85 or older | 15 | 19 | 26.7 |
| **Total, New Jersey** | **7,945** | **8,178** | **2.9** |
| Total aged 55 or older | 1,761 | 1,827 | 3.7 |
| Aged 55 to 64 | 670 | 737 | 10.0 |
| Aged 65 to 74 | 613 | 565 | -7.8 |
| Aged 75 to 84 | 364 | 395 | 8.5 |
| Aged 85 or older | 114 | 130 | 14.0 |
| **Total, New Mexico** | **1,685** | **1,860** | **10.4** |
| Total aged 55 or older | 318 | 364 | 14.5 |
| Aged 55 to 64 | 135 | 158 | 17.0 |
| Aged 65 to 74 | 107 | 114 | 6.5 |
| Aged 75 to 84 | 58 | 70 | 20.7 |
| Aged 85 or older | 18 | 22 | 22.2 |
| **Total, New York** | **18,136** | **18,146** | **0.1** |
| Total aged 55 or older | 3,958 | 3,980 | 0.6 |
| Aged 55 to 64 | 1,534 | 1,622 | 5.7 |
| Aged 65 to 74 | 1,349 | 1,239 | -8.2 |
| Aged 75 to 84 | 798 | 826 | 3.5 |
| Aged 85 or older | 277 | 293 | 5.8 |
| **Total, North Carolina** | **7,195** | **7,777** | **8.1** |
| Total aged 55 or older | 1,508 | 1,714 | 13.7 |
| Aged 55 to 64 | 609 | 723 | 18.7 |
| Aged 65 to 74 | 523 | 539 | 3.1 |
| Aged 75 to 84 | 289 | 341 | 18.0 |
| Aged 85 or older | 87 | 111 | 27.6 |

*(continued)*

*(continued from previous page)*

| | 1995 | 2000 | percent change |
|---|---|---|---|
| **Total, North Dakota** | **641** | **662** | **3.3%** |
| Total aged 55 or older | 146 | 155 | 6.2 |
| Aged 55 to 64 | 53 | 56 | 5.7 |
| Aged 65 to 74 | 46 | 48 | 4.3 |
| Aged 75 to 84 | 34 | 35 | 2.9 |
| Aged 85 or older | 13 | 16 | 23.1 |
| **Total, Ohio** | **11,151** | **11,319** | **1.5** |
| Total aged 55 or older | 2,435 | 2,536 | 4.1 |
| Aged 55 to 64 | 944 | 1,011 | 7.1 |
| Aged 65 to 74 | 842 | 795 | -5.6 |
| Aged 75 to 84 | 492 | 547 | 11.2 |
| Aged 85 or older | 157 | 183 | 16.6 |
| **Total, Oklahoma** | **3,278** | **3,373** | **2.9** |
| Total aged 55 or older | 732 | 795 | 8.6 |
| Aged 55 to 64 | 289 | 323 | 11.8 |
| Aged 65 to 74 | 242 | 249 | 2.9 |
| Aged 75 to 84 | 148 | 160 | 8.1 |
| Aged 85 or older | 53 | 63 | 18.9 |
| **Total, Oregon** | **3,141** | **3,397** | **8.2** |
| Total aged 55 or older | 681 | 796 | 16.9 |
| Aged 55 to 64 | 255 | 325 | 27.5 |
| Aged 65 to 74 | 230 | 236 | 2.6 |
| Aged 75 to 84 | 149 | 173 | 16.1 |
| Aged 85 or older | 47 | 62 | 31.9 |
| **Total, Pennsylvania** | **12,072** | **12,202** | **1.1** |
| Total aged 55 or older | 2,969 | 3,021 | 1.8 |
| Aged 55 to 64 | 1,053 | 1,122 | 6.6 |
| Aged 65 to 74 | 1,064 | 956 | -10.2 |
| Aged 75 to 84 | 651 | 709 | 8.9 |
| Aged 85 or older | 201 | 234 | 16.4 |
| **Total, Rhode Island** | **990** | **998** | **0.8** |
| Total aged 55 or older | 231 | 230 | -0.4 |
| Aged 55 to 64 | 75 | 82 | 9.3 |
| Aged 65 to 74 | 84 | 70 | -16.7 |
| Aged 75 to 84 | 54 | 57 | 5.6 |
| Aged 85 or older | 18 | 21 | 16.7 |

*(continued)*

*(continued from previous page)*

| | 1995 | 2000 | percent change |
|---|---|---|---|
| **Total, South Carolina** | **3,673** | **3,858** | **5.0%** |
| Total aged 55 or older | 745 | 837 | 12.3 |
| Aged 55 to 64 | 305 | 359 | 17.7 |
| Aged 65 to 74 | 261 | 263 | 0.8 |
| Aged 75 to 84 | 139 | 165 | 18.7 |
| Aged 85 or older | 40 | 50 | 25.0 |
| **Total, South Dakota** | **729** | **777** | **6.6** |
| Total aged 55 or older | 164 | 174 | 6.1 |
| Aged 55 to 64 | 59 | 64 | 8.5 |
| Aged 65 to 74 | 54 | 54 | 0.0 |
| Aged 75 to 84 | 37 | 39 | 5.4 |
| Aged 85 or older | 14 | 17 | 21.4 |
| **Total, Tennessee** | **5,256** | **5,657** | **7.6** |
| Total aged 55 or older | 1,120 | 1,242 | 10.9 |
| Aged 55 to 64 | 462 | 535 | 15.8 |
| Aged 65 to 74 | 373 | 382 | 2.4 |
| Aged 75 to 84 | 215 | 242 | 12.6 |
| Aged 85 or older | 70 | 83 | 18.6 |
| **Total, Texas** | **18,724** | **20,119** | **7.5** |
| Total aged 55 or older | 3,313 | 3,714 | 12.1 |
| Aged 55 to 64 | 1,398 | 1,613 | 15.4 |
| Aged 65 to 74 | 1,104 | 1,154 | 4.5 |
| Aged 75 to 84 | 608 | 704 | 15.8 |
| Aged 85 or older | 203 | 243 | 19.7 |
| **Total, Utah** | **1,951** | **2,207** | **13.1** |
| Total aged 55 or older | 293 | 352 | 20.1 |
| Aged 55 to 64 | 121 | 150 | 24.0 |
| Aged 65 to 74 | 96 | 107 | 11.5 |
| Aged 75 to 84 | 58 | 71 | 22.4 |
| Aged 85 or older | 18 | 24 | 33.3 |
| **Total, Vermont** | **585** | **617** | **5.5** |
| Total aged 55 or older | 116 | 127 | 9.5 |
| Aged 55 to 64 | 45 | 54 | 20.0 |
| Aged 65 to 74 | 39 | 38 | -2.6 |
| Aged 75 to 84 | 23 | 25 | 8.7 |
| Aged 85 or older | 9 | 10 | 11.1 |

*(continued)*

*(continued from previous page)*

| | 1995 | 2000 | percent change |
|---|---|---|---|
| **Total, Virginia** | **6,618** | **6,997** | **5.7%** |
| Total aged 55 or older | 1,261 | 1,405 | 11.4 |
| Aged 55 to 64 | 524 | 617 | 17.7 |
| Aged 65 to 74 | 428 | 422 | -1.4 |
| Aged 75 to 84 | 237 | 276 | 16.5 |
| Aged 85 or older | 72 | 90 | 25.0 |
| | | | |
| **Total, Washington** | **5,431** | **5,858** | **7.9** |
| Total aged 55 or older | 1,038 | 1,198 | 15.4 |
| Aged 55 to 64 | 410 | 513 | 25.1 |
| Aged 65 to 74 | 345 | 350 | 1.4 |
| Aged 75 to 84 | 215 | 248 | 15.3 |
| Aged 85 or older | 68 | 87 | 27.9 |
| | | | |
| **Total, West Virginia** | **1,828** | **1,841** | **0.7** |
| Total aged 55 or older | 457 | 481 | 5.3 |
| Aged 55 to 64 | 178 | 194 | 9.0 |
| Aged 65 to 74 | 158 | 155 | -1.9 |
| Aged 75 to 84 | 92 | 100 | 8.7 |
| Aged 85 or older | 29 | 32 | 10.3 |
| | | | |
| **Total, Wisconsin** | **5,123** | **5,326** | **4.0** |
| Total aged 55 or older | 1,097 | 1,166 | 6.3 |
| Aged 55 to 64 | 414 | 461 | 11.4 |
| Aged 65 to 74 | 363 | 357 | -1.7 |
| Aged 75 to 84 | 236 | 250 | 5.9 |
| Aged 85 or older | 84 | 98 | 16.7 |
| | | | |
| **Total, Wyoming** | **480** | **525** | **9.4** |
| Total aged 55 or older | 94 | 109 | 16.0 |
| Aged 55 to 64 | 40 | 47 | 17.5 |
| Aged 65 to 74 | 31 | 34 | 9.7 |
| Aged 75 to 84 | 17 | 21 | 23.5 |
| Aged 85 or older | 6 | 7 | 16.7 |

*Source: Bureau of the Census,* Population Projections for States by Age, Sex, Race, and Hispanic Origin: 1995 to 2025, *PPL-47, 1996; calculations by New Strategist*

# Where Boomers Will Live in Retirement

## The South and the West should gain the most from the surge in older Americans as boomers age.

Overall, the number of Americans aged 65 or older is projected to increase an enormous 59 percent between 1995 and 2025 as the large baby-boom generation enters the age group. By 2025, boomers will be aged 61 to 79.

The Census Bureau's projections of the elderly population by state in 2025 reveal where the boomer hot spots will be. Not surprisingly, states with year-round warm weather will see above-average growth in elderly populations, while states in the Midwest and the Northeast will see below-average growth. Connecticut, Illinois, Massachusetts, New Jersey, New York, Pennsylvania and Rhode Island will see elderly populations grow less than 35 percent between 1995 and 2025.

By contrast, the elderly populations of Alaska, Colorado, Idaho, Nevada, and Utah will surge more than 135 percent between 1995 and 2025. By 2025, California will have 5.4 million people aged 65 or older. Florida will rank second with 4.6 million, and Texas will be third with 3.7 million.

◆ In retirement, baby boomers will create booming economies wherever they go. According to the Hudson Institute's study, *Workforce 2020*, states with rapid growth in elderly population will also experience extraordinary demand for a variety of service jobs ranging from entertainment to home repair to nursing services.

# Projections of the Population Aged 65 or Older by State, 1995 and 2025

*(number of persons aged 65 or older by state, 1995 and 2025; percent change, 1995-2025; numbers in thousands)*

|  | 1995 | 2025 | percent change |
|---|---|---|---|
| **United States** | **33,547** | **53,221** | **58.6%** |
| Alabama | 552 | 920 | 66.7 |
| Alaska | 30 | 80 | 166.7 |
| Arizona | 560 | 1,158 | 106.8 |
| Arkansas | 360 | 628 | 74.4 |
| California | 3,473 | 5,352 | 54.1 |
| Colorado | 375 | 892 | 137.9 |
| Connecticut | 467 | 590 | 26.3 |
| Delaware | 91 | 141 | 54.9 |
| District of Columbia | 77 | 80 | 3.9 |
| Florida | 2,631 | 4,574 | 73.9 |
| Georgia | 718 | 1,404 | 95.5 |
| Hawaii | 150 | 248 | 65.3 |
| Idaho | 132 | 317 | 140.2 |
| Illinois | 1,484 | 1,960 | 32.1 |
| Indiana | 734 | 1,102 | 50.1 |
| Iowa | 432 | 608 | 40.7 |
| Kansas | 350 | 522 | 49.1 |
| Kentucky | 487 | 797 | 63.7 |
| Louisiana | 494 | 821 | 66.2 |
| Maine | 173 | 259 | 49.7 |
| Maryland | 572 | 882 | 54.2 |
| Massachusetts | 861 | 1,092 | 26.8 |
| Michigan | 1,182 | 1,610 | 36.2 |
| Minnesota | 573 | 938 | 63.7 |
| Mississippi | 331 | 532 | 60.7 |
| Missouri | 740 | 1,088 | 47.0 |
| Montana | 114 | 237 | 107.9 |
| Nebraska | 228 | 353 | 54.8 |
| Nevada | 176 | 415 | 135.8 |
| New Hampshire | 136 | 230 | 69.1 |
| New Jersey | 1,091 | 1,444 | 32.4 |
| New Mexico | 183 | 372 | 103.3 |
| New York | 2,424 | 2,913 | 20.2 |
| North Carolina | 899 | 1,708 | 90.0 |
| North Dakota | 93 | 146 | 57.0 |
| Ohio | 1,491 | 2,039 | 36.8 |

*(continued)*

*(continued from previous page)*

|  | 1995 | 2025 | percent change |
|---|---|---|---|
| Oklahoma | 443 | 765 | 72.7% |
| Oregon | 426 | 899 | 111.0 |
| Pennsylvania | 1,916 | 2,352 | 22.8 |
| Rhode Island | 156 | 185 | 18.6 |
| South Carolina | 440 | 824 | 87.3 |
| South Dakota | 105 | 161 | 53.3 |
| Tennessee | 658 | 1,167 | 77.4 |
| Texas | 1,915 | 3,686 | 92.5 |
| Utah | 172 | 414 | 140.7 |
| Vermont | 71 | 119 | 67.6 |
| Virginia | 737 | 1,298 | 76.1 |
| Washington | 628 | 1,324 | 110.8 |
| West Virginia | 279 | 412 | 47.7 |
| Wisconsin | 683 | 1,039 | 52.1 |
| Wyoming | 54 | 124 | 129.6 |

*Source: Bureau of the Census,* Population Projections for States by Age, Sex, Race, and Hispanic Origin: 1995 to 2025, *PPL-47, 1996; calculations by New Strategist*

# 8

# Spending

◆ Householders aged 65 to 74 spent 4 percent more in 1995 than in 1990, after adjusting for inflation; spending among householders aged 75 or older rose 3 percent.

◆ After adjusting for household size, the spending of retirees is only 7 percent less than that of the average household.

◆ Retiree households spend more than average on such items as eggs, fresh fruits, major appliances, books and newspapers, and maintenance of owned homes.

◆ Householders aged 55 to 64 spend well above average on such items as sirloin steak, owned vacation homes, lawn and garden supplies, radios, and lamps.

◆ Householders aged 65 to 74 spend well above average on cakes, nuts, whiskey, bathroom linens, new cars, and magazine and newspaper subscriptions.

◆ Householders aged 75 or older spend more than average on jams, whiskey, women's hairdressers, newspaper subscriptions, and contributions to churches.

# Householders Aged 65+ Are Spending More

**But the spending of householders aged 55 to 64 fell between 1990 and 1995, after adjusting for inflation.**

Between 1990 and 1995, householders aged 55 to 64 cut their spending 4 percent, after adjusting for inflation. This was slightly greater than the 2.5 percent decline in spending for all householders. In contrast, householders aged 65 to 74 spent 4 percent more in 1995 than in 1990, after adjusting for inflation. The spending of householders aged 75 or older rose 3 percent during those years.

Two factors account for the spending cuts among 55-to-64-year-olds. The recession of the early 1990s contributed to the 7 percent decline in average before-tax household income in this age group. Spending cuts followed the income decline. In addition, the continuing popularity of early retirement reduced spending as the growing ranks of retirees adapted to a lower-cost lifestyle.

Every older age group cut its spending on a range of discretionary items between 1990 and 1995. After adjusting for inflation, householders aged 55 to 64 spent 20 percent less on food away from home (primarily restaurant meals), 10 percent less on housekeeping supplies, 18 percent less on shoes, 15 percent less on alcohol, 16 percent less on new cars and trucks, and 10 percent less on entertainment.

### Most Older Americans Are Spending More

*(percent change in spending of consumer units aged 55 or older, 1990 to 1995; in 1995 dollars)*

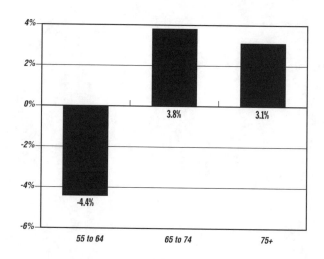

Spending patterns among householders aged 65 to 74 were mixed, with more ups than downs. The average householder in this age group spent 8 percent less on food away from home in 1995 than in 1990, but 6 percent more on alcohol. Householders in this age group spent 14 percent more on housekeeping supplies but 11 percent less on household textiles. They spent 18 percent less on women's clothes, but 25 percent more on men's clothes. Householders in this age group spent 9 percent more on entertainment in 1995 than in 1990.

Householders aged 75 or older spent 20 percent less on food away from home in 1995 than in 1990, but they spent 56 percent more on alcohol. Householders in this age group spent 31 percent more on men's clothes, but 2 percent less on women's clothes. They spent 52 percent less on new cars and trucks, but 32 percent more on entertainment.

◆ The spending of 55-to-64-year-olds is likely to rise in the years ahead as early retirement becomes less common. With more people in the age group at work, household incomes—and spending—will be higher.

◆ The spending of older Americans is rising to meet the average as the affluence of people aged 65 or older grows. This trend will intensify as well-educated boomers enter old age.

# Average Spending of Householders Aged 55 or Older, 1990 to 1995

*(average annual spending of total consumer units (CUs) and consumer units aged 55 or older, 1995 and 1990; percent change, 1990-95; in 1995 dollars)*

| | total consumer units | | | aged 55 to 64 | | | aged 65 to 74 | | | aged 75 or older | | |
|---|---|---|---|---|---|---|---|---|---|---|---|---|
| | 1995 | 1990 | % change | 1995 | 1990 | % change | 1995 | 1990 | % change | 1995 | 1990 | % change |
| Avg. before-tax income of CU | $36,948 | $37,183 | -0.6% | $38,306 | $41,170 | -7.0% | $25,589 | $25,070 | 2.1% | $18,025 | $17,997 | 0.2% |
| Avg. spending of CU, total | 32,277 | 33,092 | -2.5 | 32,604 | 34,121 | -4.4 | 25,302 | 24,371 | 3.8 | 18,573 | 18,015 | 3.1 |
| **FOOD** | **$4,505** | **$5,009** | **-10.1%** | **$4,539** | **$5,165** | **-12.1%** | **$3,895** | **$3,854** | **1.1%** | **$2,767** | **$2,805** | **-1.4%** |
| **Food at home** | **2,803** | **2,898** | **-3.3** | **2,832** | **3,033** | **-6.6** | **2,610** | **2,456** | **6.3** | **2,069** | **1,929** | **7.3** |
| Cereals and bakery products | 441 | 429 | 2.8 | 425 | 441 | -3.6 | 419 | 378 | 10.9 | 344 | 312 | 10.1 |
| Cereals and cereal products | 165 | 150 | 9.7 | 151 | 150 | 0.4 | 141 | 120 | 17.4 | 117 | 103 | 14.0 |
| Bakery products | 276 | 280 | -1.4 | 274 | 290 | -5.6 | 277 | 258 | 7.5 | 227 | 209 | 8.8 |
| Meats, poultry, fish, and eggs | 752 | 779 | -3.5 | 807 | 871 | -7.3 | 699 | 697 | 0.2 | 500 | 472 | 5.9 |
| Beef | 228 | 254 | -10.3 | 253 | 269 | -6.1 | 205 | 241 | -15.1 | 140 | 135 | 3.5 |
| Pork | 156 | 154 | 1.4 | 169 | 178 | -5.3 | 136 | 136 | -0.3 | 116 | 99 | 17.0 |
| Other meats | 104 | 115 | -9.9 | 111 | 134 | -17.2 | 91 | 96 | -4.8 | 79 | 64 | 23.2 |
| Poultry | 138 | 126 | 9.6 | 127 | 146 | -12.9 | 137 | 114 | 19.9 | 84 | 82 | 2.9 |
| Fish and seafood | 97 | 96 | 1.5 | 114 | 105 | 8.6 | 101 | 77 | 31.2 | 56 | 66 | -15.7 |
| Eggs | 30 | 35 | -14.2 | 33 | 38 | -14.2 | 29 | 31 | -7.9 | 26 | 26 | 1.4 |
| Dairy products | 297 | 344 | -13.7 | 293 | 339 | -13.6 | 274 | 288 | -4.9 | 217 | 234 | -7.4 |
| Fresh milk and cream | 123 | 163 | -24.7 | 121 | 149 | -18.9 | 110 | 142 | -22.7 | 84 | 118 | -28.7 |
| Other dairy products | 174 | 181 | -3.7 | 171 | 190 | -10.0 | 164 | 147 | 11.6 | 133 | 118 | 12.9 |
| Fruits and vegetables | 457 | 476 | -3.9 | 496 | 521 | -4.8 | 459 | 457 | 0.4 | 409 | 405 | 1.1 |
| Fresh fruits | 144 | 148 | -2.8 | 153 | 181 | -15.3 | 160 | 149 | 7.2 | 139 | 140 | -0.7 |
| Fresh vegetables | 137 | 138 | -0.4 | 157 | 153 | 2.8 | 142 | 134 | 5.9 | 120 | 99 | 21.1 |

*(continued)*

*(continued from previous page)*

| | total consumer units | | | aged 55 to 64 | | | aged 65 to 74 | | | aged 75 or older | | |
|---|---|---|---|---|---|---|---|---|---|---|---|---|
| | 1995 | 1990 | % change | 1995 | 1990 | % change | 1995 | 1990 | % change | 1995 | 1990 | % change |
| Processed fruits | $96 | $108 | -11.5% | $102 | $103 | -0.6% | $86 | $104 | -17.1% | $89 | $105 | -15.2% |
| Processed vegetables | 80 | 82 | -2.0 | 84 | 84 | 0.1 | 71 | 71 | -0.2 | 61 | 61 | 0.6 |
| Other food at home | 856 | 870 | -1.6 | 811 | 859 | -5.6 | 759 | 635 | 19.4 | 599 | 505 | 18.6 |
| Sugar and other sweets | 112 | 110 | 2.2 | 113 | 111 | 2.0 | 103 | 92 | 11.8 | 104 | 80 | 29.3 |
| Fats and oils | 82 | 79 | 3.4 | 86 | 84 | 2.4 | 89 | 75 | 19.3 | 66 | 56 | 17.9 |
| Miscellaneous foods | 377 | 392 | -3.8 | 325 | 353 | -8.0 | 316 | 258 | 22.6 | 252 | 212 | 18.7 |
| Nonalcoholic beverages | 240 | 248 | -3.4 | 230 | 252 | -8.7 | 201 | 180 | 11.9 | 159 | 145 | 10.0 |
| Food prepared by CU, out-of-town trips | 45 | 41 | 10.3 | 58 | 59 | -2.5 | 50 | 31 | 58.8 | 18 | 12 | 54.4 |
| **Food away from home** | **1,702** | **2,112** | **-19.4** | **1,707** | **2,134** | **-20.0** | **1,285** | **1,398** | **-8.1** | **698** | **877** | **-20.4** |
| **ALCOHOLIC BEVS.** | **277** | **342** | **-18.9** | **253** | **296** | **-14.6** | **206** | **194** | **6.4** | **129** | **83** | **55.8** |
| **HOUSING** | **10,465** | **10,148** | **3.1** | **10,291** | **9,863** | **4.3** | **7,927** | **7,520** | **5.4** | **7,184** | **6,377** | **12.7** |
| **Shelter** | **5,932** | **5,639** | **5.2** | **5,358** | **4,921** | **8.9** | **4,018** | **3,717** | **8.1** | **3,243** | **3,259** | **-0.5** |
| Owned dwellings | 3,754 | 3,443 | 9.0 | 3,799 | 3,349 | 13.4 | 2,819 | 2,426 | 16.2 | 1,895 | 1,888 | 0.4 |
| Mortgage interest/charges | 2,107 | 2,119 | -0.5 | 1,719 | 1,456 | 18.0 | 732 | 662 | 10.5 | 242 | 125 | 94.0 |
| Property taxes | 932 | 696 | 33.9 | 1,117 | 991 | 12.7 | 1,071 | 961 | 11.5 | 855 | 789 | 8.3 |
| Maintenance, repairs, insurance, etc. | 716 | 630 | 13.7 | 963 | 900 | 7.0 | 1,015 | 803 | 26.3 | 798 | 974 | -18.0 |
| Rented dwellings | 1,786 | 1,787 | -0.1 | 986 | 1,018 | -3.1 | 783 | 856 | -8.5 | 1,111 | 1,136 | -2.2 |
| Other lodging | 392 | 407 | -3.7 | 572 | 555 | 3.1 | 416 | 435 | -4.3 | 238 | 236 | 1.0 |
| **Utilities, fuels, public svcs.** | **2,193** | **2,204** | **-0.5** | **2,442** | **2,519** | **-3.0** | **2,152** | **2,143** | **0.4** | **1,777** | **1,766** | **0.6** |
| Natural gas | 268 | 287 | -6.6 | 322 | 339 | -5.1 | 295 | 333 | -11.5 | 271 | 251 | 8.1 |

*(continued)*

| | total consumer units | | | aged 55 to 64 | | | aged 65 to 74 | | | aged 75 or older | | |
|---|---|---|---|---|---|---|---|---|---|---|---|---|
| | 1995 | 1990 | % change | 1995 | 1990 | % change | 1995 | 1990 | % change | 1995 | 1990 | % change |
| Electricity | $870 | $884 | -1.6% | $984 | $1,070 | -8.1% | $888 | $855 | 3.9% | $697 | $707 | -1.4% |
| Fuel oil and other fuels | 87 | 117 | -25.4 | 105 | 150 | -30.2 | 120 | 150 | -20.2 | 139 | 173 | -19.5 |
| Telephone | 708 | 690 | 2.6 | 723 | 688 | 5.1 | 578 | 555 | 4.1 | 443 | 438 | 1.0 |
| Water and other public services | 260 | 225 | 15.5 | 308 | 271 | 13.9 | 271 | 251 | 8.1 | 226 | 197 | 14.7 |
| **Household services** | **508** | **520** | **-2.3** | **374** | **450** | **-16.9** | **343** | **399** | **-14.0** | **615** | **536** | **14.7** |
| Personal services | 258 | 255 | 1.0 | 65 | 66 | -2.2 | 26 | 34 | -23.1 | 249 | 220 | 13.0 |
| Other household services | 250 | 265 | -5.5 | 309 | 382 | -19.2 | 317 | 365 | -13.1 | 366 | 316 | 15.8 |
| **Housekeeping supplies** | **430** | **473** | **-9.2** | **514** | **569** | **-9.7** | **481** | **422** | **14.0** | **351** | **318** | **10.3** |
| Laundry and cleaning supplies | 110 | 132 | -16.5 | 129 | 146 | -11.5 | 112 | 100 | 11.7 | 62 | 82 | -24.0 |
| Other household products | 194 | 199 | -2.7 | 243 | 262 | -7.4 | 224 | 171 | 30.7 | 160 | 122 | 30.7 |
| Postage and stationery | 125 | 142 | -12.1 | 141 | 161 | -12.4 | 145 | 152 | -4.3 | 130 | 114 | 13.8 |
| **Household furnishings and equipment** | **1,403** | **1,312** | **7.0** | **1,603** | **1,405** | **14.1** | **934** | **837** | **11.6** | **1,197** | **496** | **141.5** |
| Household textiles | 100 | 115 | -13.4 | 126 | 142 | -11.4 | 93 | 105 | -11.4 | 36 | 40 | -9.2 |
| Furniture | 327 | 361 | -9.5 | 279 | 431 | -35.3 | 172 | 170 | 1.0 | 107 | 106 | 0.8 |
| Floor coverings | 177 | 107 | 65.0 | 167 | 106 | 57.4 | 85 | 65 | 30.2 | 712 | 62 | 1,052.1 |
| Major appliances | 155 | 171 | -9.6 | 176 | 219 | -19.7 | 159 | 134 | 18.6 | 98 | 104 | -5.6 |
| Small appliances, misc. housewares | 85 | 87 | -2.8 | 143 | 105 | 36.3 | 70 | 71 | -1.6 | 44 | 47 | -5.7 |
| Misc. household equipment | 557 | 469 | 18.8 | 712 | 402 | 77.0 | 353 | 292 | 21.1 | 200 | 136 | 46.6 |

*(continued)*

(continued from previous page)

| | total consumer units | | | aged 55 to 64 | | | aged 65 to 74 | | | aged 75 or older | | |
|---|---|---|---|---|---|---|---|---|---|---|---|---|
| | 1995 | 1990 | % change | 1995 | 1990 | % change | 1995 | 1990 | % change | 1995 | 1990 | % change |
| **APPAREL, ACCESSORIES, RELATED SERVICES** | **$1,704** | **$1,887** | **-9.7%** | **$1,833** | **$1,819** | **0.8%** | **$1,117** | **$1,133** | **-1.4%** | **$582** | **$570** | **2.1%** |
| **Men and boys** | **425** | **458** | **-7.3** | **431** | **417** | **3.3** | **252** | **203** | **24.2** | **116** | **87** | **32.6** |
| Men, aged 16 and over | 329 | 378 | -12.9 | 369 | 379 | -2.6 | 222 | 177 | 25.3 | 108 | 83 | 30.5 |
| Boys, aged 2 to 15 | 96 | 82 | 17.6 | 62 | 40 | 56.4 | 30 | 26 | 16.9 | 9 | 5 | 93.0 |
| **Women and girls** | **660** | **785** | **-15.9** | **830** | **805** | **3.2** | **513** | **605** | **-15.2** | **277** | **281** | **-1.4** |
| Women, aged 16 and over | 559 | 683 | -18.2 | 765 | 770 | -0.6 | 470 | 571 | -17.7 | 264 | 269 | -2.0 |
| Girls, aged 2 to 15 | 101 | 101 | -0.4 | 65 | 35 | 85.8 | 43 | 34 | 27.2 | 13 | 12 | 11.5 |
| **Babies under age 2** | **81** | **82** | **-0.8** | **45** | **59** | **-24.3** | **20** | **22** | **-9.7** | **17** | **15** | **12.2** |
| **Footwear** | **278** | **262** | **6.0** | **207** | **253** | **-18.2** | **176** | **156** | **12.6** | **107** | **101** | **5.5** |
| **Other apparel products/svcs.** | **259** | **301** | **-13.9** | **320** | **283** | **12.9** | **156** | **148** | **5.3** | **66** | **85** | **-22.5** |
| **TRANSPORTATION** | **6,016** | **5,970** | **0.8** | **5,726** | **6,176** | **-7.3** | **4,484** | **4,038** | **11.0** | **2,035** | **2,485** | **-18.1** |
| **Vehicle purchases** | **2,639** | **2,482** | **6.3** | **2,108** | **2,348** | **-10.2** | **1,712** | **1,356** | **26.2** | **503** | **1,074** | **-53.2** |
| Cars and trucks, new | 1,194 | 1,351 | -11.6 | 1,118 | 1,334 | -16.2 | 980 | 819 | 19.7 | 316 | 655 | -51.8 |
| Cars and trucks, used | 1,411 | 1,105 | 27.6 | 953 | 995 | -4.2 | 731 | 538 | 36.0 | 187 | 419 | -55.3 |
| Other vehicles | 34 | 26 | 32.5 | 37 | 19 | 98.3 | 1 | 1 | -14.2 | 0 | 0 | |
| **Gasoline and motor oil** | **1,006** | **1,221** | **-17.6** | **1,063** | **1,322** | **-19.6** | **749** | **923** | **-18.9** | **429** | **462** | **-7.1** |
| **Other vehicle expenses** | **2,016** | **1,915** | **5.3** | **2,142** | **2,024** | **5.8** | **1,599** | **1,444** | **10.8** | **904** | **737** | **22.7** |
| Vehicle finance charges | 261 | 350 | -25.4 | 223 | 305 | -27.0 | 113 | 166 | -31.8 | 36 | 33 | 10.3 |
| Maintenance and repairs | 653 | 687 | -4.9 | 709 | 766 | -7.4 | 587 | 571 | 2.7 | 336 | 289 | 16.2 |
| Vehicle insurance | 713 | 656 | 8.6 | 792 | 753 | 5.1 | 621 | 548 | 13.3 | 422 | 345 | 22.3 |

(continued)

*(continued from previous page)*

| | total consumer units | | | aged 55 to 64 | | | aged 65 to 74 | | | aged 75 or older | | |
|---|---|---|---|---|---|---|---|---|---|---|---|---|
| | 1995 | 1990 | % change | 1995 | 1990 | % change | 1995 | 1990 | % change | 1995 | 1990 | % change |
| Vehicle rental, leasing, licensing, etc. | $390 | $222 | 76.0% | $419 | $198 | 111.4% | $277 | $157 | 76.0% | $110 | $70 | 57.2% |
| Public transportation | 355 | 352 | 0.8 | 413 | 483 | -14.4 | 424 | 316 | 34.2 | 199 | 212 | -6.2 |
| **HEALTH CARE** | **1,732** | **1,726** | **0.4** | **1,909** | **2,088** | **-8.6** | **2,617** | **2,562** | **2.2** | **2,683** | **2,592** | **3.5** |
| Health insurance | 860 | 677 | 26.9 | 896 | 816 | 9.8 | 1,528 | 1,182 | 29.2 | 1,557 | 1,119 | 39.1 |
| Medical services | 511 | 655 | -22.0 | 587 | 763 | -23.0 | 471 | 765 | -38.4 | 487 | 786 | -38.0 |
| Drugs | 280 | 294 | -4.7 | 344 | 396 | -13.2 | 536 | 531 | 1.0 | 555 | 584 | -5.0 |
| Medical supplies | 80 | 99 | -19.3 | 83 | 112 | -25.9 | 82 | 85 | -3.7 | 84 | 103 | -18.1 |
| **ENTERTAINMENT** | **1,612** | **1,658** | **-2.8** | **1,577** | **1,757** | **-10.3** | **1,156** | **1,066** | **8.5** | **652** | **493** | **32.2** |
| Fees and admissions | 433 | 433 | 0.1 | 418 | 426 | -1.8 | 377 | 384 | -1.7 | 223 | 178 | 25.0 |
| Television, radios, sound equip. | 542 | 529 | 2.4 | 492 | 455 | 8.2 | 397 | 358 | 10.9 | 260 | 188 | 38.5 |
| Pets, toys, playground equip. | 322 | 322 | 0.1 | 316 | 297 | 6.3 | 182 | 188 | -3.1 | 100 | 97 | 3.3 |
| Other supplies, equip., services | 315 | 374 | -15.8 | 350 | 580 | -39.6 | 200 | 135 | 47.9 | 70 | 30 | 130.9 |
| **PERSONAL CARE PDTS. AND SERVICES** | **403** | **424** | **-5.0** | **407** | **480** | **-15.3** | **380** | **356** | **6.9** | **260** | **254** | **2.3** |
| **READING** | **163** | **178** | **-8.6** | **188** | **190** | **-1.1** | **180** | **182** | **-1.0** | **138** | **131** | **5.7** |
| **EDUCATION** | **471** | **473** | **-0.5** | **366** | **438** | **-16.5** | **237** | **56** | **323.5** | **55** | **71** | **-22.7** |
| **TOBACCO PRODUCTS & SMOKING SUPPLIES** | **269** | **319** | **-15.8** | **314** | **380** | **-17.4** | **183** | **244** | **-24.9** | **85** | **106** | **-19.9** |
| **MISCELLANEOUS** | **766** | **982** | **-22.0** | **948** | **965** | **-1.8** | **629** | **826** | **-23.8** | **571** | **412** | **38.7** |

*(continued)*

(continued from previous page)

| | total consumer units | | | aged 55 to 64 | | | aged 65 to 74 | | | aged 75 or older | | |
|---|---|---|---|---|---|---|---|---|---|---|---|---|
| | 1995 | 1990 | % change | 1995 | 1990 | % change | 1995 | 1990 | % change | 1995 | 1990 | % change |
| CASH CONTRIBUTIONS | $925 | $951 | -2.8% | $1,043 | $1,053 | -0.9% | $1,165 | $1,093 | 6.6% | $1,023 | $1,330 | -23.1% |
| PERSONAL INSURANCE AND PENSIONS | 2,967 | 3,022 | -1.8 | 3,211 | 3,449 | -6.9 | 1,127 | 1,249 | -9.8 | 409 | 304 | 34.4 |
| Life/other personal insurance | 374 | 402 | -7.0 | 555 | 545 | 1.9 | 304 | 398 | -23.5 | 172 | 153 | 12.6 |
| Pensions and Social Security | 2,593 | 2,621 | -1.1 | 2,656 | 2,905 | -8.6 | 823 | 851 | -3.3 | 236 | 152 | 55.7 |
| GIFTS OF GOODS AND SERVICES | 987 | 1,062 | -7.1 | 1,361 | 1,332 | 2.2 | 801 | 856 | -6.4 | 562 | 631 | -10.9 |
| Food | 88 | 111 | -20.6 | 127 | 154 | -17.5 | 56 | 68 | -17.2 | 71 | 65 | 8.7 |
| Housing | 250 | 271 | -7.6 | 289 | 302 | -4.3 | 207 | 217 | -4.6 | 129 | 169 | -23.7 |
| Housekeeping supplies | 38 | 41 | -6.9 | 46 | 50 | -8.3 | 34 | 43 | -21.2 | 27 | 22 | 21.9 |
| Household textiles | 10 | 16 | -38.7 | 12 | 19 | -35.7 | 11 | 24 | -55.1 | 4 | 3 | 14.4 |
| Appliances/misc. housewares | 27 | 31 | -14.2 | 60 | 51 | 16.9 | 31 | 33 | -5.0 | 9 | 23 | -61.4 |
| Major appliances | 5 | 8 | -38.7 | 9 | 9 | -3.5 | 8 | 9 | -14.2 | 1 | 7 | -85.7 |
| Small appliances and misc. housewares | 23 | 23 | -1.4 | 50 | 42 | 19.1 | 22 | 23 | -5.7 | 8 | 16 | -51.0 |
| Misc. household equipment | 66 | 58 | 13.2 | 77 | 69 | 11.9 | 82 | 45 | 80.3 | 33 | 9 | 253.8 |
| Other housing | 109 | 125 | -12.6 | 93 | 113 | -17.8 | 49 | 72 | -32.2 | 57 | 111 | -48.5 |
| Apparel and services | 258 | 275 | -6.2 | 457 | 323 | 41.5 | 180 | 280 | -35.7 | 101 | 87 | 15.5 |
| Males, aged 2 or older | 70 | 71 | -1.6 | 120 | 114 | 5.0 | 48 | 58 | -17.7 | 32 | 35 | -8.5 |
| Females, aged 2 or older | 94 | 111 | -15.1 | 240 | 100 | 139.3 | 67 | 153 | -56.1 | 41 | 35 | 17.2 |
| Babies under age 2 | 39 | 36 | 7.9 | 39 | 43 | -9.6 | 18 | 20 | -9.2 | 16 | 7 | 128.7 |

(continued)

(continued from previous page)

| | total consumer units | | | aged 55 to 64 | | | aged 65 to 74 | | | aged 75 or older | | |
|---|---|---|---|---|---|---|---|---|---|---|---|---|
| | 1995 | 1990 | % change | 1995 | 1990 | % change | 1995 | 1990 | % change | 1995 | 1990 | % change |
| Other apparel pdts. and svcs. | $55 | $56 | -1.7% | $58 | $66 | -12.7% | $46 | $48 | -3.8% | $13 | $10 | 23.9% |
| Jewelry and watches | 27 | 29 | -7.4 | 23 | 34 | -32.0 | 32 | 21 | 52.5 | 4 | 6 | -31.4 |
| All other apparel pdts./svcs. | 29 | 27 | 8.1 | 35 | 33 | 7.2 | 14 | 27 | -47.8 | 9 | 5 | 93.0 |
| **Transportation** | **48** | **62** | **-22.3** | **76** | **121** | **-37.3** | **48** | **40** | **21.1** | **44** | **15** | **190.3** |
| **Health care** | **22** | **52** | **-58.1** | **23** | **43** | **-46.7** | **10** | **62** | **-83.8** | **56** | **120** | **-53.4** |
| **Entertainment** | **86** | **77** | **11.8** | **134** | **120** | **11.6** | **78** | **66** | **17.4** | **42** | **34** | **24.2** |
| Toys, games, hobbies, tricycles | 29 | 29 | -0.5 | 57 | 57 | -0.2 | 30 | 28 | 7.2 | 9 | 13 | -29.8 |
| Other entertainment | 57 | 48 | 19.2 | 77 | 63 | 22.3 | 48 | 38 | 24.7 | 33 | 21 | 57.2 |
| **Education** | **120** | **112** | **7.2** | **131** | **176** | **-25.6** | **84** | **16** | **414.6** | **20** | **54** | **-62.7** |
| **All other gifts** | **114** | **103** | **11.1** | **123** | **93** | **31.9** | **138** | **107** | **28.6** | **98** | **86** | **13.6** |

Note: The Bureau of Labor Statistics uses consumer units rather than households as the sampling unit in the Consumer Expenditure Survey. For the definition of consumer unit, see the glossary.

Source: Bureau of Labor Statistics, 1995 and 1990 Consumer Expenditure Surveys; calculations by New Strategist

# Spending of Retirees Is below Average

**The spending of retirees is less than that of the average household because their households are smaller.**

Households headed by retirees spent an average of $21,631 in 1995, 33 percent less than the $32,277 spent by the average household. This difference in spending is almost entirely accounted for by differences in household size. While the average household is home to 2.5 people, households headed by retirees average just 1.8 people. After adjusting for household size, the spending of retirees is only 7 percent less than that of the average household.

Households headed by retirees spend about as much or even more than the average household on items such as eggs (with an index of 100—meaning households headed by retirees spend the same amount as the average household on this item), fresh fruits (with an index of 103), maintenance and repairs on owned homes (126), postage and stationery (106), health care (142), reading materials (98), and cash contributions (118).

◆ As better-educated and more affluent generations of Americans reach retirement age, the spending of retirees is likely to rise. This higher spending, combined with the growth of the segment, will make retirees an important market for most businesses in the decades ahead.

## Retirees Spend above Average on Some Items

*(indexed spending of consumer units headed by retirees on selected items, 1995)*

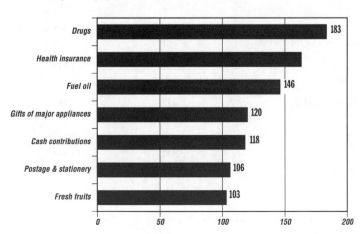

# Average and Indexed Spending of Retirees, 1995

*(average annual and indexed spending of consumer units (CUs) headed by retirees, 1995)*

| | average spending of total consumer units | consumer units headed by retirees | |
| --- | --- | --- | --- |
| | | average spending | indexed spending* |
| **Number of consumer units (in thousands)** | *103,024* | *18,636* | - |
| **Average before-tax income** | *$36,948* | *$20,241* | *55* |
| **Total average annual spending** | *32,277* | *21,631* | *67* |
| **FOOD** | **$4,505** | **$3,484** | **77** |
| **Food at home** | **2,803** | **2,451** | **87** |
| Cereals and bakery products | 441 | 387 | 88 |
| Cereals and cereal products | 165 | 139 | 84 |
| Bakery products | 276 | 249 | 90 |
| Meats, poultry, fish, and eggs | 752 | 639 | 85 |
| Beef | 228 | 191 | 84 |
| Pork | 156 | 135 | 87 |
| Other meats | 104 | 95 | 91 |
| Poultry | 138 | 111 | 80 |
| Fish and seafood | 97 | 77 | 79 |
| Eggs | 30 | 30 | 100 |
| Dairy products | 297 | 263 | 89 |
| Fresh milk and cream | 123 | 108 | 88 |
| Other dairy products | 174 | 155 | 89 |
| Fruits and vegetables | 457 | 438 | 96 |
| Fresh fruits | 144 | 149 | 103 |
| Fresh vegetables | 137 | 129 | 94 |
| Processed fruits | 96 | 89 | 93 |
| Processed vegetables | 80 | 71 | 89 |
| Other food at home | 856 | 724 | 85 |
| Sugar and other sweets | 112 | 111 | 99 |
| Fats and oils | 82 | 79 | 96 |
| Miscellaneous foods | 377 | 303 | 80 |
| Nonalcoholic beverages | 240 | 192 | 80 |
| Food prepared by CU, out-of-town trips | 45 | 39 | 87 |
| **Food away from home** | **1,702** | **1,033** | **61** |
| **ALCOHOLIC BEVERAGES** | **277** | **180** | **65** |
| **HOUSING** | **10,465** | **7,188** | **69** |
| **Shelter** | **5,932** | **3,644** | **61** |
| Owned dwellings** | 3,754 | 2,321 | 62 |

*(continued)*

*(continued from previous page)*

| | average spending of total consumer units | consumer units headed by retirees | |
|---|---|---|---|
| | | average spending | indexed spending* |
| Mortgage interest and charges | $2,107 | $494 | 23 |
| Property taxes | 932 | 928 | 100 |
| Maintenance, repairs, insurance, etc. | 716 | 899 | 126 |
| Rented dwellings | 1,786 | 978 | 55 |
| Other lodging | 392 | 345 | 88 |
| **Utilities, fuels, and public services** | **2,193** | **1,959** | **89** |
| Natural gas | 268 | 277 | 103 |
| Electricity | 870 | 787 | 90 |
| Fuel oil and other fuels | 87 | 127 | 146 |
| Telephone | 708 | 516 | 73 |
| Water and other public services | 260 | 253 | 97 |
| **Household services** | **508** | **401** | **79** |
| Personal services | 258 | 134 | 52 |
| Other household services | 250 | 267 | 107 |
| **Housekeeping supplies** | **430** | **427** | **99** |
| Laundry and cleaning supplies | 110 | 96 | 87 |
| Other household products | 194 | 199 | 103 |
| Postage and stationery | 125 | 132 | 106 |
| **Household furnishings and equipment** | **1,403** | **757** | **54** |
| Household textiles | 100 | 58 | 58 |
| Furniture | 327 | 150 | 46 |
| Floor coverings | 177 | 52 | 29 |
| Major appliances | 155 | 141 | 91 |
| Small appliances, misc. housewares | 85 | 57 | 67 |
| Miscellaneous household equipment | 557 | 298 | 54 |
| **APPAREL, ACCESSORIES, AND RELATED SERVICES** | **1,704** | **898** | **53** |
| **Men and boys** | **425** | **193** | **45** |
| Men, aged 16 and over | 329 | 170 | 52 |
| Boys, aged 2 to 15 | 96 | 23 | 24 |
| **Women and girls** | **660** | **418** | **63** |
| Women, aged 16 and over | 559 | 382 | 68 |
| Girls, aged 2 to 15 | 101 | 36 | 36 |
| **Babies under age 2** | **81** | **26** | **32** |
| **Footwear** | **278** | **145** | **52** |
| **Other apparel products and services** | **259** | **116** | **45** |
| **TRANSPORTATION** | **6,016** | **3,423** | **57** |
| **Vehicle purchases** | **2,639** | **1,202** | **46** |

*(continued)*

*(continued from previous page)*

| | average spending of total consumer units | consumer units headed by retirees | |
| --- | --- | --- | --- |
| | | average spending | indexed spending* |
| Cars and trucks, new | $1,194 | $651 | 55 |
| Cars and trucks, used | 1,411 | 525 | 37 |
| Other vehicles | 34 | 26 | 76 |
| **Gasoline and motor oil** | **1,006** | **634** | **63** |
| **Other vehicle expenses** | **2,016** | **1,309** | **65** |
| **Vehicle finance charges** | **261** | **75** | **29** |
| **Maintenance and repairs** | **653** | **503** | **77** |
| **Vehicle insurance** | **713** | **527** | **74** |
| **Vehicle rental, leasing, licensing, etc.** | **390** | **204** | **52** |
| **Public transportation** | **355** | **278** | **78** |
| **HEALTH CARE** | **1,732** | **2,454** | **142** |
| Health insurance | 860 | 1,399 | 163 |
| Medical services | 511 | 456 | 89 |
| Drugs | 280 | 511 | 183 |
| Medical supplies | 80 | 89 | 111 |
| **ENTERTAINMENT** | **1,612** | **995** | **62** |
| Fees and admissions | 433 | 321 | 74 |
| Television, radios, sound equipment | 542 | 339 | 63 |
| Pets, toys, and playground equipment | 322 | 168 | 52 |
| Other supplies, equip., and services | 315 | 167 | 53 |
| **PERSONAL CARE PRODUCTS AND SERVICES** | **403** | **320** | **79** |
| **READING** | **163** | **160** | **98** |
| **EDUCATION** | **471** | **189** | **40** |
| **TOBACCO PRODUCTS AND SMOKING SUPPLIES** | **269** | **144** | **54** |
| **MISCELLANEOUS** | **766** | **552** | **72** |
| **CASH CONTRIBUTIONS** | **925** | **1,089** | **118** |
| **PERSONAL INSURANCE AND PENSIONS** | **2,967** | **555** | **19** |
| Life and other personal insurance | 374 | 244 | 65 |
| Pensions and Social Security | 2,593 | 311 | 12 |
| **GIFTS OF GOODS AND SERVICES*** | **987** | **714** | **72** |
| **Food** | **88** | **67** | **76** |

*(continued)*

*(continued from previous page)*

| | average spending of total consumer units | consumer units headed by retirees | |
|---|---|---|---|
| | | average spending | indexed spending* |
| **Housing** | $250 | $151 | 60 |
| Housekeeping supplies | 38 | 33 | 87 |
| Household textiles | 10 | 5 | 50 |
| Appliances and misc. housewares | 27 | 18 | 67 |
|   Major appliances | 5 | 6 | 120 |
|   Small appliances and misc. housewares | 23 | 12 | 52 |
| Miscellaneous household equipment | 66 | 55 | 83 |
| Other housing | 109 | 40 | 37 |
| **Apparel and services** | 258 | 150 | 58 |
| Males, aged 2 or older | 70 | 41 | 59 |
| Females, aged 2 or older | 94 | 67 | 71 |
| Babies under age 2 | 39 | 20 | 51 |
| Other apparel products and services | 55 | 22 | 40 |
|  Jewelry and watches | 27 | 12 | 44 |
|  All other apparel products and services | 29 | 10 | 34 |
| **Transportation** | 48 | 52 | 108 |
| **Health care** | 22 | 33 | 150 |
| **Entertainment** | 86 | 72 | 84 |
| Toys, games, hobbies, and tricycles | 29 | 20 | 69 |
| Other entertainment | 57 | 52 | 91 |
| **Education** | 120 | 78 | 65 |
| **All other gifts** | 114 | 111 | 97 |

*\* The index compares the spending of consumer units headed by retirees with the spending of the average consumer unit by dividing the spending of retirees by average spending in each category and multiplying by 100. An index of 100 means that the spending of retirees in that category equals average spending. An index of 132 means that the spending of retirees is 32 percent above average, while an index of 75 means that the spending of retirees is 25 percent below average.*
*\*\* This figure does not include the amount paid for mortgage principle, which is considered an asset.*
*\*\*\* Expenditures on gifts are also included in the preceding product and service categories. Food spending, for example, includes the amount spent on food gifts.*
*Note: The Bureau of Labor Statistics uses consumer units rather than households as the sampling unit in the Consumer Expenditure Survey. For the definition of consumer unit, see the Glossary.*
*Source: Bureau of Labor Statistics, unpublished tables from the 1995 Consumer Expenditure Survey; calculations by New Strategist*

# Householders Aged 55 to 64 Are Average Spenders

## The average household headed by a 55-to-64-year-old spent $32,604 in 1995.

The spending of householders aged 55 to 64 was just 1 percent above average in 1995. Behind the average spending of this group are two very different lifestyles, however. At one extreme are the many householders aged 55 to 64 who are still working and enjoying high incomes. Their spending is well above average. At the other extreme, millions of householders in the age group are retired and have cut their spending as they adjust to lower retirement incomes.

Householders aged 55 to 64 spend well above average on many items. These include sirloin steak (with a spending index of 147—meaning householders in this age group spend 47 percent more than the average household on this item), prepared desserts (index of 149), catered affairs (214), owned vacation homes (174), lawn and garden supplies (184), lamps (260), auto rentals on out-of-town trips (173), ship fares (169), radios (188), and political contributions (287).

Householders aged 55 to 64 spend well below average on most items associated with children since most of their children are grown. The spending index of these

## 55-to-65-Year-Olds Spend More on Some Items

*(indexed spending of consumer units headed by 55-to-64-year-olds on selected items, 1995)*

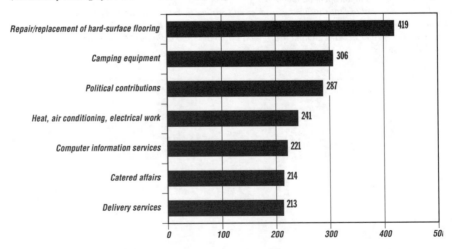

householders for baby food, for example, is just 35, meaning they spend 65 percent less than the average household on this item. Their spending is also below average on mortgage interest (index of 77) since many own their home free and clear. They do not spend much for personal services (index of 25), because most expenses in this category are for day care. They spend relatively little on items such as kitchen and dining room furniture (51), used cars and trucks (68), video game hardware and software (63), and winter sports equipment (38).

◆ Many businesses pursue the young-adult market and ignore older consumers because they think older people don't want to spend money. In fact, the spending of 55-to-64-year-olds is equal to or higher than that of young adults (under age 35) in most categories.

# Average and Indexed Spending of Householders Aged 55 to 64, 1995

*(average annual and indexed spending of consumer units (CUs) headed by 55-to-64-year-olds, 1995)*

| | average spending of total consumer units | consumer units headed by 55-to-64-year-olds | |
| --- | --- | --- | --- |
| | | average spending | indexed spending* |
| **Number of consumer units (in thousands)** | 103,024 | 12,626 | - |
| **Average before-tax income** | $36,948.00 | $38,306.00 | 104 |
| **Total average annual spending** | 32,276.59 | 32,603.57 | 101 |
| **FOOD** | $4,505.34 | $4,538.70 | 101 |
| **FOOD AT HOME** | 2,802.91 | 2,831.61 | 101 |
| **Cereals and bakery products** | 441.13 | 424.84 | 96 |
| Cereals and cereal products | 165.23 | 150.52 | 91 |
| Flour | 8.42 | 7.07 | 84 |
| Prepared flour mixes | 12.80 | 14.59 | 114 |
| Ready-to-eat and cooked cereal | 97.00 | 78.83 | 81 |
| Rice | 20.17 | 20.94 | 104 |
| Pasta, cornmeal, and other cereal products | 26.84 | 29.09 | 108 |
| **Bakery products** | 275.90 | 274.32 | 99 |
| Bread | 75.70 | 84.63 | 112 |
| White bread | 36.77 | 38.36 | 104 |
| Bread, other than white | 38.92 | 46.26 | 119 |
| Crackers and cookies | 67.33 | 68.94 | 102 |
| Cookies | 44.90 | 48.68 | 108 |
| Crackers | 22.43 | 20.26 | 90 |
| Frozen and refrigerated bakery products | 21.92 | 18.16 | 83 |
| Other bakery products | 110.95 | 102.59 | 92 |
| Biscuits and rolls | 38.49 | 40.31 | 105 |
| Cakes and cupcakes | 34.63 | 28.01 | 81 |
| Bread and cracker products | 4.23 | 3.81 | 90 |
| Sweetrolls, coffee cakes, doughnuts | 20.80 | 18.07 | 87 |
| Pies, tarts, turnovers | 12.80 | 12.40 | 97 |
| **Meats, poultry, fish, and eggs** | 752.43 | 807.19 | 107 |
| Beef | 227.60 | 252.68 | 111 |
| Ground beef | 84.47 | 77.53 | 92 |
| Roast | 40.09 | 45.16 | 113 |
| Chuck roast | 12.63 | 11.45 | 91 |
| Round roast | 13.18 | 13.86 | 105 |
| Other roast | 14.28 | 19.85 | 139 |
| Steak | 86.84 | 106.42 | 123 |
| Round steak | 18.82 | 21.61 | 115 |

*(continued)*

*(continued from previous page)*

| | average spending of total consumer units | consumer units headed by 55-to-64-year-olds | |
| --- | --- | --- | --- |
| | | average spending | indexed spending* |
| Sirloin steak | $23.42 | $34.38 | 147 |
| Other steak | 44.61 | 50.42 | 113 |
| Other beef | 16.19 | 23.57 | 146 |
| Pork | 156.00 | 169.19 | 108 |
| Bacon | 20.32 | 18.85 | 93 |
| Pork chops | 39.69 | 41.82 | 105 |
| Ham | 37.06 | 43.85 | 118 |
| Ham, not canned | 34.76 | 41.66 | 120 |
| Canned ham | 2.31 | 2.19 | 95 |
| Sausage | 22.12 | 28.35 | 128 |
| Other pork | 36.79 | 36.33 | 99 |
| Other meats | 103.63 | 110.84 | 107 |
| Frankfurters | 22.13 | 20.23 | 91 |
| Lunch meats (cold cuts) | 69.66 | 73.90 | 106 |
| Bologna, liverwurst, salami | 25.45 | 28.76 | 113 |
| Other lunchmeats | 44.22 | 45.14 | 102 |
| Lamb, organ meats, and others | 11.84 | 16.71 | 141 |
| Lamb and organ meats | 9.31 | 14.88 | 160 |
| Mutton, goat and game | 2.54 | 1.82 | 72 |
| Poultry | 137.65 | 126.75 | 92 |
| Fresh and frozen chicken | 105.14 | 98.68 | 94 |
| Fresh and frozen whole chicken | 28.21 | 28.75 | 102 |
| Fresh and frozen chicken parts | 76.93 | 69.94 | 91 |
| Other poultry | 32.51 | 28.07 | 86 |
| Fish and seafood | 97.33 | 114.34 | 117 |
| Canned fish and seafood | 17.11 | 21.59 | 126 |
| Fresh fish and shellfish | 52.43 | 65.21 | 124 |
| Frozen fish and shellfish | 27.79 | 27.54 | 99 |
| Eggs | 30.23 | 33.39 | 110 |
| **Dairy products** | **296.61** | **292.52** | **99** |
| Fresh milk and cream | 123.00 | 121.28 | 99 |
| Fresh milk, all types | 113.81 | 108.00 | 95 |
| Cream | 9.19 | 13.28 | 145 |
| Other dairy products | 173.60 | 171.24 | 99 |
| Butter | 12.31 | 11.94 | 97 |
| Cheese | 88.00 | 87.65 | 100 |
| Ice cream and related products | 51.24 | 50.89 | 99 |
| Miscellaneous dairy products | 22.05 | 20.76 | 94 |
| **Fruits and vegetables** | **456.67** | **495.83** | **109** |
| Fresh fruits | 144.14 | 152.72 | 106 |
| Apples | 29.15 | 29.36 | 101 |

*(continued)*

*(continued from previous page)*

| | average spending of total consumer units | consumer units headed by 55-to-64-year-olds | |
|---|---|---|---|
| | | average spending | indexed spending* |
| Bananas | $30.26 | $35.59 | 118 |
| Oranges | 16.27 | 17.04 | 105 |
| Citrus fruits, excl. oranges | 12.03 | 13.63 | 113 |
| Fresh vegetables | 137.31 | 156.72 | 114 |
| Potatoes | 28.50 | 34.25 | 120 |
| Lettuce | 18.22 | 17.23 | 95 |
| Tomatoes | 21.64 | 22.12 | 102 |
| Other fresh vegetables | 68.95 | 83.11 | 121 |
| Processed fruits | 95.70 | 102.09 | 107 |
| Frozen fruits and fruit juices | 17.00 | 13.74 | 81 |
| Frozen orange juice | 8.66 | 7.11 | 82 |
| Frozen fruits | 1.81 | 2.20 | 122 |
| Frozen fruit juices | 6.53 | 4.43 | 68 |
| Canned fruits | 13.88 | 15.69 | 113 |
| Dried fruit | 5.86 | 9.04 | 154 |
| Fresh fruit juice | 17.55 | 19.39 | 110 |
| Canned and bottled fruit juice | 41.40 | 44.24 | 107 |
| Processed vegetables | 79.52 | 84.30 | 106 |
| Frozen vegetables | 28.07 | 27.86 | 99 |
| Canned and dried vegetables and juices | 51.44 | 56.44 | 110 |
| Canned beans | 11.26 | 10.68 | 95 |
| Canned corn | 6.91 | 5.84 | 85 |
| Canned misc. vegetables | 16.68 | 20.72 | 124 |
| Dried peas | 0.17 | 0.14 | 82 |
| Dried beans | 2.88 | 3.54 | 123 |
| Dried misc. vegetables | 6.14 | 4.23 | 69 |
| Dried processed vegetables | 0.23 | - | - |
| Frozen vegetable juices | 0.31 | 0.22 | 71 |
| Fresh and canned vegetable juices | 6.87 | 11.08 | 161 |
| **Other food at home** | **856.08** | **811.22** | **95** |
| Sugar and other sweets | 112.08 | 112.57 | 100 |
| Candy and chewing gum | 67.43 | 65.70 | 97 |
| Sugar | 17.44 | 17.63 | 101 |
| Artificial sweeteners | 4.51 | 5.12 | 114 |
| Jams, preserves, other sweets | 22.70 | 24.12 | 106 |
| Fats and oils | 82.22 | 85.90 | 104 |
| Margarine | 12.74 | 15.60 | 122 |
| Fats and oils | 24.60 | 25.92 | 105 |
| Salad dressings | 26.16 | 27.51 | 105 |
| Nondairy cream and imitation milk | 7.15 | 7.11 | 99 |
| Peanut butter | 11.58 | 9.77 | 84 |

*(continued)*

*(continued from previous page)*

| | average spending of total consumer units | consumer units headed by 55-to-64-year-olds | |
|---|---|---|---|
| | | average spending | indexed spending* |
| Miscellaneous foods | $376.59 | $324.51 | 86 |
| Frozen prepared foods | 66.03 | 49.21 | 75 |
| Frozen meals | 19.87 | 17.37 | 87 |
| Other frozen prepared foods | 46.16 | 31.84 | 69 |
| Canned and packaged soups | 31.25 | 30.50 | 98 |
| Potato chips, nuts, and other snacks | 80.50 | 72.27 | 90 |
| Potato chips and other snacks | 62.33 | 54.29 | 87 |
| Nuts | 18.17 | 17.98 | 99 |
| Condiments and seasonings | 86.51 | 86.92 | 100 |
| Salt, spices and other seasonings | 20.29 | 21.70 | 107 |
| Olives, pickles, relishes | 10.14 | 11.43 | 113 |
| Sauces and gravies | 39.88 | 38.92 | 98 |
| Baking needs and misc. products | 16.20 | 14.88 | 92 |
| Other canned/packaged prepared foods | 112.30 | 85.60 | 76 |
| Prepared salads | 13.51 | 13.98 | 103 |
| Prepared desserts | 8.99 | 13.37 | 149 |
| Baby food | 25.02 | 8.79 | 35 |
| Misc. prepared foods | 64.79 | 49.46 | 76 |
| Nonalcoholic beverages | 240.27 | 229.94 | 96 |
| Cola | 89.20 | 82.03 | 92 |
| Other carbonated drinks | 42.50 | 34.50 | 81 |
| Coffee | 46.33 | 60.72 | 131 |
| Roasted coffee | 30.90 | 37.21 | 120 |
| Instant and freeze-dried coffee | 15.43 | 23.50 | 152 |
| Noncarbonated fruit flavored drinks, incl. nonfrozen lemonade | 24.83 | 17.69 | 71 |
| Tea | 15.64 | 15.71 | 100 |
| Nonalcoholic beer | 1.01 | 1.91 | 189 |
| Other nonalcoholic beverages and ice | 20.75 | 17.39 | 84 |
| **Food prepared by CU on out-of-town trips** | **44.91** | **58.31** | **130** |
| **FOOD AWAY FROM HOME** | **1,702.43** | **1,707.09** | **100** |
| **Meals at restaurants, carry-outs, other** | **1,331.44** | **1,260.93** | **95** |
| Lunch | 464.83 | 412.96 | 89 |
| Dinner | 653.29 | 650.08 | 100 |
| Snacks and nonalcoholic beverages | 111.73 | 87.30 | 78 |
| Breakfast and brunch | 101.59 | 110.59 | 109 |
| **Board (including at school)** | **54.60** | **38.88** | **71** |
| **Catered affairs** | **43.89** | **93.85** | **214** |
| **Food on out-of-town trips** | **196.85** | **287.25** | **146** |
| **School lunches** | **49.41** | **12.52** | **25** |
| **Meals as pay** | **26.23** | **13.66** | **52** |

*(continued)*

*(continued from previous page)*

| | average spending of total consumer units | consumer units headed by 55-to-64-year-olds | |
| --- | --- | --- | --- |
| | | average spending | indexed spending* |
| **ALCOHOLIC BEVERAGES** | **$277.28** | **$252.80** | **91** |
| **AT HOME** | **165.34** | **141.57** | **86** |
| Beer and ale | 87.91 | 60.15 | 68 |
| Whiskey | 13.37 | 10.42 | 78 |
| Wine | 48.68 | 47.59 | 98 |
| Other alcoholic beverages | 15.39 | 23.42 | 152 |
| **Away from home** | **111.94** | **111.23** | **99** |
| Beer and ale | 33.45 | 27.12 | 81 |
| Wine | 20.29 | 20.88 | 103 |
| Other alcoholic beverages | 29.77 | 30.29 | 102 |
| Alcoholic beverages purchased on trips | 28.43 | 32.94 | 116 |
| **HOUSING** | **$10,464.95** | **$10,290.68** | **98** |
| **SHELTER** | **5,931.76** | **5,358.08** | **90** |
| **Owned dwellings**\*\* | **3,754.44** | **3,799.17** | **101** |
| Mortgage interest and charges | 2,106.99 | 1,718.75 | 82 |
| Mortgage interest | 1,991.49 | 1,539.67 | 77 |
| Interest paid, home equity loan | 53.32 | 90.53 | 170 |
| Interest paid, home equity line of credit | 61.81 | 88.55 | 143 |
| Prepayment penalty charges | 0.37 | - | - |
| Property taxes | 931.76 | 1,116.93 | 120 |
| Maintenance, repairs, insurance, other expenses | 715.68 | 963.50 | 135 |
| Homeowner's and related insurance | 225.32 | 294.50 | 131 |
| Fire and extended coverage | 6.69 | 14.45 | 216 |
| Homeowner's insurance | 218.63 | 280.05 | 128 |
| Ground rent | 31.63 | 41.60 | 132 |
| Maintenance and repair services | 365.24 | 515.88 | 141 |
| Painting and papering | 41.18 | 78.25 | 190 |
| Plumbing and water heating | 33.28 | 47.65 | 143 |
| Heat, air conditioning, electrical work | 72.49 | 174.49 | 241 |
| Roofing and gutters | 65.15 | 76.05 | 117 |
| Other repair and maintenance services | 130.33 | 127.69 | 98 |
| Repair/replacement of hard surface flooring | 21.23 | 9.93 | 47 |
| Repair of built-in appliances | 1.59 | 1.83 | 115 |
| Maintenance and repair materials | 71.32 | 75.48 | 106 |
| Paints, wallpaper and supplies | 19.60 | 21.91 | 112 |
| Tools/equipment for painting, wallpapering | 2.11 | 2.35 | 111 |
| Plumbing supplies and equipment | 7.26 | 6.37 | 88 |
| Electrical supplies, heating/cooling equip. | 5.22 | 3.15 | 60 |
| Hard surface flooring, repair and replacement | 3.51 | 5.72 | 163 |
| Roofing and gutters | 4.30 | 3.55 | 83 |

*(continued)*

*(continued from previous page)*

| | average spending of total consumer units | consumer units headed by 55-to-64-year-olds | |
| --- | --- | --- | --- |
| | | average spending | indexed spending* |
| Plaster, paneling, siding, windows, doors, screens, awnings | $11.53 | $5.88 | 51 |
| Patio, walk, fence, driveway, masonry, brick and stucco work | 0.88 | 0.78 | 89 |
| Landscape maintenance | 1.78 | 1.58 | 89 |
| Miscellaneous supplies and equipment | 15.13 | 24.18 | 160 |
| Insulation, other maintenance/repair | 11.41 | 17.46 | 153 |
| Finish basement, remodel rooms or build patios, walks, etc. | 3.72 | 6.73 | 181 |
| Property management and security | 22.17 | 36.03 | 163 |
| Property management | 16.64 | 29.10 | 175 |
| Management and upkeep services for security | 5.53 | 6.93 | 125 |
| **Rented dwellings** | **1,785.64** | **986.44** | **55** |
| Rent | 1,716.25 | 903.81 | 53 |
| Rent as pay | 48.68 | 66.44 | 136 |
| Maintenance, insurance and other expenses | 20.71 | 16.19 | 78 |
| Tenant's insurance | 7.35 | 3.53 | 48 |
| Maintenance and repair services | 5.32 | 9.89 | 186 |
| Repair or maintenance services | 4.93 | 8.52 | 173 |
| Repair and replacement of hard surface flooring | 0.32 | 1.34 | 419 |
| Repair of built-in appliances | 0.07 | 0.03 | 43 |
| Maintenance and repair materials | 8.04 | 2.77 | 34 |
| Paint, wallpaper and supplies | 1.48 | 0.81 | 55 |
| Painting and wallpapering | 0.16 | 0.09 | 56 |
| Plastering, panels, roofing, gutters, etc. | 0.71 | 0.82 | 115 |
| Patio, walk, fence, driveway, masonry, brick and stucco work | 0.03 | 0.01 | 33 |
| Plumbing supplies and equipment | 1.14 | 0.03 | 3 |
| Electrical supplies, heating and cooling equip. | 0.31 | 0.32 | 103 |
| Misc. supplies and equipment | 3.53 | 0.18 | 5 |
| Insulation, other maintenance and repair | 1.43 | 0.06 | 4 |
| Materials for additions, finishing basements, remodeling rooms | 2.07 | 0.12 | 6 |
| Construction materials for jobs not started | 0.04 | - | - |
| Hard surface flooring | 0.22 | - | - |
| Landscape maintenance | 0.46 | 0.51 | 111 |
| **Other lodging** | **391.68** | **572.47** | **146** |
| Owned vacation homes | 127.18 | 221.78 | 174 |
| Mortgage interest and charges | 48.74 | 73.15 | 150 |
| Mortgage interest | 47.03 | 62.58 | 133 |
| Interest paid, home equity loan | 0.12 | - | - |

*(continued)*

| | average spending of total consumer units | consumer units headed by 55-to-64-year-olds | |
| --- | --- | --- | --- |
| | | average spending | indexed spending* |
| Interest paid, home equity line of credit | $1.59 | $10.57 | 665 |
| Property taxes | 54.14 | 89.59 | 165 |
| Maintenance, insurance and other expenses | 24.29 | 59.05 | 243 |
| Homeowner's and related insurance | 6.10 | 16.40 | 269 |
| Homeowner's insurance | 5.90 | 15.64 | 265 |
| Fire and extended coverage | 0.20 | 0.76 | 380 |
| Ground rent | 2.33 | 6.39 | 274 |
| Maintenance and repair services | 10.56 | 14.37 | 136 |
| Maintenance and repair materials | 2.00 | 10.52 | 526 |
| Property management and security | 2.64 | 5.90 | 223 |
| Property management | 1.88 | 4.88 | 260 |
| Management and upkeep services for security | 0.75 | 1.02 | 136 |
| Parking | 0.67 | 5.47 | 816 |
| Housing while attending school | 54.91 | 51.34 | 93 |
| Lodging on out-of-town trips | 209.59 | 299.35 | 143 |
| **UTILITIES, FUELS & PUBLIC SERVICES** | **2,192.58** | **2,442.21** | **111** |
| **Natural gas** | **268.26** | **321.84** | **120** |
| Natural gas (renter) | 58.60 | 36.05 | 62 |
| Natural gas (owner) | 207.94 | 280.27 | 135 |
| Natural gas (vacation) | 1.58 | 5.27 | 334 |
| **Electricity** | **869.67** | **984.24** | **113** |
| Electricity (renter) | 205.17 | 108.66 | 53 |
| Electricity (owner) | 655.26 | 850.93 | 130 |
| Electricity (vacation) | 8.41 | 21.98 | 261 |
| **Fuel oil and other fuels** | **86.66** | **105.44** | **122** |
| Fuel oil | 50.69 | 63.53 | 125 |
| Fuel oil (renter) | 4.34 | 1.19 | 27 |
| Fuel oil (owner) | 45.58 | 58.56 | 128 |
| Fuel oil (vacation) | 0.73 | 3.49 | 478 |
| Coal | 2.13 | 0.88 | 41 |
| Coal (renter) | 0.10 | - | - |
| Coal (owner) | 2.03 | 0.88 | 43 |
| Bottled/tank gas | 28.02 | 36.15 | 129 |
| Gas (renter) | 3.72 | 2.30 | 62 |
| Gas (owner) | 21.86 | 28.04 | 128 |
| Gas (vacation) | 2.43 | 5.81 | 239 |
| Wood and other fuels | 5.83 | 4.88 | 84 |
| Wood and other fuels (renter) | 0.73 | 0.14 | 19 |
| Wood and other fuels (owner) | 5.06 | 4.48 | 89 |

(continued)

*(continued from previous page)*

| | average spending of total consumer units | consumer units headed by 55-to-64-year-olds | |
|---|---|---|---|
| | | average spending | indexed spending* |
| **Telephone services** | **$708.40** | **$723.10** | **102** |
| Telephone services in home city, excl. mobile car phones | 682.65 | 702.44 | 103 |
| Telephone services for mobile car phones | 25.75 | 20.66 | 80 |
| **Water and other public services** | **259.59** | **307.60** | **118** |
| Water and sewerage maintenance | 187.25 | 224.08 | 120 |
| Water and sewerage maintenance (renter) | 25.89 | 14.08 | 54 |
| Water and sewerage maintenance (owner) | 159.68 | 204.86 | 128 |
| Water and sewerage maintenance (vacation) | 1.53 | 4.58 | 299 |
| Trash and garbage collection | 70.49 | 81.47 | 116 |
| Trash and garbage collection (renter) | 8.59 | 4.22 | 49 |
| Trash and garbage collection (owner) | 60.92 | 76.00 | 125 |
| Trash and garbage collection (vacation) | 0.95 | 1.20 | 126 |
| Septic tank cleaning | 1.84 | 2.04 | 111 |
| Septic tank cleaning (renter) | 0.02 | - | - |
| Septic tank cleaning (owner) | 1.76 | 1.87 | 106 |
| Septic tank cleaning (vacation) | 0.07 | 0.17 | 243 |
| **HOUSEHOLD OPERATIONS** | **508.34** | **373.82** | **74** |
| **Personal services** | **258.04** | **64.70** | **25** |
| Babysitting and child care in own home | 39.63 | 3.46 | 9 |
| Babysitting and child care in someone else's home | 36.48 | 1.54 | 4 |
| Care for elderly, invalids, handicapped, etc. | 35.33 | 49.35 | 140 |
| Adult day care centers | 1.05 | - | - |
| Day care centers, nurseries and preschools | 145.55 | 10.36 | 7 |
| **Other household services** | **250.30** | **309.12** | **123** |
| Housekeeping services | 85.16 | 88.63 | 104 |
| Gardening, lawn care service | 63.96 | 87.96 | 138 |
| Water softening service | 2.90 | 4.02 | 139 |
| Nonclothing laundry and dry cleaning, sent out | 1.69 | 3.27 | 193 |
| Nonclothing laundry and dry cleaning, coin-operated | 4.83 | 3.96 | 82 |
| Termite/pest control services | 11.70 | 17.46 | 149 |
| Other home services | 16.60 | 27.62 | 166 |
| Termite/pest control products | 0.16 | 0.21 | 131 |
| Moving, storage, and freight express | 27.71 | 20.55 | 74 |
| Appliance repair, incl. service center | 14.07 | 16.48 | 117 |
| Reupholstering and furniture repair | 10.80 | 21.52 | 199 |
| Repairs and rental of equipment and power tools | 5.79 | 6.26 | 108 |
| Appliance rental | 1.67 | 0.85 | 51 |
| Rental of office equipment for nonbusiness use | 0.29 | 0.38 | 131 |
| Repair of misc. household equip. and furnishings | 1.75 | 8.10 | 463 |

*(continued)*

*(continued from previous page)*

| | average spending of total consumer units | consumer units headed by 55-to-64-year-olds | |
|---|---|---|---|
| | | average spending | indexed spending* |
| Repair of computer systems for nonbusiness use | $0.82 | $0.99 | 121 |
| Computer information services | 0.39 | 0.86 | 221 |
| **HOUSEKEEPING SUPPLIES** | **429.59** | **513.87** | **120** |
| **Laundry and cleaning supplies** | **110.26** | **129.37** | **117** |
| Soaps and detergents | 63.62 | 72.70 | 114 |
| Other laundry cleaning products | 46.64 | 56.67 | 122 |
| **Other household products** | **193.90** | **243.36** | **126** |
| Cleansing and toilet tissue, paper towels and napkins | 60.03 | 64.40 | 107 |
| Misc. household products | 71.57 | 64.61 | 90 |
| Lawn and garden supplies | 62.29 | 114.35 | 184 |
| **Postage and stationery** | **125.43** | **141.14** | **113** |
| Stationery, stationery supplies, giftwrap | 61.49 | 71.07 | 116 |
| Postage | 62.40 | 66.79 | 107 |
| Delivery services | 1.54 | 3.28 | 213 |
| **HOUSEHOLD FURNISHINGS & EQUIP.** | **1,402.69** | **1,602.69** | **114** |
| **Household textiles** | **100.47** | **125.85** | **125** |
| Bathroom linens | 15.50 | 14.58 | 94 |
| Bedroom linens | 45.50 | 63.11 | 139 |
| Kitchen and dining room linens | 9.26 | 13.20 | 143 |
| Curtains and draperies | 17.36 | 14.81 | 85 |
| Slipcovers and decorative pillows | 1.74 | 4.90 | 282 |
| Sewing materials for household items | 10.01 | 14.19 | 142 |
| Other linens | 1.09 | 1.06 | 97 |
| **Furniture** | **327.49** | **279.16** | **85** |
| Mattress and springs | 41.36 | 42.86 | 104 |
| Other bedroom furniture | 51.66 | 36.26 | 70 |
| Sofas | 77.20 | 71.74 | 93 |
| Living room chairs | 39.35 | 36.97 | 94 |
| Living room tables | 16.51 | 16.31 | 99 |
| Kitchen and dining room furniture | 46.95 | 23.80 | 51 |
| Infants' furniture | 6.74 | 3.16 | 47 |
| Outdoor furniture | 10.77 | 11.90 | 110 |
| Wall units, cabinets and other furniture | 36.95 | 36.16 | 98 |
| **Floor coverings** | **177.25** | **166.92** | **94** |
| Wall-to-wall carpeting | 38.41 | 55.82 | 145 |
| Wall-to-wall carpeting (renter) | 3.96 | 1.12 | 28 |
| Wall-to-wall carpet (replacement)(owned home) | 34.45 | 54.70 | 159 |
| Room-size rugs/other floor covering, nonpermanent | 138.84 | 111.10 | 80 |

*(continued)*

*(continued from previous page)*

| | average spending of total consumer units | consumer units headed by 55-to-64-year-olds | |
|---|---|---|---|
| | | average spending | indexed spending* |
| **Major appliances** | **$154.88** | **$176.34** | **114** |
| Dishwashers (built-in), garbage disposals, range hoods (renter) | 0.95 | 0.44 | 46 |
| Dishwashers (built-in), garbage disposals, range hoods (owner) | 10.23 | 11.05 | 108 |
| Refrigerators and freezers (renter) | 6.69 | 3.09 | 46 |
| Refrigerators and freezers (owner) | 42.27 | 51.64 | 122 |
| Washing machines (renter) | 5.26 | 2.53 | 48 |
| Washing machines (owner) | 14.58 | 17.02 | 117 |
| Clothes dryers (renter) | 3.25 | 0.43 | 13 |
| Clothes dryers (owner) | 10.62 | 14.17 | 133 |
| Cooking stoves, ovens (renter) | 2.57 | 5.25 | 204 |
| Cooking stoves, ovens (owner) | 18.72 | 24.43 | 131 |
| Microwave ovens (renter) | 2.87 | 1.78 | 62 |
| Microwave ovens (owner) | 6.01 | 7.03 | 117 |
| Portable dishwasher (renter) | 0.17 | - | - |
| Portable dishwasher (owner) | 0.52 | 0.11 | 21 |
| Window air conditioners (renter) | 2.75 | 1.20 | 44 |
| Window air conditioners (owner) | 8.64 | 10.85 | 126 |
| Electric floor cleaning equipment | 12.94 | 14.83 | 115 |
| Sewing machines | 4.81 | 9.22 | 192 |
| Misc. household appliances | 1.03 | 1.29 | 125 |
| **Small appliances and misc. housewares** | **85.16** | **142.58** | **167** |
| Housewares | 62.80 | 117.46 | 187 |
| Plastic dinnerware | 1.48 | 1.30 | 88 |
| China and other dinnerware | 11.29 | 17.79 | 158 |
| Flatware | 4.01 | 5.01 | 125 |
| Glassware | 6.91 | 11.10 | 161 |
| Silver serving pieces | 2.03 | 3.76 | 185 |
| Other serving pieces | 1.28 | 1.47 | 115 |
| Nonelectric cookware | 16.04 | 31.64 | 197 |
| Tableware, nonelectric kitchenware | 19.77 | 45.39 | 230 |
| Small appliances | 22.36 | 25.12 | 112 |
| Small electric kitchen appliances | 15.65 | 20.31 | 130 |
| Portable heating and cooling equipment | 6.70 | 4.81 | 72 |
| **Miscellaneous household equipment** | **557.43** | **711.84** | **128** |
| Window coverings | 10.64 | 10.69 | 100 |
| Infants' equipment | 8.02 | 2.86 | 36 |
| Laundry and cleaning equipment | 11.33 | 11.29 | 100 |
| Outdoor equipment | 4.08 | 5.36 | 131 |
| Clocks | 3.37 | 6.69 | 199 |

*(continued)*

*(continued from previous page)*

| | average spending of total consumer units | consumer units headed by 55-to-64-year-olds | |
| --- | --- | --- | --- |
| | | average spending | indexed spending* |
| Lamps and lighting fixtures | $29.77 | $77.54 | 260 |
| Other household decorative items | 137.82 | 138.68 | 101 |
| Telephones and accessories | 14.44 | 19.47 | 135 |
| Lawn and garden equipment | 42.14 | 58.02 | 138 |
| Power tools | 15.61 | 16.16 | 104 |
| Small misc. furnishings | 2.02 | 2.42 | 120 |
| Hand tools | 10.16 | 13.21 | 130 |
| Indoor plants and fresh flowers | 46.82 | 55.91 | 119 |
| Closet and storage items | 6.93 | 8.51 | 123 |
| Rental of furniture | 3.24 | 2.97 | 92 |
| Luggage | 9.25 | 11.39 | 123 |
| Computers and computer hardware nonbusiness use | 135.02 | 143.18 | 106 |
| Computer software and accessories for nonbusiness use | 18.23 | 20.01 | 110 |
| Telephone answering devices | 3.58 | 4.19 | 117 |
| Calculators | 1.88 | 1.11 | 59 |
| Business equipment for home use | 4.11 | 5.32 | 129 |
| Other hardware | 13.63 | 59.79 | 439 |
| Smoke alarms (owner) | 1.21 | 1.83 | 151 |
| Smoke alarms (renter) | 0.17 | 0.04 | 24 |
| Other household appliances (owner) | 4.71 | 4.40 | 93 |
| Other household appliances (renter) | 1.04 | 0.80 | 77 |
| Misc. household equipment and parts | 18.22 | 30.00 | 165 |
| **APPAREL AND SERVICES** | **$1,703.63** | **$1,833.21** | **108** |
| **MEN'S APPAREL** | **329.46** | **369.28** | **112** |
| Suits | 33.42 | 38.57 | 115 |
| Sportcoats and tailored jackets | 13.23 | 16.98 | 128 |
| Coats and jackets | 30.16 | 30.12 | 100 |
| Underwear | 17.80 | 25.30 | 142 |
| Hosiery | 12.85 | 9.74 | 76 |
| Sleepwear | 3.50 | 7.34 | 210 |
| Accessories | 34.98 | 50.69 | 145 |
| Sweaters and vests | 12.43 | 15.67 | 126 |
| Active sportswear | 10.14 | 8.65 | 85 |
| Shirts | 76.52 | 94.71 | 124 |
| Pants | 63.37 | 56.53 | 89 |
| Shorts and shorts sets | 16.23 | 10.23 | 63 |
| Uniforms | 3.67 | 3.75 | 102 |
| Costumes | 1.17 | 0.98 | 84 |

*(continued)*

*(continued from previous page)*

| | average spending of total consumer units | consumer units headed by 55-to-64-year-olds | |
|---|---|---|---|
| | | average spending | indexed spending* |
| **BOYS' (AGED 2 TO 15) APPAREL** | **$95.86** | **$61.94** | **65** |
| Coats and jackets | 9.27 | 15.30 | 165 |
| Sweaters | 1.92 | 1.43 | 74 |
| Shirts | 20.82 | 10.60 | 51 |
| Underwear | 5.76 | 5.67 | 98 |
| Sleepwear | 1.12 | 2.32 | 207 |
| Hosiery | 4.01 | 1.56 | 39 |
| Accessories | 6.66 | 6.39 | 96 |
| Suits, sportcoats, and vests | 3.59 | 2.34 | 65 |
| Pants | 24.03 | 9.92 | 41 |
| Shorts and shorts sets | 11.44 | 3.52 | 31 |
| Uniforms | 4.06 | 2.26 | 56 |
| Active sportswear | 2.25 | 0.38 | 17 |
| Costumes | 0.93 | 0.25 | 27 |
| **WOMEN'S APPAREL** | **559.19** | **765.29** | **137** |
| Coats and jackets | 41.43 | 58.97 | 142 |
| Dresses | 83.48 | 89.34 | 107 |
| Sportcoats and tailored jackets | 4.29 | 9.89 | 231 |
| Sweaters and vests | 28.51 | 54.88 | 192 |
| Shirts, blouses, and tops | 100.86 | 139.69 | 138 |
| Skirts | 20.49 | 26.11 | 127 |
| Pants | 70.73 | 104.60 | 148 |
| Shorts and shorts sets | 26.72 | 24.73 | 93 |
| Active sportswear | 27.19 | 30.20 | 111 |
| Sleepwear | 23.65 | 51.53 | 218 |
| Undergarments | 30.37 | 40.44 | 133 |
| Hosiery | 20.88 | 24.00 | 115 |
| Suits | 32.66 | 48.81 | 149 |
| Accessories | 43.56 | 53.20 | 122 |
| Uniforms | 2.42 | 6.82 | 282 |
| Costumes | 1.93 | 2.08 | 108 |
| **GIRLS' (AGED 2 TO 15) APPAREL** | **101.30** | **64.73** | **64** |
| Coats and jackets | 6.86 | 2.57 | 37 |
| Dresses and suits | 13.17 | 10.14 | 77 |
| Shirts, blouses, and sweaters | 20.67 | 14.24 | 69 |
| Skirts and pants | 18.18 | 7.20 | 40 |
| Shorts and shorts sets | 9.89 | 4.29 | 43 |
| Active sportswear | 11.39 | 13.81 | 121 |
| Underwear and sleepwear | 7.47 | 4.38 | 59 |
| Hosiery | 4.78 | 1.93 | 40 |
| Accessories | 4.51 | 4.26 | 94 |

*(continued)*

*(continued from previous page)*

| | average spending of total consumer units | consumer units headed by 55-to-64-year-olds | |
| --- | --- | --- | --- |
| | | *average spending* | *indexed spending** |
| Uniforms | $1.92 | $1.20 | 63 |
| Costumes | 2.47 | 0.73 | 30 |
| **CHILDREN UNDER AGE 2** | **80.61** | **44.62** | **55** |
| Coats, jackets, and snowsuits | 3.10 | 2.69 | 87 |
| Outerwear including dresses | 22.66 | 23.49 | 104 |
| Underwear | 46.09 | 12.16 | 26 |
| Sleepwear and loungewear | 3.76 | 3.40 | 90 |
| Accessories | 4.99 | 2.88 | 58 |
| **FOOTWEAR** | **278.36** | **207.41** | **75** |
| Men's | 94.82 | 72.61 | 77 |
| Boys' | 30.48 | 5.21 | 17 |
| Women's | 117.81 | 117.83 | 100 |
| Girls' | 35.24 | 11.76 | 33 |
| **OTHER APPAREL PRODUCTS & SERVICES** | **258.84** | **319.94** | **124** |
| Material for making clothes | 4.95 | 5.31 | 107 |
| Sewing patterns and notions | 1.92 | 2.34 | 122 |
| Watches | 19.16 | 15.43 | 81 |
| Jewelry | 104.17 | 171.86 | 165 |
| Shoe repair and other shoe services | 2.66 | 3.11 | 117 |
| Coin-operated apparel laundry and dry cleaning | 39.46 | 23.76 | 60 |
| Apparel alteration, repair, and tailoring services | 5.82 | 5.75 | 99 |
| Clothing rental | 3.48 | 2.74 | 79 |
| Watch and jewelry repair | 5.07 | 6.50 | 128 |
| Professional laundry, dry cleaning | 71.68 | 82.36 | 115 |
| Clothing storage | 0.47 | 0.80 | 170 |
| **TRANSPORTATION** | **$6,015.97** | **$5,725.82** | **95** |
| **VEHICLE PURCHASES** | **2,639.33** | **2,108.05** | **80** |
| **Cars and trucks, new** | **1,194.00** | **1,118.34** | **94** |
| New cars | 670.88 | 764.31 | 114 |
| New trucks | 523.11 | 354.03 | 68 |
| **Cars and trucks, used** | **1,410.96** | **952.71** | **68** |
| Used cars | 916.45 | 735.00 | 80 |
| Used trucks | 494.51 | 217.71 | 44 |
| **Other vehicles** | **34.38** | **37.00** | **108** |
| New motorcycles | 21.74 | 36.84 | 169 |
| Used motorcycles | 12.64 | 0.15 | 1 |

*(continued)*

*(continued from previous page)*

| | average spending of total consumer units | consumer units headed by 55-to-64-year-olds | |
|---|---|---|---|
| | | average spending | indexed spending* |
| **GASOLINE AND MOTOR OIL** | **$1,006.05** | **$1,062.82** | **106** |
| Gasoline | 901.97 | 926.60 | 103 |
| Diesel fuel | 10.15 | 12.60 | 124 |
| Gasoline on out-of-town trips | 81.98 | 112.15 | 137 |
| Motor oil | 11.13 | 10.33 | 93 |
| Motor oil on out-of-town trips | 0.83 | 1.13 | 136 |
| **OTHER VEHICLE EXPENSES** | **2,015.78** | **2,142.37** | **106** |
| **Vehicle finance charges** | **260.57** | **223.31** | **86** |
| **Maintenance and repairs** | **652.77** | **708.61** | **109** |
| Coolant, additives, brake, transmission fluids | 5.63 | 5.36 | 95 |
| Tires | 87.06 | 91.40 | 105 |
| Parts, equipment, and accessories | 60.29 | 67.74 | 112 |
| Vehicle audio equipment | 10.31 | 0.82 | 8 |
| Vehicle products | 3.37 | 3.96 | 118 |
| Misc. auto repair, servicing | 33.68 | 46.29 | 137 |
| Body work and painting | 29.52 | 30.36 | 103 |
| Clutch, transmission repair | 45.69 | 54.41 | 119 |
| Drive shaft and rear-end repair | 6.14 | 3.34 | 54 |
| Brake work | 39.22 | 37.38 | 95 |
| Repair to steering or front-end | 20.68 | 15.31 | 74 |
| Repair to engine cooling system | 23.28 | 23.41 | 101 |
| Motor tune-up | 42.61 | 48.19 | 113 |
| Lube, oil change, and oil filters | 42.90 | 46.07 | 107 |
| Front-end alignment, wheel balance, rotation | 11.11 | 13.97 | 126 |
| Shock absorber replacement | 7.35 | 9.65 | 131 |
| Brake adjustment | 3.18 | 4.51 | 142 |
| Gas tank repair, replacement | 1.54 | 1.91 | 124 |
| Repair tires and other repair work | 33.28 | 43.07 | 129 |
| Vehicle air conditioning repair | 14.28 | 12.43 | 87 |
| Exhaust system repair | 20.87 | 19.27 | 92 |
| Electrical system repair | 29.58 | 27.99 | 95 |
| Motor repair, replacement | 67.64 | 81.34 | 120 |
| Auto repair service policy | 5.94 | 11.11 | 187 |
| **Vehicle insurance** | **712.81** | **791.78** | **111** |
| **Vehicle rental, leases, licenses, etc.** | **389.63** | **418.67** | **107** |
| Leased and rented vehicles | 235.64 | 259.24 | 110 |
| Rented vehicles | 37.70 | 55.40 | 147 |
| Auto rental | 7.09 | 8.32 | 117 |
| Auto rental, out-of-town trips | 25.95 | 44.80 | 173 |
| Truck rental | 1.19 | 0.94 | 79 |

*(continued)*

*(continued from previous page)*

| | average spending of total consumer units | consumer units headed by 55-to-64-year-olds | |
|---|---|---|---|
| | | average spending | indexed spending* |
| Truck rental, out-of-town trips | $3.26 | $1.34 | 41 |
| Leased vehicles | 197.94 | 203.84 | 103 |
| State and local registration | 84.53 | 87.04 | 103 |
| Driver's license | 6.92 | 6.65 | 96 |
| Vehicle inspection | 8.76 | 9.93 | 113 |
| Parking fees | 25.38 | 25.39 | 100 |
| Tolls | 11.19 | 9.04 | 81 |
| Tolls on out-of-town trips | 4.53 | 5.95 | 131 |
| Towing charges | 4.86 | 4.65 | 96 |
| Automobile service clubs | 7.83 | 10.78 | 138 |
| **PUBLIC TRANSPORTATION** | **354.81** | **412.58** | **116** |
| Airline fares | 225.58 | 257.84 | 114 |
| Intercity bus fares | 14.09 | 17.06 | 121 |
| Intracity mass transit fares | 48.51 | 42.05 | 87 |
| Local trans. on out-of-town trips | 8.46 | 10.42 | 123 |
| Taxi fares on trips | 4.97 | 6.12 | 123 |
| Taxi fares | 6.95 | 4.24 | 61 |
| Intercity train fares | 18.41 | 28.52 | 155 |
| Ship fares | 27.31 | 46.11 | 169 |
| School bus | 0.53 | 0.22 | 42 |
| **HEALTH CARE** | **$1,732.33** | **$1,909.20** | **110** |
| **HEALTH INSURANCE** | **860.45** | **895.82** | **104** |
| **Commercial health insurance** | **241.22** | **334.54** | **139** |
| Commercial health insurance | 202.64 | 280.51 | 138 |
| Traditional fee for service health plan (not BCBS) | 15.73 | 23.47 | 149 |
| Preferred provider health plan (not BCBS) | 22.86 | 30.56 | 134 |
| **Blue Cross, Blue Shield** | **171.78** | **209.70** | **122** |
| Blue Cross, Blue Shield | 143.85 | 172.10 | 120 |
| Traditional fee for service health plan (BCBS) | 13.74 | 21.95 | 160 |
| Preferred provider health plan (BCBS) | 7.06 | 6.90 | 98 |
| Health maintenance organization (BCBS) | 6.90 | 8.49 | 123 |
| Commercial Medicare supplement (BCBS) | 0.18 | - | - |
| Other health insurance (BCBS) | 0.04 | 0.26 | 650 |
| **Health maintenance plans (HMOs)** | **146.87** | **166.59** | **113** |
| Health maintenance plans | 118.87 | 134.67 | 113 |
| Health maintenance organization (not BCBS) | 28.00 | 31.92 | 114 |
| **Medicare payments** | **172.13** | **87.39** | **51** |

*(continued)*

*(continued from previous page)*

| | average spending of total consumer units | consumer units headed by 55-to-64-year-olds | |
|---|---|---|---|
| | | average spending | indexed spending* |
| **Commercial Medicare supplements/ other health insurance** | **$128.44** | **$97.61** | **76** |
| Commercial Medicare supplements/ other health insurance | 107.27 | 80.08 | 75 |
| Commercial Medicare supplement (not BCBS) | 8.30 | 0.94 | 11 |
| Other health insurance (not BCBS) | 12.88 | 16.58 | 129 |
| **MEDICAL SERVICES** | **511.47** | **586.79** | **115** |
| Physician's services | 146.97 | 150.87 | 103 |
| Dental services | 186.29 | 230.81 | 124 |
| Eye care services | 28.83 | 32.16 | 112 |
| Service by professionals other than physician | 38.24 | 32.46 | 85 |
| Lab tests, x-rays | 21.92 | 26.32 | 120 |
| Hospital room | 33.04 | 40.62 | 123 |
| Hospital services other than room | 37.16 | 57.07 | 154 |
| Care in convalescent or nursing home | 7.90 | 1.04 | 13 |
| Other medical services | 10.01 | 15.44 | 154 |
| **DRUGS** | **279.96** | **343.67** | **123** |
| Non-prescription drugs | 79.03 | 96.60 | 122 |
| Prescription drugs | 200.94 | 247.06 | 123 |
| **MEDICAL SUPPLIES** | **80.45** | **82.92** | **103** |
| Eyeglasses and contact lenses | 52.06 | 53.76 | 103 |
| Topicals and dressings | 20.73 | 22.79 | 110 |
| Medical equipment for general use | 2.53 | 2.81 | 111 |
| Supportive/convalescent medical equipment | 3.83 | 2.17 | 57 |
| **ENTERTAINMENT** | **$1,612.09** | **$1,576.78** | **98** |
| **FEES AND ADMISSIONS** | **432.91** | **418.44** | **97** |
| Recreation expenses, out-of-town trips | 21.21 | 25.49 | 120 |
| Social, recreation, civic club membership | 80.67 | 78.68 | 98 |
| Fees for participant sports | 66.55 | 60.12 | 90 |
| Participant sports, out-of-town trips | 29.25 | 49.29 | 169 |
| Movie, theater, opera, ballet | 73.42 | 66.80 | 91 |
| Movie, other admissions, out-of-town trips | 40.50 | 45.60 | 113 |
| Admission to sporting events | 28.71 | 25.14 | 88 |
| Admission to sports events, out-of-town trips | 13.50 | 15.20 | 113 |
| Fees for recreational lessons | 57.91 | 26.64 | 46 |
| Other entertainment svcs., out-of-town trips | 21.21 | 25.49 | 120 |
| **TELEVISION, RADIOS, SOUND EQUIPMENT** | **541.77** | **492.40** | **91** |
| **Televisions** | **370.32** | **384.96** | **104** |
| Community antenna or cable TV | 219.69 | 244.65 | 111 |

*(continued)*

*(continued from previous page)*

| | average spending of total consumer units | consumer units headed by 55-to-64-year-olds | |
|---|---|---|---|
| | | average spending | indexed spending* |
| Color TV, console | $29.53 | $33.13 | 112 |
| Color TV, portable, table model | 44.90 | 33.63 | 75 |
| VCRs and video disc players | 27.33 | 32.41 | 119 |
| Video cassettes, tapes, and discs | 24.05 | 24.13 | 100 |
| Video game hardware and software | 14.68 | 9.30 | 63 |
| Repair of TV, radio, and sound equipment | 7.19 | 7.10 | 99 |
| Rental of televisions | 1.06 | 0.61 | 58 |
| **Radios and sound equipment** | **171.45** | **107.44** | **63** |
| Radios | 10.61 | 19.99 | 188 |
| Tape recorders and players | 11.26 | 2.17 | 19 |
| Sound components and component systems | 32.12 | 11.46 | 36 |
| Sound equipment accessories | 4.46 | 2.30 | 52 |
| Compact disc, tape, record, video mail order clubs | 11.99 | 7.73 | 64 |
| Records, CDs, audio tapes, needles | 38.49 | 25.69 | 67 |
| Rental of VCR, radio, sound equipment | 0.27 | - | - |
| Musical instruments and accessories | 17.75 | 8.83 | 50 |
| Rental and repair of musical instruments | 1.65 | 0.79 | 48 |
| Rental of video cassettes, tapes, discs, films | 42.38 | 26.68 | 63 |
| **PETS, TOYS, PLAYGROUND EQUIPMENT** | **322.19** | **315.64** | **98** |
| **Pets** | **199.89** | **202.14** | **101** |
| Pet food | 79.56 | 101.62 | 128 |
| Pet purchase, supplies, and medicines | 47.03 | 34.21 | 73 |
| Pet services | 18.78 | 14.38 | 77 |
| Veterinary services | 54.52 | 51.93 | 95 |
| **Toys, games, hobbies, and tricycles** | **120.29** | **113.11** | **94** |
| **Playground equipment** | **2.00** | **0.39** | **20** |
| **OTHER ENTERTAINMENT SUPPLIES, EQUIPMENT, SERVICES** | **315.22** | **350.31** | **111** |
| **Unmotored recreational vehicles** | **28.10** | **9.09** | **32** |
| Boat without motor and boat trailers | 3.69 | 2.05 | 56 |
| Trailer and other attachable campers | 24.41 | 7.05 | 29 |
| **Motorized recreational vehicles** | **77.41** | **107.97** | **139** |
| Motorized camper | 21.18 | 29.31 | 138 |
| Other vehicle | 11.89 | 17.57 | 148 |
| Motor boats | 44.34 | 61.10 | 138 |
| **Rental of recreational vehicles** | **3.42** | **2.87** | **84** |
| **Outboard motors** | **0.36** | **0.32** | **89** |
| **Docking and landing fees** | **4.49** | **10.72** | **239** |

*(continued)*

*(continued from previous page)*

| | average spending of total consumer units | consumer units headed by 55-to-64-year-olds | |
|---|---|---|---|
| | | average spending | indexed spending* |
| **Sports, recreation, exercise equipment** | **$110.81** | **$131.14** | **118** |
| **Athletic gear, game tables, exercise equipment** | **50.33** | **54.84** | **109** |
| Bicycles | 12.59 | 6.38 | 51 |
| Camping equipment | 6.51 | 19.91 | 306 |
| Hunting and fishing equipment | 17.00 | 19.90 | 117 |
| Winter sports equipment | 3.78 | 1.45 | 38 |
| Water sports equipment | 9.47 | 17.91 | 189 |
| Other sports equipment | 9.50 | 9.61 | 101 |
| Rental and repair of misc. sports equipment | 1.64 | 1.15 | 70 |
| **Photographic equipment and supplies** | **81.18** | **80.37** | **99** |
| Film | 20.27 | 21.80 | 108 |
| Film processing | 28.56 | 33.44 | 117 |
| Photographic equipment | 12.56 | 18.64 | 148 |
| Photographer fees | 18.39 | 1.58 | 9 |
| **Fireworks** | **2.03** | **0.05** | **2** |
| **Souvenirs** | **0.14** | - | - |
| **Visual goods** | **1.51** | **1.85** | **123** |
| **Pinball, electronic video games** | **5.78** | **5.91** | **102** |
| **PERSONAL CARE PRODUCTS AND SERVICES** | **$403.47** | **$407.15** | **101** |
| **PERSONAL CARE PRODUCTS** | **213.44** | **209.19** | **98** |
| Hair care products | 38.65 | 33.85 | 88 |
| Hair accessories | 4.43 | 2.32 | 52 |
| Wigs and hairpieces | 0.95 | 0.65 | 68 |
| Oral hygiene products | 22.19 | 27.66 | 125 |
| Shaving products | 11.91 | 14.87 | 125 |
| Cosmetics, perfume, and bath products | 105.36 | 101.09 | 96 |
| Deodorants, feminine hygiene, misc. products | 26.10 | 23.86 | 91 |
| Electric personal care appliances | 3.85 | 4.90 | 127 |
| **PERSONAL CARE SERVICES** | **190.03** | **197.97** | **104** |
| Personal care services/female | 97.61 | 110.61 | 113 |
| Personal care services/male | 92.19 | 87.09 | 94 |
| **READING** | **$162.57** | **$187.61** | **115** |
| Newspaper subscriptions | 51.79 | 67.26 | 130 |
| Newspaper, non-subscriptions | 17.40 | 17.91 | 103 |
| Magazine subscriptions | 24.74 | 30.20 | 122 |
| Magazines, non-subscriptions | 11.00 | 10.16 | 92 |
| Books purchased through book clubs | 9.33 | 10.94 | 117 |

*(continued)*

| | average spending of total consumer units | consumer units headed by 55-to-64-year-olds | |
|---|---|---|---|
| | | average spending | indexed spending* |
| Books not purchased through book clubs | $46.51 | $50.65 | 109 |
| Encyclopedia and other reference book sets | 1.52 | 0.50 | 33 |
| **EDUCATION** | **$471.47** | **$366.12** | **78** |
| College tuition | 265.22 | 251.38 | 95 |
| Elementary/high school tuition | 81.97 | 39.40 | 48 |
| Other schools tuition | 14.06 | 12.87 | 92 |
| Other school expenses incl. rentals | 17.30 | 5.49 | 32 |
| Books, supplies for college | 36.06 | 15.50 | 43 |
| Books, supplies for elementary, high school | 8.56 | 2.73 | 32 |
| Books, supplies for day care, nursery school | 2.09 | 1.63 | 78 |
| Misc. school expenses and supplies | 46.21 | 37.11 | 80 |
| **TOBACCO PRODUCTS AND SMOKING SUPPLIES** | **$268.82** | **$313.69** | **117** |
| Cigarettes | 243.09 | 278.94 | 115 |
| Other tobacco products | 24.30 | 34.39 | 142 |
| Smoking accessories | 1.43 | 0.37 | 26 |
| **FINANCIAL PRODUCTS & SERVICES** | **$766.23** | **$947.69** | **124** |
| Miscellaneous fees, gambling losses | 54.70 | 79.51 | 145 |
| Legal fees | 98.35 | 101.70 | 103 |
| Funeral expenses | 86.83 | 134.54 | 155 |
| Safe deposit box rental | 5.51 | 7.54 | 137 |
| Checking accounts, other bank service charges | 25.62 | 20.00 | 78 |
| Cemetery lots, vaults, and maintenance fees | 15.50 | 47.35 | 305 |
| Accounting fees | 40.94 | 55.35 | 135 |
| Miscellaneous personal services | 21.64 | 9.08 | 42 |
| Finance charges, except mortgage and vehicles | 229.82 | 276.73 | 120 |
| Occupational expenses, union and prof. fees | 97.90 | 86.18 | 88 |
| Expenses for other properties | 85.37 | 125.07 | 147 |
| Credit card memberships | 3.92 | 4.63 | 118 |
| **CASH CONTRIBUTIONS** | **$925.39** | **$1,042.68** | **113** |
| Cash contributions to non-CU members, incl. students, alimony, child support | 233.28 | 150.37 | 64 |
| Gifts of cash, stocks, bonds to non-CU member | 174.20 | 198.80 | 114 |
| Contributions to charities | 85.58 | 123.42 | 144 |
| Contributions to church | 385.94 | 534.87 | 139 |
| Contributions to educational organizations | 35.65 | 14.19 | 40 |
| Political contributions | 3.39 | 9.72 | 287 |
| Other contributions | 7.35 | 11.32 | 154 |

*(continued)*

*(continued from previous page)*

| | average spending of total consumer units | consumer units headed by 55-to-64-year-olds | |
|---|---|---|---|
| | | average spending | indexed spending* |
| **PERSONAL INSURANCE & PENSIONS** | **$2,967.05** | **$3,211.44** | **108** |
| **LIFE & OTHER PERSONAL INSURANCE** | **374.03** | **555.01** | **148** |
| Life, endowment, annuity, other pers. insurance | 361.44 | 527.99 | 146 |
| Other nonhealth insurance | 12.59 | 27.02 | 215 |
| | | | |
| **PENSIONS AND SOCIAL SECURITY** | **2,593.02** | **2,656.43** | **102** |
| Deductions for government retirement | 66.21 | 71.29 | 108 |
| Deductions for railroad retirement | 5.28 | 20.37 | 386 |
| Deductions for private pensions | 325.82 | 310.56 | 95 |
| Non-payroll deposit to retirement plans | 312.41 | 467.28 | 150 |
| Deductions for Social Security | 1,883.30 | 1,786.93 | 95 |
| | | | |
| **GIFTS*** | **$986.63** | **$1,361.05** | **138** |
| **FOOD** | **87.72** | **127.35** | **145** |
| Cakes and cupcakes | 1.97 | 2.88 | 146 |
| Cheese | 1.90 | 3.58 | 188 |
| Fresh fruits | 1.83 | 2.78 | 152 |
| Candy and chewing gum | 12.79 | 11.88 | 93 |
| Misc. prepared foods | 2.52 | 1.39 | 55 |
| **HOUSING** | **249.80** | **288.51** | **115** |
| **Housekeeping supplies** | **37.72** | **45.77** | **121** |
| Misc. household products | 4.39 | 4.93 | 112 |
| Lawn and garden supplies | 3.51 | 2.62 | 75 |
| Stationery, stationery supplies, giftwraps | 22.53 | 26.87 | 119 |
| Postage | 4.17 | 5.21 | 125 |
| **Household textiles** | **10.20** | **12.39** | **121** |
| Bedroom linens | 4.44 | 5.48 | 123 |
| **Appliances and misc. housewares** | **27.44** | **59.93** | **218** |
| Major appliances | 4.79 | 9.46 | 197 |
| Small appliances and misc. housewares | 22.65 | 50.47 | 223 |
| China and other dinnerware | 2.91 | 4.76 | 164 |
| Glassware | 3.60 | 3.01 | 84 |
| Nonelectric cookware | 3.98 | 15.00 | 377 |
| Tableware, nonelectric kitchenware | 4.98 | 17.74 | 356 |
| Small electric kitchen appliances | 3.64 | 4.98 | 137 |
| **Miscellaneous household equipment** | **65.94** | **77.14** | **117** |
| Infants' equipment | 2.26 | 1.85 | 82 |
| Lamps and lighting fixtures | 3.33 | 6.96 | 209 |
| Household decorative items | 21.54 | 27.53 | 128 |
| Indoor plants, fresh flowers | 20.72 | 17.10 | 83 |

*(continued)*

*(continued from previous page)*

| | average spending of total consumer units | consumer units headed by 55-to-64-year-olds | |
| --- | --- | --- | --- |
| | | average spending | indexed spending* |
| Computers and hardware, nonbusiness use | $4.01 | $5.92 | 148 |
| Misc. household equipment | 3.08 | 2.37 | 77 |
| **Other housing** | **108.51** | **93.29** | **86** |
| Electricity (renter) | 10.47 | 5.14 | 49 |
| Telephone services in home city, excl. mobile car phone | 12.23 | 2.85 | 23 |
| Day care centers, nursery, and preschools | 15.05 | 2.47 | 16 |
| Housekeeping services | 3.90 | 5.59 | 143 |
| Gardening, lawn care service | 2.74 | 4.57 | 167 |
| **APPAREL AND SERVICES** | **258.22** | **457.29** | **177** |
| **Men and boys, aged 2 or older** | **69.77** | **120.24** | **172** |
| Men's coats and jackets | 4.70 | 1.64 | 35 |
| Men's accessories | 6.98 | 6.12 | 88 |
| Men's sweaters and vests | 3.46 | 5.89 | 170 |
| Men's shirts | 17.03 | 21.04 | 124 |
| Men's pants | 9.29 | 12.35 | 133 |
| Boys' shirts | 4.31 | 8.40 | 195 |
| **Women and girls, aged 2 or older** | **93.61** | **240.27** | **257** |
| Women's coats and jackets | 5.41 | 22.56 | 417 |
| Women's dresses | 5.36 | 9.00 | 168 |
| Women's vests and sweaters | 8.05 | 22.57 | 280 |
| Women's shirts, tops, blouses | 14.11 | 27.52 | 195 |
| Women's pants | 9.09 | 34.50 | 380 |
| Women's active sportswear | 6.11 | 2.05 | 34 |
| Women's sleepwear | 7.35 | 22.37 | 304 |
| Women's accessories | 9.16 | 15.30 | 167 |
| Girls' shirts, blouses, sweaters | 4.16 | 8.86 | 213 |
| Girls' active sportswear | 4.37 | 13.44 | 308 |
| **Children under age 2** | **39.47** | **38.57** | **98** |
| Infant dresses, outerwear | 13.60 | 22.56 | 166 |
| Infant underwear | 19.47 | 7.82 | 40 |
| **Other apparel products and services** | **55.37** | **58.21** | **105** |
| Watches | 26.56 | 23.47 | 88 |
| Jewelry | 23.90 | 20.81 | 87 |
| Men's footwear | 7.15 | 2.97 | 42 |
| Women's footwear | 10.36 | 17.23 | 166 |
| Girls' footwear | 7.76 | 6.60 | 85 |
| **TRANSPORTATION** | **47.84** | **76.01** | **159** |
| Used cars | 3.19 | - | - |

*(continued)*

*(continued from previous page)*

| | average spending of total consumer units | consumer units headed by 55-to-64-year-olds | |
|---|---|---|---|
| | | average spending | indexed spending* |
| Gasoline on out-of-town trips | $13.01 | $21.10 | 162 |
| Airline fares | 10.75 | 17.64 | 164 |
| **HEALTH CARE** | **22.21** | **23.33** | **105** |
| Dental services | 4.70 | 3.32 | 71 |
| Care in convalescent or nursing home | 4.50 | - | - |
| **ENTERTAINMENT** | **86.44** | **134.08** | **155** |
| **Toys, games, hobbies, tricycles** | **29.34** | **57.34** | **195** |
| **Other entertainment** | **57.10** | **76.73** | **134** |
| Movie, other admissions, out-of-town trips | 7.07 | 11.93 | 169 |
| Color TV, portable, table model | 3.47 | 7.59 | 219 |
| Pet purchase, supplies, medicine | 6.35 | 2.18 | 34 |
| Veterinary services | 3.05 | 3.20 | 105 |
| **EDUCATION** | **120.19** | **131.41** | **109** |
| College tuition | 96.63 | 110.22 | 114 |
| Elementary, high school tuition | 8.17 | 3.80 | 47 |
| College books, supplies | 6.55 | 5.71 | 87 |
| Misc. school supplies | 5.29 | 10.03 | 190 |
| **ALL OTHER GIFTS** | **114.22** | **123.07** | **108** |
| Out-of-town trip expenses | 36.21 | 53.39 | 147 |

*The index compares the spending of consumer units headed by 55-to-64-year-olds with the spending of the average consumer unit by dividing the spending of 55-to-64-year-olds by average spending in each category and multiplying by 100. An index of 100 means that the spending of 55-to-64-year-olds in that category equals average spending. An index of 132 means that the spending of 55-to-64-year-olds is 32 percent above average, while an index of 75 means that the spending of 55-to-64-year-olds is 25 percent below average.*

**This figure does not include the amount paid for mortgage principle, which is considered an asset.*

***Expenditures on gifts are also included in the preceding product and service categories. Food spending, for example, includes the amount spent on food gifts. Not all gift categories are shown.*

*Note: The Bureau of Labor Statistics uses consumer units rather than households as the sampling unit in the Consumer Expenditure Survey. For the definition of consumer unit, see the Glossary. (-) means the sample is too small to make a reliable estimate.*

*Source: Bureau of Labor Statistics, unpublished tables from the 1995 Consumer Expenditure Survey; calculations by New Strategist.*

# Householders Aged 65 to 74 Spend Big on Some Items

**Households headed by 65-to-74-year-olds spent $25,302 in 1995, versus the $32,277 spent by the average household.**

Householders aged 65 to 74 spend less than average because their households are relatively small and because most are retired and living on Social Security and pension benefits. Nevertheless, the spending of householders aged 65 to 74 is rising to meet the average as more educated and affluent people enter the age group. In 1990, householders aged 65 to 74 spent 26 percent less than the average household. By 1995, they spent a smaller 22 percent less.

Householders aged 65 to 74 spend well above average on many items, however. These include cakes and cupcakes (with a spending index of 132—meaning householders in this age group spend 32 percent more than the average household on this item), nuts (an index of 160), whiskey (272), lodging on out-of-town trips (124), bathroom linens (162), new cars (122), intercity bus fares (248), ship fares (219), motorized campers (296), newspaper subscriptions (151), and magazine subscriptions (134).

Householders aged 65 to 74 spend less than the average household on many grocery items because they are shopping for only one or two people rather than for

### Some Above Average Spending by 65-to-74-Year-Olds

*(indexed spending of consumer units headed by 65-to-74-year-olds on selected items, 1995)*

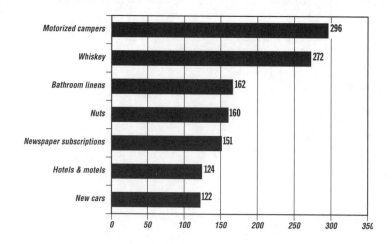

three or four. They spend 25 percent less than the average household on restaurant meals, but only 12 percent less than average on restaurant breakfasts. They spend 68 percent less than the average household on mortgage interest because most own their home free and clear. But they spend 54 percent more than the average household on maintenance and repair services for their homes. While this age group spends less than average on entertainment overall, it spends more than average on entertainment while on out-of-town trips.

◆ As better-educated and more affluent generations age into their 60s and 70s, older Americans aren't acting so old anymore. As the sophistication of older consumers grows, businesses must abandon their overly simplistic "mature market" campaigns and find new ways to reach this group.

# Average and Indexed Spending of Householders Aged 65 to 74, 1995

*(average annual and indexed spending of consumer units (CUs) headed by 65-to-74-year-olds, 1995)*

| | average spending of total consumer units | consumer units headed by 65-to-74-year-olds | |
|---|---|---|---|
| | | average spending | indexed spending* |
| **Number of consumer units (in thousands)** | 103,024 | 11,924 | - |
| **Average before-tax income** | $36,948.00 | $25,589.00 | 69 |
| **Total average annual spending** | 32,276.59 | 25,301.66 | 78 |
| **FOOD** | $4,505.34 | $3,894.85 | 86 |
| **FOOD AT HOME** | 2,802.91 | 2,609.80 | 93 |
| **Cereals and bakery products** | 441.13 | 418.57 | 95 |
| Cereals and cereal products | 165.23 | 141.36 | 86 |
| Flour | 8.42 | 9.32 | 111 |
| Prepared flour mixes | 12.80 | 13.29 | 104 |
| Ready-to-eat and cooked cereal | 97.00 | 83.85 | 86 |
| Rice | 20.17 | 15.24 | 76 |
| Pasta, cornmeal, and other cereal products | 26.84 | 19.66 | 73 |
| **Bakery products** | **275.90** | **277.21** | **100** |
| Bread | 75.70 | 74.54 | 98 |
| White bread | 36.77 | 31.16 | 85 |
| Bread, other than white | 38.92 | 43.38 | 111 |
| Crackers and cookies | 67.33 | 67.60 | 100 |
| Cookies | 44.90 | 43.06 | 96 |
| Crackers | 22.43 | 24.54 | 109 |
| Frozen and refrigerated bakery products | 21.92 | 20.60 | 94 |
| Other bakery products | 110.95 | 114.47 | 103 |
| Biscuits and rolls | 38.49 | 32.24 | 84 |
| Cakes and cupcakes | 34.63 | 45.73 | 132 |
| Bread and cracker products | 4.23 | 5.01 | 118 |
| Sweetrolls, coffee cakes, doughnuts | 20.80 | 20.18 | 97 |
| Pies, tarts, turnovers | 12.80 | 11.30 | 88 |
| **Meats, poultry, fish, and eggs** | **752.43** | **698.83** | **93** |
| Beef | 227.60 | 204.58 | 90 |
| Ground beef | 84.47 | 68.29 | 81 |
| Roast | 40.09 | 51.01 | 127 |
| Chuck roast | 12.63 | 10.61 | 84 |
| Round roast | 13.18 | 17.73 | 135 |
| Other roast | 14.28 | 22.67 | 159 |
| Steak | 86.84 | 73.37 | 84 |
| Round steak | 18.82 | 15.03 | 80 |

*(continued)*

*(continued from previous page)*

| | average spending of total consumer units | consumer units headed by 65-to-74-year-olds | |
| --- | --- | --- | --- |
| | | average spending | indexed spending* |
| Sirloin steak | $23.42 | $21.75 | 93 |
| Other steak | 44.61 | 36.58 | 82 |
| Other beef | 16.19 | 11.91 | 74 |
| Pork | 156.00 | 136.27 | 87 |
| Bacon | 20.32 | 22.43 | 110 |
| Pork chops | 39.69 | 29.54 | 74 |
| Ham | 37.06 | 30.05 | 81 |
| Ham, not canned | 34.76 | 25.39 | 73 |
| Canned ham | 2.31 | 4.66 | 202 |
| Sausage | 22.12 | 19.46 | 88 |
| Other pork | 36.79 | 34.79 | 95 |
| Other meats | 103.63 | 91.47 | 88 |
| Frankfurters | 22.13 | 17.66 | 80 |
| Lunch meats (cold cuts) | 69.66 | 67.36 | 97 |
| Bologna, liverwurst, salami | 25.45 | 29.18 | 115 |
| Other lunchmeats | 44.22 | 38.19 | 86 |
| Lamb, organ meats and others | 11.84 | 6.45 | 54 |
| Lamb and organ meats | 9.31 | 6.07 | 65 |
| Mutton, goat and game | 2.54 | 0.38 | 15 |
| Poultry | 137.65 | 136.52 | 99 |
| Fresh and frozen chickens | 105.14 | 102.14 | 97 |
| Fresh and frozen whole chicken | 28.21 | 24.96 | 88 |
| Fresh and frozen chicken parts | 76.93 | 77.18 | 100 |
| Other poultry | 32.51 | 34.38 | 106 |
| Fish and seafood | 97.33 | 101.22 | 104 |
| Canned fish and seafood | 17.11 | 21.27 | 124 |
| Fresh fish and shellfish | 52.43 | 54.18 | 103 |
| Frozen fish and shellfish | 27.79 | 25.77 | 93 |
| Eggs | 30.23 | 28.76 | 95 |
| **Dairy products** | **296.61** | **274.11** | **92** |
| Fresh milk and cream | 123.00 | 109.98 | 89 |
| Fresh milk, all types | 113.81 | 102.45 | 90 |
| Cream | 9.19 | 7.53 | 82 |
| Other dairy products | 173.60 | 164.13 | 95 |
| Butter | 12.31 | 10.55 | 86 |
| Cheese | 88.00 | 83.21 | 95 |
| Ice cream and related products | 51.24 | 53.35 | 104 |
| Miscellaneous dairy products | 22.05 | 17.02 | 77 |
| **Fruits and vegetables** | **456.67** | **459.22** | **101** |
| Fresh fruits | 144.14 | 160.22 | 111 |
| Apples | 29.15 | 31.59 | 108 |

*(continued)*

*(continued from previous page)*

| | average spending of total consumer units | consumer units headed by 65-to-74-year-olds | |
| --- | --- | --- | --- |
| | | average spending | indexed spending* |
| Bananas | $30.26 | $35.85 | 118 |
| Oranges | 16.27 | 13.20 | 81 |
| Citrus fruits, excl. oranges | 12.03 | 13.85 | 115 |
| Fresh vegetables | 137.31 | 141.76 | 103 |
| Potatoes | 28.50 | 30.49 | 107 |
| Lettuce | 18.22 | 18.24 | 100 |
| Tomatoes | 21.64 | 24.22 | 112 |
| Other fresh vegetables | 68.95 | 68.81 | 100 |
| Processed fruits | 95.70 | 85.77 | 90 |
| Frozen fruits and fruit juices | 17.00 | 11.24 | 66 |
| Frozen orange juice | 8.66 | 8.38 | 97 |
| Frozen fruits | 1.81 | 0.48 | 27 |
| Frozen fruit juices | 6.53 | 2.38 | 36 |
| Canned fruits | 13.88 | 15.95 | 115 |
| Dried fruit | 5.86 | 6.79 | 116 |
| Fresh fruit juice | 17.55 | 17.55 | 100 |
| Canned and bottled fruit juice | 41.40 | 34.24 | 83 |
| Processed vegetables | 79.52 | 71.46 | 90 |
| Frozen vegetables | 28.07 | 23.62 | 84 |
| Canned and dried vegetables and juices | 51.44 | 47.84 | 93 |
| Canned beans | 11.26 | 9.61 | 85 |
| Canned corn | 6.91 | 4.82 | 70 |
| Canned misc. vegetables | 16.68 | 16.10 | 97 |
| Dried peas | 0.17 | 0.17 | 100 |
| Dried beans | 2.88 | 3.48 | 121 |
| Dried misc. vegetables | 6.14 | 5.58 | 91 |
| Dried processed vegetables | 0.23 | - | - |
| Frozen vegetable juices | 0.31 | 0.02 | 6 |
| Fresh and canned vegetable juices | 6.87 | 8.06 | 117 |
| **Other food at home** | **856.08** | **759.07** | **89** |
| Sugar and other sweets | 112.08 | 103.32 | 92 |
| Candy and chewing gum | 67.43 | 59.16 | 88 |
| Sugar | 17.44 | 13.61 | 78 |
| Artificial sweeteners | 4.51 | 7.11 | 158 |
| Jams, preserves, other sweets | 22.70 | 23.44 | 103 |
| Fats and oils | 82.22 | 88.94 | 108 |
| Margarine | 12.74 | 17.20 | 135 |
| Fats and oils | 24.60 | 25.39 | 103 |
| Salad dressings | 26.16 | 28.01 | 107 |
| Nondairy cream and imitation milk | 7.15 | 7.28 | 102 |
| Peanut butter | 11.58 | 11.06 | 96 |

*(continued)*

*(continued from previous page)*

| | average spending of total consumer units | consumer units headed by 65-to-74-year-olds | |
|---|---|---|---|
| | | average spending | indexed spending* |
| Miscellaneous foods | $376.59 | $315.90 | 84 |
| Frozen prepared foods | 66.03 | 62.05 | 94 |
| Frozen meals | 19.87 | 21.26 | 107 |
| Other frozen prepared foods | 46.16 | 40.80 | 88 |
| Canned and packaged soups | 31.25 | 31.17 | 100 |
| Potato chips, nuts, and other snacks | 80.50 | 75.00 | 93 |
| Potato chips and other snacks | 62.33 | 45.86 | 74 |
| Nuts | 18.17 | 29.13 | 160 |
| Condiments and seasonings | 86.51 | 76.59 | 89 |
| Salt, spices and other seasonings | 20.29 | 17.41 | 86 |
| Olives, pickles, relishes | 10.14 | 12.17 | 120 |
| Sauces and gravies | 39.88 | 31.37 | 79 |
| Baking needs and misc. products | 16.20 | 15.64 | 97 |
| Other canned/packaged prepared foods | 112.30 | 71.09 | 63 |
| Prepared salads | 13.51 | 12.11 | 90 |
| Prepared desserts | 8.99 | 7.24 | 81 |
| Baby food | 25.02 | 4.79 | 19 |
| Misc. prepared foods | 64.79 | 46.96 | 72 |
| Nonalcoholic beverages | 240.27 | 200.74 | 84 |
| Cola | 89.20 | 60.30 | 68 |
| Other carbonated drinks | 42.50 | 34.65 | 82 |
| Coffee | 46.33 | 56.43 | 122 |
| Roasted coffee | 30.90 | 36.14 | 117 |
| Instant and freeze-dried coffee | 15.43 | 20.29 | 131 |
| Noncarbonated fruit flavored drinks, incl. nonfrozen lemonade | 24.83 | 21.12 | 85 |
| Tea | 15.64 | 13.16 | 84 |
| Nonalcoholic beer | 1.01 | 0.10 | 10 |
| Other nonalcoholic beverages and ice | 20.75 | 14.99 | 72 |
| **Food prepared by CU, out-of-town trips** | **44.91** | **50.17** | **112** |
| **FOOD AWAY FROM HOME** | **1,702.43** | **1,285.05** | **75** |
| **Meals at restaurants, carry-outs, other** | **1,331.44** | **997.46** | **75** |
| Lunch | 464.83 | 322.63 | 69 |
| Dinner | 653.29 | 529.99 | 81 |
| Snacks and nonalcoholic beverages | 111.73 | 55.06 | 49 |
| Breakfast and brunch | 101.59 | 89.78 | 88 |
| **Board (including at school)** | **54.60** | **26.00** | **48** |
| **Catered affairs** | **43.89** | **33.51** | **76** |
| **Food on out-of-town trips** | **196.85** | **208.88** | **106** |
| **School lunches** | **49.41** | **6.01** | **12** |
| **Meals as pay** | **26.23** | **13.21** | **50** |

*(continued)*

*(continued from previous page)*

| | average spending of total consumer units | consumer units headed by 65-to-74-year-olds | |
| --- | --- | --- | --- |
| | | average spending | indexed spending* |
| **ALCOHOLIC BEVERAGES** | **$277.28** | **$205.71** | **74** |
| **AT HOME** | **165.34** | **125.01** | **76** |
| Beer and ale | 87.91 | 38.18 | 43 |
| Whiskey | 13.37 | 36.34 | 272 |
| Wine | 48.68 | 38.65 | 79 |
| Other alcoholic beverages | 15.39 | 11.84 | 77 |
| **AWAY FROM HOME** | **111.94** | **80.70** | **72** |
| Beer and ale | 33.45 | 20.62 | 62 |
| Wine | 20.29 | 15.35 | 76 |
| Other alcoholic beverages | 29.77 | 20.82 | 70 |
| Alcoholic beverages purchased on trips | 28.43 | 23.92 | 84 |
| **HOUSING** | **$10,464.95** | **$7,927.02** | **76** |
| **SHELTER** | **5,931.76** | **4,017.77** | **68** |
| **Owned dwellings**** | **3,754.44** | **2,818.61** | **75** |
| Mortgage interest and charges | 2,106.99 | 732.33 | 35 |
| Mortgage interest | 1,991.49 | 641.30 | 32 |
| Interest paid, home equity loan | 53.32 | 44.16 | 83 |
| Interest paid, home equity line of credit | 61.81 | 46.86 | 76 |
| Prepayment penalty charges | 0.37 | - | - |
| Property taxes | 931.76 | 1,071.26 | 115 |
| Maintenance, repairs, insurance, other expenses | 715.68 | 1,015.02 | 142 |
| Homeowner's and related insurance | 225.32 | 316.11 | 140 |
| Fire and extended coverage | 6.69 | 7.40 | 111 |
| Homeowner's insurance | 218.63 | 308.71 | 141 |
| Ground rent | 31.63 | 51.14 | 162 |
| Maintenance and repair services | 365.24 | 562.59 | 154 |
| Painting and papering | 41.18 | 43.61 | 106 |
| Plumbing and water heating | 33.28 | 60.96 | 183 |
| Heat, air conditioning, electrical work | 72.49 | 79.50 | 110 |
| Roofing and gutters | 65.15 | 123.20 | 189 |
| Other repair and maintenance services | 130.33 | 230.36 | 177 |
| Repair/replacement of hard surface flooring | 21.23 | 22.12 | 104 |
| Repair of built-in appliances | 1.59 | 2.85 | 179 |
| Maintenance and repair materials | 71.32 | 55.96 | 78 |
| Paints, wallpaper and supplies | 19.60 | 12.12 | 62 |
| Tools/equipment for painting, wallpapering | 2.11 | 1.30 | 62 |
| Plumbing supplies and equipment | 7.26 | 6.32 | 87 |
| Electrical supplies, heating/cooling equip. | 5.22 | 3.39 | 65 |
| Hard surface flooring, repair and replacement | 3.51 | 4.36 | 124 |
| Roofing and gutters | 4.30 | 5.86 | 136 |

*(continued)*

*(continued from previous page)*

| | average spending of total consumer units | consumer units headed by 65-to-74-year-olds | |
|---|---|---|---|
| | | average spending | indexed spending* |
| Plaster, paneling, siding, windows, doors, screens, awnings | $11.53 | $13.95 | 121 |
| Patio, walk, fence, driveway, masonry, brick and stucco work | 0.88 | 0.71 | 81 |
| Landscape maintenance | 1.78 | 0.55 | 31 |
| Miscellaneous supplies and equipment | 15.13 | 7.40 | 49 |
| Insulation, other maintenance/repair | 11.41 | 6.91 | 61 |
| Finish basement, remodel rooms or build patios, walks, etc. | 3.72 | 0.49 | 13 |
| Property management and security | 22.17 | 29.21 | 132 |
| Property management | 16.64 | 19.49 | 117 |
| Management and upkeep services for security | 5.53 | 9.72 | 176 |
| **Rented dwellings** | **1,785.64** | **783.45** | **44** |
| Rent | 1,716.25 | 755.89 | 44 |
| Rent as pay | 48.68 | 12.00 | 25 |
| Maintenance, insurance and other expenses | 20.71 | 15.56 | 75 |
| Tenant's insurance | 7.35 | 4.44 | 60 |
| Maintenance and repair services | 5.32 | 9.03 | 170 |
| Repair or maintenance services | 4.93 | 8.92 | 181 |
| Repair and replacement of hard surface flooring | 0.32 | - | - |
| Repair of built-in appliances | 0.07 | 0.11 | 157 |
| Maintenance and repair materials | 8.04 | 2.09 | 26 |
| Paint, wallpaper and supplies | 1.48 | 0.37 | 25 |
| Painting and wallpapering | 0.16 | 0.04 | 25 |
| Plastering, panels, roofing, gutters, etc. | 0.71 | 0.12 | 17 |
| Patio, walk, fence, driveway, masonry, brick and stucco work | 0.03 | - | - |
| Plumbing supplies and equipment | 1.14 | 0.26 | 23 |
| Electrical supplies, heating and cooling equip. | 0.31 | - | - |
| Misc. supplies and equipment | 3.53 | 1.30 | 37 |
| Insulation, other maintenance and repair | 1.43 | 0.09 | 6 |
| Materials for additions, finishing basements, remodeling rooms | 2.07 | 1.22 | 59 |
| Construction materials for jobs not started | 0.04 | - | - |
| Hard surface flooring | 0.22 | - | - |
| Landscape maintenance | 0.46 | - | - |
| **Other lodging** | **391.68** | **415.71** | **106** |
| Owned vacation homes | 127.18 | 147.58 | 116 |
| Mortgage interest and charges | 48.74 | 35.93 | 74 |
| Mortgage interest | 47.03 | 35.93 | 76 |
| Interest paid, home equity loan | 0.12 | - | - |

*(continued)*

*(continued from previous page)*

| | average spending of total consumer units | consumer units headed by 65-to-74-year-olds | |
|---|---|---|---|
| | | average spending | indexed spending* |
| Interest paid, home equity line of credit | $1.59 | - | - |
| Property taxes | 54.14 | $77.67 | 143 |
| Maintenance, insurance and other expenses | 24.29 | 33.98 | 140 |
| Homeowner's and related insurance | 6.10 | 7.01 | 115 |
| Homeowner's insurance | 5.90 | 6.92 | 117 |
| Fire and extended coverage | 0.20 | 0.09 | 45 |
| Ground rent | 2.33 | 4.42 | 190 |
| Maintenance and repair services | 10.56 | 18.22 | 173 |
| Maintenance and repair materials | 2.00 | 0.39 | 20 |
| Property management and security | 2.64 | 3.93 | 149 |
| Property management | 1.88 | 2.14 | 114 |
| Management and upkeep services for security | 0.75 | 1.79 | 239 |
| Parking | 0.67 | - | - |
| Housing while attending school | 54.91 | 8.07 | 15 |
| Lodging on out-of-town trips | 209.59 | 260.07 | 124 |
| **UTILITIES, FUELS & PUBLIC SERVICES** | **2,192.58** | **2,151.56** | **98** |
| **Natural gas** | **268.26** | **294.56** | **110** |
| Natural gas (renter) | 58.60 | 25.75 | 44 |
| Natural gas (owner) | 207.94 | 266.44 | 128 |
| Natural gas (vacation) | 1.58 | 2.12 | 134 |
| **Electricity** | **869.67** | **887.77** | **102** |
| Electricity (renter) | 205.17 | 96.80 | 47 |
| Electricity (owner) | 655.26 | 777.15 | 119 |
| Electricity (vacation) | 8.41 | 12.47 | 148 |
| **Fuel oil and other fuels** | **86.66** | **120.12** | **139** |
| Fuel oil | 50.69 | 64.99 | 128 |
| Fuel oil (renter) | 4.34 | 1.45 | 33 |
| Fuel oil (owner) | 45.58 | 62.79 | 138 |
| Fuel oil (vacation) | 0.73 | 0.75 | 103 |
| Coal | 2.13 | 0.93 | 44 |
| Coal (renter) | 0.10 | - | - |
| Coal (owner) | 2.03 | 0.93 | 46 |
| Bottled/tank gas | 28.02 | 47.34 | 169 |
| Gas (renter) | 3.72 | 4.48 | 120 |
| Gas (owner) | 21.86 | 38.30 | 175 |
| Gas (vacation) | 2.43 | 4.56 | 188 |
| Wood and other fuels | 5.83 | 6.86 | 118 |
| Wood and other fuels (renter) | 0.73 | 0.18 | 25 |
| Wood and other fuels (owner) | 5.06 | 6.68 | 132 |

*(continued)*

*(continued from previous page)*

| | average spending of total consumer units | consumer units headed by 65-to-74-year-olds | |
| --- | --- | --- | --- |
| | | average spending | indexed spending* |
| **Telephone services** | **$708.40** | **$577.72** | **82** |
| Telephone services in home city, excl. mobile car phones | 682.65 | 563.56 | 83 |
| Telephone services for mobile car phones | 25.75 | 14.16 | 55 |
| **Water and other public services** | **259.59** | **271.38** | **105** |
| Water and sewerage maintenance | 187.25 | 192.74 | 103 |
| Water and sewerage maintenance (renter) | 25.89 | 9.45 | 37 |
| Water and sewerage maintenance (owner) | 159.68 | 180.79 | 113 |
| Water and sewerage maintenance (vacation) | 1.53 | 2.20 | 144 |
| Trash and garbage collection | 70.49 | 75.45 | 107 |
| Trash and garbage collection (renter) | 8.59 | 3.51 | 41 |
| Trash and garbage collection (owner) | 60.92 | 69.55 | 114 |
| Trash and garbage collection (vacation) | 0.95 | 2.16 | 227 |
| Septic tank cleaning | 1.84 | 3.19 | 173 |
| Septic tank cleaning (renter) | 0.02 | - | - |
| Septic tank cleaning (owner) | 1.76 | 2.86 | 163 |
| Septic tank cleaning (vacation) | 0.07 | 0.32 | 457 |
| **HOUSEHOLD SERVICES** | **508.34** | **343.01** | **67** |
| **Personal services** | **258.04** | **26.19** | **10** |
| Babysitting and child care in own home | 39.63 | 1.13 | 3 |
| Babysitting and child care in someone else's home | 36.48 | 2.16 | 6 |
| Care for elderly, invalids, handicapped, etc. | 35.33 | 9.30 | 26 |
| Adult day care centers | 1.05 | - | - |
| Day care centers, nursery and preschools | 145.55 | 13.59 | 9 |
| **Other household services** | **250.30** | **316.82** | **127** |
| Housekeeping services | 85.16 | 91.70 | 108 |
| Gardening, lawn care service | 63.96 | 106.04 | 166 |
| Water softening service | 2.90 | 5.24 | 181 |
| Nonclothing laundry and dry cleaning, sent out | 1.69 | 2.52 | 149 |
| Nonclothing laundry and dry cleaning, coin-operated | 4.83 | 2.06 | 43 |
| Termite/pest control services | 11.70 | 13.92 | 119 |
| Other home services | 16.60 | 14.86 | 90 |
| Termite/pest control products | 0.16 | 0.02 | 13 |
| Moving, storage, and freight express | 27.71 | 26.91 | 97 |
| Appliance repair, incl. service center | 14.07 | 18.33 | 130 |
| Reupholstering and furniture repair | 10.80 | 16.78 | 155 |
| Repairs and rental of equipment and power tools | 5.79 | 11.40 | 197 |
| Appliance rental | 1.67 | 0.76 | 46 |
| Rental of office equipment for nonbusiness use | 0.29 | 0.07 | 24 |
| Repair of misc. household equip. and furnishings | 1.75 | 3.96 | 226 |

*(continued)*

*(continued from previous page)*

| | average spending of total consumer units | consumer units headed by 65-to-74-year-olds | |
|---|---|---|---|
| | | average spending | indexed spending* |
| Repair of computer systems for nonbusiness use | $0.82 | $0.98 | 120 |
| Computer information services | 0.39 | 1.29 | 331 |
| **HOUSEKEEPING SUPPLIES** | **429.59** | **481.05** | **112** |
| **Laundry and cleaning supplies** | **110.26** | **112.38** | **102** |
| Soaps and detergents | 63.62 | 59.85 | 94 |
| Other laundry cleaning products | 46.64 | 52.53 | 113 |
| **Other household products** | **193.90** | **224.12** | **116** |
| Cleansing and toilet tissue, paper towels and napkins | 60.03 | 70.80 | 118 |
| Misc. household products | 71.57 | 63.52 | 89 |
| Lawn and garden supplies | 62.29 | 89.80 | 144 |
| **Postage and stationery** | **125.43** | **144.56** | **115** |
| Stationery, stationery supplies, giftwrap | 61.49 | 54.36 | 88 |
| Postage | 62.40 | 89.08 | 143 |
| Delivery services | 1.54 | 1.12 | 73 |
| **HOUSEHOLD FURNISHINGS & EQUIP.** | **1,402.69** | **933.63** | **67** |
| **Household textiles** | **100.47** | **92.57** | **92** |
| Bathroom linens | 15.50 | 25.72 | 166 |
| Bedroom linens | 45.50 | 21.07 | 46 |
| Kitchen and dining room linens | 9.26 | 11.07 | 120 |
| Curtains and draperies | 17.36 | 21.17 | 122 |
| Slipcovers and decorative pillows | 1.74 | 0.80 | 46 |
| Sewing materials for household items | 10.01 | 11.29 | 113 |
| Other linens | 1.09 | 1.44 | 132 |
| **Furniture** | **327.49** | **172.44** | **53** |
| Mattress and springs | 41.36 | 27.65 | 67 |
| Other bedroom furniture | 51.66 | 15.08 | 29 |
| Sofas | 77.20 | 36.69 | 48 |
| Living room chairs | 39.35 | 30.56 | 78 |
| Living room tables | 16.51 | 11.03 | 67 |
| Kitchen and dining room furniture | 46.95 | 18.47 | 39 |
| Infants' furniture | 6.74 | 2.65 | 39 |
| Outdoor furniture | 10.77 | 9.01 | 84 |
| Wall units, cabinets and other furniture | 36.95 | 21.30 | 58 |
| **Floor coverings** | **177.25** | **85.37** | **48** |
| Wall-to-wall carpeting | 38.41 | 44.63 | 116 |
| Wall-to-wall carpeting (renter) | 3.96 | 6.29 | 159 |
| Wall-to-wall carpet (replacement)(owned home) | 34.45 | 38.34 | 111 |
| Room-size rugs/other floor covering, nonpermanent | 138.84 | 40.74 | 29 |

*(continued)*

*(continued from previous page)*

| | average spending of total consumer units | consumer units headed by 65-to-74-year-olds | |
|---|---|---|---|
| | | average spending | indexed spending* |
| Major appliances | $154.88 | $159.50 | 103 |
| Dishwashers (built-in), garbage disposals, range hoods (renter) | 0.95 | - | - |
| Dishwashers (built-in), garbage disposals, range hoods (owner) | 10.23 | 9.11 | 89 |
| Refrigerators and freezers (renter) | 6.69 | 1.58 | 24 |
| Refrigerators and freezers (owner) | 42.27 | 55.80 | 132 |
| Washing machines (renter) | 5.26 | 0.67 | 13 |
| Washing machines (owner) | 14.58 | 19.81 | 136 |
| Clothes dryers (renter) | 3.25 | - | - |
| Clothes dryers (owner) | 10.62 | 12.20 | 115 |
| Cooking stoves, ovens (renter) | 2.57 | - | - |
| Cooking stoves, ovens (owner) | 18.72 | 17.57 | 94 |
| Microwave ovens (renter) | 2.87 | 1.35 | 47 |
| Microwave ovens (owner) | 6.01 | 5.48 | 91 |
| Portable dishwasher (renter) | 0.17 | 1.25 | 735 |
| Portable dishwasher (owner) | 0.52 | 1.82 | 350 |
| Window air conditioners (renter) | 2.75 | - | - |
| Window air conditioners (owner) | 8.64 | 15.70 | 182 |
| Electric floor cleaning equipment | 12.94 | 12.90 | 100 |
| Sewing machines | 4.81 | 3.13 | 65 |
| Misc. household appliances | 1.03 | 1.12 | 109 |
| **Small appliances and misc. housewares** | **85.16** | **70.33** | **83** |
| Housewares | 62.80 | 45.78 | 73 |
| Plastic dinnerware | 1.48 | 3.84 | 259 |
| China and other dinnerware | 11.29 | 5.34 | 47 |
| Flatware | 4.01 | 5.16 | 129 |
| Glassware | 6.91 | 3.44 | 50 |
| Silver serving pieces | 2.03 | 0.60 | 30 |
| Other serving pieces | 1.28 | 0.78 | 61 |
| Nonelectric cookware | 16.04 | 10.74 | 67 |
| Tableware, nonelectric kitchenware | 19.77 | 15.88 | 80 |
| Small appliances | 22.36 | 24.55 | 110 |
| Small electric kitchen appliances | 15.65 | 16.26 | 104 |
| Portable heating and cooling equipment | 6.70 | 8.28 | 124 |
| **Miscellaneous household equipment** | **557.43** | **353.42** | **63** |
| Window coverings | 10.64 | 7.99 | 75 |
| Infants' equipment | 8.02 | 1.83 | 23 |
| Laundry and cleaning equipment | 11.33 | 11.39 | 101 |
| Outdoor equipment | 4.08 | 2.88 | 71 |
| Clocks | 3.37 | 1.14 | 34 |

*(continued)*

*(continued from previous page)*

| | average spending of total consumer units | consumer units headed by 65-to-74-year-olds | |
|---|---|---|---|
| | | average spending | indexed spending* |
| Lamps and lighting fixtures | $29.77 | $12.96 | 44 |
| Other household decorative items | 137.82 | 94.20 | 68 |
| Telephones and accessories | 14.44 | 9.05 | 63 |
| Lawn and garden equipment | 42.14 | 42.48 | 101 |
| Power tools | 15.61 | 10.00 | 64 |
| Small misc. furnishings | 2.02 | 0.23 | 11 |
| Hand tools | 10.16 | 8.12 | 80 |
| Indoor plants and fresh flowers | 46.82 | 44.86 | 96 |
| Closet and storage items | 6.93 | 10.86 | 157 |
| Rental of furniture | 3.24 | 2.04 | 63 |
| Luggage | 9.25 | 6.82 | 74 |
| Computers and computer hardware nonbusiness use | 135.02 | 48.08 | 36 |
| Computer software and accessories for nonbusiness use | 18.23 | 9.08 | 50 |
| Telephone answering devices | 3.58 | 2.24 | 63 |
| Calculators | 1.88 | 1.74 | 93 |
| Business equipment for home use | 4.11 | 0.80 | 19 |
| Other hardware | 13.63 | 4.34 | 32 |
| Smoke alarms (owner) | 1.21 | 1.25 | 103 |
| Smoke alarms (renter) | 0.17 | 0.43 | 253 |
| Other household appliances (owner) | 4.71 | 2.08 | 44 |
| Other household appliances (renter) | 1.04 | 0.68 | 65 |
| Misc. household equipment and parts | 18.22 | 15.84 | 87 |
| **APPAREL AND SERVICES** | **$1,703.63** | **$1,116.53** | **66** |
| **MEN'S APPAREL** | **329.46** | **222.02** | **67** |
| Suits | 33.42 | 18.85 | 56 |
| Sportcoats and tailored jackets | 13.23 | 14.40 | 109 |
| Coats and jackets | 30.16 | 21.29 | 71 |
| Underwear | 17.80 | 8.42 | 47 |
| Hosiery | 12.85 | 9.18 | 71 |
| Sleepwear | 3.50 | 1.67 | 48 |
| Accessories | 34.98 | 17.09 | 49 |
| Sweaters and vests | 12.43 | 9.56 | 77 |
| Active sportswear | 10.14 | 6.84 | 67 |
| Shirts | 76.52 | 50.04 | 65 |
| Pants | 63.37 | 46.49 | 73 |
| Shorts and shorts sets | 16.23 | 16.12 | 99 |
| Uniforms | 3.67 | 0.95 | 26 |
| Costumes | 1.17 | 1.14 | 97 |

*(continued)*

*(continued from previous page)*

| | average spending of total consumer units | consumer units headed by 65-to-74-year-olds | |
|---|---|---|---|
| | | average spending | indexed spending* |
| **BOYS' (AGED 2 TO 15) APPAREL** | **$95.86** | **$29.86** | **31** |
| Coats and jackets | 9.27 | 0.45 | 5 |
| Sweaters | 1.92 | 1.31 | 68 |
| Shirts | 20.82 | 7.67 | 37 |
| Underwear | 5.76 | 1.34 | 23 |
| Sleepwear | 1.12 | - | - |
| Hosiery | 4.01 | 1.53 | 38 |
| Accessories | 6.66 | 2.07 | 31 |
| Suits, sportcoats, and vests | 3.59 | 0.70 | 19 |
| Pants | 24.03 | 10.60 | 44 |
| Shorts and shorts sets | 11.44 | 0.85 | 7 |
| Uniforms | 4.06 | 1.81 | 45 |
| Active sportswear | 2.25 | 1.14 | 51 |
| Costumes | 0.93 | 0.38 | 41 |
| **WOMEN'S APPAREL** | **559.19** | **470.13** | **84** |
| Coats and jackets | 41.43 | 27.84 | 67 |
| Dresses | 83.48 | 65.84 | 79 |
| Sportcoats and tailored jackets | 4.29 | 1.04 | 24 |
| Sweaters and vests | 28.51 | 26.98 | 95 |
| Shirts, blouses, and tops | 100.86 | 93.37 | 93 |
| Skirts | 20.49 | 27.62 | 135 |
| Pants | 70.73 | 60.79 | 86 |
| Shorts and shorts sets | 26.72 | 15.87 | 59 |
| Active sportswear | 27.19 | 22.42 | 82 |
| Sleepwear | 23.65 | 24.23 | 102 |
| Undergarments | 30.37 | 20.64 | 68 |
| Hosiery | 20.88 | 14.22 | 68 |
| Suits | 32.66 | 26.23 | 80 |
| Accessories | 43.56 | 42.33 | 97 |
| Uniforms | 2.42 | - | - |
| Costumes | 1.93 | 0.70 | 36 |
| **GIRLS' (AGED 2 TO 15) APPAREL** | **101.30** | **43.00** | **42** |
| Coats and jackets | 6.86 | 1.27 | 19 |
| Dresses and suits | 13.17 | 6.84 | 52 |
| Shirts, blouses, and sweaters | 20.67 | 9.31 | 45 |
| Skirts and pants | 18.18 | 5.58 | 31 |
| Shorts and shorts sets | 9.89 | 3.51 | 35 |
| Active sportswear | 11.39 | 6.26 | 55 |
| Underwear and sleepwear | 7.47 | 2.69 | 36 |
| Hosiery | 4.78 | 1.70 | 36 |
| Accessories | 4.51 | 4.32 | 96 |

*(continued)*

*(continued from previous page)*

| | average spending of total consumer units | consumer units headed by 65-to-74-year-olds | |
| --- | --- | --- | --- |
| | | average spending | indexed spending* |
| Uniforms | $1.92 | $0.75 | 39 |
| Costumes | 2.47 | 0.76 | 31 |
| **CHILDREN UNDER AGE 2** | **80.61** | **19.88** | **25** |
| Coats, jackets, and snowsuits | 3.10 | 1.90 | 61 |
| Outerwear including dresses | 22.66 | 10.09 | 45 |
| Underwear | 46.09 | 3.51 | 8 |
| Sleepwear and loungewear | 3.76 | 1.74 | 46 |
| Accessories | 4.99 | 2.64 | 53 |
| **FOOTWEAR** | **278.36** | **176.05** | **63** |
| Men's | 94.82 | 62.31 | 66 |
| Boys' | 30.48 | 4.37 | 14 |
| Women's | 117.81 | 92.58 | 79 |
| Girls' | 35.24 | 16.78 | 48 |
| **OTHER APPAREL PRODUCTS & SERVICES** | **258.84** | **155.60** | **60** |
| Material for making clothes | 4.95 | 4.34 | 88 |
| Sewing patterns and notions | 1.92 | 1.36 | 71 |
| Watches | 19.16 | 10.24 | 53 |
| Jewelry | 104.17 | 75.35 | 72 |
| Shoe repair and other shoe services | 2.66 | 2.48 | 93 |
| Coin-operated apparel laundry and dry cleaning | 39.46 | 14.75 | 37 |
| Apparel alteration, repair, and tailoring services | 5.82 | 5.57 | 96 |
| Clothing rental | 3.48 | 0.55 | 16 |
| Watch and jewelry repair | 5.07 | 3.14 | 62 |
| Professional laundry, dry cleaning | 71.68 | 36.98 | 52 |
| Clothing storage | 0.47 | 0.84 | 179 |
| **TRANSPORTATION** | **$6,015.97** | **$4,483.98** | **75** |
| **VEHICLE PURCHASES** | **2,639.33** | **1,711.84** | **65** |
| **Cars and trucks, new** | **1,194.00** | **979.89** | **82** |
| New cars | 670.88 | 818.73 | 122 |
| New trucks | 523.11 | 161.15 | 31 |
| **Cars and trucks, used** | **1,410.96** | **730.78** | **52** |
| Used cars | 916.45 | 617.40 | 67 |
| Used trucks | 494.51 | 113.38 | 23 |
| **Other vehicles** | **34.38** | **1.17** | **3** |
| New motorcycles | 21.74 | - | - |
| Used motorcycles | 12.64 | 1.17 | 9 |

*(continued)*

*(continued from previous page)*

| | average spending of total consumer units | consumer units headed by 65-to-74-year-olds | |
|---|---|---|---|
| | | average spending | indexed spending* |
| **GASOLINE AND MOTOR OIL** | **$1,006.05** | **$748.98** | **74** |
| Gasoline | 901.97 | 660.40 | 73 |
| Diesel fuel | 10.15 | 4.24 | 42 |
| Gasoline on out-of-town trips | 81.98 | 76.42 | 93 |
| Motor oil | 11.13 | 7.15 | 64 |
| Motor oil on out-of-town trips | 0.83 | 0.77 | 93 |
| **OTHER VEHICLE EXPENSES** | **2,015.78** | **1,598.85** | **79** |
| **Vehicle finance charges** | **260.57** | **113.06** | **43** |
| **Maintenance and repairs** | **652.77** | **587.46** | **90** |
| Coolant, additives, brake, transmission fluids | 5.63 | 3.21 | 57 |
| Tires | 87.06 | 74.32 | 85 |
| Parts, equipment, and accessories | 60.29 | 72.82 | 121 |
| Vehicle audio equipment | 10.31 | - | - |
| Vehicle products | 3.37 | 1.68 | 50 |
| Misc. auto repair, servicing | 33.68 | 23.35 | 69 |
| Body work and painting | 29.52 | 34.20 | 116 |
| Clutch, transmission repair | 45.69 | 29.99 | 66 |
| Drive shaft and rear-end repair | 6.14 | 3.57 | 58 |
| Brake work | 39.22 | 31.10 | 79 |
| Repair to steering or front-end | 20.68 | 12.97 | 63 |
| Repair to engine cooling system | 23.28 | 30.13 | 129 |
| Motor tune-up | 42.61 | 36.26 | 85 |
| Lube, oil change, and oil filters | 42.90 | 41.71 | 97 |
| Front-end alignment, wheel balance, rotation | 11.11 | 10.62 | 96 |
| Shock absorber replacement | 7.35 | 6.33 | 86 |
| Brake adjustment | 3.18 | 1.24 | 39 |
| Gas tank repair, replacement | 1.54 | 0.90 | 58 |
| Repair tires and other repair work | 33.28 | 27.09 | 81 |
| Vehicle air conditioning repair | 14.28 | 18.60 | 130 |
| Exhaust system repair | 20.87 | 19.85 | 95 |
| Electrical system repair | 29.58 | 32.29 | 109 |
| Motor repair, replacement | 67.64 | 66.16 | 98 |
| Auto repair service policy | 5.94 | 3.16 | 53 |
| **Vehicle insurance** | **712.81** | **621.45** | **87** |
| **Vehicle rental, leases, licenses, etc.** | **389.63** | **276.89** | **71** |
| Leased and rented vehicles | 235.64 | 145.38 | 62 |
| Rented vehicles | 37.70 | 32.04 | 85 |
| Auto rental | 7.09 | 3.53 | 50 |
| Auto rental, out-of-town trips | 25.95 | 22.88 | 88 |
| Truck rental | 1.19 | 0.33 | 28 |

*(continued)*

| | average spending of total consumer units | consumer units headed by 65-to-74-year-olds | |
|---|---|---|---|
| | | average spending | indexed spending* |
| Truck rental, out-of-town trips | $3.26 | $5.26 | 161 |
| Leased vehicles | 197.94 | 113.34 | 57 |
| State and local registration | 84.53 | 76.23 | 90 |
| Driver's license | 6.92 | 5.30 | 77 |
| Vehicle inspection | 8.76 | 8.20 | 94 |
| Parking fees | 25.38 | 15.14 | 60 |
| Tolls | 11.19 | 6.92 | 62 |
| Tolls on out-of-town trips | 4.53 | 4.71 | 104 |
| Towing charges | 4.86 | 3.06 | 63 |
| Automobile service clubs | 7.83 | 11.95 | 153 |
| **PUBLIC TRANSPORTATION** | **354.81** | **424.31** | **120** |
| Airline fares | 225.58 | 260.20 | 115 |
| Intercity bus fares | 14.09 | 34.92 | 248 |
| Intracity mass transit fares | 48.51 | 20.40 | 42 |
| Local trans. on out-of-town trips | 8.46 | 12.67 | 150 |
| Taxi fares on trips | 4.97 | 7.44 | 150 |
| Taxi fares | 6.95 | 5.64 | 81 |
| Intercity train fares | 18.41 | 23.06 | 125 |
| Ship fares | 27.31 | 59.82 | 219 |
| School bus | 0.53 | 0.15 | 28 |
| **HEALTH CARE** | **$1,732.33** | **$2,616.99** | **151** |
| **HEALTH INSURANCE** | **860.45** | **1,528.33** | **178** |
| **Commercial health insurance** | **241.22** | **237.77** | **99** |
| Commercial health insurance | 202.64 | 204.81 | 101 |
| Traditional fee for service health plan (not BCBS) | 15.73 | 15.59 | 99 |
| Preferred provider health plan (not BCBS) | 22.86 | 17.37 | 76 |
| **Blue Cross, Blue Shield** | **171.78** | **222.26** | **129** |
| Blue Cross, Blue Shield | 143.85 | 181.44 | 126 |
| Traditional fee for service health plan (BCBS) | 13.74 | 21.48 | 156 |
| Preferred provider health plan (BCBS) | 7.06 | 11.35 | 161 |
| Health maintenance organization (BCBS) | 6.90 | 6.78 | 98 |
| Commercial Medicare supplement (BCBS) | 0.18 | 1.21 | 672 |
| Other health insurance (BCBS) | 0.04 | - | - |
| **Health maintenance plans (HMOs)** | **146.87** | **83.53** | **57** |
| Health maintenance plans | 118.87 | 70.03 | 59 |
| Health maintenance organization (not BCBS) | 28.00 | 13.50 | 48 |
| **Medicare payments** | **172.13** | **687.90** | **400** |

*(continued)*

*(continued from previous page)*

| | average spending of total consumer units | consumer units headed by 65-to-74-year-olds | |
|---|---|---|---|
| | | average spending | indexed spending* |
| **Commercial Medicare supplements/ other health insurance** | **$128.44** | **$296.88** | **231** |
| Commercial Medicare supplements/ other health insurance | 107.27 | 248.17 | 231 |
| Commercial Medicare supplement (not BCBS) | 8.30 | 32.66 | 393 |
| Other health insurance (not BCBS) | 12.88 | 16.05 | 125 |
| **MEDICAL SERVICES** | **511.47** | **471.24** | **92** |
| Physician's services | 146.97 | 118.58 | 81 |
| Dental services | 186.29 | 224.11 | 120 |
| Eye care services | 28.83 | 41.69 | 145 |
| Service by professionals other than physician | 38.24 | 32.91 | 86 |
| Lab tests, x-rays | 21.92 | 15.97 | 73 |
| Hospital room | 33.04 | 41.93 | 127 |
| Hospital services other than room | 37.16 | -21.46 | -58 |
| Care in convalescent or nursing home | 7.90 | 2.76 | 35 |
| Other medical services | 10.01 | 5.09 | 51 |
| **DRUGS** | **279.96** | **535.52** | **191** |
| Non-prescription drugs | 79.03 | 107.58 | 136 |
| Prescription drugs | 200.94 | 427.95 | 213 |
| **MEDICAL SUPPLIES** | **80.45** | **81.90** | **102** |
| Eyeglasses and contact lenses | 52.06 | 53.30 | 102 |
| Topicals and dressings | 20.73 | 14.61 | 70 |
| Medical equipment for general use | 2.53 | 7.25 | 287 |
| Supportive/convalescent medical equipment | 3.83 | 4.93 | 129 |
| **ENTERTAINMENT** | **$1,612.09** | **$1,156.09** | **72** |
| **FEES AND ADMISSIONS** | **432.91** | **377.18** | **87** |
| Recreation expenses, out-of-town trips | 21.21 | 21.65 | 102 |
| Social, recreation, civic club membership | 80.67 | 123.72 | 153 |
| Fees for participant sports | 66.55 | 51.48 | 77 |
| Participant sports, out-of-town trips | 29.25 | 26.87 | 92 |
| Movie, theater, opera, ballet | 73.42 | 42.60 | 58 |
| Movie, other admissions, out-of-town trips | 40.50 | 42.01 | 104 |
| Admission to sporting events | 28.71 | 18.68 | 65 |
| Admission to sports events, out-of-town trips | 13.50 | 14.00 | 104 |
| Fees for recreational lessons | 57.91 | 14.52 | 25 |
| Other entertainment svcs., out-of-town trips | 21.21 | 21.65 | 102 |
| **TELEVISION, RADIOS, SOUND EQUIPMENT** | **541.77** | **397.11** | **73** |
| **Televisions** | **370.32** | **312.78** | **84** |
| Community antenna or cable TV | 219.69 | 219.65 | 100 |

*(continued)*

*(continued from previous page)*

| | average spending of total consumer units | consumer units headed by 65-to-74-year-olds | |
|---|---|---|---|
| | | average spending | indexed spending* |
| Color TV, console | $29.53 | $12.67 | 43 |
| Color TV, portable, table model | 44.90 | 36.07 | 80 |
| VCRs and video disc players | 27.33 | 13.49 | 49 |
| Video cassettes, tapes, and discs | 24.05 | 14.08 | 59 |
| Video game hardware and software | 14.68 | 4.59 | 31 |
| Repair of TV, radio, and sound equipment | 7.19 | 8.65 | 120 |
| Rental of televisions | 1.06 | - | - |
| **Radios and sound equipment** | **171.45** | **84.33** | **49** |
| Radios | 10.61 | 14.60 | 138 |
| Tape recorders and players | 11.26 | 14.67 | 130 |
| Sound components and component systems | 32.12 | 8.35 | 26 |
| Sound equipment accessories | 4.46 | 5.12 | 115 |
| Compact disc, tape, record, video mail order clubs | 11.99 | 8.18 | 68 |
| Records, CDs, audio tapes, needles | 38.49 | 14.91 | 39 |
| Rental of VCR, radio, sound equipment | 0.27 | 0.29 | 107 |
| Musical instruments and accessories | 17.75 | 4.90 | 28 |
| Rental and repair of musical instruments | 1.65 | 1.77 | 107 |
| Rental of video cassettes, tapes, discs, films | 42.38 | 11.54 | 27 |
| **PETS, TOYS, PLAYGROUND EQUIPMENT** | **322.19** | **182.17** | **57** |
| **Pets** | **199.89** | **120.98** | **61** |
| Pet food | 79.56 | 58.41 | 73 |
| Pet purchase, supplies, and medicines | 47.03 | 14.14 | 30 |
| Pet services | 18.78 | 14.00 | 75 |
| Veterinary services | 54.52 | 34.42 | 63 |
| **Toys, games, hobbies, and tricycles** | **120.29** | **60.00** | **50** |
| **Playground equipment** | **2.00** | **1.20** | **60** |
| **OTHER ENTERTAINMENT SUPPLIES, EQUIPMENT, SERVICES** | **315.22** | **199.63** | **63** |
| **Unmotored recreational vehicles** | **28.10** | **0.46** | **2** |
| Boat without motor and boat trailers | 3.69 | 0.46 | 12 |
| Trailer and other attachable campers | 24.41 | - | - |
| **Motorized recreational vehicles** | **77.41** | **90.84** | **117** |
| Motorized camper | 21.18 | 62.76 | 296 |
| Other vehicle | 11.89 | 10.71 | 90 |
| Motor boats | 44.34 | 17.37 | 39 |
| **Rental of recreational vehicles** | **3.42** | **2.00** | **58** |
| **Outboard motors** | **0.36** | **-** | **-** |
| **Docking and landing fees** | **4.49** | **1.43** | **32** |

*(continued)*

*(continued from previous page)*

| | average spending of total consumer units | consumer units headed by 65-to-74-year-olds | |
| --- | --- | --- | --- |
| | | average spending | indexed spending* |
| **Sports, recreation, exercise equipment** | **$110.81** | **$50.46** | **46** |
| **Athletic gear, game tables, exercise equipment** | **50.33** | **29.89** | **59** |
| Bicycles | 12.59 | 3.12 | 25 |
| Camping equipment | 6.51 | 0.72 | 11 |
| Hunting and fishing equipment | 17.00 | 7.50 | 44 |
| Winter sports equipment | 3.78 | 0.97 | 26 |
| Water sports equipment | 9.47 | 3.25 | 34 |
| Other sports equipment | 9.50 | 3.68 | 39 |
| Rental and repair of misc. sports equipment | 1.64 | 1.33 | 81 |
| **Photographic equipment and supplies** | **81.18** | **47.36** | **58** |
| Film | 20.27 | 14.50 | 72 |
| Film processing | 28.56 | 18.79 | 66 |
| Photographic equipment | 12.56 | 5.86 | 47 |
| Photographer fees | 18.39 | 5.63 | 31 |
| **Fireworks** | **2.03** | - | - |
| **Souvenirs** | **0.14** | - | - |
| **Visual goods** | **1.51** | **6.62** | **438** |
| **Pinball, electronic video games** | **5.78** | **0.47** | **8** |
| **PERSONAL CARE PRODUCTS AND SERVICES** | **$403.47** | **$380.00** | **94** |
| **PERSONAL CARE PRODUCTS** | **213.44** | **160.61** | **75** |
| Hair care products | 38.65 | 25.96 | 67 |
| Hair accessories | 4.43 | 1.45 | 33 |
| Wigs and hairpieces | 0.95 | 1.76 | 185 |
| Oral hygiene products | 22.19 | 16.90 | 76 |
| Shaving products | 11.91 | 10.02 | 84 |
| Cosmetics, perfume, and bath products | 105.36 | 87.96 | 83 |
| Deodorants, feminine hygiene, misc. products | 26.10 | 13.34 | 51 |
| Electric personal care appliances | 3.85 | 3.23 | 84 |
| **PERSONAL CARE SERVICES** | **190.03** | **219.39** | **115** |
| Personal care services/female | 97.61 | 151.06 | 155 |
| Personal care services/male | 92.19 | 68.31 | 74 |
| **READING** | **$162.57** | **$179.54** | **110** |
| Newspaper subscriptions | 51.79 | 77.96 | 151 |
| Newspaper, non-subscriptions | 17.40 | 15.98 | 92 |
| Magazine subscriptions | 24.74 | 33.09 | 134 |
| Magazines, non-subscriptions | 11.00 | 6.58 | 60 |
| Books purchased through book clubs | 9.33 | 9.95 | 107 |

*(continued)*

| | average spending of total consumer units | consumer units headed by 65-to-74-year-olds | |
|---|---|---|---|
| | | average spending | indexed spending* |
| Books not purchased through book clubs | $46.51 | $33.92 | 73 |
| Encyclopedia and other reference book sets | 1.52 | 2.06 | 136 |
| **EDUCATION** | **$471.47** | **$237.02** | **50** |
| College tuition | 265.22 | 90.71 | 34 |
| Elementary/high school tuition | 81.97 | 24.52 | 30 |
| Other schools tuition | 14.06 | 7.55 | 54 |
| Other school expenses incl. rentals | 17.30 | 3.75 | 22 |
| Books, supplies for college | 36.06 | 7.27 | 20 |
| Books, supplies for elementary, high school | 8.56 | 3.04 | 36 |
| Books, supplies for day care, nursery school | 2.09 | 0.90 | 43 |
| Misc. school expenses and supplies | 46.21 | 99.29 | 215 |
| **TOBACCO PRODUCTS AND SMOKING SUPPLIES** | **$268.82** | **$182.91** | **68** |
| Cigarettes | 243.09 | 146.57 | 60 |
| Other tobacco products | 24.30 | 35.62 | 147 |
| Smoking accessories | 1.43 | 0.72 | 50 |
| **FINANCIAL PRODUCTS & SERVICES** | **$766.23** | **$629.39** | **82** |
| Miscellaneous fees, gambling losses | 54.70 | 47.22 | 86 |
| Legal fees | 98.35 | 62.19 | 63 |
| Funeral expenses | 86.83 | 134.63 | 155 |
| Safe deposit box rental | 5.51 | 8.74 | 159 |
| Checking accounts, other bank service charges | 25.62 | 12.29 | 48 |
| Cemetery lots, vaults, and maintenance fees | 15.50 | 32.68 | 211 |
| Accounting fees | 40.94 | 50.77 | 124 |
| Miscellaneous personal services | 21.64 | 3.33 | 15 |
| Finance charges, except mortgage and vehicles | 229.82 | 136.48 | 59 |
| Occupational expenses, union and prof. fees | 97.90 | 60.93 | 62 |
| Expenses for other properties | 85.37 | 76.97 | 90 |
| Credit card memberships | 3.92 | 3.14 | 80 |
| **CASH CONTRIBUTIONS** | **$925.39** | **$1,164.68** | **126** |
| Cash contributions to non-CU members, incl. students, alimony, child support | 233.28 | 81.46 | 35 |
| Gifts of cash, stocks, bonds to non-CU member | 174.20 | 468.84 | 269 |
| Contributions to charities | 85.58 | 118.14 | 138 |
| Contributions to church | 385.94 | 472.36 | 122 |
| Contributions to educational organizations | 35.65 | 9.19 | 26 |
| Political contributions | 3.39 | 3.62 | 107 |
| Other contributions | 7.35 | 11.08 | 151 |

*(continued)*

*(continued from previous page)*

| | average spending of total consumer units | consumer units headed by 65-to-74-year-olds | |
|---|---|---|---|
| | | average spending | indexed spending* |
| **PERSONAL INSURANCE & PENSIONS** | **$2,967.05** | **$1,126.95** | **38** |
| **LIFE & OTHER PERSONAL INSURANCE** | **374.03** | **303.99** | **81** |
| Life, endowment, annuity, other pers. insurance | 361.44 | 294.78 | 82 |
| Other nonhealth insurance | 12.59 | 9.21 | 73 |
| | | | |
| **PENSIONS AND SOCIAL SECURITY** | **2,593.02** | **822.96** | **32** |
| Deductions for government retirement | 66.21 | 9.97 | 15 |
| Deductions for railroad retirement | 5.28 | - | - |
| Deductions for private pensions | 325.82 | 71.75 | 22 |
| Non-payroll deposit to retirement plans | 312.41 | 246.98 | 79 |
| Deductions for Social Security | 1,883.30 | 494.26 | 26 |
| | | | |
| **GIFTS*** | **$986.63** | **$801.08** | **81** |
| **FOOD** | **87.72** | **56.33** | **64** |
| Cakes and cupcakes | 1.97 | 1.98 | 101 |
| Cheese | 1.90 | 3.68 | 194 |
| Fresh fruits | 1.83 | 2.24 | 122 |
| Candy and chewing gum | 12.79 | 10.45 | 82 |
| Misc. prepared foods | 2.52 | 1.67 | 66 |
| | | | |
| **HOUSING** | **249.80** | **206.59** | **83** |
| **Housekeeping supplies** | **37.72** | **33.87** | **90** |
| Misc. household products | 4.39 | 3.28 | 75 |
| Lawn and garden supplies | 3.51 | 4.49 | 128 |
| Stationery, stationery supplies, giftwraps | 22.53 | 21.40 | 95 |
| Postage | 4.17 | 2.71 | 65 |
| | | | |
| **Household textiles** | **10.20** | **11.03** | **108** |
| Bedroom linens | 4.44 | 4.38 | 99 |
| | | | |
| **Appliances and misc. housewares** | **27.44** | **30.72** | **112** |
| Major appliances | 4.79 | 8.40 | 175 |
| Small appliances and misc. housewares | 22.65 | 22.33 | 99 |
| China and other dinnerware | 2.91 | 3.11 | 107 |
| Glassware | 3.60 | 1.85 | 51 |
| Nonelectric cookware | 3.98 | 1.01 | 25 |
| Tableware, nonelectric kitchenware | 4.98 | 4.87 | 98 |
| Small electric kitchen appliances | 3.64 | 4.45 | 122 |
| | | | |
| **Miscellaneous household equipment** | **65.94** | **81.74** | **124** |
| Infants' equipment | 2.26 | 1.83 | 81 |
| Lamps and lighting fixtures | 3.33 | 3.80 | 114 |
| Household decorative items | 21.54 | 13.17 | 61 |
| Indoor plants, fresh flowers | 20.72 | 29.60 | 143 |

*(continued)*

*(continued from previous page)*

| | average spending of total consumer units | consumer units headed by 65-to-74-year-olds | |
| --- | --- | --- | --- |
| | | average spending | indexed spending* |
| Computers and hardware, nonbusiness use | $4.01 | $13.60 | 339 |
| Misc. household equipment | 3.08 | 6.99 | 227 |
| **Other housing** | **108.51** | **49.23** | **45** |
| Electricity (renter) | 10.47 | 7.47 | 71 |
| Telephone services in home city, excl. mobile car phone | 12.23 | 5.05 | 41 |
| Day care centers, nursery, and preschools | 15.05 | 4.53 | 30 |
| Housekeeping services | 3.90 | 3.97 | 102 |
| Gardening, lawn care service | 2.74 | 3.14 | 115 |
| **APPAREL AND SERVICES** | **258.22** | **179.79** | **70** |
| **Men and boys, aged 2 or older** | **69.77** | **48.09** | **69** |
| Men's coats and jackets | 4.70 | 1.71 | 36 |
| Men's accessories | 6.98 | 5.04 | 72 |
| Men's sweaters and vests | 3.46 | 3.53 | 102 |
| Men's shirts | 17.03 | 8.65 | 51 |
| Men's pants | 9.29 | 4.53 | 49 |
| Boys' shirts | 4.31 | 4.75 | 110 |
| **Women and girls, aged 2 or older** | **93.61** | **67.12** | **72** |
| Women's coats and jackets | 5.41 | 0.96 | 18 |
| Women's dresses | 5.36 | 3.01 | 56 |
| Women's vests and sweaters | 8.05 | 3.80 | 47 |
| Women's shirts, tops, blouses | 14.11 | 4.92 | 35 |
| Women's pants | 9.09 | 0.82 | 9 |
| Women's active sportswear | 6.11 | 6.90 | 113 |
| Women's sleepwear | 7.35 | 6.92 | 94 |
| Women's accessories | 9.16 | 3.56 | 39 |
| Girls' shirts, blouses, sweaters | 4.16 | 5.15 | 124 |
| Girls' active sportswear | 4.37 | 3.77 | 86 |
| **Children under age 2** | **39.47** | **18.16** | **46** |
| Infant dresses, outerwear | 13.60 | 9.41 | 69 |
| Infant underwear | 19.47 | 3.22 | 17 |
| **Other apparel products and services** | **55.37** | **46.42** | **84** |
| Watches | 26.56 | 32.02 | 121 |
| Jewelry | 23.90 | 28.80 | 121 |
| Men's footwear | 7.15 | 0.57 | 8 |
| Women's footwear | 10.36 | 3.98 | 38 |
| Girls' footwear | 7.76 | 6.56 | 85 |
| **TRANSPORTATION** | **47.84** | **48.04** | **100** |
| Used cars | 3.19 | 4.74 | 149 |

*(continued)*

| | average spending of total consumer units | consumer units headed by 65-to-74-year-olds | |
| --- | --- | --- | --- |
| | | average spending | indexed spending* |
| Gasoline on out-of-town trips | $13.01 | $13.25 | 102 |
| Airline fares | 10.75 | 11.40 | 106 |
| **HEALTH CARE** | **22.21** | **10.25** | **46** |
| Dental services | 4.70 | 0.47 | 10 |
| Care in convalescent or nursing home | 4.50 | 0.51 | 11 |
| **ENTERTAINMENT** | **86.44** | **78.12** | **90** |
| **Toys, games, hobbies, tricycles** | **29.34** | **29.66** | **101** |
| **Other entertainment** | **57.10** | **48.46** | **85** |
| Movie, other admissions, out-of-town trips | 7.07 | 6.65 | 94 |
| Color TV, portable, table model | 3.47 | 1.00 | 29 |
| Pet purchase, supplies, medicine | 6.35 | 0.53 | 8 |
| Veterinary services | 3.05 | 1.73 | 57 |
| **EDUCATION** | **120.19** | **83.62** | **70** |
| College tuition | 96.63 | 59.77 | 62 |
| Elementary, high school tuition | 8.17 | 11.52 | 141 |
| College books, supplies | 6.55 | 2.37 | 36 |
| Misc. school supplies | 5.29 | 3.86 | 73 |
| **ALL OTHER GIFTS** | **114.22** | **138.33** | **121** |
| Out-of-town trip expenses | 36.21 | 37.45 | 103 |

*The index compares the spending of consumer units headed by 65-to-74-year-olds with the spending of the average consumer unit by dividing the spending of 65-to-74-year-olds by average spending in each category and multiplying by 100. An index of 100 means that the spending of 65-to-74-year-olds in that category equals average spending. An index of 132 means that the spending of 65-to-74-year-olds is 32 percent above average, while an index of 75 means that the spending of 65-to-74-year-olds is 25 percent below average.
** This figure does not include the amount paid for mortgage principle, which is considered an asset.
*** Expenditures on gifts are also included in the preceding product and service categories. Food spending, for example, includes the amount spent on food gifts. Not all gift categories are shown.
Note: The Bureau of Labor Statistics uses consumer units rather than households as the sampling unit in the Consumer Expenditure Survey. For the definition of consumer unit, see the Glossary. (-) means the sample is too small to make a reliable estimate.
Source: Bureau of Labor Statistics, unpublished tables from the 1995 Consumer Expenditure Survey; calculations by New Strategist

# The Spending of Householders Aged 75+ Is Rising

**The average householder aged 75 or older spent $18,573 in 1995, much less than the $32,277 spent by the average household.**

Householders aged 75 or older spend less than the average household, in part, because their households are much smaller. While the average household is home to 2.5 people, households headed by people aged 75 or older include just 1.5 persons. Nevertheless, the spending of the oldest householders is rising to meet the average. In 1990, householders aged 75 or older spent only 54 percent as much as the average household. By 1995, this figure had climbed to 58 percent.

Householders aged 75 or older spend at least an average amount on many items. These include pies, tarts, and turnovers (with a spending index of 106—meaning householders in this age group spend 6 percent more than the average household on this item), jams, preserves, and other sweets (111), whiskey (159), gardening and lawn care services (209), women's personal care services—such as hairdressers (102)—newspaper subscriptions (141), and contributions to churches (117).

Householders aged 75 or older spend less than the average household on most items because they are shopping for only one or two people rather than three or four.

## Oldest Consumers Spend Above-Average on Some Items

*(indexed spending of consumer units headed by persons aged 75 or older on selected items, 1995)*

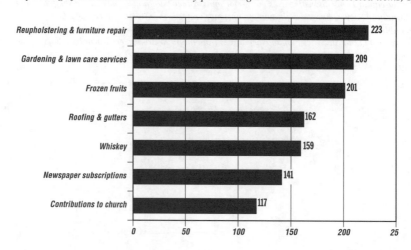

| | |
|---|---|
| Reupholstering & furniture repair | 223 |
| Gardening & lawn care services | 209 |
| Frozen fruits | 201 |
| Roofing & gutters | 162 |
| Whiskey | 159 |
| Newspaper subscriptions | 141 |
| Contributions to church | 117 |

0    50    100    150    200    25

In addition, this age group is now filled with people who remember the financial hardships of the Depression, making them hesitant to spend on anything but necessities.

◆ The spending patterns of the 75-plus age group will change as it is filled by younger generations without memories of the Depression. Look for the spending of householders aged 75 or older to continue to rise toward the average.

# Average and Indexed Spending of Householders Aged 75 or Older, 1995

*(average annual and indexed spending of consumer units (CUs) headed by persons aged 75 or older, 1995)*

| | average spending of total consumer units | consumer units headed by persons aged 75+ | |
|---|---|---|---|
| | | average spending | indexed spending* |
| Number of consumer units (in thousands) | 103,024 | 9,835 | - |
| Average before-tax income | $36,948.00 | $18,025.00 | 49 |
| Total average annual spending | 32,276.59 | 18,572.88 | 58 |
| **FOOD** | **$4,505.34** | **$2,766.81** | **61** |
| **FOOD AT HOME** | **2,802.91** | **2,068.83** | **74** |
| **Cereals and bakery products** | **441.13** | **343.56** | **78** |
| Cereals and cereal products | 165.23 | 116.91 | 71 |
| Flour | 8.42 | 6.87 | 82 |
| Prepared flour mixes | 12.80 | 10.56 | 83 |
| Ready-to-eat and cooked cereal | 97.00 | 72.96 | 75 |
| Rice | 20.17 | 11.45 | 57 |
| Pasta, cornmeal, and other cereal products | 26.84 | 15.07 | 56 |
| **Bakery products** | **275.90** | **226.65** | **82** |
| Bread | 75.70 | 66.91 | 88 |
| White bread | 36.77 | 30.16 | 82 |
| Bread, other than white | 38.92 | 36.75 | 94 |
| Crackers and cookies | 67.33 | 60.04 | 89 |
| Cookies | 44.90 | 40.64 | 91 |
| Crackers | 22.43 | 19.41 | 87 |
| Frozen and refrigerated bakery products | 21.92 | 13.90 | 63 |
| Other bakery products | 110.95 | 85.80 | 77 |
| Biscuits and rolls | 38.49 | 27.45 | 71 |
| Cakes and cupcakes | 34.63 | 26.74 | 77 |
| Bread and cracker products | 4.23 | 2.22 | 52 |
| Sweetrolls, coffee cakes, doughnuts | 20.80 | 15.75 | 76 |
| Pies, tarts, turnovers | 12.80 | 13.63 | 106 |
| **Meats, poultry, fish, and eggs** | **752.43** | **500.33** | **66** |
| Beef | 227.60 | 139.63 | 61 |
| Ground beef | 84.47 | 50.91 | 60 |
| Roast | 40.09 | 28.27 | 71 |
| Chuck roast | 12.63 | 8.23 | 65 |
| Round roast | 13.18 | 10.48 | 80 |
| Other roast | 14.28 | 9.56 | 67 |
| Steak | 86.84 | 44.28 | 51 |
| Round steak | 18.82 | 9.39 | 50 |

*(continued)*

*(continued from previous page)*

| | average spending of total consumer units | consumer units headed by persons aged 75+ | |
| --- | --- | --- | --- |
| | | average spending | indexed spending* |
| Sirloin steak | $23.42 | $10.07 | 43 |
| Other steak | 44.61 | 24.82 | 56 |
| Other beef | 16.19 | 16.17 | 100 |
| Pork | 156.00 | 115.91 | 74 |
| Bacon | 20.32 | 18.72 | 92 |
| Pork chops | 39.69 | 26.07 | 66 |
| Ham | 37.06 | 31.79 | 86 |
| Ham, not canned | 34.76 | 29.49 | 85 |
| Canned ham | 2.31 | 2.30 | 100 |
| Sausage | 22.12 | 14.88 | 67 |
| Other pork | 36.79 | 24.45 | 66 |
| Other meats | 103.63 | 78.94 | 76 |
| Frankfurters | 22.13 | 14.33 | 65 |
| Lunch meats (cold cuts) | 69.66 | 55.98 | 80 |
| Bologna, liverwurst, salami | 25.45 | 19.56 | 77 |
| Other lunchmeats | 44.22 | 36.42 | 82 |
| Lamb, organ meats and others | 11.84 | 8.64 | 73 |
| Lamb and organ meats | 9.31 | 7.60 | 82 |
| Mutton, goat and game | 2.54 | 1.03 | 41 |
| Poultry | 137.65 | 83.76 | 61 |
| Fresh and frozen chickens | 105.14 | 64.64 | 61 |
| Fresh and frozen whole chicken | 28.21 | 16.98 | 60 |
| Fresh and frozen chicken parts | 76.93 | 47.66 | 62 |
| Other poultry | 32.51 | 19.12 | 59 |
| Fish and seafood | 97.33 | 56.04 | 58 |
| Canned fish and seafood | 17.11 | 11.29 | 66 |
| Fresh fish and shellfish | 52.43 | 31.88 | 61 |
| Frozen fish and shellfish | 27.79 | 12.86 | 46 |
| Eggs | 30.23 | 26.05 | 86 |
| **Dairy products** | **296.61** | **216.68** | **73** |
| Fresh milk and cream | 123.00 | 84.12 | 68 |
| Fresh milk, all types | 113.81 | 77.41 | 68 |
| Cream | 9.19 | 6.71 | 73 |
| Other dairy products | 173.60 | 132.56 | 76 |
| Butter | 12.31 | 10.15 | 82 |
| Cheese | 88.00 | 60.05 | 68 |
| Ice cream and related products | 51.24 | 46.70 | 91 |
| Miscellaneous dairy products | 22.05 | 15.66 | 71 |
| **Fruits and vegetables** | **456.67** | **408.77** | **90** |
| Fresh fruits | 144.14 | 138.87 | 96 |
| Apples | 29.15 | 24.78 | 85 |

*(continued)*

*(continued from previous page)*

| | average spending of total consumer units | consumer units headed by persons aged 75+ | |
|---|---|---|---|
| | | average spending | indexed spending* |
| Bananas | $30.26 | $32.29 | 107 |
| Oranges | 16.27 | 16.33 | 100 |
| Citrus fruits, excl. oranges | 12.03 | 11.89 | 99 |
| Fresh vegetables | 137.31 | 119.95 | 87 |
| Potatoes | 28.50 | 28.09 | 99 |
| Lettuce | 18.22 | 13.83 | 76 |
| Tomatoes | 21.64 | 16.51 | 76 |
| Other fresh vegetables | 68.95 | 61.52 | 89 |
| Processed fruits | 95.70 | 89.33 | 93 |
| Frozen fruits and fruit juices | 17.00 | 15.10 | 89 |
| Frozen orange juice | 8.66 | 8.47 | 98 |
| Frozen fruits | 1.81 | 3.63 | 201 |
| Frozen fruit juices | 6.53 | 3.00 | 46 |
| Canned fruits | 13.88 | 16.03 | 115 |
| Dried fruit | 5.86 | 8.94 | 153 |
| Fresh fruit juice | 17.55 | 16.70 | 95 |
| Canned and bottled fruit juice | 41.40 | 32.55 | 79 |
| Processed vegetables | 79.52 | 60.61 | 76 |
| Frozen vegetables | 28.07 | 18.02 | 64 |
| Canned and dried vegetables and juices | 51.44 | 42.59 | 83 |
| Canned beans | 11.26 | 10.12 | 90 |
| Canned corn | 6.91 | 5.45 | 79 |
| Canned misc. vegetables | 16.68 | 14.50 | 87 |
| Dried peas | 0.17 | 0.15 | 88 |
| Dried beans | 2.88 | 0.97 | 34 |
| Dried misc. vegetables | 6.14 | 4.87 | 79 |
| Dried processed vegetables | 0.23 | 0.42 | 183 |
| Frozen vegetable juices | 0.31 | 0.04 | 13 |
| Fresh and canned vegetable juices | 6.87 | 6.08 | 89 |
| **Other food at home** | **856.08** | **599.49** | **70** |
| Sugar and other sweets | 112.08 | 104.03 | 93 |
| Candy and chewing gum | 67.43 | 60.71 | 90 |
| Sugar | 17.44 | 13.40 | 77 |
| Artificial sweeteners | 4.51 | 4.61 | 102 |
| Jams, preserves, other sweets | 22.70 | 25.30 | 111 |
| Fats and oils | 82.22 | 66.17 | 80 |
| Margarine | 12.74 | 12.36 | 97 |
| Fats and oils | 24.60 | 19.53 | 79 |
| Salad dressings | 26.16 | 16.24 | 62 |
| Nondairy cream and imitation milk | 7.15 | 9.67 | 135 |
| Peanut butter | 11.58 | 8.38 | 72 |

*(continued)*

*(continued from previous page)*

| | average spending of total consumer units | consumer units headed by persons aged 75+ | |
| --- | --- | --- | --- |
| | | average spending | indexed spending* |
| Miscellaneous foods | $376.59 | $251.92 | 67 |
| Frozen prepared foods | 66.03 | 42.07 | 64 |
| Frozen meals | 19.87 | 19.80 | 100 |
| Other frozen prepared foods | 46.16 | 22.27 | 48 |
| Canned and packaged soups | 31.25 | 31.22 | 100 |
| Potato chips, nuts, and other snacks | 80.50 | 44.32 | 55 |
| Potato chips and other snacks | 62.33 | 27.96 | 45 |
| Nuts | 18.17 | 16.36 | 90 |
| Condiments and seasonings | 86.51 | 60.83 | 70 |
| Salt, spices and other seasonings | 20.29 | 16.08 | 79 |
| Olives, pickles, relishes | 10.14 | 8.13 | 80 |
| Sauces and gravies | 39.88 | 23.83 | 60 |
| Baking needs and misc. products | 16.20 | 12.80 | 79 |
| Other canned/packaged prepared foods | 112.30 | 73.49 | 65 |
| Prepared salads | 13.51 | 9.82 | 73 |
| Prepared desserts | 8.99 | 10.83 | 120 |
| Baby food | 25.02 | 4.92 | 20 |
| Misc. prepared foods | 64.79 | 47.92 | 74 |
| Nonalcoholic beverages | 240.27 | 159.03 | 66 |
| Cola | 89.20 | 44.38 | 50 |
| Other carbonated drinks | 42.50 | 21.49 | 51 |
| Coffee | 46.33 | 49.50 | 107 |
| Roasted coffee | 30.90 | 31.83 | 103 |
| Instant and freeze-dried coffee | 15.43 | 17.67 | 115 |
| Noncarbonated fruit flavored drinks, incl. nonfrozen lemonade | 24.83 | 19.04 | 77 |
| Tea | 15.64 | 11.21 | 72 |
| Nonalcoholic beer | 1.01 | - | - |
| Other nonalcoholic beverages and ice | 20.75 | 13.40 | 65 |
| **Food prepared by CU, on out-of-town trips** | **44.91** | **18.34** | **41** |
| **FOOD AWAY FROM HOME** | **1,702.43** | **697.98** | **41** |
| **Meals at restaurants, carry-outs, other** | **1,331.44** | **579.99** | **44** |
| Lunch | 464.83 | 201.31 | 43 |
| Dinner | 653.29 | 310.44 | 48 |
| Snacks and nonalcoholic beverages | 111.73 | 20.28 | 18 |
| Breakfast and brunch | 101.59 | 47.96 | 47 |
| **Board (including at school)** | **54.60** | **24.25** | **44** |
| **Catered affairs** | **43.89** | **5.95** | **14** |
| **Food on out-of-town trips** | **196.85** | **85.75** | **44** |
| **School lunches** | **49.41** | **1.48** | **3** |
| **Meals as pay** | **26.23** | **0.55** | **2** |

*(continued)*

*(continued from previous page)*

| | average spending of total consumer units | consumer units headed by persons aged 75+ | |
|---|---|---|---|
| | | average spending | indexed spending* |
| **ALCOHOLIC BEVERAGES** | **$277.28** | **$129.04** | **47** |
| **AT HOME** | **165.34** | **95.30** | **58** |
| Beer and ale | 87.91 | 22.05 | 25 |
| Whiskey | 13.37 | 21.22 | 159 |
| Wine | 48.68 | 43.90 | 90 |
| Other alcoholic beverages | 15.39 | 8.13 | 53 |
| **AWAY FROM HOME** | **111.94** | **33.74** | **30** |
| Beer and ale | 33.45 | 6.68 | 20 |
| Wine | 20.29 | 5.30 | 26 |
| Other alcoholic beverages | 29.77 | 8.68 | 29 |
| Alcoholic beverages purchased on trips | 28.43 | 13.07 | 46 |
| **HOUSING** | **$10,464.95** | **$7,183.55** | **69** |
| **SHELTER** | **5,931.76** | **3,242.97** | **55** |
| **Owned dwellings**** | **3,754.44** | **1,894.64** | **50** |
| Mortgage interest and charges | 2,106.99 | 241.69 | 11 |
| Mortgage interest | 1,991.49 | 207.85 | 10 |
| Interest paid, home equity loan | 53.32 | 17.26 | 32 |
| Interest paid, home equity line of credit | 61.81 | 16.58 | 27 |
| Prepayment penalty charges | 0.37 | - | - |
| Property taxes | 931.76 | 854.70 | 92 |
| Maintenance, repairs, insurance, other expenses | 715.68 | 798.24 | 112 |
| Homeowner's and related insurance | 225.32 | 251.74 | 112 |
| Fire and extended coverage | 6.69 | 9.22 | 138 |
| Homeowner's insurance | 218.63 | 242.52 | 111 |
| Ground rent | 31.63 | 36.14 | 114 |
| Maintenance and repair services | 365.24 | 420.65 | 115 |
| Painting and papering | 41.18 | 63.56 | 154 |
| Plumbing and water heating | 33.28 | 42.21 | 127 |
| Heat, air conditioning, electrical work | 72.49 | 53.02 | 73 |
| Roofing and gutters | 65.15 | 105.31 | 162 |
| Other repair and maintenance services | 130.33 | 147.46 | 113 |
| Repair/replacement of hard surface flooring | 21.23 | 8.17 | 38 |
| Repair of built-in appliances | 1.59 | 0.92 | 58 |
| Maintenance and repair materials | 71.32 | 26.05 | 37 |
| Paints, wallpaper and supplies | 19.60 | 4.78 | 24 |
| Tools/equipment for painting, wallpapering | 2.11 | 0.51 | 24 |
| Plumbing supplies and equipment | 7.26 | 3.23 | 44 |
| Electrical supplies, heating/cooling equip. | 5.22 | 2.10 | 40 |
| Hard surface flooring, repair and replacement | 3.51 | 3.13 | 89 |
| Roofing and gutters | 4.30 | 4.41 | 103 |

*(continued)*

*(continued from previous page)*

| | average spending of total consumer units | consumer units headed by persons aged 75+ | |
| --- | --- | --- | --- |
| | | average spending | indexed spending* |
| Plaster, paneling, siding, windows, doors, screens, awnings | $11.53 | $1.50 | 13 |
| Patio, walk, fence, driveway, masonry, brick and stucco work | 0.88 | 0.17 | 19 |
| Landscape maintenance | 1.78 | 0.54 | 30 |
| Miscellaneous supplies and equipment | 15.13 | 5.68 | 38 |
| Insulation, other maintenance/repair | 11.41 | 5.68 | 50 |
| Finish basement, remodel rooms or build patios, walks, etc. | 3.72 | - | - |
| Property management and security | 22.17 | 63.66 | 287 |
| Property management | 16.64 | 40.87 | 246 |
| Management and upkeep services for security | 5.53 | 22.79 | 412 |
| **Rented dwellings** | **1,785.64** | **1,110.58** | **62** |
| Rent | 1,716.25 | 1,090.48 | 64 |
| Rent as pay | 48.68 | 7.71 | 16 |
| Maintenance, insurance and other expenses | 20.71 | 12.39 | 60 |
| Tenant's insurance | 7.35 | 9.57 | 130 |
| Maintenance and repair services | 5.32 | 2.75 | 52 |
| Repair or maintenance services | 4.93 | 2.75 | 56 |
| Repair and replacement of hard surface flooring | 0.32 | - | - |
| Repair of built-in appliances | 0.07 | - | - |
| Maintenance and repair materials | 8.04 | 0.07 | 1 |
| Paint, wallpaper and supplies | 1.48 | 0.06 | 4 |
| Painting and wallpapering | 0.16 | 0.01 | 6 |
| Plastering, panels, roofing, gutters, etc. | 0.71 | - | - |
| Patio, walk, fence, driveway, masonry, brick and stucco work | 0.03 | - | - |
| Plumbing supplies and equipment | 1.14 | - | - |
| Electrical supplies, heating and cooling equip. | 0.31 | 0.01 | 3 |
| Misc. supplies and equipment | 3.53 | - | - |
| Insulation, other maintenance and repair | 1.43 | - | - |
| Materials for additions, finishing basements, remodeling rooms | 2.07 | - | - |
| Construction materials for jobs not started | 0.04 | - | - |
| Hard surface flooring | 0.22 | - | - |
| Landscape maintenance | 0.46 | - | - |
| **Other lodging** | **391.68** | **237.75** | **61** |
| Owned vacation homes | 127.18 | 100.22 | 79 |
| Mortgage interest and charges | 48.74 | 19.26 | 40 |
| Mortgage interest | 47.03 | 17.92 | 38 |
| Interest paid, home equity loan | 0.12 | 1.24 | 1,033 |

*(continued)*

| | average spending of total consumer units | consumer units headed by persons aged 75+ | |
| --- | --- | --- | --- |
| | | *average spending* | *indexed spending\** |
| Interest paid, home equity line of credit | $1.59 | $0.11 | 7 |
| Property taxes | 54.14 | 51.02 | 94 |
| Maintenance, insurance and other expenses | 24.29 | 29.94 | 123 |
| Homeowner's and related insurance | 6.10 | 6.13 | 100 |
| Homeowner's insurance | 5.90 | 5.51 | 93 |
| Fire and extended coverage | 0.20 | 0.62 | 310 |
| Ground rent | 2.33 | 9.88 | 424 |
| Maintenance and repair services | 10.56 | 9.98 | 95 |
| Maintenance and repair materials | 2.00 | 1.26 | 63 |
| Property management and security | 2.64 | 2.70 | 102 |
| Property management | 1.88 | 1.82 | 97 |
| Management and upkeep services for security | 0.75 | 0.88 | 117 |
| Parking | 0.67 | - | - |
| Housing while attending school | 54.91 | 14.99 | 27 |
| Lodging on out-of-town trips | 209.59 | 122.54 | 58 |
| **UTILITIES, FUELS & PUBLIC SERVICES** | **2,192.58** | **1,777.35** | **81** |
| **Natural gas** | **268.26** | **271.42** | **101** |
| Natural gas (renter) | 58.60 | 28.76 | 49 |
| Natural gas (owner) | 207.94 | 241.55 | 116 |
| Natural gas (vacation) | 1.58 | 1.00 | 63 |
| **Electricity** | **869.67** | **696.64** | **80** |
| Electricity (renter) | 205.17 | 94.92 | 46 |
| Electricity (owner) | 655.26 | 593.06 | 91 |
| Electricity (vacation) | 8.41 | 8.29 | 99 |
| **Fuel oil and other fuels** | **86.66** | **139.47** | **161** |
| Fuel oil | 50.69 | 94.60 | 187 |
| Fuel oil (renter) | 4.34 | 3.59 | 83 |
| Fuel oil (owner) | 45.58 | 90.96 | 200 |
| Fuel oil (vacation) | 0.73 | 0.05 | 7 |
| Coal | 2.13 | 2.93 | 138 |
| Coal (renter) | 0.10 | - | - |
| Coal (owner) | 2.03 | 2.93 | 144 |
| Bottled/tank gas | 28.02 | 32.72 | 117 |
| Gas (renter) | 3.72 | 1.61 | 43 |
| Gas (owner) | 21.86 | 30.30 | 139 |
| Gas (vacation) | 2.43 | 0.81 | 33 |
| Wood and other fuels | 5.83 | 9.22 | 158 |
| Wood and other fuels (renter) | 0.73 | 0.01 | 1 |
| Wood and other fuels (owner) | 5.06 | 9.22 | 182 |

*(continued)*

*(continued from previous page)*

| | average spending of total consumer units | consumer units headed by persons aged 75+ | |
|---|---|---|---|
| | | average spending | indexed spending* |
| **Telephone services** | **$708.40** | **$443.47** | **63** |
| Telephone services in home city, | | | |
| excl. mobile car phones | 682.65 | 441.49 | 65 |
| Telephone services for mobile car phones | 25.75 | 1.98 | 8 |
| **Water and other public services** | **259.59** | **226.36** | **87** |
| Water and sewerage maintenance | 187.25 | 151.27 | 81 |
| Water and sewerage maintenance (renter) | 25.89 | 7.23 | 28 |
| Water and sewerage maintenance (owner) | 159.68 | 143.07 | 90 |
| Water and sewerage maintenance (vacation) | 1.53 | 0.97 | 63 |
| Trash and garbage collection | 70.49 | 74.36 | 105 |
| Trash and garbage collection (renter) | 8.59 | 4.19 | 49 |
| Trash and garbage collection (owner) | 60.92 | 69.29 | 114 |
| Trash and garbage collection (vacation) | 0.95 | 0.88 | 93 |
| Septic tank cleaning | 1.84 | 0.72 | 39 |
| Septic tank cleaning (renter) | 0.02 | - | - |
| Septic tank cleaning (owner) | 1.76 | 0.72 | 41 |
| Septic tank cleaning (vacation) | 0.07 | - | - |
| **HOUSEHOLD SERVICES** | **508.34** | **615.30** | **121** |
| **Personal services** | **258.04** | **249.19** | **97** |
| Babysitting and child care in own home | 39.63 | 2.38 | 6 |
| Babysitting and child care in someone else's home | 36.48 | 0.09 | 0 |
| Care for elderly, invalids, handicapped, etc. | 35.33 | 220.45 | 624 |
| Adult day care centers | 1.05 | 9.28 | 884 |
| Day care centers, nursery and preschools | 145.55 | 17.00 | 12 |
| **Other household services** | **250.30** | **366.11** | **146** |
| Housekeeping services | 85.16 | 142.91 | 168 |
| Gardening, lawn care service | 63.96 | 133.43 | 209 |
| Water softening service | 2.90 | 3.65 | 126 |
| Nonclothing laundry and dry cleaning, sent out | 1.69 | 0.85 | 50 |
| Nonclothing laundry and dry cleaning, coin-operated | 4.83 | 2.38 | 49 |
| Termite/pest control services | 11.70 | 9.72 | 83 |
| Other home services | 16.60 | 15.60 | 94 |
| Termite/pest control products | 0.16 | - | - |
| Moving, storage, and freight express | 27.71 | 10.90 | 39 |
| Appliance repair, incl. service center | 14.07 | 13.74 | 98 |
| Reupholstering and furniture repair | 10.80 | 24.13 | 223 |
| Repairs and rental of equipment and power tools | 5.79 | 4.87 | 84 |
| Appliance rental | 1.67 | - | - |
| Rental of office equipment for nonbusiness use | 0.29 | 0.67 | 231 |
| Repair of misc. household equip. and furnishings | 1.75 | 3.03 | 173 |

*(continued)*

*(continued from previous page)*

| | average spending of total consumer units | consumer units headed by persons aged 75+ | |
|---|---|---|---|
| | | average spending | indexed spending* |
| Repair of computer systems for nonbusiness use | $0.82 | $0.24 | 29 |
| Computer information services | 0.39 | - | - |
| **HOUSEKEEPING SUPPLIES** | **429.59** | **351.18** | **82** |
| **Laundry and cleaning supplies** | **110.26** | **61.78** | **56** |
| Soaps and detergents | 63.62 | 34.82 | 55 |
| Other laundry cleaning products | 46.64 | 26.96 | 58 |
| **Other household products** | **193.90** | **159.52** | **82** |
| Cleansing and toilet tissue, paper towels and napkins | 60.03 | 44.27 | 74 |
| Misc. household products | 71.57 | 50.98 | 71 |
| Lawn and garden supplies | 62.29 | 64.27 | 103 |
| **Postage and stationery** | **125.43** | **129.88** | **104** |
| Stationery, stationery supplies, giftwrap | 61.49 | 49.54 | 81 |
| Postage | 62.40 | 77.07 | 124 |
| Delivery services | 1.54 | 3.27 | 212 |
| **HOUSEHOLD FURNISHINGS & EQUIP.** | **1,402.69** | **1,196.74** | **85** |
| **Household textiles** | **100.47** | **35.56** | **35** |
| Bathroom linens | 15.50 | 6.76 | 44 |
| Bedroom linens | 45.50 | 5.88 | 13 |
| Kitchen and dining room linens | 9.26 | 7.79 | 84 |
| Curtains and draperies | 17.36 | 7.84 | 45 |
| Slipcovers and decorative pillows | 1.74 | 0.47 | 27 |
| Sewing materials for household items | 10.01 | 6.14 | 61 |
| Other linens | 1.09 | 0.67 | 61 |
| **Furniture** | **327.49** | **106.95** | **33** |
| Mattress and springs | 41.36 | 23.47 | 57 |
| Other bedroom furniture | 51.66 | 8.81 | 17 |
| Sofas | 77.20 | 19.12 | 25 |
| Living room chairs | 39.35 | 29.05 | 74 |
| Living room tables | 16.51 | 1.28 | 8 |
| Kitchen and dining room furniture | 46.95 | 14.27 | 30 |
| Infants' furniture | 6.74 | 0.12 | 2 |
| Outdoor furniture | 10.77 | 0.44 | 4 |
| Wall units, cabinets and other furniture | 36.95 | 10.38 | 28 |
| **Floor coverings** | **177.25** | **712.22** | **402** |
| Wall-to-wall carpeting | 38.41 | 21.57 | 56 |
| Wall-to-wall carpeting (renter) | 3.96 | 1.33 | 34 |
| Wall-to-wall carpet (replacement)(owned home) | 34.45 | 20.24 | 59 |
| Room-size rugs/other floor covering, nonpermanent | 138.84 | 690.65 | 497 |

*(continued)*

*(continued from previous page)*

| | average spending of total consumer units | consumer units headed by persons aged 75+ | |
| --- | --- | --- | --- |
| | | average spending | indexed spending* |
| **Major appliances** | **$154.88** | **$98.32** | **63** |
| Dishwashers (built-in), garbage disposals, range hoods (renter) | 0.95 | - | - |
| Dishwashers (built-in), garbage disposals, range hoods (owner) | 10.23 | 6.42 | 63 |
| Refrigerators and freezers (renter) | 6.69 | 2.74 | 41 |
| Refrigerators and freezers (owner) | 42.27 | 25.80 | 61 |
| Washing machines (renter) | 5.26 | 0.11 | 2 |
| Washing machines (owner) | 14.58 | 8.15 | 56 |
| Clothes dryers (renter) | 3.25 | - | - |
| Clothes dryers (owner) | 10.62 | 5.94 | 56 |
| Cooking stoves, ovens (renter) | 2.57 | - | - |
| Cooking stoves, ovens (owner) | 18.72 | 18.50 | 99 |
| Microwave ovens (renter) | 2.87 | 2.90 | 101 |
| Microwave ovens (owner) | 6.01 | 8.59 | 143 |
| Portable dishwasher (renter) | 0.17 | - | - |
| Portable dishwasher (owner) | 0.52 | - | - |
| Window air conditioners (renter) | 2.75 | - | - |
| Window air conditioners (owner) | 8.64 | 8.68 | 100 |
| Electric floor cleaning equipment | 12.94 | 8.10 | 63 |
| Sewing machines | 4.81 | 2.40 | 50 |
| Misc. household appliances | 1.03 | - | - |
| **Small appliances and misc. housewares** | **85.16** | **44.10** | **52** |
| Housewares | 62.80 | 30.80 | 49 |
| Plastic dinnerware | 1.48 | 0.21 | 14 |
| China and other dinnerware | 11.29 | 3.24 | 29 |
| Flatware | 4.01 | 1.16 | 29 |
| Glassware | 6.91 | 2.47 | 36 |
| Silver serving pieces | 2.03 | 1.11 | 55 |
| Other serving pieces | 1.28 | 0.70 | 55 |
| Nonelectric cookware | 16.04 | 16.88 | 105 |
| Tableware, nonelectric kitchenware | 19.77 | 5.03 | 25 |
| Small appliances | 22.36 | 13.30 | 59 |
| Small electric kitchen appliances | 15.65 | 8.50 | 54 |
| Portable heating and cooling equipment | 6.70 | 4.80 | 72 |
| **Miscellaneous household equipment** | **557.43** | **199.59** | **36** |
| Window coverings | 10.64 | 7.52 | 71 |
| Infants' equipment | 8.02 | 4.23 | 53 |
| Laundry and cleaning equipment | 11.33 | 7.55 | 67 |
| Outdoor equipment | 4.08 | 3.92 | 96 |
| Clocks | 3.37 | 2.35 | 70 |

*(continued)*

*(continued from previous page)*

| | average spending of total consumer units | consumer units headed by persons aged 75+ | |
|---|---|---|---|
| | | average spending | indexed spending* |
| Lamps and lighting fixtures | $29.77 | $13.52 | 45 |
| Other household decorative items | 137.82 | 32.47 | 24 |
| Telephones and accessories | 14.44 | 7.04 | 49 |
| Lawn and garden equipment | 42.14 | 37.75 | 90 |
| Power tools | 15.61 | 7.66 | 49 |
| Small misc. furnishings | 2.02 | 0.65 | 32 |
| Hand tools | 10.16 | 1.73 | 17 |
| Indoor plants and fresh flowers | 46.82 | 28.66 | 61 |
| Closet and storage items | 6.93 | 1.12 | 16 |
| Rental of furniture | 3.24 | 3.71 | 115 |
| Luggage | 9.25 | 1.26 | 14 |
| Computers and computer hardware nonbusiness use | 135.02 | 24.94 | 18 |
| Computer software and accessories for nonbusiness use | 18.23 | 0.70 | 4 |
| Telephone answering devices | 3.58 | 0.25 | 7 |
| Calculators | 1.88 | 0.31 | 16 |
| Business equipment for home use | 4.11 | 0.10 | 2 |
| Other hardware | 13.63 | 1.50 | 11 |
| Smoke alarms (owner) | 1.21 | 1.72 | 142 |
| Smoke alarms (renter) | 0.17 | - | - |
| Other household appliances (owner) | 4.71 | 1.20 | 25 |
| Other household appliances (renter) | 1.04 | 0.06 | 6 |
| Misc. household equipment and parts | 18.22 | 7.67 | 42 |
| **APPAREL AND SERVICES** | **$1,703.63** | **$582.34** | **34** |
| **MEN'S APPAREL** | **329.46** | **107.60** | **33** |
| Suits | 33.42 | 5.10 | 15 |
| Sportcoats and tailored jackets | 13.23 | 4.48 | 34 |
| Coats and jackets | 30.16 | 10.79 | 36 |
| Underwear | 17.80 | 12.25 | 69 |
| Hosiery | 12.85 | 3.16 | 25 |
| Sleepwear | 3.50 | 7.39 | 211 |
| Accessories | 34.98 | 7.27 | 21 |
| Sweaters and vests | 12.43 | 4.04 | 33 |
| Active sportswear | 10.14 | 2.07 | 20 |
| Shirts | 76.52 | 21.83 | 29 |
| Pants | 63.37 | 24.93 | 39 |
| Shorts and shorts sets | 16.23 | 3.87 | 24 |
| Uniforms | 3.67 | 0.05 | 1 |
| Costumes | 1.17 | 0.37 | 32 |

*(continued)*

*(continued from previous page)*

| | average spending of total consumer units | consumer units headed by persons aged 75+ | |
| --- | --- | --- | --- |
| | | average spending | indexed spending* |
| **BOYS' (AGED 2 TO 15) APPAREL** | $95.86 | $8.68 | 9 |
| Coats and jackets | 9.27 | - | - |
| Sweaters | 1.92 | 0.81 | 42 |
| Shirts | 20.82 | 2.28 | 11 |
| Underwear | 5.76 | 1.55 | 27 |
| Sleepwear | 1.12 | - | - |
| Hosiery | 4.01 | 1.20 | 30 |
| Accessories | 6.66 | 0.65 | 10 |
| Suits, sportcoats, and vests | 3.59 | - | - |
| Pants | 24.03 | 0.57 | 2 |
| Shorts and shorts sets | 11.44 | 0.46 | 4 |
| Uniforms | 4.06 | 0.68 | 17 |
| Active sportswear | 2.25 | 0.46 | 20 |
| Costumes | 0.93 | - | - |
| | | | |
| **WOMEN'S APPAREL** | 559.19 | 263.67 | 47 |
| Coats and jackets | 41.43 | 28.05 | 68 |
| Dresses | 83.48 | 19.18 | 23 |
| Sportcoats and tailored jackets | 4.29 | - | - |
| Sweaters and vests | 28.51 | 14.85 | 52 |
| Shirts, blouses, and tops | 100.86 | 51.79 | 51 |
| Skirts | 20.49 | 6.39 | 31 |
| Pants | 70.73 | 29.08 | 41 |
| Shorts and shorts sets | 26.72 | 6.78 | 25 |
| Active sportswear | 27.19 | 17.41 | 64 |
| Sleepwear | 23.65 | 9.99 | 42 |
| Undergarments | 30.37 | 24.26 | 80 |
| Hosiery | 20.88 | 10.23 | 49 |
| Suits | 32.66 | 20.84 | 64 |
| Accessories | 43.56 | 24.21 | 56 |
| Uniforms | 2.42 | - | - |
| Costumes | 1.93 | 0.61 | 32 |
| | | | |
| **GIRLS' (AGED 2 TO 15) APPAREL** | 101.30 | 12.86 | 13 |
| Coats and jackets | 6.86 | 0.48 | 7 |
| Dresses and suits | 13.17 | 2.60 | 20 |
| Shirts, blouses, and sweaters | 20.67 | 1.52 | 7 |
| Skirts and pants | 18.18 | 1.49 | 8 |
| Shorts and shorts sets | 9.89 | 0.53 | 5 |
| Active sportswear | 11.39 | 2.96 | 26 |
| Underwear and sleepwear | 7.47 | 0.81 | 11 |
| Hosiery | 4.78 | 0.79 | 17 |
| Accessories | 4.51 | 0.23 | 5 |

*(continued)*

| | average spending of total consumer units | consumer units headed by persons aged 75+ | |
|---|---|---|---|
| | | average spending | indexed spending* |
| Uniforms | $1.92 | $0.19 | 10 |
| Costumes | 2.47 | 1.26 | 51 |
| **CHILDREN UNDER AGE 2** | **80.61** | **16.73** | **21** |
| Coats, jackets, and snowsuits | 3.10 | 1.01 | 33 |
| Outerwear including dresses | 22.66 | 4.10 | 18 |
| Underwear | 46.09 | 10.22 | 22 |
| Sleepwear and loungewear | 3.76 | 0.80 | 21 |
| Accessories | 4.99 | 0.60 | 12 |
| **FOOTWEAR** | **278.36** | **106.79** | **38** |
| Men's | 94.82 | 32.11 | 34 |
| Boys' | 30.48 | 1.49 | 5 |
| Women's | 117.81 | 71.17 | 60 |
| Girls' | 35.24 | 2.02 | 6 |
| **OTHER APPAREL PRODUCTS & SERVICES** | **258.84** | **66.01** | **26** |
| Material for making clothes | 4.95 | 1.40 | 28 |
| Sewing patterns and notions | 1.92 | 0.76 | 40 |
| Watches | 19.16 | 4.57 | 24 |
| Jewelry | 104.17 | 17.24 | 17 |
| Shoe repair and other shoe services | 2.66 | 0.95 | 36 |
| Coin-operated apparel laundry and dry cleaning | 39.46 | 14.43 | 37 |
| Apparel alteration, repair, and tailoring services | 5.82 | 2.70 | 46 |
| Clothing rental | 3.48 | 0.29 | 8 |
| Watch and jewelry repair | 5.07 | 4.13 | 81 |
| Professional laundry, dry cleaning | 71.68 | 18.73 | 26 |
| Clothing storage | 0.47 | 0.82 | 174 |
| **TRANSPORTATION** | **$6,015.97** | **$2,034.91** | **34** |
| **VEHICLE PURCHASES** | **2,639.33** | **503.22** | **19** |
| **Cars and trucks, new** | **1,194.00** | **316.21** | **26** |
| New cars | 670.88 | 316.21 | 47 |
| New trucks | 523.11 | - | - |
| **Cars and trucks, used** | **1,410.96** | **187.01** | **13** |
| Used cars | 916.45 | 177.48 | 19 |
| Used trucks | 494.51 | 9.53 | 2 |
| **Other vehicles** | **34.38** | **-** | **-** |
| New motorcycles | 21.74 | - | - |
| Used motorcycles | 12.64 | - | - |

*(continued)*

*(continued from previous page)*

| | average spending of total consumer units | consumer units headed by persons aged 75+ | |
| --- | --- | --- | --- |
| | | average spending | indexed spending* |
| **GASOLINE AND MOTOR OIL** | **$1,006.05** | **$428.75** | **43** |
| Gasoline | 901.97 | 384.05 | 43 |
| Diesel fuel | 10.15 | 3.07 | 30 |
| Gasoline on out-of-town trips | 81.98 | 37.32 | 46 |
| Motor oil | 11.13 | 3.93 | 35 |
| Motor oil on out-of-town trips | 0.83 | 0.38 | 46 |
| **OTHER VEHICLE EXPENSES** | **2,015.78** | **903.64** | **45** |
| **Vehicle finance charges** | **260.57** | **36.44** | **14** |
| **Maintenance and repairs** | **652.77** | **335.68** | **51** |
| Coolant, additives, brake, transmission fluids | 5.63 | 1.68 | 30 |
| Tires | 87.06 | 39.38 | 45 |
| Parts, equipment, and accessories | 60.29 | 35.32 | 59 |
| Vehicle audio equipment | 10.31 | - | - |
| Vehicle products | 3.37 | 1.02 | 30 |
| Misc. auto repair, servicing | 33.68 | 32.11 | 95 |
| Body work and painting | 29.52 | 15.50 | 53 |
| Clutch, transmission repair | 45.69 | 15.63 | 34 |
| Drive shaft and rear-end repair | 6.14 | 1.19 | 19 |
| Brake work | 39.22 | 15.84 | 40 |
| Repair to steering or front-end | 20.68 | 11.05 | 53 |
| Repair to engine cooling system | 23.28 | 7.78 | 33 |
| Motor tune-up | 42.61 | 33.42 | 78 |
| Lube, oil change, and oil filters | 42.90 | 27.53 | 64 |
| Front-end alignment, wheel balance, rotation | 11.11 | 5.20 | 47 |
| Shock absorber replacement | 7.35 | 4.21 | 57 |
| Brake adjustment | 3.18 | 1.97 | 62 |
| Gas tank repair, replacement | 1.54 | 1.36 | 88 |
| Repair tires and other repair work | 33.28 | 14.27 | 43 |
| Vehicle air conditioning repair | 14.28 | 11.86 | 83 |
| Exhaust system repair | 20.87 | 11.78 | 56 |
| Electrical system repair | 29.58 | 19.26 | 65 |
| Motor repair, replacement | 67.64 | 22.06 | 33 |
| Auto repair service policy | 5.94 | 0.99 | 17 |
| **Vehicle insurance** | **712.81** | **421.55** | **59** |
| **Vehicle rental, leases, licenses, etc.** | **389.63** | **109.97** | **28** |
| Leased and rented vehicles | 235.64 | 34.93 | 15 |
| Rented vehicles | 37.70 | 8.93 | 24 |
| Auto rental | 7.09 | 0.45 | 6 |
| Auto rental, out-of-town trips | 25.95 | 8.47 | 33 |
| Truck rental | 1.19 | - | - |

*(continued)*

*(continued from previous page)*

| | average spending of total consumer units | consumer units headed by persons aged 75+ | |
|---|---|---|---|
| | | average spending | indexed spending* |
| Truck rental, out-of-town trips | $3.26 | - | - |
| Leased vehicles | 197.94 | $26.01 | 13 |
| State and local registration | 84.53 | 45.72 | 54 |
| Driver's license | 6.92 | 4.43 | 64 |
| Vehicle inspection | 8.76 | 4.74 | 54 |
| Parking fees | 25.38 | 6.04 | 24 |
| Tolls | 11.19 | 1.77 | 16 |
| Tolls on out-of-town trips | 4.53 | 2.44 | 54 |
| Towing charges | 4.86 | 1.30 | 27 |
| Automobile service clubs | 7.83 | 8.59 | 110 |
| **PUBLIC TRANSPORTATION** | **354.81** | **199.31** | **56** |
| Airline fares | 225.58 | 130.92 | 58 |
| Intercity bus fares | 14.09 | 9.33 | 66 |
| Intracity mass transit fares | 48.51 | 14.49 | 30 |
| Local trans. on out-of-town trips | 8.46 | 9.82 | 116 |
| Taxi fares on trips | 4.97 | 5.77 | 116 |
| Taxi fares | 6.95 | 10.46 | 151 |
| Intercity train fares | 18.41 | 11.19 | 61 |
| Ship fares | 27.31 | 6.96 | 25 |
| School bus | 0.53 | 0.37 | 70 |
| **HEALTH CARE** | **$1,732.33** | **$2,683.50** | **155** |
| **HEALTH INSURANCE** | **860.45** | **1,557.09** | **181** |
| **Commercial health insurance** | **241.22** | **156.72** | **65** |
| Commercial health insurance | 202.64 | 131.34 | 65 |
| Traditional fee for service health plan (not BCBS) | 15.73 | 10.39 | 66 |
| Preferred provider health plan (not BCBS) | 22.86 | 14.98 | 66 |
| **Blue Cross, Blue Shield** | **171.78** | **312.31** | **182** |
| Blue Cross, Blue Shield | 143.85 | 260.47 | 181 |
| Traditional fee for service health plan (BCBS) | 13.74 | 37.01 | 269 |
| Preferred provider health plan (BCBS) | 7.06 | 7.68 | 109 |
| Health maintenance organization (BCBS) | 6.90 | 7.05 | 102 |
| Commercial Medicare supplement (BCBS) | 0.18 | 0.10 | 56 |
| Other health insurance (BCBS) | 0.04 | - | - |
| **Health maintenance plans (HMOs)** | **146.87** | **53.80** | **37** |
| Health maintenance plans | 118.87 | 40.37 | 34 |
| Health maintenance organization (not BCBS) | 28.00 | 13.43 | 48 |
| **Medicare payments** | **172.13** | **708.87** | **412** |

*(continued)*

*(continued from previous page)*

| | average spending of total consumer units | consumer units headed by persons aged 75+ | |
|---|---|---|---|
| | | average spending | indexed spending* |
| **Commercial Medicare supplements/ other health insurance** | **$128.44** | **$325.40** | **253** |
| Commercial Medicare supplements/ other health insurance | 107.27 | 267.55 | 249 |
| Commercial Medicare supplement (not BCBS) | 8.30 | 40.11 | 483 |
| Other health insurance (not BCBS) | 12.88 | 17.74 | 138 |
| **MEDICAL SERVICES** | **511.47** | **487.50** | **95** |
| Physician's services | 146.97 | 103.60 | 70 |
| Dental services | 186.29 | 169.63 | 91 |
| Eye care services | 28.83 | 33.64 | 117 |
| Service by professionals other than physician | 38.24 | 22.61 | 59 |
| Lab tests, x-rays | 21.92 | 14.84 | 68 |
| Hospital room | 33.04 | 20.44 | 62 |
| Hospital services other than room | 37.16 | 26.24 | 71 |
| Care in convalescent or nursing home | 7.90 | 69.50 | 880 |
| Other medical services | 10.01 | 27.00 | 270 |
| **DRUGS** | **279.96** | **555.31** | **198** |
| Non-prescription drugs | 79.03 | 99.59 | 126 |
| Prescription drugs | 200.94 | 455.72 | 227 |
| **MEDICAL SUPPLIES** | **80.45** | **83.60** | **104** |
| Eyeglasses and contact lenses | 52.06 | 33.02 | 63 |
| Topicals and dressings | 20.73 | 26.60 | 128 |
| Medical equipment for general use | 2.53 | 5.13 | 203 |
| Supportive/convalescent medical equipment | 3.83 | 14.55 | 380 |
| **ENTERTAINMENT** | **$1,612.09** | **$652.40** | **40** |
| **FEES AND ADMISSIONS** | **432.91** | **222.62** | **51** |
| Recreation expenses, out-of-town trips | 21.21 | 6.87 | 32 |
| Social, recreation, civic club membership | 80.67 | 70.43 | 87 |
| Fees for participant sports | 66.55 | 61.25 | 92 |
| Participant sports, out-of-town trips | 29.25 | 12.79 | 44 |
| Movie, theater, opera, ballet | 73.42 | 21.55 | 29 |
| Movie, other admissions, out-of-town trips | 40.50 | 16.18 | 40 |
| Admission to sporting events | 28.71 | 11.91 | 41 |
| Admission to sports events, out-of-town trips | 13.50 | 5.39 | 40 |
| Fees for recreational lessons | 57.91 | 9.38 | 16 |
| Other entertainment svcs., out-of-town trips | 21.21 | 6.87 | 32 |
| **TELEVISION, RADIOS, SOUND EQUIPMENT** | **541.77** | **260.35** | **48** |
| **Televisions** | **370.32** | **228.25** | **62** |
| Community antenna or cable TV | 219.69 | 161.07 | 73 |

*(continued)*

*(continued from previous page)*

| | average spending of total consumer units | consumer units headed by persons aged 75+ | |
|---|---|---|---|
| | | average spending | indexed spending* |
| Color TV, console | $29.53 | $7.95 | 27 |
| Color TV, portable, table model | 44.90 | 27.65 | 62 |
| VCRs and video disc players | 27.33 | 8.31 | 30 |
| Video cassettes, tapes, and discs | 24.05 | 7.86 | 33 |
| Video game hardware and software | 14.68 | 8.47 | 58 |
| Repair of TV, radio, and sound equipment | 7.19 | 6.93 | 96 |
| Rental of televisions | 1.06 | - | - |
| **Radios and sound equipment** | **171.45** | **32.10** | **19** |
| Radios | 10.61 | 1.43 | 13 |
| Tape recorders and players | 11.26 | 0.35 | 3 |
| Sound components and component systems | 32.12 | 3.43 | 11 |
| Sound equipment accessories | 4.46 | 1.68 | 38 |
| Compact disc, tape, record, video mail order clubs | 11.99 | 4.30 | 36 |
| Records, CDs, audio tapes, needles | 38.49 | 5.39 | 14 |
| Rental of VCR, radio, sound equipment | 0.27 | - | - |
| Musical instruments and accessories | 17.75 | 11.56 | 65 |
| Rental and repair of musical instruments | 1.65 | 0.94 | 57 |
| Rental of video cassettes, tapes, discs, films | 42.38 | 2.91 | 7 |
| **PETS, TOYS, PLAYGROUND EQUIPMENT** | **322.19** | **99.89** | **31** |
| **Pets** | **199.89** | **77.61** | **39** |
| Pet food | 79.56 | 41.44 | 52 |
| Pet purchase, supplies, and medicines | 47.03 | 9.05 | 19 |
| Pet services | 18.78 | 4.13 | 22 |
| Veterinary services | 54.52 | 22.99 | 42 |
| **Toys, games, hobbies, and tricycles** | **120.29** | **22.24** | **18** |
| **Playground equipment** | **2.00** | **0.04** | **2** |
| **OTHER ENTERTAINMENT SUPPLIES, EQUIPMENT, SERVICES** | **315.22** | **69.54** | **22** |
| **Unmotored recreational vehicles** | **28.10** | **9.83** | **35** |
| Boat without motor and boat trailers | 3.69 | 9.83 | 266 |
| Trailer and other attachable campers | 24.41 | - | - |
| **Motorized recreational vehicles** | **77.41** | **-** | **-** |
| Motorized camper | 21.18 | - | - |
| Other vehicle | 11.89 | - | - |
| Motor boats | 44.34 | - | - |
| **Rental of recreational vehicles** | **3.42** | **0.29** | **8** |
| **Outboard motors** | **0.36** | **0.29** | **81** |
| **Docking and landing fees** | **4.49** | **7.76** | **173** |

*(continued)*

*(continued from previous page)*

| | average spending of total consumer units | consumer units headed by persons aged 75+ | |
|---|---|---|---|
| | | average spending | indexed spending* |
| **Sports, recreation, exercise equipment** | **$110.81** | **$31.85** | **29** |
| **Athletic gear, game tables, exercise equipment** | **50.33** | **10.54** | **21** |
| Bicycles | 12.59 | 5.29 | 42 |
| Camping equipment | 6.51 | 0.81 | 12 |
| Hunting and fishing equipment | 17.00 | 7.95 | 47 |
| Winter sports equipment | 3.78 | - | - |
| Water sports equipment | 9.47 | 0.15 | 2 |
| Other sports equipment | 9.50 | 6.92 | 73 |
| Rental and repair of misc. sports equipment | 1.64 | 0.19 | 12 |
| **Photographic equipment and supplies** | **81.18** | **16.47** | **20** |
| Film | 20.27 | 6.41 | 32 |
| Film processing | 28.56 | 8.16 | 29 |
| Photographic equipment | 12.56 | 1.90 | 15 |
| Photographer fees | 18.39 | - | - |
| **Fireworks** | **2.03** | - | - |
| **Souvenirs** | **0.14** | - | - |
| **Visual goods** | **1.51** | **2.66** | **176** |
| **Pinball, electronic video games** | **5.78** | **0.39** | **7** |
| **PERSONAL CARE PRODUCTS AND SERVICES** | **$403.47** | **$259.68** | **64** |
| **PERSONAL CARE PRODUCTS** | **213.44** | **114.90** | **54** |
| Hair care products | 38.65 | 14.08 | 36 |
| Hair accessories | 4.43 | 0.74 | 17 |
| Wigs and hairpieces | 0.95 | 0.43 | 45 |
| Oral hygiene products | 22.19 | 16.84 | 76 |
| Shaving products | 11.91 | 5.58 | 47 |
| Cosmetics, perfume, and bath products | 105.36 | 62.75 | 60 |
| Deodorants, feminine hygiene, misc. products | 26.10 | 13.70 | 52 |
| Electric personal care appliances | 3.85 | 0.77 | 20 |
| **PERSONAL CARE SERVICES** | **190.03** | **144.78** | **76** |
| Personal care services/female | 97.61 | 99.37 | 102 |
| Personal care services/male | 92.19 | 44.16 | 48 |
| **READING** | **$162.57** | **$138.44** | **85** |
| Newspaper subscriptions | 51.79 | 73.03 | 141 |
| Newspaper, non-subscriptions | 17.40 | 14.32 | 82 |
| Magazine subscriptions | 24.74 | 22.43 | 91 |
| Magazines, non-subscriptions | 11.00 | 3.55 | 32 |
| Books purchased through book clubs | 9.33 | 5.56 | 60 |

*(continued)*

*(continued from previous page)*

| | average spending of total consumer units | consumer units headed by persons aged 75+ | |
|---|---|---|---|
| | | average spending | indexed spending* |
| Books not purchased through book clubs | $46.51 | $18.88 | 41 |
| Encyclopedia and other reference book sets | 1.52 | 0.68 | 45 |
| **EDUCATION** | **$471.47** | **$54.53** | **12** |
| College tuition | 265.22 | 30.83 | 12 |
| Elementary/high school tuition | 81.97 | 4.02 | 5 |
| Other schools tuition | 14.06 | 5.07 | 36 |
| Other school expenses incl. rentals | 17.30 | 2.75 | 16 |
| Books, supplies for college | 36.06 | 3.15 | 9 |
| Books, supplies for elementary, high school | 8.56 | 0.91 | 11 |
| Books, supplies for day care, nursery school | 2.09 | 0.11 | 5 |
| Misc. school expenses and supplies | 46.21 | 7.69 | 17 |
| **TOBACCO PRODUCTS AND SMOKING SUPPLIES** | **$268.82** | **$84.96** | **32** |
| Cigarettes | 243.09 | 66.25 | 27 |
| Other tobacco products | 24.30 | 18.11 | 75 |
| Smoking accessories | 1.43 | 0.60 | 42 |
| **FINANCIAL PRODUCTS & SERVICES** | **$766.23** | **$570.81** | **74** |
| Miscellaneous fees, gambling losses | 54.70 | 27.67 | 51 |
| Legal fees | 98.35 | 36.87 | 37 |
| Funeral expenses | 86.83 | 285.49 | 329 |
| Safe deposit box rental | 5.51 | 10.30 | 187 |
| Checking accounts, other bank service charges | 25.62 | 5.93 | 23 |
| Cemetery lots, vaults, and maintenance fees | 15.50 | 20.73 | 134 |
| Accounting fees | 40.94 | 44.73 | 109 |
| Miscellaneous personal services | 21.64 | 36.56 | 169 |
| Finance charges, except mortgage and vehicles | 229.82 | 52.68 | 23 |
| Occupational expenses, union and prof. fees | 97.90 | 6.63 | 7 |
| Expenses for other properties | 85.37 | 41.47 | 49 |
| Credit card memberships | 3.92 | 1.65 | 42 |
| **CASH CONTRIBUTIONS** | **$925.39** | **$1,023.20** | **111** |
| Cash contributions to non-CU members, inc. students, alimony, child support | 233.28 | 89.95 | 39 |
| Gifts of cash, stocks, bonds to non-CU member | 174.20 | 361.52 | 208 |
| Contributions to charities | 85.58 | 88.12 | 103 |
| Contributions to church | 385.94 | 451.59 | 117 |
| Contributions to educational organizations | 35.65 | 19.52 | 55 |
| Political contributions | 3.39 | 3.74 | 110 |
| Other contributions | 7.35 | 8.77 | 119 |

*(continued)*

*(continued from previous page)*

| | average spending of total consumer units | consumer units headed by persons aged 75+ | |
|---|---|---|---|
| | | average spending | indexed spending* |
| **PERSONAL INSURANCE & PENSIONS** | **$2,967.05** | **$408.69** | **14** |
| **LIFE & OTHER PERSONAL INSURANCE** | **374.03** | **172.40** | **46** |
| Life, endowment, annuity, other pers. insurance | 361.44 | 158.83 | 44 |
| Other nonhealth insurance | 12.59 | 13.57 | 108 |
| | | | |
| **PENSIONS AND SOCIAL SECURITY** | **2,593.02** | **236.29** | **9** |
| Deductions for government retirement | 66.21 | 2.19 | 3 |
| Deductions for railroad retirement | 5.28 | - | - |
| Deductions for private pensions | 325.82 | 14.37 | 4 |
| Non-payroll deposit to retirement plans | 312.41 | 63.27 | 20 |
| Deductions for Social Security | 1,883.30 | 156.46 | 8 |
| | | | |
| **GIFTS**\*** | **$986.63** | **$561.62** | **57** |
| **FOOD** | **87.72** | **70.54** | **80** |
| Cakes and cupcakes | 1.97 | 1.88 | 95 |
| Cheese | 1.90 | 2.80 | 147 |
| Fresh fruits | 1.83 | 2.19 | 120 |
| Candy and chewing gum | 12.79 | 20.63 | 161 |
| Misc. prepared foods | 2.52 | 0.28 | 11 |
| | | | |
| **HOUSING** | **249.80** | **128.95** | **52** |
| **Housekeeping supplies** | **37.72** | **26.98** | **72** |
| Misc. household products | 4.39 | 0.60 | 14 |
| Lawn and garden supplies | 3.51 | 0.32 | 9 |
| Stationery, stationery supplies, giftwraps | 22.53 | 17.81 | 79 |
| Postage | 4.17 | 6.62 | 159 |
| | | | |
| **Household textiles** | **10.20** | **3.93** | **39** |
| Bedroom linens | 4.44 | 0.65 | 15 |
| | | | |
| **Appliances and misc. housewares** | **27.44** | **8.74** | **32** |
| Major appliances | 4.79 | 0.92 | 19 |
| Small appliances and misc. housewares | 22.65 | 7.83 | 35 |
| China and other dinnerware | 2.91 | 1.94 | 67 |
| Glassware | 3.60 | 2.11 | 59 |
| Nonelectric cookware | 3.98 | - | - |
| Tableware, nonelectric kitchenware | 4.98 | 0.18 | 4 |
| Small electric kitchen appliances | 3.64 | 1.54 | 42 |
| | | | |
| **Miscellaneous household equipment** | **65.94** | **32.55** | **49** |
| Infants' equipment | 2.26 | 3.10 | 137 |
| Lamps and lighting fixtures | 3.33 | 0.38 | 11 |
| Household decorative items | 21.54 | 5.79 | 27 |
| Indoor plants, fresh flowers | 20.72 | 12.17 | 59 |

*(continued)*

*(continued from previous page)*

| | average spending of total consumer units | consumer units headed by persons aged 75+ | |
| --- | --- | --- | --- |
| | | average spending | indexed spending* |
| Computers and hardware, nonbusiness use | $4.01 | $1.20 | 30 |
| Misc. household equipment | 3.08 | 0.36 | 12 |
| **Other housing** | **108.51** | **56.75** | **52** |
| Electricity (renter) | 10.47 | 7.99 | 76 |
| Telephone services in home city, excl. mobile car phone | 12.23 | 5.19 | 42 |
| Day care centers, nursery, and preschools | 15.05 | 3.37 | 22 |
| Housekeeping services | 3.90 | 4.70 | 121 |
| Gardening, lawn care service | 2.74 | 4.17 | 152 |
| **APPAREL AND SERVICES** | **258.22** | **101.08** | **39** |
| **Men and boys, aged 2 or older** | **69.77** | **31.64** | **45** |
| Men's coats and jackets | 4.70 | - | - |
| Men's accessories | 6.98 | 0.38 | 5 |
| Men's sweaters and vests | 3.46 | 2.14 | 62 |
| Men's shirts | 17.03 | 5.79 | 34 |
| Men's pants | 9.29 | 9.72 | 105 |
| Boys' shirts | 4.31 | 1.42 | 33 |
| **Women and girls, aged 2 or older** | **93.61** | **40.53** | **43** |
| Women's coats and jackets | 5.41 | - | - |
| Women's dresses | 5.36 | 4.16 | 78 |
| Women's vests and sweaters | 8.05 | - | - |
| Women's shirts, tops, blouses | 14.11 | 5.99 | 42 |
| Women's pants | 9.09 | 3.58 | 39 |
| Women's active sportswear | 6.11 | 3.11 | 51 |
| Women's sleepwear | 7.35 | 0.71 | 10 |
| Women's accessories | 9.16 | 8.81 | 96 |
| Girls' shirts, blouses, sweaters | 4.16 | 1.52 | 37 |
| Girls' active sportswear | 4.37 | 2.96 | 68 |
| **Children under age 2** | **39.47** | **16.09** | **41** |
| Infant dresses, outerwear | 13.60 | 4.04 | 30 |
| Infant underwear | 19.47 | 9.64 | 50 |
| **Other apparel products and services** | **55.37** | **12.83** | **23** |
| Watches | 26.56 | 3.52 | 13 |
| Jewelry | 23.90 | 2.35 | 10 |
| Men's footwear | 7.15 | - | - |
| Women's footwear | 10.36 | 6.35 | 61 |
| Girls' footwear | 7.76 | 2.02 | 26 |
| **TRANSPORTATION** | **47.84** | **44.31** | **93** |
| Used cars | 3.19 | - | - |

*(continued)*

| | average spending of total consumer units | consumer units headed by persons aged 75+ | |
|---|---|---|---|
| | | average spending | indexed spending* |
| Gasoline on out-of-town trips | $13.01 | $6.21 | 48 |
| Airline fares | 10.75 | 11.10 | 103 |
| **HEALTH CARE** | **22.21** | **56.21** | **253** |
| Dental services | 4.70 | 0.32 | 7 |
| Care in convalescent or nursing home | 4.50 | 46.54 | 1,034 |
| **ENTERTAINMENT** | **86.44** | **42.24** | **49** |
| Toys, games, hobbies, tricycles | 29.34 | 9.23 | 31 |
| Other entertainment | 57.10 | 33.01 | 58 |
| Movie, other admissions, out-of-town trips | 7.07 | 2.97 | 42 |
| Color TV, portable, table model | 3.47 | 0.49 | 14 |
| Pet purchase, supplies, medicine | 6.35 | 0.63 | 10 |
| Veterinary services | 3.05 | 0.08 | 3 |
| **EDUCATION** | **120.19** | **19.97** | **17** |
| College tuition | 96.63 | 11.31 | 12 |
| Elementary, high school tuition | 8.17 | 2.87 | 35 |
| College books, supplies | 6.55 | 0.57 | 9 |
| Misc. school supplies | 5.29 | 2.94 | 56 |
| **ALL OTHER GIFTS** | **114.22** | **98.31** | **86** |
| Out-of-town trip expenses | 36.21 | 27.84 | 77 |

*The index compares the spending of consumer units headed by persons aged 75 or older with the spending of the average consumer unit by dividing the spending of persons aged 75 or older by average spending in each category and multiplying by 100. An index of 100 means that the spending of persons aged 75 or older in that category equals average spending. An index of 132 means that the spending of persons aged 75 or older is 32 percent above average, while an index of 75 means that the spending of persons aged 75 or older is 25 percent below average.

** This figure does not include the amount paid for mortgage principle, which is considered an asset.

*** Expenditures on gifts are also included in the preceding product and service categories. Food spending, for example, includes the amount spent on food gifts. Not all gift categories are shown.

Note: The Bureau of Labor Statistics uses consumer units rather than households as the sampling unit in the Consumer Expenditure Survey. For the definition of consumer unit, see the Glossary. (-) means the sample is too small to make a reliable estimate.

Source: Bureau of Labor Statistics, unpublished tables from the 1995 Consumer Expenditure Survey; calculations by New Strategist

# 9

# Wealth

◆ Net worth peaks at $110,800 among householders aged 55 to 64, falling to $95,000 among those aged 75 or older.

◆ The most-valuable financial asset owned by householders aged 55 to 64 is mutual funds; bonds are the most-valuable asset among 65-to-74-year-olds.

◆ Stocks account for 45 percent of the financial assets of 55-to-64-year-old householders, 34 percent among those aged 65 to 74, and 40 percent among those aged 75 or older.

◆ Median home value stood at $85,000 among householders aged 55 to 64 in 1995 and $80,000 among those aged 65 or older, compared with $90,000 for all Americans.

◆ A majority of older Americans are homeowners, ranging from 56 percent of women living alone to over 90 percent of couples aged 55 or older.

◆ Among householders aged 65 or older with debt, the median amount owed is just $7,700, compared with $22,500 owed by the average American household.

◆ Fifty-three percent of workers aged 51 to 60 are vested in a pension plan.

◆ Among people aged 51 to 61, 29 percent had $100,000 or more in retirement savings, compared with 15 percent of all Americans aged 22 or older.

# Net Worth of Older Americans Fell

**Between 1992 and 1995, the median net worth of householders aged 55 to 64 fell 10 percent, after adjusting for inflation.**

The net worth of all households rose 7 percent between 1992 and 1995, after adjusting for inflation—to $56,400. But the net worth of householders aged 55 to 74 declined. One factor behind the 10 percent decline in the net worth of 55-to-64-year-olds is early retirement, with older householders withdrawing savings to maintain their standard of living in retirement. Among householders aged 65 to 74, the 2 percent decline in net worth is due, in part, to declining interest rates during the recession of the early 1990s.

The youngest age groups saw the biggest gains in wealth. The net worth of householders under age 35 rose 13 percent between 1992 and 1995, after adjusting for inflation. Despite this increase, the youngest householders have little net worth, a median of just $11,400 in 1995. Net worth peaks at $110,800 among householders aged 55 to 64, then falls slightly with age as people spend their retirement savings. Even so, the $95,000 net worth of householders aged 75 or older surpasses that of all other householders except those aged 55 to 74.

◆ If the early retirement trend comes to an end, as seems likely, the net worth of householders aged 55 to 74 should grow.

### Net Worth Up and Down

*(percent change in median net worth of households by age of householder, 1992 to 1995; in 1995 dollars)*

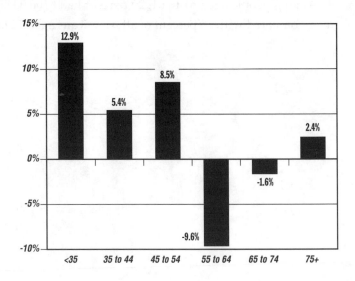

# Net Worth of Households by Age of Householder, 1992 and 1995

*(median net worth of households by age of householder, 1992 and 1995; percent change 1992-95; in 1995 dollars)*

| | 1995 | 1992 | percent change 1992-95 |
|---|---|---|---|
| **Total households** | **$56,400** | **$52,800** | **6.8%** |
| Under age 35 | 11,400 | 10,100 | 12.9 |
| Aged 35 to 44 | 48,500 | 46,000 | 5.4 |
| Aged 45 to 54 | 90,500 | 83,400 | 8.5 |
| Aged 55 to 64 | 110,800 | 122,500 | -9.6 |
| Aged 65 to 74 | 104,100 | 105,800 | -1.6 |
| Aged 75 or older | 95,000 | 92,800 | 2.4 |

*Source: Federal Reserve Board,* Family Finances in the U.S.: Recent Evidence from the Survey of Consumer Finances, *Federal Reserve Bulletin, January 1997; calculations by New Strategist*

# Financial Assets of Older Americans Are above Average

**The financial assets of older householders surpassed the $13,000 median held by the average household in 1995.**

Householders aged 55 to 64 owned a median of $32,300 in financial assets in 1995—more than twice as much as the average household. Those aged 65 to 74 held $19,100 in financial assets, while the oldest householders had $20,900.

At least 90 percent of householders aged 55 or older own at least one type of financial asset, with transaction accounts (i.e., checking accounts) most common. Retirement accounts rank second among 55-to-64-year-olds (owned by 47 percent, and worth a median of $32,800), while life insurance is the second most common financial asset owned by householders aged 65 or older. Life insurance is owned by at least 35 percent of householders aged 65 or older, but it is worth only about $5,000.

The most-valuable financial asset owned by householders aged 55 to 64 are mutual funds, worth a median of $55,000 in 1995. Only 15 percent of 55-to-64-year-olds own mutual funds, however. Among 65-to-74-year-olds, bonds are the most-valuable financial asset, worth a median of $58,000. Few householders in the age group own bonds—only 5 percent in 1995. Among householders aged 75 or older, the most-valuable financial asset is "other" managed assets, worth a median of $100,000 in 1995. Just 6 percent own these assets, however.

◆ As younger generations enter the 55-plus age groups, the proportion of householders with retirement accounts, and the value of these accounts, will rise.

# Financial Assets of Households Headed by Persons Aged 55 or Older, 1995

*(percent of total households and households headed by persons aged 55 or older owning selected financial assets, and median value of assets for owners, by type of asset, 1995)*

| | total households | aged 55 to 64 | aged 65 to 74 | aged 75 or older |
|---|---|---|---|---|
| **Percent owning asset** | | | | |
| Any financial asset | 90.8% | 90.5% | 92.0% | 93.8% |
| Transaction accounts | 87.1 | 88.2 | 91.1 | 93.0 |
| Certificates of deposit | 14.1 | 16.2 | 23.9 | 34.1 |
| Savings bonds | 22.9 | 19.6 | 17.0 | 15.3 |
| Bonds | 3.0 | 2.9 | 5.1 | 7.0 |
| Stocks | 15.3 | 14.9 | 18.0 | 21.3 |
| Mutual funds | 12.0 | 15.2 | 13.7 | 10.4 |
| Retirement accounts | 43.0 | 47.2 | 35.0 | 16.5 |
| Life insurance | 31.4 | 37.5 | 37.0 | 35.1 |
| Other managed assets | 3.8 | 7.1 | 5.6 | 5.7 |
| Other financial assets | 11.0 | 9.0 | 10.4 | 5.3 |
| **Median value of asset for owners** | | | | |
| Any financial asset | $13,000 | $32,300 | $19,100 | $20,900 |
| Transaction accounts | 2,100 | 3,000 | 3,000 | 5,000 |
| Certificates of deposit | 10,000 | 14,000 | 17,000 | 11,000 |
| Savings bonds | 1,000 | 1,100 | 1,500 | 4,000 |
| Bonds | 26,200 | 10,000 | 58,000 | 40,000 |
| Stocks | 8,000 | 17,000 | 15,000 | 25,000 |
| Mutual funds | 19,000 | 55,000 | 50,000 | 50,000 |
| Retirement accounts | 15,600 | 32,800 | 28,500 | 17,500 |
| Life insurance | 5,000 | 6,000 | 5,000 | 5,000 |
| Other managed assets | 30,000 | 42,000 | 26,000 | 100,000 |
| Other financial assets | 3,000 | 9,000 | 9,000 | 35,000 |

*Source: Federal Reserve Board,* Family Finances in the U.S.: Recent Evidence from the Survey of Consumer Finances, *Federal Reserve Bulletin, January 1997*

# Stock Ownership Is Lower in Older Age Groups

## Householders aged 35 to 54 are most likely to own stock.

Stock ownership is average among householders aged 55 to 64, at 41 percent. It falls below average among householders aged 65 or older. Only 34 percent of householders aged 65 or older own stock, as do 28 percent of householders aged 75 or older.

Among older Americans who own stock, however, the median value of the stock they own is far above average. For stock-owning households overall, the median value of stock was $13,500 in 1995. But among stock-owning householders aged 55 to 64, the median value of stock stood at $20,000. The value peaked at $28,100 among householders aged 75 or older.

Stocks account for 40 percent of the financial assets of all households. This proportion is highest among householders aged 55 to 64—at 45 percent. Stocks account for 34 percent of the financial assets of householders aged 65 to 74, and for 40 percent of the financial assets of householders aged 75 or older.

◆ Stock ownership has been rising along with the stock market over the past few years. If stock values retreat significantly, American households could shift their financial assets into other types of investments.

### Stock Value Increases with Age

*(median value of stock for owners, by age of householder, 1995)*

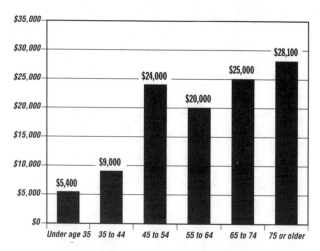

# Stock Ownership by Age of Householder, 1995

*(percentage of households owning stocks directly or indirectly, median value of stocks for owners, and share of total household financial assets accounted for by stock holdings, by age of householder, 1995)*

|  | percent owning stock | median value of stock | stock as a share of total financial assets |
|---|---|---|---|
| **Total households** | **41.1%** | **$13,500** | **40.4%** |
| Under age 35 | 38.5 | 5,400 | 32.4 |
| Aged 35 to 44 | 46.7 | 9,000 | 41.4 |
| Aged 45 to 54 | 49.3 | 24,000 | 44.2 |
| Aged 55 to 64 | 41.4 | 20,000 | 45.3 |
| Aged 65 to 74 | 34.0 | 25,000 | 34.3 |
| Aged 75 or older | 28.1 | 28,100 | 39.5 |

*Source: Federal Reserve Board,* Family Finances in the U.S.: Recent Evidence from the Survey of Consumer Finances, *Federal Reserve Bulletin, January 1997*

# Over 90 Percent of Older Householders Own Nonfinancial Assets

## The most commonly owned nonfinancial assets are vehicles and homes.

While 65 percent of all households own their home, the figure is significantly higher among householders aged 55 or older—ranging from 82 percent among 55-to-64-year-olds to 73 percent among householders aged 75 or older. The homes owned by householders aged 55 to 64 were worth a median of $85,000 in 1995, slightly less than the $90,000 median value of the homes owned by all Americans. Among householders aged 65 or older, median home value stood at $80,000 in 1995.

Vehicles are the most commonly owned financial asset for householders overall—84 percent own at least one. The proportion of householders aged 55 to 64 who own a vehicle is above average at 89 percent, but the figure for householders aged 65 or older is below average.

◆ With millions of Americans investing in stocks, look for little change in the ownership or value of nonfinancial assets in the next few years. If stocks tumble, however, real estate may once again look like a good investment.

# Nonfinancial Assets of Households Headed by Persons Aged 55 or Older, 1995

*(percent of total households and households headed by persons aged 55 or older owning selected non-financial assets, and median value of assets for owners, by type of asset, 1995)*

| | total households | aged 55 to 64 | aged 65 to 74 | aged 75 or older |
|---|---|---|---|---|
| **Percent owning asset** | | | | |
| Any nonfinancial asset | 91.1% | 94.0% | 92.5% | 90.2% |
| Vehicles | 84.2 | 88.7 | 82.0 | 72.8 |
| Primary residence | 64.7 | 82.1 | 79.0 | 73.0 |
| Investment real estate | 17.5 | 26.9 | 26.5 | 16.6 |
| Business | 11.0 | 11.7 | 7.9 | 3.8 |
| Other nonfinancial | 9.0 | 9.8 | 8.9 | 5.4 |
| **Median value of asset for owners** | | | | |
| Any nonfinancial asset | $83,000 | $107,000 | $93,500 | $79,000 |
| Vehicles | 10,000 | 11,900 | 8,000 | 5,300 |
| Primary residence | 90,000 | 85,000 | 80,000 | 80,000 |
| Investment real estate | 50,000 | 82,500 | 55,000 | 20,000 |
| Business | 41,000 | 75,000 | 100,000 | 30,000 |
| Other nonfinancial | 10,000 | 10,000 | 16,000 | 15,000 |

*Source: Federal Reserve Board,* Family Finances in the U.S.: Recent Evidence from the Survey of Consumer Finances, *Federal Reserve Bulletin, January 1997*

# Homeownership Is Well above Average for Older Americans

**The homeownership rate is rising for householders aged 55 or older.**

The 55-to-64 age group saw homeownership rise 0.7 percentage points between 1990 and 1996, while the rate rose 2.6 percentage points for those aged 65 or older. Behind these rising homeownership rates is the growing affluence of older Americans.

By household type, married couples are most likely to own a home, with a homeownership rate of over 90 percent among couples aged 55 or older. Regardless of household type, however, a majority of older Americans are homeowners. This includes 81 percent of families headed by women aged 65 or older as well as 67 percent of women in this age group living alone.

By age, homeownership among older Americans declined for three types of households in the 55-to-59 age group. Homeownership fell less than 1 percentage point among female-headed families and women living alone. It fell 3 percentage points for male-headed families. The biggest gain in homeownership was for families headed by 65-to-69-year-old men, rising 8 percentage points between 1990 and 1996.

◆ Because baby boomers and younger adults have bought homes more slowly than today's older Americans, homeownership rates in the 55-plus age groups could fall as younger generations age.

# Homeownership Rates of Householders Aged 55 or Older, 1990 and 1996

*(percent of total households and households headed by persons aged 55 or older who own their home, by type of household, 1990 and 1996; percentage point change in homeownership, 1990-96)*

| | total households | | | married couples | | | female-headed families | | |
|---|---|---|---|---|---|---|---|---|---|
| | 1996 | 1990 | percentage point change | 1996 | 1990 | percentage point change | 1996 | 1990 | percentage point change |
| **Total households** | **65.4%** | **63.9%** | **1.5** | **80.2%** | **78.1%** | **2.1** | **46.1%** | **44.0%** | **2.1** |
| Aged 55 to 64 | 80.0 | 79.3 | 0.7 | 90.3 | 89.7 | 0.6 | 69.2 | 67.9 | 1.3 |
| Aged 65 or older | 78.9 | 76.3 | 2.6 | 91.3 | 89.2 | 2.1 | 81.1 | 76.6 | 4.5 |
| Aged 55 to 59 | 79.4 | 78.8 | 0.6 | 89.8 | 88.9 | 0.9 | 66.4 | 66.8 | -0.4 |
| Aged 60 to 64 | 80.7 | 79.8 | 0.9 | 90.8 | 90.4 | 0.4 | 72.5 | 69.2 | 3.3 |
| Aged 65 to 69 | 82.4 | 80.0 | 2.4 | 92.4 | 90.7 | 1.7 | 76.1 | 74.4 | 1.7 |
| Aged 70 to 74 | 81.4 | 78.4 | 3.0 | 91.7 | 89.5 | 2.2 | 81.7 | 76.2 | 5.5 |
| Aged 75 or older | 75.3 | 72.3 | 3.0 | 89.9 | 87.1 | 2.8 | 84.0 | 79.2 | 4.8 |

| | male-headed families | | | men living alone | | | women living alone | | |
|---|---|---|---|---|---|---|---|---|---|
| | 1996 | 1990 | percentage point change | 1996 | 1990 | percentage point change | 1996 | 1990 | percentage point change |
| **Total households** | **55.5%** | **55.2%** | **0.3** | **44.9%** | **42.4%** | **2.5** | **56.0%** | **53.6%** | **2.4** |
| Aged 55 to 64 | 74.5 | 74.9 | -0.4 | 55.1 | 51.7 | 3.4 | 63.8 | 62.8 | 1.0 |
| Aged 65 or older | 85.6 | 80.7 | 4.9 | 65.2 | 62.4 | 2.8 | 67.2 | 64.0 | 3.2 |
| Aged 55 to 59 | 72.7 | 75.8 | -3.1 | 54.5 | 50.5 | 4.0 | 61.2 | 61.7 | -0.5 |
| Aged 60 to 64 | 76.8 | 73.9 | 2.9 | 55.8 | 52.8 | 3.0 | 66.2 | 63.6 | 2.6 |
| Aged 65 to 69 | 87.7 | 79.3 | 8.4 | 60.4 | 56.7 | 3.7 | 70.1 | 66.8 | 3.3 |
| Aged 70 to 74 | 79.6 | 78.9 | 0.7 | 66.2 | 63.6 | 2.6 | 70.6 | 66.8 | 3.8 |
| Aged 75 or older | 88.1 | 83.0 | 5.1 | 67.2 | 65.2 | 2.0 | 65.0 | 61.8 | 3.2 |

*Source: Bureau of the Census, Internet web site,* http://www.census.gov; *calculations by New Strategist*

# Householders Aged 65 or Older Have Little Debt

## But householders aged 55 to 64 have more debt than the average household.

While 75 percent of all households have debts, a much smaller share of householders aged 65 or older are in debt. Among those aged 65 to 74, only 55 percent owe money. The figure for householders aged 75 or older is just 30 percent. Householders aged 55 to 64 are as likely to be in debt is the average household.

Among householders aged 65 or older with debt, the median amount is far less than that carried by the average household—$7,700 among those aged 65 to 74 and only $2,000 for householders aged 75 or older. This compares with a median of $22,500 owed by the average household. Householders aged 55 to 64 owed slightly more—a median of $25,800 in 1995.

The most commonly held debt among householders aged 55 to 64 is a mortgage. This age group owed a median of $36,000 in mortgage debt in 1995, which—although it is the largest of their debts—is far below what the average household owes on a mortgage ($51,000).

Among householders aged 65 or older, credit card debt is most common. But this age group owes little on its credit cards. Its biggest I.O.U.s are for investment real estate among 65-to-74-year-olds and mortgages among householders aged 75 or older.

◆ As older Americans become more willing to spend, the proportion holding credit card debt is rising. Expect to see continued growth in credit card debt among older Americans as younger generations enter the age group.

# Debt of Households Headed by Persons Aged 55 or Older, 1995

*(percent of total households and households headed by persons aged 55 or older with debt, and median value of debt for those with debts, 1995)*

| | total households | aged 55 to 64 | aged 65 to 74 | aged 75 or older |
|---|---|---|---|---|
| **Percent with debt** | | | | |
| Any debt | 75.2% | 75.2% | 54.5% | 30.1% |
| Mortgage and home equity | 41.1 | 45.8 | 24.8 | 7.1 |
| Installment | 46.5 | 36.0 | 16.7 | 9.6 |
| Other lines of credit | 1.9 | 1.4 | 1.3 | - |
| Credit card | 47.8 | 43.4 | 31.3 | 18.3 |
| Investment real estate | 6.3 | 12.5 | 5.0 | 1.5 |
| Other debt | 9.0 | 7.5 | 5.5 | 3.6 |
| **Median value of debt for debtors** | | | | |
| Any debt | $22,500 | $25,800 | $7,700 | $2,000 |
| Mortgage and home equity | 51,000 | 36,000 | 19,000 | 15,900 |
| Installment | 6,100 | 5,900 | 4,900 | 3,900 |
| Other lines of credit | 3,500 | 3,500 | 3,800 | - |
| Credit card | 1,500 | 1,300 | 800 | 400 |
| Investment real estate | 28,000 | 26,000 | 36,000 | 8,000 |
| Other debt | 2,000 | 4,000 | 2,000 | 3,000 |

*Note: (-) means sample is too small to make a reliable estimate.*
*Source: Federal Reserve Board,* Family Finances in the U.S.: Recent Evidence from the Survey of Consumer Finances, *Federal Reserve Bulletin, January 1997*

# Many Older Workers Are Covered by Pensions

**Over 60 percent of workers aged 51 to 64 work for organizations offering pension plans.**

Among the nation's civilian, nonagricultural workers, 40 percent are vested in a pension plan—meaning they will receive at least some pension income when they retire. Among workers aged 51 to 60, a 53 percent majority are vested in a pension. This share falls to 48 percent among workers aged 61 to 64, and to just 27 percent among workers aged 65 or older. Many older workers are part-timers, having already retired from their primary career. Thus, they are less likely to be covered by pension plans at their current employer.

Among people who work for companies sponsoring pension plans, participation peaks at 89 percent among those aged 51 to 60. It is a slightly lower 82 percent among those aged 61 to 64, and stands at 63 percent among those aged 65 or older.

◆ Many pension plans offered to workers today are defined contribution (where employees must contribute their own money to the plan) rather than defined benefit (where employers guarantee a retirement benefit after a certain number of years of work). Consequently, the pension income many older workers will receive after they retire may not amount to much.

# Pension Plan Participation by Sex and Age, 1993

*(total number of civilian, nonagricultural workers aged 16 or older; percent with employers who sponsor a pension plan, participation rates of total workers and those with plans, and vesting rates of total workers and those with plans, by sex and age, 1993; numbers in thousands)*

| | total workers | sponsorship rate | participation rate (total workers) | sponsored participation rate | vesting rate (total workers) | participant vesting rate |
|---|---|---|---|---|---|---|
| **Total** | **105,815** | **62.1%** | **47.1%** | **75.9%** | **40.3%** | **85.8%** |
| Men | 55,582 | 62.3 | 50.0 | 80.2 | 42.8 | 85.6 |
| Women | 50,233 | 61.8 | 44.0 | 71.2 | 37.6 | 85.3 |
| Aged 16 to 20 | 6,634 | 32.2 | 3.5 | 11.0 | 1.6 | 45.6 |
| Aged 21 to 30 | 26,359 | 56.6 | 33.8 | 59.8 | 25.8 | 76.2 |
| Aged 31 to 40 | 31,047 | 65.8 | 52.7 | 80.1 | 45.0 | 85.3 |
| Aged 41 to 50 | 23,459 | 70.6 | 61.5 | 87.1 | 54.5 | 88.7 |
| Aged 51 to 60 | 13,164 | 66.8 | 59.3 | 88.8 | 53.3 | 89.9 |
| Aged 61 to 64 | 2,781 | 62.4 | 51.3 | 82.3 | 47.7 | 92.9 |
| Aged 65 or older | 2,371 | 46.1 | 29.0 | 63.0 | 26.6 | 91.6 |

*Note: Sponsorship rate is the percent of total workers who work for an employer where a plan was sponsored for any of the employees. Participation rate is the percent of total workers who participated in a pension plan. Sponsored participation is the percent of employees working for an employer where a retirement plan was sponsored who participated in the plan. Vesting rate is the percent of all workers who are vested in a pension plan. Participant vesting rate is the percent of workers who participated in an employer-sponsored plan who are vested in the plan.*
*Source: Employee Benefit Research Institute,* Baby Boomers in Retirement: What Are Their Prospects? *Special Report and Issue Brief Number 151, July, 1994*

# Older Americans Are Struggling to Save for Retirement

## A substantial proportion have saved very little for retirement.

Among all Americans aged 22 or older, 15 percent had at least $100,000 saved for retirement in 1997, according to a nationally representative survey by the New York City-based research organization, Public Agenda. Among people aged 51 to 61, a larger 29 percent had $100,000 or more in retirement savings. But among these pre-retirees, a substantial 13 percent had nothing saved for retirement, while another 17 percent had less than $10,000 in retirement saving.

One reason why so many pre-retirees have little saved for retirement is their live-for-today attitude. While baby boomers usually get blamed for spending rather than saving, older Americans are actually more likely to espouse this attitude. Sixty-six percent of boomers agree with the statement, "I don't want to worry so much about saving for my retirement that I end up not enjoying my life now." Among people aged 51 to 61, a larger 73 percent agree with that statement.

People aged 51 to 61 are less likely than younger adults to buy things without thinking, however. And only 38 percent say shopping makes them feel good.

◆ Although the stereotypical older American is a penny pincher who would rather save than spend, that attitude is most descriptive of the Depression-era generation now in its 60s and 70s. Americans in their 50s are much more willing to spend—good news for retailers, but bad news for their own financial well-being in retirement.

# Retirement Savings by Age, 1997

*(percent distribution of persons aged 22 or older by level of retirement savings, by age, 1997)*

|  | total persons | young adults (22-32) | baby boomers (33-50) | pre-retirees (51-61) |
|---|---|---|---|---|
| None | 15% | 22% | 12% | 13% |
| Less than $10,000 | 31 | 47 | 26 | 17 |
| $10,000-$49,999 | 24 | 18 | 28 | 20 |
| $50,000-$99,999 | 13 | 7 | 16 | 17 |
| $100,000 or more | 15 | 5 | 16 | 29 |

*Source: Public Agenda,* Miles to Go: A Status Report on Americans' Plans for Retirement, *by Steve Farkas and Jean Johnson, with Ali Bers and Ann Duffett, New York, 1997*

## Attitudes of Consumers toward Retirement Savings by Age, 1997

*(percent of persons aged 22 or older agreeing with statement, by age, 1997)*

| | total persons | young adults (22-32) | baby boomers (33-50) | pre-retirees (51-61) |
|---|---|---|---|---|
| I don't want to worry so much about saving for my retirement that I end up not enjoying my life now | 68% | 71% | 66% | 73% |
| Shopping makes me feel good | 41 | 48 | 38 | 38 |
| I sometimes buy things without thinking and then realize that it was a waste of money | 38 | 46 | 35 | 33 |

*Source: Public Agenda,* Miles to Go: A Status Report on Americans' Plans for Retirement, *by Steve Farkas and Jean Johnson, with Ali Bers and Ann Duffett, New York, 1997*

# Glossary

**adjusted for inflation** Income or a change in income that has been adjusted for the rise in the cost of living, or the consumer price index (CPI-U-X1).

**baby-boom generation** Americans born between 1946 and 1964, aged 33 to 51 in 1997.

**consumer unit** For convenience, consumer units are sometimes called households in this book, although consumer units are somewhat different from the Census Bureau's households. Consumer units are all related members of a household, or financially independent members of a household. A Census Bureau-defined household may include more than one consumer unit.

**dual-earner couples** A married couple in which both the householder and the householder's spouse are in the labor force. Also called two-income couples.

**earnings** One type of income. See also income.

**employed** All civilians who did any work as a paid employee or farmer/self-employed worker, or who worked 15 hours or more as an unpaid farm worker or in a family-owned business during the reference period. All those who have jobs but who are temporarily absent from their jobs due to illness, bad weather, vacation, labor management disputes, or personal reasons are considered employed.

**expenditure** The transaction cost includes excise and sales taxes of goods and services acquired during the survey period. The full cost of each purchase is recorded even though full payment may not have been made at the date of purchase. Expenditure estimates include money spent on gifts for others.

**family household** A household maintained by a householder who lives with one or more people related to him or her by blood, marriage, or adoption.

**female/male householder** A women or man who maintains a household without a spouse present. May head family or nonfamily households.

**full-time, year-round** Fifty or more weeks of full-time employment during the previous calendar year.

**Generation X** Americans born between 1965 and 1976; also known as the baby bust. Generation Xers were aged 21 to 32 in 1997.

**geographic regions** The four major regions and nine census divisions of the United States are grouped as shown below:

*Northeast:*
—New England: Connecticut, Maine, Massachusetts, New Hampshire, Rhode Island, and Vermont
—Middle Atlantic: New Jersey, New York, and Pennsylvania

*Midwest :*
—East North Central: Illinois, Indiana, Michigan, Ohio, and Wisconsin
—West North Central: Iowa, Kansas, Minnesota, Missouri, Nebraska, North Dakota, and South Dakota

*South:*

—East South Central: Alabama, Kentucky, Mississippi, and Tennessee

—South Atlantic: Delaware, District of Columbia, Florida, Georgia, Maryland, North Carolina, South Carolina, Virginia, and West Virginia

*West:*

—West South Central: Arkansas, Louisiana, Oklahoma, and Texas

—Mountain: Arizona, Colorado, Idaho, Montana, Nevada, New Mexico, Utah, and Wyoming

—Pacific: Alaska, California, Hawaii, Oregon, and Washington

**Hispanic** Persons or householders who identify their origin as Mexican, Puerto Rican, Central or South American, or some other Hispanic origin. Unless otherwise noted, persons of Hispanic origin may be of any race. In other words, there are black Hispanics, white Hispanics, and Asian Hispanics

**household** All the persons who occupy a housing unit. A household includes the related family members and all the unrelated persons, if any, such as lodgers, foster children, wards, or employees who share the housing unit. A person living alone is counted as a household. A group of unrelated people who share a housing unit as roommates or unmarried partners is also counted as a household. Households do not include group quarters such as college dormitories, prisons, or nursing homes.

**household, race/ethnicity of** Households are categorized according to the race or ethnicity of the householder only.

**householder** The householder is the person (or one of the persons) in whose name the housing unit is owned or rented or, if there is no such person, any adult member. With married couples, the householder may be either the husband or wife. The householder is the reference person for the household.

**householder, age of** The age of the householder is used to categorize households into age groups. Married couples, for example, are classified according to the age of either the husband or wife, depending on which one identified him or herself as the householder.

**income** Money received in the preceding calendar year by each person aged 15 or older from each of the following sources: (1) earnings from longest job (or self-employment); (2) earnings from jobs other than longest job; (3) unemployment compensation; (4) workers' compensation; (5) Social Security; (6) Supplemental Security income; (7) public assistance; (8) veterans' payments; (9) survivor benefits; (10) disability benefits; (11) retirement pensions; (12) interest; (13) dividends; (14) rents and royalties or estates and trusts; (15) educational assistance; (16) alimony; (17) child support; (18) financial assistance from outside the household, and other periodic income. Household income is the combined income of all household members. Income of persons is all income accruing to a person from all sources. Earnings is the amount of money a person received from his or her job.

**labor force** The labor force tables are based on the civilian labor force, which includes all employed civilians, as well as those who are looking for work (the unemployed).

**labor force participation rate** The percent of the civilian population in the labor force.

**married couples with or without children under age 18** Refers to married couples with or without children under age 18 living in the same household. Couples without children under age 18 may be childless couples or parents of grown children who live elsewhere.

**median** The amount that divides the population or households into two equal halves; one below and one above the median. Medians can be calculated for income, age, and many other characteristics.

**median income** The amount that divides the income distribution into two equal groups, half having incomes above the median, half having incomes below the median. The medians for households or families are based on all households or families. The median for persons are based on all persons aged 15 or older with income.

**nonfamily household** A household maintained by a householder who lives alone or who lives with people to whom he or she is not related.

**nonfamily householder** A householder who lives alone or with nonrelatives only.

**occupation** Occupational classification is based on the kind of work a person did at his or her job during the previous calendar year. For persons who changed jobs during the year, the data refer to the occupation of the job held the longest during that year.

**part-time or full-time employment** Part-time is less than 35 hours of work per week in a majority of the weeks worked during the year. Full-time is 35 or more hours of work per week during a majority of the weeks worked.

**percent change** The change (either positive or negative) in a measure that is expressed as a proportion of the starting measure. When median income changes from $20,000 to $25,000, for example, it is a 25 percent increase.

**percentage point change** The change (either positive or negative) in a value which is already expressed as a percentage. When a labor force participation rate changes from 70 percent to 75 percent, for example, it is a 5 percentage point increase.

**poverty level** The official income threshold below which families and persons are classified as living in poverty. The threshold rises each year with inflation and varies depending on family size and age of householder. In 1995, the poverty threshold for one person under age 65 was $7,929. The threshold for a family of four was $15,569.

**proportion or share** The value of a part expressed as a percentage of the whole. If there are a total of 4 million people and 3 million are white, then the white proportion is 75 percent.

**race** Race is self-reported. A household is assigned the race of the householder.

**rounding** Percentages are rounded to the nearest tenth of a percent; therefore, the percentages in a distribution do not always add exactly to 100.0 percent. The totals, however, are always shown as 100.0. Moreover, individual figures are rounded to the nearest thousand without being adjusted to group totals, which are independently rounded; percentages are based on the unrounded numbers.

**self-employment** A person is categorized as self-employed in this book if he or she was self-employed in the job held longest during the reference period. Persons who report self-employment from a second job are excluded, but those who report wage-and-salary income from a second job are included. Unpaid workers in family businesses are excluded. Self-employment statistics in this book include only nonagricultural workers and exclude people who work for themselves in an incorporated business.

**sex ratio** The number of men per women.

**unemployed** Unemployed persons are those who, during the survey period, had no employment but were available and looking for work. Those who were laid off from their jobs and were waiting to be recalled are also classified as unemployed.

# Index